The Human Resources Scorecard
Measuring the Return on Investment

The Human Resources Scorecard
Measuring the Return on Investment

Jack J. Phillips
Ron D. Stone
Patricia Pulliam Phillips

BUTTERWORTH
HEINEMANN

Boston   Oxford   Auckland   Johannesburg   Melbourne   New Delhi

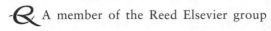

Library of Congress Cataloging-in-Publication Data
Phillips, Jack J., 1945–
    The human resources scorecard: measuring the return on investment / Jack J. Phillips, Ron D. Stone, Patricia Pulliam Phillips.
        p. cm.
    Includes index.
    ISBN 0-87719-367-3
    1. Wages and labor productivity—Measurement. 2. Labor costs Accounting. 3. Human capital—Cost effectiveness. 4. Manpower planning. 5. Labor ecomonics. 6. Rate of return. I. Stone, Ron D. II. Phillips, Patricia Pulliam. III. Title.

HD 4945.P44 2000
331—dc21
                                                                    00-062236

British Library Cataloguing-in-Publication Data
A complete record for this title is available from the British Library
The publisher offers special discounts on bulk orders of this book.
For information, please contact:
Manager of Special Sales
Butterworth–Heinemann
225 Wildwood Avenue
Woburn, MA 01801–2041
Tel: 781-904-2500
Fax: 781-904-2620
For information on all Butterworth–Heinemann publications available, contact our World Wide Web home page at: http://www.bh.com

10 9 8 7 6 5 4 3 2 1
Printed in the United States of America

Contents

v

viii

Preface

Interest in ROI

Today's HR professionals need a balanced set of measures and processes to show the value of the HR contribution. Measuring the return on investment (ROI) is emerging as a promising tool to provide convincing data about the contribution of specific human resources programs and processes. It is now a part of the measurement mix.

The interest in ROI has been phenomenal. The topic appears on almost every HR conference and convention agenda. Articles about ROI appear regularly in HR practitioner and research journals. Several related books have been developed about the topic, and consulting firms have sprung up almost overnight to tackle this critical and important issue.

Several issues are driving the increased interest in ROI and its application to a variety of HR programs. Pressure from clients and senior managers to show the return on their HR investment is probably the most influential driver. Competitive economic pressures are causing intense scrutiny of all expenditures, including all human resources costs. Total quality management, reengineering, and continuous process improvement have created a renewed interest in measurement and evaluation, including measuring the effectiveness of HR. The general trend toward accountability with all staff support groups is causing some HR departments to measure their contribution. A few progressive HR departments have taken a proactive approach by using ROI to measure their contribution without prodding or encouragement. In all, these and other factors have created an unprecedented wave of applications of the ROI process.

NEEDED: AN EFFECTIVE ROI PROCESS

Return on investment has become one of the most challenging and intriguing issues facing the human resources field. The challenging aspect of the process is the nature and accuracy of its development. It sometimes seems confusing, surrounded by models, formulas, and statistics that often frighten the most capable practitioners. Coupled with this concern are misunderstandings about the process and the gross misuse of ROI techniques in some organizations. These issues sometimes leave HR practitioners with a distaste for the process. Unfortunately, ROI cannot be ignored. To admit to clients and senior managers that the impact of HR cannot be measured is to admit that HR programs do not add value or that HR should not be subjected to accountability processes. In practice, ROI must be explored, considered, and ultimately implemented in most organizations.

What is needed is a rational, logical approach that can be simplified and implemented within the current budget constraints and resources of the organization. This book presents a proven ROI process based on almost twenty years of development and refinement. It is a process that is rich in tradition and modified to meet the demands facing the diversity of current HR programs.

The ROI process described in this book meets the requirements of three very important groups. First, HR practitioners who have used this model and implemented the ROI process in their organizations continue to report their satisfaction with the process and the success that it has achieved. The ROI process presented here is user-friendly, is easy to understand, and has been proven to pay for itself time and time again. A second important group, the clients and senior managers, who approve HR budgets, need measurable results, preferably expressed as a return on investment. The ROI process presented here has fared well with these groups. Senior managers view the process as credible, logical, practical, and easy to understand. More importantly, they buy into the process, which is critical for their future support. The third important group is the evaluation researchers who develop, explore, and analyze new processes and techniques. When exposed to this ROI process in a two-day or one-week workshop, the researchers, without exception, give this process high marks. They often applaud the strategies for isolating the effects of HR and the strategies for converting data to monetary values. Unanimously, they characterize the process as an important contribution to the HR field and to measurement science.

WHY THIS BOOK AT THIS TIME?

When examining current publications related to ROI, we discovered there is no book with a comprehensive, practical presentation about ROI for HR using a process that meets the demands of the three groups previously described. Most models and representations of the ROI process ignore or provide little insight into the two key elements essential to developing the ROI: isolating the effects of HR and converting data to monetary values. Recognizing that many other factors will influence output results, this book provides ten strategies to isolate the effects of HR, far more than any other presentation on the topic. Not enough attention has been provided to the issue of assigning monetary values to the data derived from HR programs. This book presents ten strategies for converting data to monetary values.

This book was developed at the request of many clients and colleagues who asked for a simplified, concise description of the ROI process, presented in a step-by-step approach. Our earlier contributions to the ROI process include two successful books, *Return on Investment in Training and Performance Improvement Programs* (Gulf Publishing) and *The Consultant's Scorecard* (McGraw-Hill). What is needed, according to practitioners, is a book that addresses the ROI process for HR and presents a model that is rational, feasible, and understandable to the typical HR practitioner. This book should meet this need.

TARGET AUDIENCE

HR professionals are the primary audience for this book. Whether an individual is involved in the process of analysis, design, implementation, coordination, or evaluation, this book will be an indispensable reference. Individuals involved in all function aspects of HR should find the book valuable. These include recruiting and staffing, education and learning, compensation and benefits, labor relations, compliance, fair employment practices, human resource information systems, and HR consulting and services. The ROI process described in the book has been used to measure a variety of human resources programs.

Individuals in HR leadership positions (managers, supervisors, team leaders, directors, vice presidents) make up the second audience. These HR leaders will find this book a helpful guide to ROI. With its step-by-step approach and case applications, it will also be useful as a self-study guide.

A third audience is the management group. Because of the tremendous interest among the management team and clients involved in ROI studies, this book should be a useful reference for them. In a simple, easy-to-implement process, it shows how the ROI is developed, in language that managers understand.

The fourth target audience is consultants, professionals, researchers, and seminar presenters who find this process to be an effective way to measure the impact of HR programs. It provides a workable model for consultants to evaluate change initiatives or consulting interventions. The book provides researchers with a sound tool for evaluating a variety of HR programs. Its content should stimulate thought and debate about how the ROI is developed. The book should be a useful textbook or supplemental book for a course on evaluation.

STRUCTURE OF THE BOOK

This book has two unique features that make it a useful guide. First, it presents the ROI model in a step-by-step process. Typically, a chapter is devoted to each major part of the model as the pieces of the ROI puzzle are methodically assembled. At the conclusion, the reader has a clear understanding of the overall ROI process.

The second unique feature is an application of the model in detailed cases based on actual situations. The cases reflect a variety of HR issues and programs. Readers can work through each case step-by-step, exploring the issues and learning how to apply them to their own organizations. The actual results are presented for each case. Case presentations represent a proven learning tool to develop an understanding of the ROI process.

CHAPTER DESCRIPTIONS

Chapter 1, **The Business Case for ROI**, describes how the ROI process has evolved in recent years and how organizations are tackling this important issue. The chapter begins with a presentation of the leading-edge approaches to measuring the HR contribution, of which the ROI process is one. Best practices for ROI, which form the basis for the book, are briefly described next. Various ROI criteria and requirements are presented to build a foundation for the remainder of the book. This chapter presents a brief summary of the model for those who are being introduced to the process for the first time.

Chapter 2, **Initial Analysis and Planning**, shows the initial analysis needed for an effective evaluation process. In some situations the up-front analysis is the key to a successful evaluation. Planning for an ROI evaluation is fully described with an introduction of the tools necessary to capture the details for a comprehensive impact study.

Chapter 3, **Collecting Data During HR Program Implementation**, provides tools and techniques for capturing data to measure reaction, satisfaction, and learning as the HR program is being implemented. These measures are essential to provide important feedback, make process adjustments, and capture important building-block information needed to make the evaluation complete.

Chapter 4, **Collecting Data After HR Program Implementation**, presents a variety of approaches to one of the most fundamental issues. Ranging from conducting surveys to monitoring performance data, the most common ways to collect data after an HR program has been implemented are described in this chapter. Useful tips and techniques to help select the appropriate method for a specific situation are presented.

Chapter 5, **Isolating the Effects of an HR Program**, presents what is perhaps the most important aspect of the ROI process. Ranging from the use of a control group arrangement to obtaining estimates directly from participants, several strategies are presented that can determine the amount of improvement directly linked to the HR program. The premise of this chapter is that there are many influences on business performance measures with HR being only one of them.

Chapter 6, **Converting Data to Monetary Value**, presents an essential step for developing an economic benefit from HR. Ranging from determining the profit contribution of an increased output to using expert opinion to assign a value to data, several strategies to convert both hard and soft data to monetary values are presented, along with many examples.

Chapter 7, **Monitoring the Cost of Human Resource Programs**, details specifically what types of costs should be included in the ROI formula. Different categories and classifications of costs are explored in this chapter, with the goal of developing a fully loaded cost profile for each ROI calculation.

Chapter 8, **Calculating the Actual Return on Investment**, describes the actual ROI calculation and presents several issues surrounding its development, calculation, and use. Examples are presented to illustrate the process.

Chapter 9, **Identifying Intangible Measures**, is a brief chapter that focuses on nonmonetary benefits from programs. Recognizing that not all the output measures from HR can or should be converted to monetary values, this chapter shows how the intangible measures should be identified, monitored, and reported. Common intangible measures are examined.

Chapter 10, **Communicating Results**, provides insight into the most appropriate and effective ways to communicate results to a variety of target audiences. Communication is critical and must be planned early in the process. This chapter shows how to carefully select appropriate messages to meet the unique needs of important audiences.

Chapter 11, **Forecasting the ROI**, shows how the return on investment can be developed at different time frames, ranging from a pre-program measure to using post-program data. Several examples are presented to highlight each concept. This chapter underscores the range of possibilities available for forecasting the ROI.

Chapter 12, **Implementation Issues**, addresses a variety of issues needed to implement the ROI process effectively. Following logical steps and overcoming several hurdles, this chapter identifies the important issues that must be tackled for the ROI process to become a useful and long-lasting process.

The first case application, **Sexual Harassment Prevention (Healthcare Inc.)**, shows how the return on investment is developed for a program aimed at reducing the number of sexual harassment complaints. This case clearly shows that preventive programs can add to the bottom line when the appropriate process is developed and an adequate measurement system is in place.

The next case, **Competency-Based Pay System (National Crushed Stone)**, shows the impact and return on investment of a competency-based pay system installed in construction aggregate plants. The case shows how the indisputable data were developed to show the contribution of a new pay scheme and the effects that it had on operations.

The third case, **Absenteeism Reduction Program (Metro Transit Authority)**, shows how an absenteeism reduction program adds to the bottom line, including a return on investment. The case reveals how comprehensive measurements are critical and how the costing of absenteeism is a difficult and complex issue.

Stress Management (Midwest Electric Inc.) shows how the impact of a stress management program is developed using a pilot group of six intact workteams. The analysis is comprehensive but necessary to show senior management the actual value of this type of program.

Safety Incentive Program (National Steel) shows how the implementation of the simple safety incentive program has dramatically lowered accidents and provided both short-term and long-term payoffs, including a significant, positive ROI. Several important issues are uncovered as the plan is implemented.

Case six, **Executive Leadership Development (Imperial National Bank)**, shows the monetary impact of the executive leadership program. This case underscores the complexity of measuring the impact of leadership development using an action learning process. More importantly, this case shows how changes in program design can significantly increase the actual return on investment.

The final case application, **Technology-Based Learning (United Petroleum International)**, shows how technology assisted learning can add bottom-line value. This case illustrates how the use of nontraditional training and delivery can add financial benefits to produce a positive ROI.

Acknowledgments

No book is a work of the authors alone. We have received much help along the way to make this book a reality. Many of the concepts, issues, and techniques have been developed from earlier research and application. Our previous, much publicized work on the ROI process provided the basic foundation for this book. In addition, many of our clients have provided helpful suggestions and allowed us to use their organizations to develop new tools and processes. Collectively they have made this an important and rich new publication. To them we owe a debt of gratitude, particularly for their interest in exploring new frontiers of measurement and evaluation.

Two individuals who stand out as pioneers in the early development of HR measurement and evaluation have influenced us. First, in the training and development field, Donald Kirkpatrick has been a pioneer in the evaluation process. His ingenious framework for the levels of evaluation have provided the foundation for many evaluation processes and models. Second, Jac Fitzenz has been a pioneer in the development of HR measurements and HR benchmarking. Through his work at Saratoga Institute, Jac has made his mark on the HR field, clearly demonstrating and challenging us with the measurement imperative. We are fortunate to count Jac and Don among our colleagues and are very proud to continue their work through ours.

Finally, we owe much appreciation to our staff at The Chelsea Group, Performance Resources Organization, and Gulf. Kelly Perkins has served us superbly in the managing and editing role for this publication and has kept us on schedule (or at least almost on schedule). Kelly Chappell and Jaime Beard provided excellent support in developing the manuscripts. At Gulf Publishing, we are indebted to Kim Kilmer, who understood the tremendous time pressures we encountered as we attempted to develop this detailed manuscript. To the folks at Gulf, PRO, and The Chelsea Group, we appreciate their support, encouragement, and understanding.

Jack J. Phillips
Ron D. Stone
Patricia Pulliam Phillips
Birmingham, Alabama

PART I

The Need for ROI in Human Resources

CHAPTER 1

The Business Case
for ROI

There has been great debate about measuring the return on investment (ROI) in human resources (HR). Rarely does a topic stir up emotions to the degree the ROI issue does. Some individuals characterize ROI as inappropriate. Others passionately characterize ROI as the answer to their accountability concerns. The truth lies somewhere between these two extreme viewpoints. Understanding the drivers for the ROI process and the inherent weaknesses and advantages of ROI makes it possible to take a rational approach to the issue and implement an appropriate mix of evaluation strategies within the HR function. This book presents the ROI process, a revolutionary approach to evaluating an HR program that generates six types of measures representing a scorecard of results.

One thing is certain—ROI is not a fad. The concept of ROI has been used for centuries. The seventy-fifth anniversary issue of *Harvard Business Review* traced the tools used to measure results in organizations [1]. During the 1920s, ROI was the emerging tool to place a value on the payoff of investments. In recent years, the application of the concept has been expanded to all types of investments including human resources, training and education, change initiatives, and technology. Today, hundreds of organizations are developing ROI calculations for HR programs. Two casebooks have been developed to show specific applications [2]. As long as there is a need for accountability of human resource expenditures and as long as the concept of an investment payoff is desired, the ROI will be used to evaluate major HR investments.

APPROACHES TO HR ACCOUNTABILITY

Fortunately, the HR profession has made much progress with measurement and evaluation in recent years. Since the 1960s, several approaches have been used. These measurement approaches have changed over time. Figure 1-1 illustrates the approximate time frame for the use of particular measurement approaches. There is no argument that human resource functions must be measured, but determining the right approach is a significant challenge. Following is a description of each of the twelve approaches. Although each one is presented separately, the techniques, processes, and focus of some approaches often overlap.

Early Approaches

The early approaches include those tried-and-true approaches we are all so familiar with. Although these are still being used

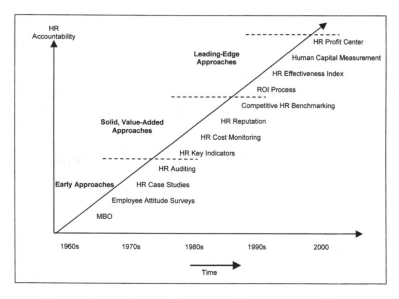

Figure 1-1. Approaches to HR accountability.

by many organizations, other approaches are also being incorporated as organizations work toward more effective measurement processes.

HR Management by Objectives (MBO). The evaluation process of measuring progress toward HR performance objectives gained popularity in the 1960s because of the widespread use of MBO [3]. With this approach, the HR department develops specific objectives and evaluates performance against those objectives. Objectives are based on what management wants accomplished or on what is perceived to be necessary to achieve an adequate level of performance. Measures of turnover, absenteeism, job satisfaction, employee health, and compensation expenses are quantifiable and are considered objectives for many HR functions. Whatever measures are determined, they must be related to organization performance in order to represent meaningful approaches to reflecting the contribution HR makes to the organization.

Employee Attitude Surveys. Many organizations still use employee attitude surveys to evaluate the effectiveness of their HR departments. These surveys attempt to link employee attitudes to organizational performance. One study designed to measure the impact of surveys on an organization compared the use of employee surveys with the profitability of the company. As expected, those organizations responding as more profitable than most of the industry were high users of employees surveys. On the other hand, those organizations describing themselves as less profitable rarely used surveys [4]. Other studies of organizations using employee surveys have proven positive relationships between organization performance and the attitudes of employees. Although this is one method to collect information regarding organization performance, it is often used in conjunction with other methodologies.

HR Case Studies. Another approach to evaluate the success of HR programs is to present results in a case study format to selected audiences. For example, an organization may report the success of a labor-management program in a case study report to all employees. These case studies have significant value and can be presented with little cost. They are developed using data about HR performance, reaction from individuals, or interviews with participants involved in HR programs or services.

The case study approach does have some weaknesses, however. It does not represent a balanced measure of the performance of the HR function but provides some evidence that certain programs are successful. It usually does not represent an ongoing evaluation of any particular program or the overall function—only a one-shot examination. Also, it is often subjectively based, and a program's success is usually judged by those providing the data that is to be included in the case study. Finally quantitative data are not always a part of these studies. Even with these weaknesses, however, the case study approach of evaluation should be an important part of an organization's overall measurement and evaluation program.

HR Auditing. A human resource audit is an investigative, analytical, and comparative process that attempts to reflect the effectiveness of the HR function. It undertakes a systematic search that gathers, compiles, and analyzes data in depth for an extended period, usually one year, instead of with daily formal and informal reports. The use of HR audits has increased significantly. One reason for this is a commitment to moving the HR function from service to the strategic arena [5].

HR auditing is an extension of traditional auditing, which until recent years was limited to the financial practices of the organization. There has been a tremendous expansion in the extent, scope, and types of information being audited. In addition to human resources, auditing has now moved into production, operations, sales, quality, data processing, and engineering. It has become a critical analytical tool to assess how well—or how poorly—an activity is performed. HR auditing provides the necessary baseline data so that actions can be taken to improve HR performance. HR auditing is an important process that can help improve the efficiency of the HR function; it does, however, fall short of a valid approach to measuring the contribution of the HR function.

Solid, Value-Added Approaches

The four techniques illustrated in the center group of Figure 1-1 are considered sound approaches to generate increased accountability to the HR function. These approaches are being used regularly by most progressive organizations.

HR Key Indicators. In some HR evaluation efforts, key measures are developed that reflect the major efforts of the HR function. In some cases, these measures are linked to organizational performance. The key indicators approach is perhaps the best known and established method of HR evaluation. It uses a set of quantitative measures such as accident frequency rate, absenteeism rate, turnover rate, and average time to fill requisitions. Key indicators may come from areas such as:

☐ Employment
☐ Compensation administration
☐ Diversity
☐ Employee benefits
☐ Learning and development
☐ Work environment/safety
☐ Performance
☐ Labor relations
☐ Careers
☐ Overall effectiveness

Although this approach of tying key measures to organizational performance seems sound, there is little empirical evidence to show this direct connection. This area still needs additional support, research, and study.

HR Cost Monitoring. Although most executives are aware of the total cost of payroll and benefits, they do not understand that changes in HR practices can result in a tremendous increase in costs. One approach to evaluating HR performance is to develop HR costs and use them in comparisons with cost standards. Some organizations compare these costs with other internal costs; these comparisons, however, could possibly reinforce complacency. Comparisons with other similar organizations may be more effective. Examples of HR costs monitored by organizations include:

☐ Employment
  —Cost per hire
  —Orientation cost

☐ Learning and development
—Cost per employee
—Total costs as a percent of payroll
☐ Benefits
—Costs as a percent of payroll
—Healthcare costs per employee
☐ Compensation
—Compensation expense as a percent of operating expense
—Total compensation costs
☐ Fair employment
—Cost per complaint
—Cost of litigation
☐ Labor relations
—Cost per grievance
—Cost of work stoppages
☐ Safety and health
—Accident costs
—Costs of citations/fines
☐ Overall HR
—HR costs as a percent of operating expenses
—Turnover costs

Tracking costs alone is no guarantee of a direct link to organizational performance. Also, although costs comparisons are helpful, standard HR cost data are not yet available. From a practical approach, HR costs monitoring is necessary as input for other approaches to evaluation. For example, in the benefit/cost analysis, HR cost data are required for comparisons.

HR Reputation. Some HR professionals suggest that the effectiveness of the HR function should be judged by feedback from those it is designed to serve, often referred to as constituencies or clients. Constituencies depend on, or exert control over, the HR function. Proponents of this approach argue that effectiveness is a value judgment. Even objective criteria are only one step removed from subjectivity. Someone has to determine what level of objective performance is considered effective and what level is considered ineffective. For these proponents, it is more important to measure the perception of the function in the mind of constituents [6].

It is important that the HR function is perceived as effective and its clients and users are satisfied. However, there is little concrete evidence of a relationship between levels of satisfaction among constituencies and overall organizational performance. This process ignores HR outcomes that may directly impact the bottom line.

Competitive HR Benchmarking. A few organizations developed key measures that represent the output of the HR function. The measures are compared with measures from other organizations regarded as having best practices within a given industry. This process, known as competitive benchmarking, began as an important development in the American quality movement. Despite the surge of interest in the process, few companies know what they are doing when they undertake a benchmarking study. Some see the process as merely a comparison of processes to ensure functional similarity with other companies. Others take the process more seriously and view it as a learning process that can improve overall HR effectiveness. Although benchmarking has proven successful in quality and other areas, it is slow to develop within the human resources function, though progress is being made.

Leading-Edge Approaches

The last four techniques are often considered the leading-edge approaches based on interest in the issue. Although some organizations have made progress with these techniques, they are still in a developmental stage within the vast majority of organizations.

Return on Investment. Probably the most convincing approach to HR evaluation is to compare the cost of HR programs with the benefits derived from them. In most cases, the cost of HR programs can be developed or monitored. Although confusion sometimes exists concerning ways to allocate specific costs, overall program costs can usually be pinpointed. The difficulty lies in determining program benefits. In many cases, expert input is used to assign monetary values to benefits derived from programs, particularly for intangible benefits. Consequently, this approach is sometimes avoided as an evaluation tool. However, reliable techniques to generate accurate estimates do exist, and these are presented in detail in the following chapters.

The ROI process is experiencing success in the HR field and even more so in training and development, quality, technology, and change management. This approach to measurement and evaluation is used in the private and public sectors around the world. The process is built around the basic financial equation, earnings divided by investment, or net benefits divided by costs. And although there are various processes on the market today that measure some level of impact of HR programs, most do not meet the criteria and credibility test needed for an effective ROI process. As compared with the other leading approaches presented below, the ROI approach presented in this book seems to have the greatest promise as an evaluation methodology for today's organizations.

HR Effectiveness Index. A few organizations have attempted to develop a single composite index of effectiveness for the HR function. One of the first examples of such an index was developed and used by General Electric in the 1950s [7]. This Employee Relations Index (ERI) was based on eight indicators selected from a detailed study of employee behavior. Among the indicators were absenteeism, initial dispensary visits, terminations, grievances, and work stoppages.

Another index attempt was the Human Resource Performance Index (HRPX), which uses massive data banks made available by human resources systems [8]. According to its developer, the HRPX has been successfully used to evaluate HR functions such as selection, compensation, development, and retention. No attempt was made to validate this index against organizational performance.

The most comprehensive study about this issue was conducted to develop and test a Human Resources Effectiveness Index (HREI) [9]. The study, involving seventy-one organizations from eight industry segments, provided additional empirical evidence of the relationship between HR performance and organizational effectiveness. Six measures of HR department performance were identified for use in the study:

☐ HR expenses/total operating expenses
☐ Total compensation/total operating expenses
☐ Total cost of benefits/total operating expenses
☐ Training and development expenses/total employees
☐ Absence rate
☐ Turnover rate

The HREI represented a composite of the six measures, and significant correlations were developed with revenue/employees, assets/employee costs, operating income/employee costs, and operating income/stockholders' equity (ROE).

An index is appealing because it is simple to compute and easy to understand. Many have been useful for comparing one organization with another and can be used for internal control and goal setting.

Human Capital Measurement. In the early 1960s and 1970s a novel approach to evaluation was taken: human resources accounting (HRA). Interest in this approach seemed to diminish in the early 1980s; however, it has recently obtained renewed emphasis. This concept, currently labeled human capital measurement, attempts to place a value on employees as assets in an organization and to measure improvements or changes in these values using standard accounting principles. It is an extension of the accounting principles of matching cost and revenues and of organizing data to communicate relevant information in financial terms. Human resources are viewed as assets or investments of the organization. Methods of measuring these assets are similar to those for measuring other assets.

Although the concept of measuring human capital has regained popularity, it is not without its share of critics. The concept developed slowly, primarily because of controversies surrounding three important issues: (1) if human beings are indeed assets, (2) what costs should be capitalized, and (3) what methods are most appropriate for establishing a value for employees with the eventual allocation of such value to expense. There are legitimate problems concerning the concept that employees can be owned or controlled by an organization, which is a prerequisite for defining them as assets. Even with these concerns, however, promising signs indicate many corporations will begin listing the financial value of their human assets on the balance sheet. This action can lead to benefits that greatly outweigh the cost of implementing an accounting system to measure human capital [10].

HR Profit Center. According to some researchers and practitioners, the ultimate approach to evaluation is the profit-center approach. This concept requires a shift from the traditional view of the HR department as an expense center in which costs are accumulated, to a view of HR as an investment that can achieve a bottom-line contribution and, in some cases, actually operate as a profit center. Increases in the investment in HR through additional staff, programs, and resources are expected to improve the performance of the organization. This is an important shift in the perception of the HR function [11].

The underlying premise of this approach is that user departments such as production, operations, sales, and engineering are charged for the services of the HR department and, in some cases, have the option of using external services in lieu of those offered by the HR function. In effect, the HR department either makes a profit, breaks even, or experiences a loss. Assuming the services are priced on a competitive basis, the profit represents a financial return on the investment allocated to the HR function [12].

Adoption of this approach requires the HR department to become client-oriented and quality conscious in delivering services and programs. Some organizations have expanded this concept to include selling HR services to outside clients, thus generating additional income for the organization. Although the profit-center approach has made some progress and is generating considerable interest, some legitimate barriers exist in its implementation. The profit center represents a significant departure from the traditional HR management practices, and because of this, it may never be fully implemented in most organizations.

Summary of Approaches

Although there are many approaches to bringing accountability to the HR function, using a variety of tools and based on a variety of assumptions, HR departments still have difficulty achieving success with current approaches. Unfortunately, there are few success stories about comprehensive HR evaluation programs that show the contribution of the function. Many researchers question the quantitative approach to evaluation, suggesting that a return on investment in employees must be approached cautiously and judiciously, and that any such return may be the result of activities initiated by others rather than the HR staff. Some professionals even question the requirement of bottom-line results from HR programs by arguing that it is not possible to isolate monetary benefits an organization may receive from an HR program. Although there is an important trend toward HR accountability, a major problem is that evaluation approaches have been unable to deliver what top management and even HR practitioners want them to deliver: objective data showing the contribution of the HR function to organizational effectiveness.

The twelve approaches presented provide an array of useful tools to help the HR department develop a comprehensive strategy to show its contribution. Table 1-1 shows a comparison of these approaches, as they are used to collect both qualitative and quantitative data from a multitude of sources. The measurement focus is outlined, the relative cost is provided, and the relative value of the information (from the perspective of the client) is presented. Table 1-2 shows how each approach could be used to provide input about a particular issue—in this case, reporting employee turnover [13]. Although use of multiple approaches is necessary to measure important issues such as turnover, use of all approaches would be a tremendous overkill.

Of the twelve approaches, the ROI process, described in detail in this book, provides a balanced approach to measuring the bottom-line impact of HR initiatives. It is being used by organizations around the world and can be implemented within the budget and resource constraints of most organizations. The remainder of this chapter will present critical ROI issues, as well as the business case for implementing the ROI process within an organization.

WHY ROI?

Developing a balanced set of measures, including measuring the ROI, has earned a place among the critical issues in the HR field. The topic routinely appears on conference agendas and at professional meetings. Journals and newsletters embrace the concept with increasing print space. Clients are asking that ROI calculations be conducted for specific programs and initiatives. Even top executives have increased their interest in ROI information.

Although the interest in ROI has heightened and progress is being made, it is still an issue that challenges even the most sophisticated and progressive organizations. Some argue that it

(text continued on page 16)

Table 1-1
Comparison of Approaches to Measure the HR Contribution

Approach	Measurement Focus	Relative Cost	Relative Value of Information
1. HR Management by Objectives	Goal Setting for HR Performance Measures	Low	Moderate
2. Surveys	Attitudes/Perceptions	Moderate	Moderate
3. HR Case Studies	Qualitative Description with Data	Low	Low
4. HR Auditing	Efficiency/Existence of Practices	Low	Low
5. HR Key Indicators	Program/Function Performance Measures	Moderate	Moderate
6. HR Cost Monitoring	Program/Function	Low	Low
7. HR Reputation	Attitudes/Perceptions	Moderate	Moderate
8. Competitive Benchmarking	Performance Measures/Practices	High	High
9. ROI	Benefits vs. Costs	High	High
10. HR Effectiveness Index	Multiple Key Indicators	High	High
11. Human Capital/ HR Accounting	Value of Skills/ Capabilities/ Performance of Employees	High	Moderate
12. HR Profit Centers	Profit Contribution of Programs/Services	High	High

Table 1-2

Integrating the Various Approaches to Measuring HR Contribution:
Monitoring, Analyzing, and Reporting Information Related to Employee Turnover

	Approach to Measure the HR Contribution	Major Focus of the Approach	How the Approach Can Be Used to Reflect Information About Turnover
1.	Management by Objectives (MBO)	Here's our target for turnover for the next year . . .	Specific objectives are established for turnover measures, reflecting previous performance, external factors, environmental pressures, and planned efforts to prevent/reduce turnover.
2.	Employee Survey Data	Our turnover is linked to . . .	Job satisfaction measures, which correlate with employee turnover, are monitored. Correlations are established from research or from analysis within the firm.
3.	Case Studies	In one situation, we prevented turnover by . . .	Successful cases are documented in which turnover reduction projects resulted in a reduction of turnover. Also, turnover prevention initiatives that have prevented turnover from rising to expected levels, local benchmarks, or industry standards are highlighted in case studies.
4.	HR Auditing	Here's how well we adhere to our practices to prevent turnover . . .	Various policies, procedures, and practices that prevent, monitor, and analyze turnover are audited for completeness, accuracy, and effectiveness. The scope of this audit includes practices such as exit interviews, competitive pay, and complaint resolution systems.
5.	Key Indicators	Here's our progress with this important measure of HR performance . . .	Turnover is one of the key indicators tracked in most organizations and compared with historical trends internally and with other organizations through reports such as the Saratoga Human Resource Effectiveness report.

6. HR Cost Monitoring	Here's the cost of turnover . . .	The fully loaded cost of turnover is calculated or estimated based on comparative turnover studies. Absent an actual turnover cost study, it is helpful to reach an agreement about the approximate cost of turnover and report it routinely to the operating areas in which turnover is excessive.
7. HR Reputation	Here's how well we address the turnover issue . . .	The various stakeholders report how well the organization prevents turnover, reacts to turnover issues, and resolves turnover problems.
8. Competitive Benchmarking	Here's what our competitors are experiencing with turnover . . .	Employee turnover data by job category, classification, region, organization, and company are all benchmark items in an HR competitive benchmarking project. In addition, specific programs and practices to prevent turnover or reduce excessive turnover are also benchmarked in this type of project.
9. Return on Investment	Here's the ROI for our turnover reduction program . . .	Specific programs, designed to either prevent or reduce turnover, are developed and implemented and the actual return on investment is calculated. The ROI compares the monetary benefit of the program with the actual cost of the program.
10. HR Effectiveness Index	Turnover is one of several measures in our HR index.	The HR Effectiveness Index is composed of several measures, with turnover reflecting the most important measure. When combined, the index is correlated with the productivity and profitability of the firm.
11. Human Capital/ HR Accounting	How we address turnover reflects our progress with human capital . . .	Employee turnover is one critical measure of human capital for most organizations. Low turnover is an indication that the organization is retaining talented employees. High turnover reflects a drain on intellectual capital, whereas zero turnover reflects a lack of new ideas from new employees.
12. Profit Center	Here's what it would cost us to reduce turnover . . .	A department, division, region, operating unity, or subsidiary is charged fees for specific programs or services related to turnover prevention or reduction. The client pays competitive rates for these services or programs and is usually free to buy the same services externally.

(text continued from page 12)

is not possible to calculate the ROI in HR programs, while others quietly and deliberately proceed to develop measures and ROI calculations. Regardless of the position taken on the issue, the reasons for measuring the ROI remain. Most HR staff members share a concern that they must eventually show a return on the investment in their programs. Otherwise, resources may be reduced, or the function as a whole may lose credibility with the organization.

Rationale for Developing ROI

Although the rationale for focusing on ROI may be obvious, it helps to explore the various reasons why now is the time to pursue the actual calculations for the ROI. The HR function has existed for many years and is a core activity of most medium-sized and large organizations. Several issues create an explanation as to why now is the time to begin measuring HR programs and initiatives more aggressively than ever before.

Client Demands. Today, more clients—those funding the HR initiative—are requesting evaluation data, up to and including measuring the actual ROI. Clients commonly ask the key question at the beginning of most HR programs: "How do I know if this will pay off for me, and will this be a good return on my investment?" Although the accountability issue has always been present, it has never existed at today's level. When the client demands a process, it must be explored and implemented, and the process must be credible enough for the client to believe the results. Client questions must be addressed in a simple, rational way. Avoiding the issue will create distrust between the client and the HR staff and ultimately may cause the program to get off track.

Competitive Advantage. Perhaps one of the most important reasons to pursue a more comprehensive measurement and evaluation, including ROI, is to meet or beat the competition for scarce resources. Many HR functions are beginning to develop the ROI around initiatives and programs to stay competitive or perhaps to stay ahead of other functions competing for internal resources and funding. It is imperative to address the issue in a proactive manner with a comprehensive approach to developing ROI for HR programs.

Resource Allocation. When HR can show the actual contribution of an initiative in monetary terms, an excellent case can be made for additional resources. Some organizations are even using the ROI process to drive additional funding and increased budgets, for example, by placing annual budgets at risk by basing them on a threshold ROI. If the minimum ROI is met for key HR programs, the budget will remain level. Exceeding the threshold can result in increased budget; falling below the threshold can cause a reduction of budget. Although this provides an excellent means by which to focus only on those programs and initiatives that positively impact the bottom line, the process needs to be carefully managed. Measuring the ROI should never be used to assess individual performance, and much can be learned from a negative ROI. Therefore, the HR function should not focus only on those programs that are expected to result in a positive ROI. A clear set of criteria should be used to select programs for ROI evaluation. Program selection is discussed later in this book.

Case Study Database. Developing a history of ROI applications ultimately builds an important database of results. The database not only shows clients and executive management the success with previous programs, but it can eventually show various trends and patterns of HR interventions within the organization. A substantial database of projects using a credible, accepted process can be a crucial advantage and a persuasive selling point when pursuing new initiatives.

Self-Satisfaction. Individuals engaged in professional work want to know that their efforts make a difference. Most HR staff members want to know if they are making a contribution in terms that managers respect and appreciate. Showing the ROI may be one of the most self-satisfying parts of an excellent HR program. In addition to completing projects on schedule, within budget, and with positive client feedback, the actual value-added benefits in monetary terms with an impressive ROI adds the final touch to a major project. This provides additional evidence that what the HR function does makes a difference.

Consequences of Improper or Ineffective HR Practices. Many HR interventions have not lived up to their promises or even expectations. They have not delivered the results the client expected—at least not in the terms management understands, primarily bottom-line contribution. As more and more HR projects are undertaken, consuming precious resources in an organization, the results have simply not materialized. And when the results are reported, skepticism and concern often surrounds the credibility of the data, the objectivity of data, and the thoroughness of the analysis. This has caused executive management to rethink the role of HR, as well as the accountability of HR, and to place more restraints and demands on the HR function, including developing ROI data for selected programs.

The Need for Balanced Measures. For years a debate has ensued about what should or should not be measured and how. Some prefer soft data directly from the client or consumers. Others prefer hard data focused on key issues of output, quality, cost, and time. Still others have argued for a balance of measures, and the latter camp seems to be winning. There exists a critical need to examine data from a variety of groups at different time frames and for different purposes. This mixture of data, often referred to as a balanced approach, is driving the need for the ROI process described in this book. The ROI process develops six types of data.

Top Executive Requirement for HR Contribution. ROI is now enjoying increased interest from the executive suite. Top executives who have watched their HR budgets grow without the appropriate accountability measures have become frustrated and, in an attempt to respond to the situation, have demanded a return on investment for HR programs. Measuring the ROI of HR programs is becoming a global issue because executives from around the world are concerned about accountability. Whether the economy is mature or developing, the economic pressures of running a global enterprise make the accountability of HR an issue.

A Credible Approach

For an ROI process to be feasible, it must balance many issues, including feasibility, simplicity, credibility, and soundness. More specifically, three major target audiences must be satisfied. First, the HR staff members who use a process must have a simple approach. Unfortunately, when they attempt to look for an ROI process, they often find long formulas, complicated equations, and complex models. These make the process appear confusing and complex. This has caused many HR staff members to give up in a fit of frustration, assuming that the ROI cannot be developed or that it is too expensive for most applications. Because of these concerns, a simple, easy-to-understand process is necessary so that the steps and strategies can be implemented. Also, the process cannot take an excessive amount of time to implement, consuming too much staff time. Finally, the process should not be too expensive. Given the fierce competition for financial resources, the HR function needs a process that will not command a significant portion of the HR budget. The ROI process presented in this book meets this important challenge.

Second, an ROI process that will meet the unique requirements of the clients is needed. The clients who request the HR interventions and approve projects need a process that will provide quantitative and qualitative results. They need a process that will develop a calculation similar to the ROI formula applied to other types of investments. And, as with the HR staff, they want a process that is simple and easy to understand and that reflects their point of reference, background, and level of understanding. They neither want nor need a string of formulas, charts, or complicated models. Instead, they need a process that they can explain to others if necessary. More importantly, they need a process with which they can identify—one that is sound and realistic enough to earn their confidence. The process outlined in this book meets the important needs of the client group.

Finally, researchers in measurement and evaluation need a process that they can support—one that holds up under their scrutiny and close examination. Researchers want to use models, formulas, assumptions, and theories that are sound and based on commonly accepted practices. Also, they want a process that produces accurate values and consistent outcomes. They want a process that can be replicated from one situation to another, a reliable process that will result in the same measurements if two different practitioners are pursuing a project. They want a process that uses estimates carefully. If estimates are necessary, the researchers want a process that provides the most accuracy within the constraints of a given situation, recognizing that adjustments need to be made when there is uncertainty in the process. Fortunately, the process presented in this book has met the needs of researchers who have examined the process closely.

Along with meeting the critical challenges of these three important groups, the ROI process must meet certain criteria to be accepted and implemented fully within an organization. The following ten criteria are based on the input from HR managers and specialists.

1. **Simple**

   The ROI process must be simple and void of complex formulas, lengthy equations, and complicated methodologies. Most ROI models have failed in this requirement. In an attempt to obtain statistical perfection using many theories, several ROI models and processes have become too complex to understand and use. Consequently, they have not been implemented.

2. **Economical**

   The ROI process must be economical, with the ability to be implemented easily. The process should have the capability to become a routine part of HR without requiring significant additional resources. Sampling for ROI calculations and early planning for ROI are often necessary to make progress without adding new staff.

3. **Credible**

   The assumptions, methodology, and outcomes must be credible. Logical, methodical steps are needed to earn the respect of practitioners, senior managers, and researchers. This requires a very practical approach for the process.

4. **Theoretically Sound**

   From a research perspective, the ROI process must be theoretically sound and based on generally accepted practices. Unfortunately, this requirement can lead to an extensive, complicated process. Ideally, the process must strike a balance between maintaining a practical and sensible approach *and* a sound and theoretical basis for the procedures. This is perhaps one of the greatest challenges to those who have developed models for the ROI process.

5. **Account for Other Factors**

   An ROI process must account for other factors that influence output variables. Addressing one of the most often

overlooked issues, isolating the influence of an HR program, is necessary to build credibility and accuracy within
the process. The ROI process should pinpoint the contribution of the program when compared with other influences.

6. **Appropriate**
   The ROI process must be appropriate for a variety of HR
   programs. Some models apply to only a small number of
   programs, such as productivity improvements. Ideally, the
   process must be applicable to all types of HR initiatives.

7. **Flexible**
   The ROI process must have the flexibility to be applied
   on a pre-program basis, as well as a post-program basis.
   In some situations, an estimate of the ROI is required
   before the actual program is developed. Ideally, the process
   should be able to adjust to a range of potential time
   frames for calculating the ROI.

8. **Applicable**
   The ROI process must be applicable with all types of data,
   including hard data, which are typically represented as
   output, quality, costs, and time; *and* soft data, which
   include job satisfaction, customer satisfaction, absenteeism,
   turnover, grievances, and complaints.

9. **Inclusive of Costs**
   The ROI process must include the costs of the HR program. The ultimate level of evaluation compares the benefits with costs. Although the term *ROI* has been loosely
   used to express any benefit of HR, an acceptable ROI
   formula must include costs. Omitting or understating costs
   will only destroy the credibility of the ROI values.

10. **Successful Track Record**
    Finally, the ROI process must have a successful track
    record in a variety of applications. In far too many situa-
    tions, models are created but are never successfully applied.
    An effective ROI process should withstand the wear and
    tear of implementation and prove valuable to users.

Because these criteria are considered essential, an ROI process
should meet the vast majority of, if not all, the criteria. The bad
news is that most ROI processes do not meet these criteria. The
good news is that the ROI process presented in this book meets
the ten criteria listed above. Readers are encouraged to analyze

the process they are currently using and determine which of the above criteria are being met by that process.

Not only does the ROI process meet these ten criteria, but it also provides the HR staff with a useful, helpful tool that can serve as a routine and integral part of HR interventions. To develop a credible approach for calculating the ROI in HR, several pieces of an important puzzle must be developed. Figure 1-2 shows the major elements of the puzzle.

The Evaluation Framework

The ROI process adds a fifth level to the four levels of evaluation developed almost forty years ago by Donald Kirkpatrick [14]. The concept of different levels of evaluation is both helpful and instructive in understanding how the return on investment is calculated. Table 1-3 shows a modified version of Kirkpatrick's four-level framework—a fifth level is added to distinguish the ultimate level of evaluation, which is ROI. At Level 1, reaction and satisfaction, reaction from participants involved in an HR program is measured, along with input about a variety of issues. Almost all HR programs are evaluated at this level in one way or another, usually with generic questionnaires and surveys.

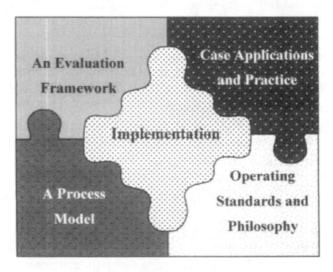

Figure 1-2. The evaluation puzzle.

Table 1-3
Characteristics of Evaluation Levels

Level	Brief Description
1. Reaction and satisfaction	Measures participants' reaction to the initiative and stakeholder satisfaction with the HR project and the planned implementation
2. Learning	Measures skills, knowledge, or attitude changes related to the HR program and implementation
3. Application and implementation	Measures changes in behavior on the job and specific application and implementation of the HR program
4. Business impact	Measures business impact changes related to the HR initiative
5. Return on investment	Compares the monetary value of the business impact with the costs for the HR program; usually expressed as a percentage

Although reaction and satisfaction is important, a favorable input does not ensure that participants will imple-ment the improvements or new process or that they will follow new guidelines or procedures.

At Level 2, learning, measurements focus on what participants learned during the HR program if there is a learning component. A learning check is helpful to ensure that participants absorb new skills and knowledge and that they know how to use it to make the HR program successful. However, a positive measure at this level is no guarantee that the program will be successfully implemented.

At Level 3, application and implementation, various follow-up methods are used to determine if participants apply on the job what is needed to make the initiative successful. The frequency and use of skills are important measures at Level 3. In addition, this measure includes all the steps, actions, tasks, and processes involved in the implementation of the initiative. Although Level 3 evaluation is important to gauge the success of the initiative's implementation, it still does not guarantee a positive impact on the organization.

At Level 4, business impact, the measurement focuses on the actual results achieved by the HR initiative. Typical Level 4 measures include output, quality, cost, time, and customer satisfaction. Although the HR initiative may produce a measurable business impact, there is still a concern that the costs of the HR program may be too high. At Level 5, return on investment, the measurement compares the program's monetary benefits with the costs. Although the ROI can be expressed in several ways, it is usually presented as a percentage or benefit/cost ratio. The evaluation cycle is not complete until the Level 5 evaluation, the ultimate level of evaluation, is conducted.

Although almost all HR functions conduct evaluations to measure satisfaction, few actually conduct evaluations at the ROI level. Perhaps the best explanation for this is that ROI evaluation is often characterized as a difficult and expensive process. Although business results and ROI are desired, it is crucial to evaluate the other levels. A chain of impact should occur through the levels, as the skills and knowledge learned (Level 2) during the HR intervention are applied on the job as implementation takes place (Level 3) to produce business impact (Level 4). If measurements are not taken at each level, it is difficult to conclude that the results achieved were actually produced by the HR initiative. Because of this, it is recommended that evaluation be conducted at all levels when a Level 5 evaluation is planned.

The ROI Process Model

The ROI process, presented briefly in this chapter and explored throughout this book, had its beginnings several years ago as the process was applied to a variety of programs and initiatives. Since then, the process has been refined and modified, and is represented by the model in Figure 1-3. As the figure illustrates, the process is comprehensive; data are developed at different times and gathered from different sources to develop the six types of measures that are the focal point of this book. To date, more than 300 case studies demonstrate the use of the ROI process, and the number is growing rapidly. Each part of the process is briefly mentioned below.

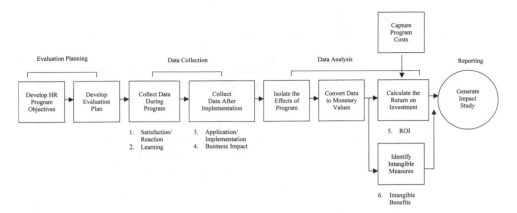

Figure 1-3. ROI process model.

Evaluation Planning. The first two parts of the ROI process focus on two critical planning issues. The first step is to develop appropriate objectives for the HR initiatives. These are often referred to as the ultimate objectives as a particular solution to a problem is implemented. These range from developing objectives for satisfaction to developing an objective for the ROI and are defined in more detail in Chapter 2.

With the objectives in hand, the next step is to develop a detailed evaluation plan. This involves two important documents. A data collection plan indicates the type of data collected, the method for data collection, data sources, the timing of collection, and the various responsibilities. The next document, the ROI analysis plan, details how the HR program is isolated from other influences, how data are converted to monetary values, the appropriate cost categories, the expected intangible measures, and the anticipated target audience for communication. These planning documents are necessary for the process to be implemented appropriately. This is also discussed in Chapter 2.

Collecting Data. Data collected during the HR program measure reaction and satisfaction at Level 1 and learning at Level 2. Collecting data during the HR program intervention ensures that adjustments are made and the process is altered as necessary to keep the assignment on track. The satisfaction and learning data are critical for immediate feedback and necessary to make the HR intervention successful.

After program implementation, post-program data are collected and compared with pre-program situations, control group differences, and expectations. Both hard data, representing output, quality, cost, and time; and soft data, including work habits, work climate, and attitudes, are collected. Data are collected using a variety of methods, such as the following:

☐ Follow-up surveys measure satisfaction from stakeholders.
☐ Follow-up questionnaires measure reaction and uncover specific application issues with HR programs.
☐ On-the-job observation captures actual application and use.
☐ Tests and assessments are used to measure the extent of learning (knowledge gained or skills enhanced).
☐ Interviews measure reaction and determine the extent to which the HR program has been implemented.
☐ Focus groups determine the degree of application of the HR solution in job situations.
☐ Action plans show progress with implementation on the job and the impact obtained.
☐ Performance contracts detail specific outcomes expected or obtained from the HR program.
☐ Business performance monitoring shows improvement in various performance records and operational data.

The important challenge in data collection is selecting the method or methods appropriate for the setting and the specific program, within the time and budget constraints. Data collection methods are covered in more detail in Chapters 3 and 4.

Isolating the Effects of the HR Program. An often-overlooked issue in most evaluations is the process of isolating the effects of an HR program. In this step of the process, specific strategies are explored that determine the amount of performance improvement directly related to the program. This step is essential because many factors will influence performance data after an HR program. The specific strategies in this step will pinpoint the amount of improvement directly related to the intervention. The result is increased accuracy and credibility of the ROI calculation. Organizations have used several strategies to tackle this important issue:

☐ A pilot group of participants in an HR program is compared with a control group not participating in the program to isolate program impact.

☐ Trendlines are used to project the values of specific output variables, and projections are compared with the actual data after an HR program.

☐ A forecasting model is used to isolate the effects of an HR program when mathematical relationships between input and output variables are known.

☐ Participants/stakeholders estimate the amount of improvement related to an HR program.

☐ Supervisors and managers estimate the impact of an HR program on the output measures.

☐ External studies provide input about the impact of an HR program.

☐ Independent experts provide estimates of the impact of an HR program on the output data performance variable.

☐ When feasible, other influencing factors are identified, and the impact is estimated or calculated, leaving the remaining unexplained improvement attributable to the HR program.

☐ Customers provide input about the extent to which the HR program has influenced their decisions to use a product or service.

Collectively, these strategies provide a comprehensive set of tools to tackle the important and critical issue of isolating the effects of an HR program. Chapter 5 is devoted to this important step in the process.

Converting Data to Monetary Values. To calculate the return on investment, business impact data are converted to monetary values and compared with intervention costs. This requires a value to be placed on each unit of data connected with the HR program. The list below shows most of the key strategies available to convert data to monetary values. The specific strategy selected usually depends on the type of data and the situation:

☐ Output data are converted to profit contribution or cost savings and reported as a standard value.

☐ The cost of a quality measure, such as number of accidents, is calculated and reported as a standard value.

☐ Employee time saved is converted to wages and benefits.
☐ Historical costs of preventing a measure, such as a customer complaint, are used when available.
☐ Internal and external experts estimate a value of a measure.
☐ External databases contain an approximate value or cost of a data item.
☐ Participants estimate the cost or value of the data item.
☐ Supervisors or managers provide estimates of costs or value when they are both willing and capable of doing so.
☐ The HR staff estimates a value of a data item.
☐ The measure is linked to other measures for which the costs are easily developed.

This step in the ROI process is critical and is absolutely necessary for determining the monetary benefits from an HR program. The process is challenging, particularly with soft data, but can be methodically accomplished using one or more of these strategies. Because of the importance of this step, Chapter 6 is devoted to this issue.

Tabulating the Cost of the HR Program. The other part of the equation in a benefit/cost analysis is the HR program cost. Tabulating the cost involves monitoring or developing the cost related to the program. A fully loaded approach is recommended in which all direct and indirect costs are tabulated. The following cost components should be included:

☐ The cost of initial analysis and assessment, possibly prorated over the expected life of the program
☐ The cost to develop solutions
☐ The cost to acquire solutions
☐ The cost for application and implementation of the program
☐ The cost of maintaining and monitoring
☐ The cost of evaluating and reporting
☐ The costs of administration and overhead for the program, allocated in some convenient way

The conservative approach is to include all these costs so that the total is fully loaded. Chapter 7 is devoted to this issue.

Calculating the Return on Investment. The return on investment is calculated using benefits and costs. The benefit/cost ratio is the benefits of the HR program or intervention divided by the costs. In formula form it is:

$$BCR = \frac{\text{HR Program Benefits}}{\text{HR Program Costs}}$$

Sometimes this ratio is stated as a return on investment, although the formula is similar to that of the BCR. The return on investment uses the net benefits divided by costs. The net benefits are the program benefits minus the costs. In formula form, the ROI becomes:

$$ROI\% = \frac{\text{Net HR Program Benefits}}{\text{HR Program Costs}} \times 100$$

This is the same basic formula used for evaluating other investments in which the ROI is traditionally reported as earnings divided by investment. Chapter 8 is devoted to ROI calculations.

The BCR and the ROI present the same general information but with slightly different perspectives. An example illustrates the use of these formulas. An HR program produced benefits of $581,000, with a cost of $229,000. Therefore, the benefit/cost ratio would be:

$$BCR = \frac{\$581,000}{\$229,000} = 2.54 \text{ (or 2.5:1)}$$

As this calculation shows, for every $1 invested, $2.50 in benefits were returned. In this example, net benefits were $581,000 − $229,000 = $352,000. Thus, the ROI would be:

$$ROI\% = \frac{\$352,000}{\$229,000} \times 100 = 154\%$$

This means each $1 invested in the HR program returned $1.50 in *net* benefits, after costs were covered. The benefits are usually expressed as annual benefits for short-term programs, representing the amount saved or gained for a complete year after the HR program has been implemented. Although the benefits may continue after the first year, the impact usually diminishes and is omitted from calculations in short-term situations. For long-term projects, the benefits are spread over several years. This conservative approach is used throughout the application of the ROI process described in this book.

Identifying Intangible Benefits. In addition to tangible, monetary benefits, most HR programs will drive intangible, non-monetary benefits. During data analysis, every attempt is made to convert all data to monetary values. All hard data—such as output, quality, and time—are converted to monetary values. The conversion of soft data is attempted for each data item. However, if the process used for conversion is too subjective or inaccurate and the resulting values lose credibility in the process, then the data are listed as intangible benefits with the appropriate explanation. For some interventions, intangible, non-monetary benefits have extreme value, often commanding as much influence as the hard data items. Intangible benefits include items such as:

- ☐ Improved public impact
- ☐ Increased job satisfaction
- ☐ Increased organizational commitment
- ☐ Enhanced technology leadership
- ☐ Reduced stress
- ☐ Improved teamwork
- ☐ Improved customer service
- ☐ Reduced customer-response time

Chapter 9 is devoted to intangible benefits.

Reporting with an Impact Study. A final operational step of the ROI process is to generate an impact study to document the results achieved by the HR program and communicate them to various target audiences. The impact study shows the basic process used to generate the six measures of data. The methodology, assumptions, key concepts, and guiding principles are all outlined before the actual results are presented. Next, the six categories of data, beginning with reaction and satisfaction and then moving through ROI and intangible measures, are presented in a rational, logical process, showing the building blocks to success for the study. This becomes the official document that presents the complete assessment of the success of the program. Its length ranges from 20 to 30 pages for a small project to 200 to 300 pages for a substantial, long-term HR program impact study.

Because there are a variety of target audiences, different reports may need to be generated. All the stakeholders involved will need some communication regarding the success of the HR initiative, including key clients who are not interested in knowing the full details. A stakeholder report may be appropriate for stakeholders who are involved but not directly responsible for the project. Still other reports may be necessary for different target audiences. The key issue in this step of the ROI process is to analyze the target audiences (detailed in the evaluation planning) and develop the appropriate report to meet their specific needs. Chapter 10 is devoted to communicating the results of measurement and evaluation, including the impact study.

The Operating Standards: Guiding Principles

To ensure that each study takes the same conservative philosophy and to increase the likelihood of replication, a set of guiding principles has been developed for the ROI process and is used throughout this book:

1. When a higher-level evaluation is conducted, data must be collected at lower levels.
2. When an evaluation is planned for a higher level, the previous level does not have to be comprehensive.
3. When collecting and analyzing data, use only the most credible sources.
4. When analyzing data, choose the most conservative approach among alternatives.
5. At least one method must be used to isolate the effects of the program/initiative.
6. If no improvement data are available for a population or from a specific source, it is assumed that little or no improvement occurred.

7. Estimates of improvement should be adjusted for the potential error of the estimate.
8. Extreme data items and unsupported claims should not be used in ROI calculations.
9. The first year of benefits (annual) should be used in the ROI analysis of short-term projects/initiatives.
10. Costs of a solution, project, or program should be fully loaded for ROI analysis.

Although the principles may be obvious, each will be explored and revisited throughout the book. However, they do need some explanation at this time. The first general principle refers to the need to report the complete story. Although data at a lower level may not impact results at higher levels, they do provide important information that may be helpful in making adjustments for future execution of a program.

The second general principle represents a way to conserve important resources. Shortcuts can perhaps be taken on lower-level evaluations, whereas more emphasis is regularly placed on higher levels. This is important when the client wants to see the business impact. In those cases, shortcuts can be taken perhaps at Levels 2 and 3 (measuring learning and application/implementation).

The third general principle refers to the credibility of data. The source from which data are collected is vital in maintaining credibility of the study. This is especially true when using estimates to convert data to monetary value and when isolating the impact of a program or initiative.

The fourth general principle addresses the need to take a conservative approach in analyzing data. Because the ROI of an HR program is often quite high, use of a conservative approach on a consistent basis helps preserve the credibility of the outcome.

Principle five also adds to the credibility of the process. Without some method to isolate the effects of the HR program, the studies are considered highly inaccurate and overstated in their results.

Principle six addresses missing data from individuals involved in programs or initiatives. If the participants are no longer on the job or no longer performing the work, it is assumed that little or no improvement occurred. This is an ultra-conservative approach.

Principles seven and eight build on the conservative approach to data analysis. Principle nine focuses on the timing of the actual stream of benefits from an HR program. A conservative approach is recommended, usually dictating one year of benefits for short-term assignments but multiple years for a more extensive program.

The last principle focuses on the issue of fully loaded costs, ensuring that all direct and indirect costs of the program are included. Collectively, these principles will ensure that the proper conservative approach is taken and that the impact study can be replicated and compared with others.

Implementation of the Process

The best tool, technique, or model will not succeed unless it is properly used and becomes a routine part of the process. As a new process, it will be resisted by both the HR staff and clients, just as with any other significant change. Some of the resistance will be based on realistic barriers, while some will be based on misunderstandings and perceived problems that may be mythical. In both cases, specific steps must be taken to overcome the resistance by carefully and methodically implementing the ROI process. Implementation involves many issues, including assigning responsibilities, building the necessary skills, and developing the plans and goals around the process. It also involves pre-paring the environment, individuals, and support teams for this type of comprehensive analysis. The firms that have the most success with this process are those that have devoted adequate resources to implementation and deliberately planned for transition from their current state to where they desire the organization to be in terms of accountability. Chapter 12 covers the implementation issues.

Case Applications: The Progress

Although a significant number of case applications have been developed, the status of ROI among HR practitioners is difficult, if not impossible, to pinpoint. Senior executives and HR staff members are often reluctant to disclose internal practices, and even in the most progressive organizations, they confess that too little progress has been made. It is difficult to find cases in the literature that show how an organization has attempted to measure the return on investment in an intervention.

Recognizing this void, the American Society for Training and Development (ASTD) undertook an ambitious project to develop a collection of cases that illustrate real-world examples of measuring the return on investment in a variety of training and HR programs. To find cases for the initial volume, more than 2,000 individuals were contacted, including practitioners, authors, researchers, consultants, and conference presenters. In addition, organizations perceived to be respected and admired were contacted. The result was the publication of *In Action: Measuring Return on Investment, Volume 1,* published in 1994, and *Volume 2,* published in 1997 [2]. *Volume 3* is planned for publication in 2001.

Combinations of books and cases have been published in other fields. For example, *The Consultant's Scorecard* [15] offers case studies about the ROI process in the consulting field. This book is the first publication to focus primarily on ROI in HR.

Although examples of the progress of measuring the ROI in HR are available, it has become a critical topic that constantly haunts the field. The need is clear. The interest in ROI will persist as long as HR budgets continue to increase and the HR function holds the promise of helping organizations improve. Much progress must be made to meet this important need.

BARRIERS TO IMPLEMENTING THE ROI PROCESS

Although progress is being made in the implementation of ROI, barriers can inhibit implementation of the concept. Some of these barriers are realistic, while others are actually myths based on false perceptions. This section briefly describes each barrier.

Costs and Time

The ROI process will add some additional costs and time to the HR program, although the added amount should not be excessive. As will be described throughout this book, a comprehensive ROI process will probably not add more than 3 to 5 percent to the HR program budget. The additional investment in ROI would perhaps be offset by the additional results achieved from these interventions and the elimination or prevention of unproductive or unprofitable interventions. This barrier alone stops many ROI implementations early in the process.

Lack of Skills and Orientation for HR Staff

Many HR staff members do not understand ROI, nor do they have the basic skills necessary to apply the process within their scope of responsibilities. Also, the typical program does not focus on results, but more on qualitative data. Consequently, a tremendous barrier to implementation is the change needed for the overall orientation, attitude, and skills of HR staff members. As Pogo, the cartoon character, once said, "We have met the enemy, and he is us." This certainly applies to ROI implementation in HR.

Faulty Initial Analysis

Many HR programs do not have an adequate initial analysis and assessment. Some of these programs have been implemented for the wrong reasons and are based on management requests or on efforts to chase a popular fad or trend in the industry. If a program is not needed, the program probably won't produce enough benefits to overcome the costs. An ROI calculation for an unnecessary HR program will likely yield a negative value. This is a realistic barrier for many programs.

Fear

Some HR staff members do not pursue ROI because of fear of failure or fear of the unknown. Fear of failure appears in many ways. They may have concerns about the consequences of a negative ROI. Also, a comprehensive measurement process can stir up the traditional fear of change. This fear, although often based on unrealistic assumptions and a lack of knowledge of the process, is so strong that it becomes a real barrier to many ROI implementations.

Discipline and Planning

A successful ROI implementation requires much planning and a disciplined approach to keep the process on track. Implementation schedules, evaluation targets, ROI analysis plans, measurement and evaluation policies, and follow-up schedules are required. The practitioner may not have enough discipline and determination to stay on course. This becomes a barrier, particularly when no immediate pressures to measure the return exist. If the client is not requiring ROI, the HR staff may not allocate time for planning and coordination. Also, other pressures and priorities often eat into the time necessary for ROI implementation. Only carefully planned implementations will succeed.

False Assumptions

Many consultants have false assumptions about the ROI process that keep them from attempting ROI. Typical false assumptions include the following:

- ☐ ROI can be applied to only a few narrowly focused projects.
- ☐ Senior managers do not want to see the results of HR interventions expressed in monetary values.
- ☐ If the client does not ask for ROI, it should not be pursued.
- ☐ If the CEO does not ask for ROI, then he or she does not expect it.

These false assumptions form realistic barriers that impede the progress of ROI implementation.

Benefits of Implementing the ROI Process

Although the benefits of adopting a comprehensive measurement and evaluation process (including ROI) may be obvious, several important benefits can be derived from the routine use of this process. A summary should be helpful.

Show the Contribution of Selected HR Interventions

With the ROI process, the HR staff and the client will know the specific contribution of the HR program in terms that were not previously developed nor in a language understood by the client group. The ROI will show the actual benefits versus the cost, elevating the evaluation data to the ultimate level of analysis. This process presents indisputable evidence that the program succeeded.

Earn the Respect of Senior Management

Measuring the ROI of an HR program or intervention is one of the best ways to earn the respect and support of the senior management team—not only for a particular project but also for other interventions as well. Managers will respect processes that add bottom-line value presented in terms they understand. The result of this analysis is comprehensive, and when applied consistently and comprehensively in several projects, it can convince management that the HR function is an important investment and not just an expense. Middle-level managers will see that HR is making a viable contribution to their immediate objectives. This is a critical step toward building an appropriate partnership with the senior management team.

Gain the Confidence of Clients

The client, who requests and authorizes a project, will now have a complete set of data to show the overall success of the process. Not hampered by a lack of qualitative or quantitative data, this data set provides a complete profile from different sources, at different time frames, and with different types of data. These data reveal the process that has occurred and validate the initial decision to move forward with the HR program.

Improve the HR Processes

Because a variety of feedback data are collected during the HR program, a comprehensive analysis (including ROI) provides data to drive changes in HR processes and make adjustments during a program. It also provides data that help improve HR interventions in the future when certain processes are revealed as nonproductive while others add value. Thus, the ROI process is an important process-improvement tool.

Develop a Results-Focused Approach

The communication of data at different time frames and with the detailed planning that is involved with the ROI process focuses the entire team, including stakeholders, on bottom-line results. This focus often enhances the results that can be achieved because the ultimate goals are clearly in mind. In essence, the process begins with the end in mind. All the processes, activities, and steps are clearly focused on the ultimate outcomes. As the HR program demonstrates success, confidence in using the process grows, which enhances the results of future programs and initiatives.

Alter or Enhance HR Programs

This benefit is twofold. First, if a program is not working effectively, and the results are not materializing, the ROI process will prompt changes or modifications to move the HR program back on track. On rare occasions, the intervention may have to be halted if it is not adding the appropriate value. Although stopping the HR program will take courage, it will reap important benefits with the client if it is clearly evident that it will not produce results. The other part of this benefit is that if the HR program succeeds greatly, perhaps the same type of intervention can be applied to other areas. It makes a convincing argument that if one division has a successful program and another division has the same needs, the program may add the same value and enhance the overall success and replication of all HR initiatives.

FINAL THOUGHTS

The need for a balanced approach to HR accountability is significant. Most organizations spend less than 1 percent of their direct budgets on accountability processes. This figure only considers the post-program analysis or comprehensive review process. Implementing the ROI process requires an expenditure closer to 5 percent, thus becoming a significant project for larger organizations.

Certain symptoms indicate an organization is ready to implement ROI within its HR function. Many of these symptoms reflect the key drivers discussed earlier in this chapter, causing pressure to pursue ROI.

Figure 1-4 is a checklist to help you determine if your organization is a candidate for ROI implementation.

This chapter provided a brief overview of the ROI process, which is presented in detail in the remainder of the book. It clearly underscored the urgency of the challenge; now is the time

Is Your Organization a Candidate for ROI Implementation?					

Read each question and check off the most appropriate level of agreement (1 = Disagree; 5 = Total Agreement). The higher the total score, the better candidate your company is for ROI.

	Disagree				Agree
	1	2	3	4	5
1. My organization is considered a large organization with a wide variety of HR programs.	☐	☐	☐	☐	☐
2. We have a large HR budget that reflects the interest of senior management.	☐	☐	☐	☐	☐
3. Our organization has a culture of measurement and is focused on establishing a variety of measures including HR.	☐	☐	☐	☐	☐
4. My organization is undergoing significant change.	☐	☐	☐	☐	☐
5. There is pressure from senior management to measure results of our HR initiatives.	☐	☐	☐	☐	☐
6. My HR function currently has a very low investment in measurement and evaluation.	☐	☐	☐	☐	☐
7. My organization has suffered more than one HR program disaster in the past.	☐	☐	☐	☐	☐
8. My organization has a new leader for HR.	☐	☐	☐	☐	☐
9. My management team would like to be the leader in HR processes.	☐	☐	☐	☐	☐
10. The image of our HR function is less than satisfactory.	☐	☐	☐	☐	☐
11. My clients are demanding that our HR processes show bottom-line results.	☐	☐	☐	☐	☐

Figure 1-4

	Disagree				Agree
	1	2	3	4	5
12. My HR function competes with other functions within our organization for resources.	☐	☐	☐	☐	☐
13. My organization has increased its focus on linking processes to the strategic direction of the company.	☐	☐	☐	☐	☐
14. My HR function is a key player in change initiatives currently taking place in my organization.	☐	☐	☐	☐	☐
15. Our overall HR budget is growing, and we are required to prove the bottom-line value of our HR processes.	☐	☐	☐	☐	☐

Total Score: _____

Figure 1-4. Continued.

to develop a comprehensive measurement and evaluation process, including the ROI. It also showed how various forces are creating this important need for a comprehensive evaluation process. This chapter also defined the pieces to the evaluation puzzle: evaluation framework, the process model, operating standards and philosophy, implementation, and case application. When these pieces come together, a reliable, credible process is developed that can be replicated from one project to another. This process is not without its concerns and barriers, but many of them can be overcome with simplified, economical methods. The remainder of the book provides details of each step of the ROI process and addresses implementation issues. Part IV provides case studies describing how the process has been implemented in various organizations.

REFERENCES

1. Sibbet, David. *Harvard Business Review, 75 Years of Management Ideas and Practice 1922–1997*. Boston: *Harvard Business Review,* 1997.

2. Phillips, Jack J. (Ed.) *Measuring the Return on Investment, Vol. 1 and Vol. 2*. In Action Series. Alexandria, Va.: American Society for Training and Development, 1994 and 1997.
3. Odiorne, G. S. *Personnel Administration by Objectives*. Homewood, Ill.: Irwin, 1971.
4. Wyner, W. E., and Parente, J. A. "Employee Surveys: What Employers Are Doing and What Works." *Employment Relations Today,* Winter 1991–92, pp. 477–484.
5. Invancevich, J. M. *Human Resource Management*. Chicago: Irwin, 1995.
6. Gómez-Mejía, L. R., Balkin, D. B., and Cardy, R. L. *Managing Human Resources*. Englewood Cliffs, N.J.: Prentice Hall, 1995.
7. Merrihue, W. V., and Katzell, R. A. "ERI—Yardstick of Employee Relations." *Harvard Business Review,* Vol. 33, No. 6, 1955, pp. 91–99.
8. LaPointe, J. R. "Human Resource Performance Indexes." *Personnel Journal,* No. 62, 1983, pp. 545, 553.
9. Phillips, Jack J. *The Development of a Human Resources Effectiveness Index*. Ph.D. dissertation, April 1988.
10. Cascio, W. F. *Managing Human Resources: Productivity, Quality of Work Life, Profits,* 4th ed. New York: McGraw-Hill, 1993.
11. Pauly, D. "HR: The New Profit Center." *Human Resource Executive,* August 1993.
12. Kromling, L. K. "CalComp Considers HR a Business Unit." *Personnel Journal,* February 1993.
13. Phillips, Jack J. *Accountability in Human Resource Management*. Houston, Tex.: Gulf Publishing, 1996.
14. Kirkpatrick, Donald L. *Evaluating Training Programs: The Four Levels*. San Francisco: Berrett-Koehler, 1994.
15. Phillips, Jack J. *The Consultant's Scorecard: Tracking Six Key Measures for Consulting Projects*. New York: McGraw-Hill, 2000.

CHAPTER 2

Initial Analysis and Planning

Few things are more important in evaluating an HR program than the initial analysis and planning, particularly the planning for accountability processes. When attempting to measure the success of an HR program after the program is implemented, an obvious conclusion is often reached: There should have been more planning. The initial analysis and planning have several advantages and involve several key issues explored in this chapter. The first issue involves specifying what the evaluation project will involve. Next, and perhaps more importantly, the chapter shows how to determine the success of the project—in advance, in specific detail. Then the chapter examines the process of ensuring that all the key measures or groups of measures are identified to reflect the success of the project, focusing on different levels of analysis. Finally, the chapter introduces a variety of planning tools that can be helpful in setting up the initial HR program evaluation.

EVALUATION: PROJECT REQUIREMENTS

When it comes to specifying the requirements of an HR program evaluation, there can never be too much detail. Evaluation projects often go astray and fail to reach their full success because of misunderstandings and differences in expectations. This section shows the key issues that must be addressed before the HR program evaluation actually begins. These issues are often outlined in the project proposal or sometimes in the outline and scope of the project's documentation. In other cases, it is the planning or implementation document for the actual evaluation project. Regardless of when it is developed, or for what purpose it is developed, each of the areas listed below should be identified in some way. More importantly, the client and the HR staff need to reach an agreement about these key issues.

Objectives of the Evaluation Project

When it comes to evaluation projects, there are two sets of objectives. First, there are the objectives for the evaluation project itself, indicating specifically what will be accomplished and delivered through the evaluation process. The other set of objectives is called the program objectives and focuses on the goals of the actual HR program that will ultimately add value to the organization. The program objectives are discussed later. Here, our focus is on the objectives of the evaluation project.

Every evaluation project should have a major project objective, and in most cases there are multiple objectives. The objectives are as specific as possible and focused directly on the assignment. Examples of evaluation project objectives are as follows:

☐ Determine if the HR program is accomplishing its objectives.
☐ Identify the strengths and weaknesses in the HR program.
☐ Determine the benefit/cost ratio of the HR program.
☐ Determine who should participate in future initiatives.
☐ Identify who benefited the most or the least from the HR program.

☐ Reinforce major points made to the target population.
☐ Gather data to assist in pursuing future initiatives.

As this list illustrates, the objectives are broad in scope, outlining from an overall perspective what is to be accomplished. The details of timing, specifications, and specific deliverables come later. The broad evaluation project objectives are critical because they bring focus to the project quickly. They define the basic parameters of the project and are often the beginning points of the discussion of the evaluation project.

Scope

The scope of the evaluation project needs to be clearly defined. The scope can pinpoint key parameters addressed by the project. The following list shows typical scoping issues that should be defined in the project:

☐ Target group for the evaluation
☐ Location of target group
☐ Time frame for the evaluation
☐ Technology necessary to conduct the evaluation
☐ Access to stakeholders
☐ Functional area for coverage
☐ Product line for coverage
☐ Type of process/activity being evaluated
☐ Constraints on data collection

Perhaps the project is limited to certain employee groups, a functional area of the business, a specific location, a unique type of system, or a precise time frame. Sometimes there is a constraint on the type of data collected or access to certain individuals, such as customers. Whatever the scope involves, it needs to be clearly defined in this section.

Timing

Timing is critical in showing specifically when activities will occur. This means not only the timing of the delivery of the final report but also the timing of particular steps and events—including when data are needed, analyzed, and reported and when presentations are made. The following list shows typical scheduled activities:

- ☐ HR solutions developed
- ☐ Implementation started
- ☐ Implementation complete
- ☐ Start of evaluation project
- ☐ Data collection design complete
- ☐ Evaluation design complete
- ☐ Data collection begins
- ☐ Data collection complete
- ☐ Specific data collection issues (for example, pilot testing, executive interviews)
- ☐ Data analysis complete
- ☐ Preliminary results available
- ☐ Report developed
- ☐ Presentation to management

Deliverables from the Evaluation Project

This section describes exactly what the client will receive when the evaluation project is completed in terms of reports, documents, systems, processes, manuals, forms, flowcharts, or rights to new technology. Whatever the specific deliverables, they are clearly defined in this section. Most projects will have a final report, but they often go much further, delivering process tools and suggested methodologies for improving the HR program evaluated.

Methodology

If a specific methodology is to be used for the evaluation project, it should be defined. A reference should be made to the appropriateness of the methodology, as well as its reliability, its validity, its previous success, and how the methodology will accomplish what is needed for the evaluation project to be successful.

Steps

The specific steps that will occur should be defined showing key milestones. This provides a step-by-step understanding and tracking of the evaluation project so that at any given time the client and the HR staff can see not only where progress is made but where the project is going next.

Resources Required for the Evaluation Project

This section will define the specific resources required to implement the evaluation. This could include access to individuals, vendors, technology, equipment, facilities, competitors, or customers. All resources that may be needed should be listed along with details regarding the timing and circumstances under which the resources will be needed.

Cost

The cost section details the specific costs tied to the different steps of the evaluation process. There is often reluctance to detail costs; however, it is important to understand the different steps of the process and their relative costs. When calculating the ROI for an HR program, all costs are considered. This includes not only development and implementation costs but also the costs of evaluating the program. Chapter 7 goes into detail about costs.

LEVELS OF OBJECTIVES FOR HR PROGRAMS

Eventually an HR program or intervention should lead to some level of impact on the business of the organization. In some situations, the intervention is aimed at softer issues, such as employee satisfaction, customer satisfaction, and stress reduction. In other situations, the program is aimed at more tangible issues, such as cost reductions, productivity, and number of accidents. Whatever the case, HR programs and interventions should have multiple levels of objectives. These levels of objectives, ranging from qualitative to quantitative, define precisely what will occur as a particular program is implemented in the organization. Table 2-1 shows the different levels of objectives. These objectives are so critical that they need special attention in their development and use.

Table 2-1
Multiple Levels of Objectives

Levels of Objectives	Focus of Objectives
Level 1 Reaction and Satisfaction	Defines a specific level of satisfaction and reaction to the HR program as it is revealed and communicated to the stakeholders
Level 2 Learning	Defines specific skills and knowledge requirements as the stakeholders learn new skills and acquire new knowledge through the HR program
Level 3 Application and Implementation	Defines key issues around the implementation of the HR program in the workplace
Level 4 Business Impact	Defines the specific business measures that will change or improve as a result of the implementation of the HR program
Level 5 ROI	Defines the specific return on investment from the implementation of the HR program, comparing costs with benefits

Satisfaction and Reaction

For any program to succeed, various stakeholders must react favorably, or at least not negatively. Ideally, the stakeholders should be satisfied with the program because the best solutions offer win-win results. The stakeholders are those who are directly involved in implementing or using the program or intervention. These can be the employees involved in implementing the work, or the supervisors or team leaders responsible for the redesigned or changed process. Stakeholders could also be managers who must support or assist the process in some way. Finally, the stakeholders could involve the teams and task forces involved in the intervention.

It is important to routinely obtain this type of information so that feedback can be used to make adjustments, keep the project on track, and perhaps even redesign certain parts of the process. One problem with many HR interventions is that specific objectives at this level are not developed, and data collection mechanisms are not put in place to ensure appropriate feedback for making needed adjustments.

Learning Objectives

Many HR programs and interventions will involve a learning objective. In some interventions, the learning component is quite significant. To ensure that the various stakeholders have learned what they need to learn to make the intervention effective, learning objectives are developed. Learning objectives are critical to the measurement process because they define the desired competence or performance necessary to make the program successful. Learning objectives provide a focus for participants, clearly indicating what they must learn.

The best learning objectives describe the observable and measurable behaviors that are necessary for success with the HR program. They are often outcome-based, clearly worded, and specific. They specify what the particular stakeholder must do as a result of implementing the HR program. Learning objectives often have three components:

1. Performance—what the participant or stakeholder will be able to do as the program is implemented
2. Conditions under which the participant or stakeholder will perform the various tasks and processes
3. Criteria—the degree or level of proficiency necessary to perform a new task, process, or procedure that is part of the HR solution

The three types of learning objectives are often defined as:

1. Awareness—familiarity with terms, concepts, and processes
2. Knowledge—general understanding of concepts, processes, or procedures
3. Performance—ability to demonstrate skills at least on a basic level

Application and Implementation Objectives

As a solution is actually implemented in the workplace, the application and implementation objectives clearly define what is expected and often what level of performance is expected. Application objectives are similar to learning objectives but reflect the actual implementation of a new HR program. They also involve particular milestones, indicating specifically when intervals of the process are implemented. Application objectives are critical because they describe the expected outcomes in the interim—that is, between the actual learning of new tasks and procedures and the actual impact that will result. Application or implementation objectives describe how things should be performed or the state of the workplace after the solution is implemented. They provide a basis for the evaluation of on-the-job changes and performance. The emphasis is on what has occurred on the job as a result of the HR program.

The best application objectives identify behaviors that are observable and measurable or action steps in a process that can easily be observed or measured. They specify what the various stakeholders will change or have changed as a result of the HR program. As with learning objectives, application or implementation objectives may have three components:

☐ Performance—describes what the stakeholders have changed or have accomplished in a specific time frame after the implementation of the HR solution

☐ Condition—specifies the circumstances under which the stakeholders have performed or are performing the tasks or implementing the solution

☐ Criteria—indicates the degree or level of proficiency under which the solution is implemented, the task is being performed, or the steps are completed

There are two types of basic application objectives. They are knowledge-based—when the general use of concepts, processes, and procedures is important—and behavior-based, which is when the participant is able to demonstrate the actual use of skills, accomplishments of particular tasks, or completion of particular milestones. Here are some typical key questions regarding application and implementation objectives:

1. What new or improved knowledge will be applied on the job?
2. What is the frequency of skill application?
3. What specific new task will be performed?
4. What new steps will be implemented?
5. What action items will be implemented?
6. What new procedures will be implemented or changed?
7. What new guidelines will be implemented?
8. What new processes will be implemented?
9. Which meetings need to be held?
10. Which tasks, steps, or procedures will be discontinued?

Application objectives have always been included to some degree in HR programs but have not been as specific as they need to be. To be effective, they must clearly define the workplace environment when the solution is successfully implemented.

Impact Objectives

Every HR program should result in improving business impact. Business impact represents the key business measures that should be improved as the application or implementation objectives are achieved. The impact objectives are critical to measuring business performance because they define the ultimate expected outcome from the HR program. They describe business-unit performance that should be connected to the HR solution. Above all, they place emphasis on achieving bottom-line results, which key client groups expect and demand.

The best impact objectives contain measures that are linked to the solution from the HR intervention. They describe measures that are easily collected and are well-known to the client group. They are results-based, are clearly worded, and specify what the stakeholders have ultimately accomplished in the business unit as a result of the HR program.

Impact objectives include output, quality, cost, and time. These four categories are often considered hard data. The major categories of soft data impact objectives are customer service, work climate, and work habits.

Return on Investment

A fifth level of objectives for HR programs is the actual expected return on investment. These objectives define the expected payoff from the HR solution and compare the input resources, the cost of the HR program, with the value of the ultimate outcome—the monetary benefits. This is typically expressed as a desired return on investment percentage that compares the annual monetary benefits minus the cost, divided by the actual cost, and multiplied by 100. A zero percent ROI indicates a break-even HR solution. A 50 percent ROI indicates that the cost of the program is recaptured and an additional 50 percent "earnings" are achieved.

For many HR interventions, the ROI objective is larger than what might be expected from the ROI of other expenditures, such as the purchase of a new company, a new building, or major equipment; but the two are related. In many organizations the ROI objective is set slightly higher than the ROI expected from other interventions because of the relative newness of applying the ROI concept to HR programs. For example, if the expected ROI from the purchase of a new company is 20 percent, the ROI from an HR program might be nearer 25 percent. The important point is that the ROI objective should be established up front through discussions with the client.

Importance of Specific Objectives

Developing specific objectives at different levels for HR interventions provides important benefits. First, objectives provide direction to the HR staff members directly involved in the process to help keep them on track. Objectives define exactly what is expected at different time frames from different individuals and involving different types of data. Also, objectives provide guidance to the support staff and the client so that they fully understand the ultimate goal and impact of the HR program. Further, objectives provide important information and motivation for the stakeholders. In most HR initiatives, the stakeholders are actively involved and will influence the results of the solution. Specific objectives provide goals and motivation for the stakeholders so that they will clearly see the gains that should be achieved. More importantly, objectives provide important information for the key client groups to clearly understand what the landscape will look like when the HR intervention is complete. Finally, from an evaluation perspective, the objectives provide a basis for measuring success.

LINKING EVALUATION WITH NEEDS

There is a distinct linkage between evaluation objectives and original needs driving an HR intervention. Chapter 1 introduced the five levels of evaluation and showed how they are critical to providing an overall assessment of the impact of an HR program. The earlier material in this chapter showed the importance of setting objectives around the HR program. The objectives define the specific improvements sought. In this section, we will make

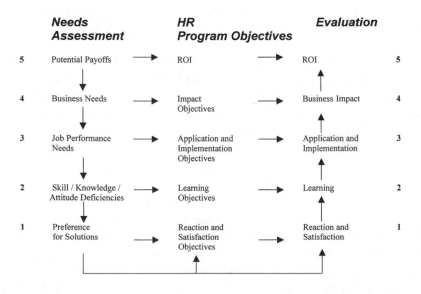

Figure 2-1.

a further connection to the original needs assessment. Figure 2-1 shows the connection between evaluation and needs assessment. This figure shows the important linkage from the initial problem or opportunity that created the need to the evaluation and measurement. Level 5 defines the potential payoff and examines the possibility for a return on investment before the project is even pursued. Level 4 analysis focuses directly on the business needs that precipitated an HR intervention. At Level 3, the specific issues in the workplace focus on job performance in detail. At Level 2, the specific knowledge, skill, or attitude deficiencies are uncovered as learning needs are identified. Finally, the preferences for the structure of the solution define the Level 1 needs. This connection is critical and important to understanding all the elements that must go into an effective HR solution.

An example will help illustrate this linkage. Figure 2-2 shows an example of linking needs assessment with the evaluation of a

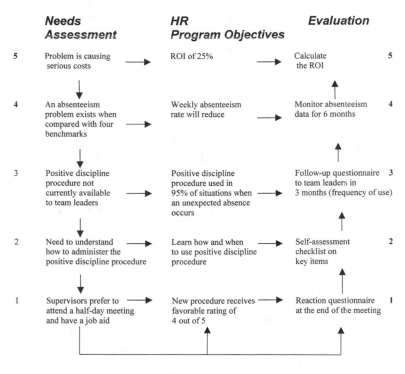

Figure 2-2.

program involving a reduction in absenteeism. As the figure shows, the first step is to see if the problem is great enough at Level 5. However, this sometimes causes a validation of the problem using Level 4 data. Four benchmarks are used to gauge the current absenteeism problem. These are:

☐ Absenteeism is higher than it used to be.
☐ Absenteeism is higher than at other locations within the company.
☐ Absenteeism is higher than at other facilities in the local area.
☐ Absenteeism is higher than the general manager desires.

With the confirmation in Level 4 that there is a problem, a potential payoff is estimated. This involves estimating the cost of absenteeism and estimating the actual potential reduction that can come from the HR intervention. This develops a profile of potential payoff to see if the problem is worth solving.

At Level 3, the causes of excessive absenteeism are explored using a variety of techniques. One issue that is uncovered is that a positive discipline procedure is not currently available to team leaders when there is an unexpected absence. A learning component at Level 2 is also uncovered because the team leaders need to understand how and when to administer the positive discipline procedure. Finally, the specific way in which the program should be implemented is explored in terms of preferences at Level 1. In this case, supervisors preferred to attend a half-day meeting to learn the procedure and leave with a job aid that helps them with the process as they apply it.

These five levels provide an overall profile for determining if the problem is worth solving to begin with, as well as aligning problems with key measures and data necessary to develop the program objectives. The HR program objectives for each level are shown in the figure as well, as are the evaluation methods needed to verify that the appropriate changes did occur. This process is important to the development and implementation of an HR solution. Many HR programs are involved in developing the actual solution and implementing the solution, as is the case in this particular example. When this occurs, the above linkage connects the needs to actual objectives and then to evaluation.

The solution to the problem or opportunity is an important part of this linkage. Some programs may be involved in uncovering needs with the initial analysis to determine the actual causes of the problem and then recommend solutions. It is up to the client to then implement the solution, or implementation becomes part of another program. In both cases, the solutions are ultimately developed. If this has not been accomplished, multiple levels of analysis may be necessary for the intervention. Although other references exist that focus more specifically on the performance analysis to uncover different levels of needs, a brief summary is presented here.

Payoff Needs

The very first part of the process is to determine if the problem is worth solving or if the opportunity is large enough to warrant serious consideration. In some cases, this is obvious when serious problems are affecting the organization's operations and strategy. Still others may not be so obvious. At Level 5, it is important not only to identify needed business improvement measures at Level 4 but to also convert them into monetary values so the actual improvement can be converted to financial measures.

The second part of the process is to develop an approximate cost for the entire HR program. This could come from a detailed proposal or may be a rough estimate. At this stage it is only an estimate because the projected cost of the project is compared to the potential benefits to roughly determine if a payoff would result from addressing the issue. This step may be omitted in some situations when the problem must be solved regardless of the cost or if it becomes obvious that it is a high-payoff activity. Still other projects may be initiated when the potential payoff is not expected to be developed. For example, as an organization strives to be a technology leader, it may be difficult to place a value on that goal.

Business Needs

In conjunction with Level 5, actual business data are examined to determine which measures need to improve. This includes an examination of organizational records and involves examining all types of hard and soft data. Usually one of the data items and its performance trigger the HR initiative or intervention—for example, market share may not be as much as it should be, costs may be excessive, quality may be deteriorating, or productivity may not be as high as it should be. These are the key issues that come directly from the data in the organization and are often found in the operating reports or records.

The supporting data may come not only from the operating reports but from annual reports, marketing data, industry data, major planning documents, or other important information sources that clearly indicate operating performance in terms of operation or strategy.

Job Performance Needs

The Level 3 analysis involves job performance or workplace needs. The task is to determine the cause of the problem as determined at Level 4 (that is, what is causing the business measure not to be at the desired level or to be inhibited in some way). Needs can vary considerably and may include, among others, the following:

1. Ineffective or inappropriate behavior
2. Dysfunctional work climate
3. Ineffective systems
4. Improper process flow
5. Ineffective procedures
6. Unsupported culture
7. Inappropriate technology
8. Unsupportive environment

These and other types of needs will have to be uncovered using a variety of problem-solving or analysis techniques. This may involve the use of data collection techniques discussed in this book such as surveys, questionnaires, focus groups, or interviews. It may involve a variety of problem-solving or analysis techniques such as root-cause analysis, fishbone diagrams, and other analysis techniques. Whatever is used, the key is to determine all the causes of the problem so that solutions can be developed. Often, multiple solutions are appropriate.

Learning Needs

Most problem analysis from Level 3 uncovers specific learning needs. It may be that learning inefficiencies, in terms of knowledge and skills, may contribute to the problem if they are not the major cause of it. In other situations, the actual solution applied may need a particular learning component as participants learn how to implement a new process, procedure, or system. The extent of learning required will determine whether formalized training is needed or if more informal, on-the-job methods can be used to build the necessary skills and knowledge. The learning would typically involve acquisition of knowledge or the development of skills necessary to improve the situation. In some cases, perceptions or attitudes may need to be altered or make the process successful in the future.

Preferences

The final level is to consider the preference for the solution. This involves determining the way in which those involved in the process prefer to have it changed or implemented. It may involve implementation preferences and/or learning preferences. Learning preferences may involve decisions such as when learning is expected and in what amounts, how it is presented, and the overall time frame. Implementation preferences may involve issues such as timing, support, expectation, and other key factors. The important point is to try to determine the specific preferences to the extent possible so that the complete profile of the solution can be adjusted accordingly.

PLANNING FOR MEASUREMENT AND EVALUATION

An important ingredient in the success of the ROI process is to properly plan early in the process. Appropriate up-front attention will save much time later when data are actually collected and analyzed, thus improving accuracy and reducing the cost of the evaluation process. It also avoids any confusion surrounding what will be accomplished, by whom, and at what time. Two planning documents are key and should be completed before the intervention is designed or developed.

Data Collection Plan

Table 2-2 shows a completed data collection plan for a sexual harassment prevention program. The program was initiated to reduce sexual harassment complaints and the resulting employee turnover. An ROI calculation was planned to show the value of preventive projects.

This document provides a place for the major elements and issues regarding collecting data for the five evaluation levels. In the first column, broad areas for objectives are stated, which are appropriate for planning. Specific, detailed objectives are developed later, before the HR program is designed. In the second column, the specific measures or data descriptors are indicated when they are necessary to explain the measures linked to the objectives. In the next column, the specific data collection method is briefly described using standard terminology. Next, the source of the data is entered. Data sources will vary considerably, but usually include participants, team leaders, company records, and the client. In the next column, the time frame for data collection is usually referenced from the beginning of the project. Finally, the responsibility for data collection is described.

The objectives for reaction and satisfaction usually include positive reactions to the intervention and suggested improvements. Planned actions may be included in the input. Reaction and satisfaction data may be collected at different intervals. In this example, feedback is taken only at one time, at the end of implementation of the solution.

Because Level 2 evaluation focuses on the measures of learning, specific objectives include those areas where participants are expected to learn new tasks, knowledge, skills, or attitudes. The evaluation method is the specific way in which learning is assessed, in this case, a test and observation of skill practice by the facilitator of the meeting. The timing for Level 2 evaluation is at the end of the implementation.

For application and implementation evaluation, the objectives represent broad areas of application, including significant on-the-job activities and implementation steps. In this example, the methods include questionnaires, surveys, and monitoring company records. This information is usually collected a matter of months after the implementation. Because responsibilities are often shared among several groups, including the HR staff, it is important to

Table 2-2
Example of Completed Data Collection Plan

Project: Preventing Sexual Harassment   Responsibility: _____   Date: _____

Data Collection Plan

Level	Broad Objectives	Measures/Data	Data Collection Method	Data Sources	Timing	Responsibilities
1. Reaction, Satisfaction, and Planned Actions	• Obtain a positive reaction to project and materials • Obtain input for suggestions for improvement • Identify planned actions		• Questionnaire	• Supervisors	• End of Implementation	• Project coordinator
2. Learning	• Knowledge of policy on sexual harassment • Knowledge of inappropriate and illegal behavior • Skills to investigate and discuss sexual harassment	• True/False statements • Skill practices	• Pre- and post-test • Observation	• Supervisors • Supervisors	• Beginning of project and end of implementation • During session	• Meeting facilitator
3. Application	• Administer policy • Conduct meeting with employees to explain policy and issues • Ensure that the workplace is free of sexual harassment	• Completed meeting records	• Questionnaire • Company records • Employee survey (25% sample)	• Supervisors • New supervisors and employees	• 6 months after program • 1 month after program • 6 months after program	• Project evaluator • HRIS staff • Employee communications
4. Business Results	• Reduce internal complaints • Reduce external complaints • Reduce employee turnover	• Formal complaints filed with HR VP • Charges filed with EEOC • Monthly voluntary termination	• Performance monitoring • Questionnaire	• Company records • Supervisors	• Monthly for 1 year before and after program • 6 months after program	• Project evaluator

clarify this issue early in the process. In this example, four groups share the responsibilities.

For impact evaluation, objectives focus on business impact measures influenced by the intervention. The measures/data column includes the way in which each item is measured. For example, if one of the objectives is to improve quality, a specific measure would indicate how that quality is actually measured, such as defects per thousand units produced. In the example, two types of complaints are defined and are very different. The third measure, turnover, is also defined. Two sources of data are used at this level: company records and questionnaires. Although the preferred data collection method is performance monitoring, other methods such as questionnaires may be appropriate as in this example. The timing depends on how quickly the intervention can generate a sustained impact on the three measures. It is usually a matter of months after the program is completed. In this example, data were collected at six-month intervals. A project evaluator is responsible for data collection at this level. If appropriate, an ROI objective (Level 5) is included. It was not considered appropriate for this example.

The data collection plan is an important part of the evaluation strategy and should be completed prior to moving forward with the intervention; the plan is completed before pursuing an ROI evaluation. The plan provides a clear direction of what types of data will be collected, how they will be collected, where they will be collected, when they will be collected, and who will collect them.

ROI Analysis Plan

Table 2-3 shows a completed ROI analysis plan for the same sexual harassment prevention program. This planning document is the continuation of the data collection plan presented in Table 2-2 and captures information on several key items that are necessary to develop the actual ROI calculation. In the first column, significant data items are listed; these are usually business impact measures (Level 4 data items), but in some cases could include Level 3 data. These items will be used in the ROI analysis. The method for isolating the effects of the HR program is listed next to each data item in the second column. For most projects, the method will be the same for each data item, but there could

Table 2-3
Example of Completed ROI Analysis Plan

Project: Preventing Sexual Harassment **Responsibility:** _____ **Date:** _____

ROI Analysis Plan

Data Items	Methods of Isolating the Effects of the Intervention	Methods of Converting Data	Cost Categories	Intangible Benefits	Communication Targets	Other Influences/Issues
Formal internal complaints of sexual harassment	• Trendline analysis • Participant estimation (as a backup)	• Historical costs with estimation form EEO/AA staff (internal expert)	• Initial analysis and assessment solution • Solution development • Coordination/ facilitation • Client time for project • Materials • Food/refreshments • Salaries and benefits for participants • Evaluation and reporting	• Job satisfaction • Absenteeism • Stress reduction • Public image • Recruiting	• All employees (condensed info.) • Senior executives (summary report with detailed backup) • All supervisors and managers (brief report) • HR/consulting staff (full report)	• Several initiatives to reduce turnover were implemented during this time period • Must not duplicate benefits from both internal and external complaints
External complaints of sexual harassment	• Trendline analysis • Participant estimation (as a backup)	• Historical costs with estimation form EEO/AA staff (internal expert)				
Employee voluntary turnover	• Forecasting using percentage of turnover related to sexual harassment	• External studies within industry				

be variations. For example, if no historical data are available for one data item, then trendline analysis is not possible for that item, although it may be appropriate for other items. In this example, a control group arrangement was not feasible, but a trendline analysis was. Participant estimates were used as a backup.

The method for converting data to monetary values is included in the third column. In this example, complaints are converted to monetary values with two approaches: using costs in the company records and collecting expert input from the staff directly involved in the process. The cost categories planned for capture are outlined in the fourth column. Instructions about how certain costs should be prorated are noted here. The cost categories will be somewhat consistent from one HR program to another. However, a specific cost that is unique to this program is also noted. The anticipated intangible benefits expected from this program are outlined in the fifth column. This list is generated from discussions about the intervention with sponsors and subject matter experts.

Communication targets are outlined in the sixth column. Although there could be many groups that should receive the information, four target groups are always recommended: senior management, managers of participants, participants, and the HR staff. Each of these four groups needs to know about the results of the ROI analysis. Finally, other issues or events that might influence program implementation are highlighted in the seventh column. Typical items include the capability of participants, the degree of access to data sources, and unique data analysis issues.

The ROI analysis plan, when combined with the data collection plan, provides detailed information on calculating the ROI, illustrating how the process will develop from beginning to end. When completed, these two plans should provide the direction necessary for an ROI evaluation and should integrate with the overall project plan.

SHORTCUT WAYS TO PLAN FOR THE EVALUATION

This chapter presents a very comprehensive approach to planning the evaluation of HR programs and interventions. The process is thorough, which is the approach often needed in most major programs. When a major program involves hundreds of thousands or even millions of dollars of investment, it is important to allocate the appropriate time and budgets for developing the actual ROI. For smaller-scale projects, a more simplified process is appropriate. Four key issues should be addressed when taking a shortcut approach to planning for the evaluation.

Define Expectations and Requirements

Even in small-scale, simple projects, it is important to detail the specific requirements needed for the program to be successful and to clearly define the expectations. Here, the client should be as specific as possible in terms of the desired conduct and expectations from the HR initiative. As much detail that can be developed is recommended. This can be included in the proposal or a very brief working document, but it should highlight the very key issues that can cause the process to go astray.

Define Workforce Changes

It is important to define the anticipated changes at the work site—changes that will be driven by the HR program and, more specifically, the solutions from the program. Thinking through the changes often will help identify potential barriers and enablers to the process. It will define what the employees and other stakeholders will experience or be expected to do to make the program successful.

Define Expected Outcomes

The various levels of objectives are helpful for the simplest projects. It is recommended that some consideration be given to developing these multiple levels of objectives. More importantly, the ultimate impact expected should be clearly defined in terms of the measures that should change or improve if the program is successful. Along with this definition would be the parameters around collecting data and methods to isolate the effects of the program. The more specifics around these outcomes, the better the program will be in terms of its results being focused and having a clear understanding of what is necessary for success.

Develop a Plan

While the two documents presented in Tables 2-2 and 2-3 may be too much detail for a simple program, there is no substitute for detailing these issues. Even a program with a $50,000 price tag is worth the few hours of planning to make sure that the key issues are covered in some way. Shortcut ways to develop some of those processes are possible and are described later in the book. The important point here is to develop some type of simplified plan, although the document may be less detailed than the two formal planning documents presented. Overall, this step is critical and cannot be ignored because the key issues must be addressed.

FINAL THOUGHTS

This chapter presented the initial analysis and planning for the evaluation of an HR program. The rationale for initial analysis and objectives was explored. The linkage of levels of evaluation, objectives, and needs was explored. This connection greatly simplifies the HR accountability process. Next, evaluation planning tools were introduced. When the ROI process is thoroughly planned, taking into consideration all potential strategies and techniques, it becomes manageable and achievable. The remaining chapters focus on the major elements of the ROI process.

FURTHER READING

Dean., Peter J., and Ripley, David E. (Eds.) "Performance Improvement Interventions: Performance Technologies in the Workplace," in *Methods for Organizational Learning*. Performance Improvement Series, Vol. 3. Washington, D.C.: The International Society for Performance Improvement, 1998.

Esque, Timm J., and Patterson, Patricia A. (Ed.) *Getting Results: Case Studies in Performance Improvement, Vol. 1.* Washington, D.C.: HRD Press/International Society for Performance Improvement, 1998.

Hiebeler, Robert, Kelly, Thomas B., and Ketteman, Charles. *Best Practices: Building Your Business With Customer-Focused Solutions.* New York: Arthur Andersen/Simon & Schuster, 1998.

Kaufman, Roger, Thiagarajan, Sivasailam, and MacGillis, Paula (Eds.) *The Guidebook for Performance Improvement: Working with Individuals and Organizations.* San Francisco: Pfeiffer, 1997.

Kaufman, Roger. *Strategic Thinking: A Guide to Identifying and Solving Problems.* Washington, D.C.: American Society for Training and Development, 1996.

Langley, Gerald J. et al. *The Improvement Guide: A Practical Approach to Enhancing Organizational Performance.* San Francisco: Jossey-Bass Publishers, 1996.

Swanson, Richard A., and Holton, Elwood F. III. *Results: How to Assess Performance, Learning, and Perceptions in Organizations.* San Francisco: Berrett-Koehler Publishers, 1999.

PART II

The ROI Process, Step-by-Step

CHAPTER 3

Collecting Data During HR Program Implementation

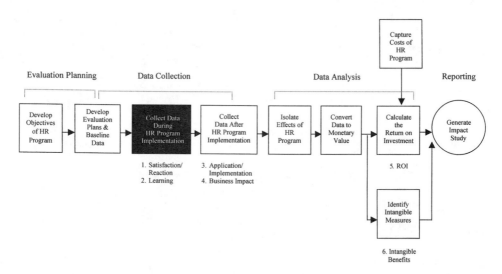

Because of the variety of approaches to collecting data at the first four levels (Level 1—reaction and satisfaction, Level 2—learning, Level 3—application and implementation, and Level 4—impact), two chapters are devoted to presenting the techniques and issues surrounding this major phase of evaluation. This chapter focuses on collecting data during implementation to measure participant reaction and satisfaction and learning. Chapter 4 covers collecting data after implementation to measure application and business impact. Although there is overlap in the methods for data collecting across the levels of evaluation, the two chapters are arranged according to the most likely method for the specific level.

Collecting data at all four levels is necessary because of the chain of impact that must exist for a program to be successful. Participants in the program should (1) experience a positive reaction to the program and its potential application, (2) acquire new skills or knowledge to implement the program, (3) change on-the-job behavior, actions, and tasks that should prompt a positive implementation, and (4) drive changes in business impact. The only way to know if the chain of impact has occurred is to collect data at all four levels.

MEASURING REACTION AND SATISFACTION

Collecting reaction and satisfaction data during the implementation of the HR program is the first operational phase of the ROI process. Client feedback data are powerful for making adjustments and measuring success. A variety of methods are available to capture reaction and satisfaction data at the appropriate time during implementation. This section outlines the most common approaches for collecting these critical data and explores several key issues about the use of the information.

Why Measure Reaction and Satisfaction?

It would be difficult to imagine an HR program being implemented without collecting feedback from those involved in the program, or at least from the client. Client feedback is critical to understanding how well the process is working or to gauge its success after it has been completed. It is always included in every HR initiative because of its crucial importance. However, the advantage of collecting this type of data goes beyond just the satisfaction of the client and includes many other key issues, making it one of the most important data collection efforts.

Customer Service Is Key. In these days of the customer service revolution, it is important to measure customer satisfaction. Without continuous improvement evidenced by customer satisfaction data and without sustained, favorable reactions to HR programs, it is difficult for an HR group to function properly. It is important to consider the different types of customers involved in programs. Three particular types of customers exist for almost every HR program. First, there are those directly involved in the program. They are key stakeholders who are directly affected by the HR program and often have to change processes and procedures, and make other job adjustments related to the program. In addition, they often have to learn new skills, tasks, and behaviors to make the program successful. These participants, as they are sometimes called, are critical to the success of the program, and their feedback is critical to making adjustments and changes in the program as it unfolds and is implemented. The second set of customers is those who are on the sidelines; those who are not directly involved, but have some interest in the HR initiative. The supporters, as they are sometimes called, are concerned about the program and are supporting it in some way. Their perception of the success of the program or potential success is important feedback, as this group will be in a position to influence the program in the future. The third set of stakeholders is perhaps the most important. This is the client group who actually pays for the program. This individual, or group of individuals, requests programs, supports programs, approves budgets, allocates resources, and ultimately must live with the success or failure of the program. This important group must be completely satisfied with the HR solution. Their level of satisfaction must be determined early, and adjustments must be made. In short, customer satisfaction is key to success and must be obtained in a variety of different ways to focus on the success.

Early Feedback Is Essential. HR initiatives can go astray quickly, and sometimes a specific program is the wrong (or incomplete) solution for the specified problem. There are times when a program can be mismatched from the beginning, so it is essential to get feedback early in the process so that adjustments can be made. This helps avoid misunderstandings, miscommunications, and, more importantly, misappropriations, as an improperly designed program is altered or changed quickly before more serious problems are created.

Making Adjustments and Changes to the Program. The concept of continuous process improvement suggests that a program must be adjusted and refined throughout its duration. There must be an important linkage between obtaining feedback and making changes and reporting changes back to the groups who provide the information. This survey-feedback-action loop is critical for any type of HR program.

Attention Is Appreciated. Many of the individuals involved in an HR program, particularly the affected population or participants, appreciate the opportunity to provide feedback. In too many situations, their input is ignored and their complaints disregarded. They appreciate the program leader or HR consultant asking for input and, more importantly, taking action as a result of that input. Other stakeholders and even clients appreciate the opportunity to provide feedback, not only early in the process, but throughout the process.

For Some, These Are the Most Important Data. Because feedback data are important to the program's success, they should be gathered in almost every HR initiative. They have become some of the most important data collected. Unfortunately, in some situations, program success is often measured by the feedback. As this book clearly shows, the feedback data are only one part of the evaluation puzzle and represent only one of the six types of data, yet their importance cannot be understated.

Comparing with Data from Other Programs. Some organizations collect reaction and satisfaction data from several sources using standard questions, and the data are then compared with data from other programs so that norms and standards can be developed. This is particularly helpful at the end of a program rollout as client satisfaction is gauged. These satisfaction data can be used not only to compare the success of the program but to relate to overall program success and even correlate with other successful measures. Data collection must be deliberately pursued in a systematic, logical, rational way. This section explores the key issues involved in collecting and using these important measures.

Sources of Data for Reaction and Satisfaction

When considering the possible data sources that will provide feedback on the success of an HR program, the categories are easily defined. The major categories of stakeholders are briefly described in this section.

Client/Senior Managers. One of the most useful data sources for ROI analysis is the client group, usually a senior management team. Whether an individual or a group, the client's perception is critical to program success. Clients can provide input on all types of issues and are usually available and willing to offer feedback. Collecting data from this source is preferred for reaction and satisfaction because the data usually reflect what is necessary to make adjustments and measure success.

HR Program Participants. The most widely used data source for an ROI analysis is the HR program participants, who are directly involved in or affected by the program. They must use the skills and knowledge acquired as a result of an HR initiative and apply them on the job. Sometimes they are asked to explain the potential impact of those actions. Participants are a rich source of data for almost every issue or part of the program. They are credible, since they are the individuals who must achieve the performance results and are often the most knowledgeable of the processes and other influencing factors. The challenge is to find an effective and efficient way to capture data in a consistent manner.

Team Leaders. Another important source of data is those individuals who directly supervise or lead program participants. This group will often have a vested interest in evaluation, since they have a stake in the process because their employees are directly involved in the program. Also, in many situations, they observe the participants as they attempt to use the knowledge and skills acquired from the initiative. Consequently, they can report on the successes linked to the initiative as well as the difficulties and problems associated with it. Although team leader input is usually best for reaction and satisfaction data, it can also be useful for other levels of evaluation data.

Team Members. In situations where entire teams are involved or affected by the HR program, all team members can provide information about the perceived changes prompted by the program. Input from team members is appropriate for issues directly involved in their work. Although collecting data from this source can be helpful and instructive, it is sometimes avoided because of the potential inaccuracies that can enter the feedback process. Team members must be capable of providing meaningful input.

Internal Customers. The individuals who serve as internal customers of the program participants are another source of data for a few types of HR programs. In these situations, internal customers provide input on perceived changes linked to the HR program. This source of data is more appropriate when HR programs directly affect the internal customers. They report on how the program has (or will) influence their work or the service they receive. Because of the subjective nature of this process and the lack of opportunity to fully evaluate the application of skills, of the participants, this source of data may be somewhat limited.

Program Implementation Leader. In some situations, the HR program implementation leader may provide input on the success of the program. The input from these sources may be based on on-the-job observations during the implementation and after it has been completed. Data from this source have limited use because program leaders may have a vested interest in the outcome of evaluation, so their input may lack objectivity.

Areas of Feedback for Reaction and Satisfaction Data

There are many topics that are critical targets for feedback because there are so many issues and processes involved in a typical HR program implementation. Feedback is needed in almost every major issue, step, or process to make sure things are moving forward properly. The following list shows the typical major areas of feedback for most programs:

☐ Appropriateness of objectives
☐ Appropriateness of plans
☐ Appropriateness of schedule
☐ Progress made with plans
☐ Relevance of program
☐ Support for program
☐ Resources for program
☐ Integration of program with other systems
☐ Program leadership
☐ Program staffing
☐ Program coordination
☐ Program communication
☐ Motivation of program participants
☐ Cooperation of program participants
☐ Capability of program participants
☐ Likelihood of program success
☐ Barriers to project success
☐ Enablers to program success
☐ Continuing administration of program

This list shows the key success factors in an HR program, beginning with the issues that reflect the initial planning of the program. Different stakeholders react to the appropriateness of the program planning schedule and objectives and the progress made with those planning tools. The relevance of the program is critical for the participants because if the program is perceived as irrelevant, more than likely it will not succeed in the workplace. The support for the program—including resources and how the program is integrated with other systems—represents important areas for feedback. Participants must see that the program has the necessary commitment. Several issues are important to management and the organization sponsoring the program, including program leadership, staffing levels, coordination, and communication. Also, it is important to gather feedback on how well the program implementation team is working to address such issues as motivation, cooperation, and capability. A dysfunctional team can spell disaster quickly. Finally, the issues that inhibit or enhance success are important, along with input on the likelihood of success. For a particular program, there can be other issues, and each can have specific parts. Each step, element, task, or part of the program represents an opportunity for feedback. The challenge is to sort out those things that are most important so the participants can provide valuable input.

Timing of Data Collection for Reaction and Satisfaction Feedback

The timing of data collection revolves around particular events connected with the HR program. Any particular activity, implementation issue, or milestone is an appropriate time to collect data, beginning with pre-program data collection and progressing to the implementation. Figure 3-1 shows the timing of feedback in a six-month program. This particular program has pre-program data collection. This is important to make sure that the environment is proper and supportive of the program. A pre-program assessment can be an eye-opening exercise, as particular inhibitors and barriers can be identified that will need adjusting or altering in the program to achieve success. In this particular example, assessment is taken at the beginning of the program as the announcement is made and the program is fully described. Next, a one-month follow-up is taken, followed by a four-month follow-up that is actually three months later. Finally, at the end of the program, the sixth month, an assessment is taken. Using five time frames for data collection may be too comprehensive for some programs, but is appropriate for major programs. In addition to these data collection opportunities, a six-month follow-up is planned after implementation. Timing will depend on the resources available, the need to obtain feedback directly from participants, and the magnitude of events or activities

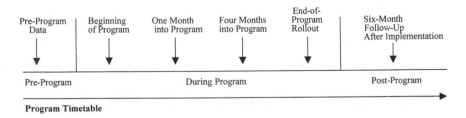

Figure 3-1. Timing of feedback in a six-month program.

scheduled throughout the program. In addition, they need to make quick adjustments and changes that will also affect the timing. Finally, the need to gain commitment and to support and measure the pulse all the way through the process are important factors in determining the actual timing.

Using Questionnaires to Measure Reaction and Satisfaction

The questionnaire is probably the most common method of data collection. Questionnaires come in all sizes, ranging from short reaction forms to detailed instruments. They can be used to obtain subjective data about participants' attitudes, as well as to document data for future use in a projected ROI analysis. With this versatility and popularity, it is important that questionnaires be designed properly to satisfy both purposes.

Types of Questions. Five basic types of questions are available. Depending on the purpose of the evaluation, the questionnaire may contain any or all of the following types of questions:

☐ Open-ended question—has an unlimited answer. The question is followed by ample blank space for the response.
☐ Checklist—a list of items. A participant is asked to check those that apply to the situation.
☐ Two-way question—has alternate responses, a yes/no, or other possibilities. This type of question can also include a range of responses from disagree to agree.
☐ Multiple choice question—has several choices, and the participant is asked to select the most appropriate.
☐ Ranking scales—requires the participant to rank a list of items.

Figure 3-2 shows examples of each of these types of questions.

Questionnaire Design. Questionnaire design is a simple and logical process. An improperly designed or worded questionnaire will not collect the desired data and is confusing, frustrating, and potentially embarrassing. The following steps will help ensure that a valid, reliable, and effective instrument is developed.

1. Open-Ended Question:

   What problems will you encounter when attempting to use the new performance management process?

2. Checklist:

   From the following list, check all of the business measures that may be influenced by the application of the new performance management process.

   ☐ Resource Allocation   ☐ Cost Control
   ☐ Productivity   ☐ Response Time
   ☐ Quality   ☐ Customer Satisfaction
   ☐ Efficiency   ☐ Job Satisfaction

3. Two-Way Question:

   As a result of this program, I have a better understanding of my job in managing performance.

   YES ☐   NO ☐

4. Multiple Choice Question:

   Since the new program has been initiated, my team's achievement of goals has:

   a. Increased
   b. Decreased
   c. Remained the same
   d. Don't know

5. Ranking Scales:

   The following list contains six important factors that will influence the success of this program. Place a one (1) by the item that is most influential, a two (2) by the item that is second most influential, and so on. The item ranked six (6) will be the least influential item on the list.

   Rewards Systems   _____   Training   _____
   Supervisor Coaching   _____   Management Support   _____
   Communications   _____   Resources   _____

Figure 3-2. Sample questions.

Determine the Information Needed. The first step of any instrument design is to itemize the topics, issues, and success factors for the program. Questions are developed later. It might be helpful to develop this information in outline form so that related questions can be grouped together.

Select the Type(s) of Questions. Determine whether open-ended questions, checklists, two-way questions, multiple choice questions, or a ranking scale is most appropriate for the purpose of the questions. Take into consideration the planned data analysis and variety of data to be collected.

Develop the Questions. The next step is to develop the questions based on the types of questions planned and the information needed. The questions should be simple and straightforward enough to avoid confusion or leading the participant to a desired response. Terms or expressions unfamiliar to the participant should be avoided.

Test the Questions. After the questions are developed, they should be tested for understanding. Ideally, the questions should be tested on a small sample of participants in the program. If this is not feasible, the questions should be tested on employees at approximately the same job level as the participants. Collect as much input and criticism as possible, and revise the questions as necessary.

Prepare a Data Summary. A data summary sheet should be developed so data can be tabulated quickly for summary and interpretation. This step will help ensure that the data can be analyzed quickly and presented in a meaningful way.

Develop the Completed Questionnaire. The questions should be finalized in a professional questionnaire with proper instructions. After completing these steps, the questionnaire is ready to be administered. Because questionnaire administration is a critical element in evaluation, several ideas will be presented later in this chapter.

Determining Questionnaire Content. The content for a particular questionnaire will vary with the particular issue explored. The questions will focus on any of the areas identified the list of areas of feedback, earlier in this chapter. For example, the issue of progress made with the program is an important topic to always include on a questionnaire. It could be presented as a range of responses, an open-ended question, or even a multiple choice response category. The content of the actual questions is just as important as the design and must have careful attention to make sure the proper topics are explored and the appropriate information is examined.

Using Surveys to Measure Reaction and Satisfaction

Attitude surveys represent a specific type of questionnaire with several applications for measuring reaction and satisfaction of HR programs designed to improve work, policies, procedures, the organization, or even the team. Pre- and post-measurements are important to show changes. Sometimes an organization will conduct a survey to assess the correct solution with one of the areas previously listed. Then, based on these results, HR initiatives are undertaken to influence change in areas where improvements are needed.

Measuring satisfaction and reaction is a complex task in which attitudes are crucial. It is impossible to measure an attitude precisely, since information gathered may not represent a participant's true feelings. Also, the behavior, beliefs, and feelings of an individual will not always correlate. Attitudes tend to change with time, and several factors can form an individual's attitude. Recognizing these shortcomings, it is possible to get a reasonable assessment of an individual's attitude.

Surveys are not the only way to measure attitudes. Interviews and observations are two other ways to measure attitudes and are discussed later.

Guidelines for Developing Surveys. The principles of survey construction are similar to those of questionnaire design. However, there are a few guidelines unique to the design or purchase of feedback surveys.

Involve Appropriate Management. The key stakeholders involved in this process must be committed to taking action based on survey results. Involve them early in the process, before the survey is constructed. Address management concerns, issues, and suggestions, and try to win commitment.

Determine Precisely the Reactions that Must Be Measured. While this is obvious, it is easy to stray into areas unrelated to the subject. "Let's check on their reaction to this" is a familiar trap. Although it may be interesting information, it should be omitted if it is unrelated.

Keep Survey Statements as Simple as Possible. Participants need to understand the meaning of a statement or question. There should be little room for differing interpretations.

Ensure that Participant Responses Are Anonymous. If feasible, participants must feel free to respond openly to statements or questions. The confidentiality of their responses is of the utmost importance. If data are collected that can identify a respondent, then a neutral third party should collect and process the data.

Communicate the Purpose of the Survey. Participants tend to cooperate in an activity when they understand its purpose. When a survey is administered, participants should be given an explanation of its purpose and told what will be done with the information. Also, they should be encouraged to give correct and proper statements or answers.

Identify Survey Comparisons. Reactions by themselves are virtually meaningless. They need to be compared with expectations, with data before or after the program, or with another group or program. Data may be compared with all employees, a division, a department, or previous programs. For purchased surveys, information may be available on a national scale in similar industries. In any case, specific comparisons should be planned before administering the survey.

Design for Easy Tabulation. In an attitude survey, yes/no remarks or varying degrees of agreement and disagreement are the usual responses. Figure 3-3 illustrates these two kinds of responses.

Yes/No Responses

		Yes	No
1.	My team leader gives us credit for our work on the project.	☐	☐
2.	My team leader secures our ideas about the project.	☐	☐

Agreement/Disagreement Responses

		Strongly Disagree	Disagree	Neutral	Agree	Strongly Agree
1.	My work environment is supportive of this project.	☐	☐	☐	☐	☐
2.	Management provides adequate resources for this project.	☐	☐	☐	☐	☐

Figure 3-3

Uniform responses make it easier for tabulation and comparisons. On a scale of strongly agree to strongly disagree, numbers are usually assigned to reflect the response. For instance, a 1 may represent strongly disagree, and a 5, strongly agree. An average response of 2.2 on a pre-program survey followed by a post-program average response of 4.3 shows a significant change in attitude. Some argue that a five-point scale merely permits the respondent to select the midpoint and not to be forced to make a choice. If this is a concern, an even-numbered scale should be used.

Using Reaction and Satisfaction Data

Sometimes participant feedback is solicited, tabulated, summarized, and then disregarded. The information must be collected and used for one or more of the purposes of evaluation. Otherwise, the exercise is a waste of the participants' time. Too often, program implementers or evaluators use the material to feed their egos and let it quietly disappear into their files, forgetting the original purposes behind its collection. A few of the more common reasons for gathering reaction and satisfaction data are summarized below.

Monitor Customer Satisfaction. Because this input is the principal measure taken from the participants, it provides a good indication of their overall reaction to, and satisfaction with, the program. Thus, program developers and owners will know how well satisfied the customers actually are with the product. Data should be reported to clients and others.

Identify Strengths and Weaknesses of the Program. Feedback is extremely helpful in identifying weaknesses as well as strengths in the program. Participant feedback on weaknesses can often lead to adjustments and changes. Identifying strengths can be helpful in future designs so processes can be replicated.

Develop Norms and Standards. Because reaction and satisfaction evaluation data can be automated and can be collected in nearly 100 percent of HR initiatives, it becomes relatively easy to develop norms and standards throughout the organization. Target ratings can be set for expectations; particular program results are then compared with those norms and standards.

Evaluate the HR Staff. Perhaps one of the most common uses of reaction and satisfaction data is HR staff evaluation. If properly constructed and collected, helpful feedback data can be provided to HR staff members so that adjustments can be made to increase effectiveness. Some caution needs to be taken, though, because these evaluations can sometimes be biased, so other evidence may be necessary to provide an overall assessment of HR staff performance.

Evaluate Planned Improvements. Feedback data from a questionnaire can provide a profile of planned actions and improvements. This can be compared with on-the-job actions as a result of the program. This provides a rich source of data in terms of what participants may be changing or implementing because of what they have learned.

Link with Follow-up Data. If a follow-up evaluation is planned, it may be helpful to link Level 1 data with follow-up data to see if planned improvements became reality. In most cases, planned actions are often inhibited in some way through on-the-job barriers.

Marketing Future Programs. For some organizations, participant feedback data provide helpful marketing information. Participants' quotes and reactions provide information that may be convincing to potential participants or business units considering implementing the HR program. Program marketing brochures often contain quotes and summaries of feedback data.

Shortcut Ways to Measure Reaction and Satisfaction

The key question for some at this point is what are some shortcut ways to measure reaction and satisfaction? Although reaction and satisfaction data should always be collected, some shortcuts that can be taken. There are some essential items that must be taken care of for very short, low-profile, inexpensive programs. Unfortunately, omitting Level 1 is not an option because of the critical importance of early feedback. Three particular issues can be helpful.

Use a Simple Questionnaire. A detailed, comprehensive, 100-item questionnaire isn't necessary for every program. A simple ten- to fifteen-item questionnaire using multiple choice, true/false, or even a scale rating will be sufficient for many small-scale programs. Although interviews, focus groups, surveys, and questionnaires are all presented as options, the questionnaire can suffice for most situations.

Collect Data Early and React Quickly. Taking an early pulse is critical. Find out if the program is being accepted and if those involved have concerns. This is very critical, and the action must be taken quickly. This will ensure that the process is kept on track and that the HR program enjoys success as planned.

Pay Attention to Participants. The key stakeholders, the program participants, are critical to the process. They can make or break any HR initiative, and their feedback is very important. A general rule is to always listen to this group and react to its concerns, issues, and recommendations. Sometimes it will need filtering because of biases. The important thing is to listen and react, when appropriate.

MEASURING SKILL AND KNOWLEDGE CHANGES

It may seem unnecessary to measure learning in an HR program or initiative. After all, when application and implementation are measured, the actual progress made in the workplace is measured. And ultimately, when business impact variables are monitored, the success of the initiative becomes quite clear. However, it is sometimes critical to understand the extent to which learning has occurred, particularly in initiatives where there are a significant amount of job changes, procedure changes, new tools, new processes, and new technology. The extent to which the participants involved in a program actually learn their new jobs and new processes may be one of the biggest determinants of the success of the HR program. This section focuses on simple techniques for measuring learning. Many of them have been used for years to measure learning in training programs in terms of formal testing and skill practices. Others are less formal in structure and can suffice when time is a concern or when costs need to be minimized.

Why Measure Learning?

There are three key areas that demonstrate why learning is an important measure in an HR initiative or program. Each of these, individually, will probably justify the need to measure learning. Collectively, they provide a major thrust for measuring the amount of skills, knowledge, or change during an intervention.

Importance of Knowledge, Expertise, and Competencies. Many organizations are focusing more on knowledge, expertise, and competencies than previously. Many of the large HR initiatives involve developing expertise with employees using tools and techniques not previously used. Some programs focus directly on core competencies and building important skills, knowledge, and behaviors into the organization. With a continuous focus on knowledge management, it is important for knowledge-based employees to understand and acquire a vast array of information, assimilate it, and use it in a productive way. This emphasis on employee knowledge and skills makes measuring learning in an HR program crucial.

The Importance of Learning in an HR Initiative or Program. Although some HR initiatives may involve plenty of new equipment, processes, procedures, and new technology, the human factor is still critical to the process. Whether there is significant restructuring or the addition of new systems, employees must learn how to work in the new environment and develop new knowledge and skills. Learning is becoming a larger part of HR initiatives than it previously was because of the variety of tools, techniques, processes, and technology that are being applied in such initiatives. Gone are the days where the simple tasks and procedures are built into work or automated within the process. Instead, there are complex environments, complex processes, and complicated tools that must be used in an intelligent way to reap the benefits from the HR initiative or program. Employees must learn in a variety of ways, not just in a formal classroom environment, but through technology-based learning and on-the-job facilitation with job aids and other tools. Also, the team leaders and managers often serve to reinforce, coach, or mentor in some initiatives. In a few cases, learning coaches or on-the-job trainers are used in conjunction with the HR initiative to ensure that learning is transferred to the job and is implemented as planned.

Finding Out What Went Wrong When There Is a Problem. When the initial program announcement and rollout do not go smoothly, the most important issue is to find out what went wrong. What areas need to be adjusted? What needs to be altered? When learning is measured, it is easy to see the degree to which the lack of learning is actually a problem or, in some cases, to eliminate the learning deficiency as a problem. Without the learning measurement, the HR consultant may not know why employees are not performing the way they should or why particular parts of the HR initiative are not being managed the way they should.

These key issues make learning an important issue in HR initiatives, requiring appropriate attention to this measure as with the other five measures in the ROI process.

Measuring Learning with Formal Tests

Testing is important for measuring learning in program evaluations. Pre- and post-intervention comparisons using tests are very common. An improvement in test scores shows the change in skill, knowledge, or attitude of the participant that is attributed to the HR initiative. By any measure, there was a dramatic increase in the use of tests in the United States throughout the 1990s. The principles of test development are similar to those for the design and development of questionnaires and attitude surveys.

The types of tests used in HR initiatives can be classified in three ways. The first is based on the medium used for administering the test. The most common media for tests are written or keyboard tests; performance tests, using simulated tools or the actual equipment; and computer-based tests, using computers and video displays. Knowledge and skills tests are usually written, because performance tests are more costly to develop and administer. Computer-based tests and those using interactive video are gaining popularity. In these tests, a computer monitor or video screen presents the questions or situations, and participants respond by typing on a keyboard or touching the screen. Interactive videos have a strong element of realism because the person being tested can react to images, often moving pictures and video vignettes that reproduce the real job situation.

The second way to classify tests is by purpose and content. In this context, tests can be divided into aptitude tests or achievement tests. Aptitude tests measure basic skills or acquired capacity to learn a job. An achievement test assesses a person's knowledge or competence in a particular subject.

A third way to classify tests is by test design. The most common are objective tests, norm-referenced tests, criterion-referenced tests, essay tests, oral examinations, and performance tests. Objective tests have answers that are specific and precise, based on the objectives of a program. Attitudes, feelings, creativity, problem-solving processes, and other intangible skills and abilities cannot be measured accurately with objective tests. A more useful form of objective test is the criterion-referenced test. Oral examinations and essay tests have limited use in evaluating HR initiatives; they are probably more useful in academic settings. The last two types of tests listed above are more common in HR initiatives: criterion-referenced tests and performance testing evaluation. Both are described in more detail below.

Criterion-Referenced Test. The criterion-referenced test (CRT) is an objective test with a predetermined cutoff score. The CRT is a measure against carefully written objectives for the learning components of the program. In a CRT, the interest lies in whether or not a participant meets the desired minimum standards, not how that participant ranks with others. The primary concern is to measure, report, and analyze participant performance as it relates to the learning objectives.

Table 3-1 examines a reporting format based on criterion-referenced testing. This format helps explain how a CRT is applied to an evaluation effort. Four participants have completed a learning component with three measurable objectives that correspond to each of the modules. Actual test scores are reported, and the minimum standard is shown. For example, on the first objective, Participant 4 received a pass rating for a test that has no numerical value and that is simply rated pass or fail. The same

Table 3-1
Reporting Format for CRT Test Data

| | Objective 1 | Objective 2 | | | Objective 3 | | | Total Objectives | Minimum | Overall |
	P/F	Raw Score	Std	P/F	Raw Score	Std	P/F	Passed	Standard	Score
Participant 1	P	4	10	F	87	90	F	1	2 of 3	Fail
Participant 2	F	12	10	P	110	90	P	2	2 of 3	Pass
Participant 3	P	10	10	P	100	90	P	3	2 of 3	Pass
Participant 4	P	14	10	P	88	90	F	2	2 of 3	Pass
Totals 4	3 Pass 1 Fail			3 Pass 1 Fail			2 Pass 2 Fail	8 Pass 4 Fail		3 Pass 1 Fail

participant met objective 2 with a score of 14 (10 was listed as the minimum passing score). The participant scored 88 on objective 3 but failed it because the standard was 90. Overall, participant 4 satisfactorily completed the learning component. The column on the far right shows that the minimum passing standard for the program is at least two of the three objectives. Participant 4 achieved two objectives, the required minimum.

Criterion-referenced testing is a popular measurement tool sometimes used in HR initiatives. The approach is helpful when it is necessary for a group of employees to learn new systems, procedures, or technology as part of an HR initiative. Its use is becoming widespread. The process is frequently computer-based, making testing more convenient. It has the advantage of being objective-based, precise, and relatively easy to administer. It requires clearly defined objectives that can be measured by tests.

Performance Testing. Performance testing allows the participant to exhibit a skill (and occasionally knowledge or attitudes) that has been learned through an HR initiative. The skill can be manual, verbal, or analytical, or a combination of the three. Performance testing is used frequently in HR programs where the participants are allowed to demonstrate what they have learned. Performance testing also comes in the form of skill practices or role playing. Participants are asked to demonstrate discussion or problem-solving skills they have acquired. To illustrate the possibilities of performance testing, two examples are presented.

Example 1. Managers are participating in an HR program that requires them to analyze the HR processes used in the organization. As part of the program, participants are given the project assignment to design and test a basic performance appraisal system. The HR staff observes participants as they check out their completed process and then carefully builds the same process and compares the results with those of the participants. These comparisons and the simulated performance of the design provide an evaluation of the project and represent an adequate reflection of the skills learned in the program.

Example 2. As part of a reorganization project, team members learn new products and sales strategies. Part of the evaluation requires team members to practice skills in an actual situation involving a sales presentation. Then, participants are asked to conduct the skill practice on another member of the group using a real situation and applying the principles and steps learned in the project. The skill practice is observed by the HR staff and a written critique is provided at the end of the practice. These critiques provide part of the evaluation of the HR initiative.

For a performance test to be effective, the following steps are recommended in the design and administration of the test:

☐ The test should be a representative sample of the work/task related to the HR initiative. The test should allow the participant to demonstrate as many skills taught in the program as possible. This increases the validity of the test and makes it more meaningful to the participant.

☐ The test should be thoroughly planned. Every phase of the test should be planned—the timing, the preparation of the participant, the collection of necessary materials and tools, and the evaluation of results.

☐ Thorough and consistent instructions are necessary. As with other tests, the quality of the instructions can influence the outcome of a performance test. All participants should be given the same instructions. They should be clear, concise, and to the point. Charts, diagrams, blueprints, and other supporting information should be provided if they are normally provided in the work setting. If appropriate and feasible, the test should be demonstrated by an HR staff member so that participants observe how the skill is practiced.

☐ Procedures should be developed for objective evaluation, and acceptable standards must be developed for a performance test. Standards are sometimes difficult to develop because varying degrees of speed, skill, and quality are associated with individual outcomes. Predetermined standards must be developed so that employees know in advance what has to be accomplished to be considered satisfactory and acceptable for test completion.

☐ Information that may bias participant reasons should not be included. The learning module is included to develop a particular skill. Participants should not be led in this direction unless they face the same obstacles in the job environment.

With these general guidelines, performance tests can be used as effective tools for evaluations where demonstration of performance is a requirement of HR initiatives. Although more costly than written tests, performance tests are essential in situations where a high degree of fidelity is required between work and test conditions.

Measuring Learning with Simulation

Another technique for measuring learning is job simulation. This method involves the construction and application of a procedure or task that simulates or models the work involved in the HR initiative. The simulation is designed to represent, as closely as possible, the actual job situation. Participants try out their performance in the simulated activity and have it evaluated based on how well the task is accomplished. Simulations may be used during the intervention, at the end of the implementation, or as part of a follow-up evaluation.

Advantages of Simulations. Simulations offer several advantages for the HR staff.

Reproducibility. Simulations permit a job or part of a job to be reproduced in a manner almost identical to the real setting. Through careful planning and design, the simulation can have all of the central characteristics of the real situation. Even complex jobs, such as that of the manager, can be simulated adequately.

Cost Effectiveness. Although sometimes expensive in the initial development, simulations can be cost effective in the long run. For example, it is cost prohibitive to train airline pilots to fly an airplane by using a $50 million aircraft. Therefore, an aircraft simulator is used to simulate all of the flying conditions and enable the pilot to learn to fly before boarding the actual aircraft. The cost involved in on-the-job learning becomes prohibitive making simulation much more attractive in other situations.

Safety Considerations. Another advantage of using simulations is safety. The safety component of many jobs requires participants to learn under simulated conditions. For example, emergency medical technicians risk injury and even life if they do not learn emergency medical techniques prior to encountering a real-life situation. Firefighters are trained in simulated conditions prior to being exposed to actual fires. CIA agents are trained in simulated conditions before being exposed to their real-world environment. Safety is an important consideration when deciding on learning methodologies.

Simulation Techniques. There are several simulation techniques used to evaluate learning that has taken place during an HR initiative. The most common techniques are briefly described.

Electrical/Mechanical Simulation. This technique uses a combination of electronics and mechanical devices to simulate real-life situations. They are used in conjunction with programs to develop operational and diagnostic skills. Expensive examples of these types include simulated patients, or a simulator for a nuclear power plant operator. Other less-expensive types of simulators have been developed to simulate equipment operation.

Task Simulation. Another approach involves a participant's performance in a simulated task as part of an evaluation. For example, in an aircraft company, technicians are trained on the safe removal, handling, and installation of a radioactive source used in a nucleonic oil-quantity indicator gauge. These technicians attend a thorough HR safety program on all of the procedures necessary for this important assignment. To become certified to perform this task, technicians are observed in a simulation, where they perform all the necessary steps on a checklist. After they have demonstrated that they possess the skills necessary for the safe performance of this assignment, they are certified by the instructor. This task simulation serves as the evaluation.

Business Games. Business games have grown in popularity in recent years. They represent simulations of a part or all of a business enterprise. Participants change the variables of the business and observe the effects of those changes. The game not only reflects the real-world situation, but may also represent an

HR initiative. The participants are provided certain objectives, play the game, and have their output monitored. Their performance can usually be documented and measured. Typical objectives are to maximize profit, sales, market share, or return on investment. Those participants who maximize the objectives are those who usually have the highest performance in the program.

In-Basket. Another simulation technique called the in-basket is particularly useful in team leader, supervisory, and management development initiatives. Portions of a supervisor's job are simulated through a series of items that normally appear in an in-basket. These items are usually memos, notes, letters, and reports that create realistic conditions facing the supervisor. The participant must decide what to do with each item while taking into consideration the principles learned. The participant's performance with the in-basket represents an evaluation of the program. In some situations, every course of action for each item in the in-basket is rated, and a combination of the chosen alternatives provides an overall rating on the in-basket. This provides a performance score representing the participant's ability to address the major issues.

Case Studies. A perhaps less-effective but still-popular technique of simulation is a case study. A case study represents a detailed description of a problem and usually contains a list of several questions posed to the participant. The participant is asked to analyze the case and determine the best course of action. The problem should reflect the conditions in the real-world setting and the content in an HR program.

The most common categories of case studies include:

☐ Exercise case studies, which provide an opportunity for participants to practice the application of specific procedures
☐ Situational case studies, which provide participants the opportunity to analyze information and make decisions surrounding their particular situation
☐ Complex case studies, which are an extension of the situational case study, where the participant is required to process a large amount of data and information, some of which may be irrelevant

☐ Decision case studies, which require the participant to go a step further than the previous categories and present plans for solving a particular problem
☐ Critical-incident case studies, which provide the participant with a certain amount of information and withhold other information until it is requested by the participant
☐ Action-maze case studies, which present a large case in a series of smaller units. The participant is required to predict at each stage what will happen next

The difficulty in a case study lies in the objectivity of the evaluation of the participant's performance. Frequently, there can be many possible courses of action, some equally as effective as others, making it extremely difficult to obtain an objective, measurable performance rating for the analysis and interpretation of the case.

Role Playing. In role playing, sometimes referred to as skill practice, participants practice a newly learned skill and are observed by other individuals. Participants are given their assigned role with specific instructions, which sometimes include an ultimate course of action. The participant then practices the skill with other individuals to accomplish the desired objectives. This is intended to simulate the real-world setting to the greatest extent possible. Difficulty sometimes arises when other participants involved in the skill practice make the practice unrealistic by not reacting the way individuals would in an actual situation. To help overcome this obstacle, trained role players (non-participants trained for the role) may be used in all roles except that of the participant. This can possibly provide a more objective evaluation. The success of this technique also lies in the judgment of those observing the role playing. The skill of effective observation is as critical as the skill of the role player. Also, the success of this method depends on the participants' willingness to participate in and adjust to the planned role. If participant resistance is extremely high, the performance in the skill practice may not reflect the actual performance on the job. Nevertheless, these skill practices can be very useful, particularly in supervisory and sales training, to enable participants to practice discussion skills.

Assessment Center Method. The final method for measuring learning with simulation is a formal procedure called the assessment center method. The feedback is provided by a group of specially trained observers called assessors. For years, the assessment center approach has been a very effective tool for employee selection. It now shows great promise as a tool for evaluating the effectiveness of a major learning module in an HR initiative.

Assessment centers are not actually centers, such as a location or building. The term refers to a procedure for evaluating the performance of individuals. In a typical assessment center, the individuals being assessed participate in a variety of exercises that enable them to demonstrate a particular skill, knowledge, or ability, usually called job dimensions. These dimensions are important to on-the-job success for individuals involved in the HR initiative. It may take anywhere from four hours to three days for the participants to complete all the exercises. The assessors then combine ratings of each exercise for each dimension, removing subjectivity to reach a final rating for each participant.

In the assessment center process, a rating or "assessment" of the participants is given prior to the HR initiative. After the initiative is implemented, the participants are assessed again to see if there are improvements in their performance within the job dimensions. The use of a control group in an evaluation design helps produce evidence of the impact of the initiative.

Although the popularity of this method seems to be growing, it still may not be feasible for many HR initiatives. The use of an assessment center is quite involved and time consuming for the participants and the assessors. The assessors have to be carefully trained to be objective and reliable. However, for programs that represent large expenditures aimed at making improvements in the soft-data area, the assessment center approach may be the most promising way to measure the impact of the program. This is particularly true for an organization in which the assessment center process is already in use for selection purposes.

In summary, simulations come in a wide variety of types and styles. They offer an opportunity for participants to practice what they have learned in an HR program and to have their performance observed in simulated job conditions. They can provide extremely accurate evaluations if the performance in the simulation is objective and can be clearly measured.

Measuring Learning with Less Structured Activities

In many situations, it is sufficient to have an informal check of learning to provide some assurance that participants have acquired the skills and knowledge, or perhaps that there have been some changes in attitudes. This approach is appropriate when other levels of evaluation are pursued. For example, if a Level 3 application and implementation evaluation is planned, it might not be so critical to conduct a comprehensive Level 2 evaluation. An informal assessment of learning is usually sufficient. After all, the resources are scarce, and a comprehensive evaluation at all levels becomes quite expensive. The following are some alternative approaches to measuring learning when inexpensive, low-key, informal assessments are needed.

Exercises/Activities. Many HR initiatives involve activities, exercises, or problems that must be explored, developed, or solved during the program. Some of these are constructed in terms of involvement exercises, while others require individual problem-solving skills. When these tools are integrated into the learning activity, there are several specific ways in which to measure learning:

☐ The results of the exercise can be submitted for review and for possible scoring by the HR staff. This becomes part of the overall score for the course and becomes a measure of learning.

☐ The results can be discussed in a group, with a comparison of the various approaches and solutions, and the group can reach an assessment of how much each individual has learned. This may not be practical in many settings, but can work in a few narrowly focused applications.

☐ The solutions to the problem or exercises can be shared with the group, and the participant can provide a self-assessment indicating the degree to which the skills and/or knowledge have been obtained from the exercise. This also serves as reinforcement in that participants quickly see the correct solution.

☐ The HR staff can review the individual progress of each participant to determine the relative success. This is appropriate

for small groups but can be cumbersome and time consuming in larger groups.

Self-Assessment. In many HR programs, self-assessment may be
appropriate. Participants are provided an opportunity to assess
their acquisition of skills and knowledge. This is particularly
applicable in cases where higher-level evaluations are planned and
it is important to know if actual learning is taking place. A few
techniques can ensure that the process is effective:

- ☐ The self-assessment should be made anonymously so that
  participants feel free to express realistic and accurate assessments of what they have learned.
- ☐ The purpose of the self-assessment should be explained,
  along with the plans for the data. Specifically, if there are
  implications for program design or individual re-testing, this
  should be discussed.
- ☐ If there has been no improvement or the self-assessment is
  unsatisfactory, there should be some explanation as to what
  that means and what the implications will be. This will help
  ensure that accurate and credible information is provided.

HR Staff Assessment. A final technique is for the HR staff and/
or facilitators to provide an assessment of the HR program
learning that has taken place. Although this approach is very
subjective, it may be appropriate when a higher-level evaluation
is planned. One of the most effective ways to accomplish this is
to provide a checklist of the specific skills that need to be
acquired in the course. Facilitators can then check off the assessment of the skills individually. Also, if there is a particular body
of knowledge that needs to be acquired, a checklist of the categories
should be developed for assuring that the individual has a good
understanding of those items. This could create a problem if the
participants have not had the appropriate time and opportunity
to demonstrate skills or knowledge acquisition, and the instructor
may have a difficult time in providing appropriate responses.
There is also the question of what to do if there is no evidence
of learning. The specific consequences need to be considered and
addressed before the method is used.

Administrative Issues

There are several administrative issues that need to be addressed for measuring learning. Each is briefly discussed below and should be part of the overall plan for administering a Level 2 measurement.

Consistency. It is extremely important that different tests, exercises, or processes for measuring learning are administered consistently from one group to another. This includes issues such as the time required to respond, the actual learning conditions in which the participants complete the process, the resources available to them, and the assistance from other members of the group. These issues can easily be addressed in the instructions.

Monitoring. In some situations, it is important for participants to be monitored as they are completing the test or other measurement processes. This ensures that each individual is working independently and also that someone is there to provide assistance or answer questions as needed. This may not be an issue in all situations but needs to be addressed in the overall plan.

Scoring. The scoring instructions need to be developed for the measurement process so that the person evaluating the responses will be objective in the process and provide consistent scores. Ideally, the potential bias from the individual scoring the instrument should be completely removed through proper scoring instructions and other information necessary to provide an objective evaluation.

Reporting. A final issue is reporting the results. In some situations, the participants are provided with the results immediately, particularly with self-scoring tests or with group-based scoring mechanisms. In other situations, the actual results may not be known until later. In these situations, a mechanism for providing scoring data should be built into the evaluation plan unless it has been predetermined that participants will not know the scores. The worst-case scenario is to promise test scores and deliver them late or not at all.

Using Learning Data

Although there can be several uses of learning data, the following uses are most common:

Providing Individual Feedback to Build Confidence. Learning data, when provided directly to participants, provides reinforcement for correct answers and enhances learning for the program. This reinforces the learning process and provides much-needed feedback to participants in HR programs.

Ensuring that Learning Has Been Acquired. Sometimes it is essential to show the extent and scope of learning. Measuring learning, even if informally, will provide input on this issue.

Improving HR Initiatives or Programs. Perhaps the most important use of learning data is to improve the HR program. Consistently low responses in certain learning measures may indicate that inadequate facilitation has been provided on that topic. Consistently low scores with all participants may indicate that the objectives and scope of coverage are too ambitious or misdirected.

Evaluating HR Program Staff or Facilitators. Just as reaction and satisfaction data can be used to evaluate HR program implementation, learning measures provide additional evidence of their success. The HR staff has a significant responsibility to ensure that participants have learned the new skills and knowledge and that testing is a reflection of the degree to which the skills/knowledge have been acquired and internalized from actual application.

CONCLUSION

This chapter is the first of two chapters about data collection and presents two of the six measures of data reported in the ROI process. Measuring reaction and satisfaction is included in every study and is a critical part of the success. Although there are many uses for the data, two important uses stand out. The first use is for making adjustments and changes throughout the implementation of the HR program as problems or barriers are uncovered. The second is for reporting the level of satisfaction with the program and having it included as one of the six key types of data. There are several ways to collect reaction and satisfaction data, including questionnaires and surveys. By far the questionnaire is the most common, and sometimes just a simple, one-page reaction questionnaire is appropriate. Whatever the method used, the important point is to collect data, react quickly, make adjustments, and summarize the data for reporting and for use in preparing the ROI impact study.

Key issues involved in measuring learning—an important ingredient in many HR initiatives—were also presented in this chapter. Even if it is accomplished informally, learning must be assessed to determine the extent to which the participants in an HR program are learning new skills, techniques, processes, tools, and procedures. Without measuring learning, it is impossible to know what may be wrong should there be an implementation problem later. Also, measuring learning provides an opportunity to make adjustments quickly so that changes can be made to enhance learning. The approach does not have to be so formal, except for major programs. A less-formal, less-structured approach—even if a self-assessment activity—is usually appropriate for most learning situations.

CHAPTER 4

Collecting Data After HR Program Implementation

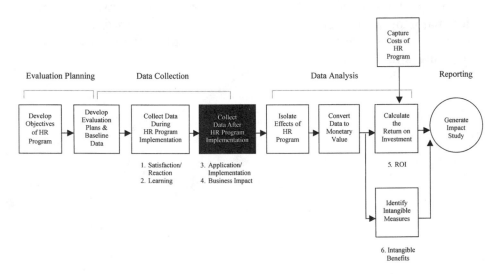

MEASURING APPLICATION AND IMPLEMENTATION

Measuring the actual application and implementation of skills and knowledge is critical because these steps play a pivotal role in the overall success or failure of an HR initiative. If learned skills and knowledge are not applied effectively, there will be no change in the business function—and no benefit from the HR initiative.

The first section of this chapter explores some of the key issues in and the most common data collection methods to evaluate HR programs. The range of possibilities varies including the use of questionnaires, interviews, focus groups, and observation. These include several specific methodologies, such as action planning and performance contracting. This section will explore the issues faced in applying these processes on the job and provide several examples.

Why Measure Application and Implementation?

In addition to the obvious reasons for measuring application and implementation, there are several specific reasons why this is one of the most important measures to track in the evaluation process.

The Value of the Information. As briefly discussed earlier in this book, the value of the information increases as progress is made through the chain of impact from Level 1 to Level 5. Thus, information concerning application and implementation at Level 3 is more valuable to the client than reaction/satisfaction (Level 1) and learning (Level 2). This is not meant to discount the importance of these two levels, but to emphasize that measuring the extent to which the HR program is implemented often provides critical data about not only the success of the project but also the factors that can contribute to greater success as the HR program is fully integrated within the organization.

A Key Transition Issue. The two previous measures, reaction/satisfaction and learning, occur during the HR initiative where there is more attention and focus directly on the HR program. Level 3, measuring application and implementation, occurs after the project has been implemented and measures the success of the application and implementation. Essentially, this measure explains the degree to which the project is handed off to those who are charged with its ultimate success. This is a key transition process and is the first measure that follows the process after the project has been fully implemented. This in itself makes it a critical issue, where various measures of success are identified and enhancements to additional success are pinpointed.

The Key Focus of Many Projects. As many HR projects focus directly on application and implementation, the project sponsor often speaks in these terms and is concerned about these measures of success. Many major HR projects designed to transform an organization and build a stronger team and customer focus will have key issues around Level 3, application and implementation. The sponsor will be interested in knowing the extent to which all of the key stakeholders are adjusting to and implementing the desired new behaviors, processes, and procedures. This interest is at the core of application and implementation.

Problems, Obstacles, and Barriers. When an HR project goes astray, the first question is, "What happened?" More importantly, when a project appears not to be adding value, the first question should be, "What can we do to change the direction of the project?" In either scenario, it is critical to have information that identifies barriers to success, problems encountered in implementation, and obstacles to the actual application of the process. It is at Level 3, measuring application and implementation, that these problems are addressed, identified, and examined for solutions. In many cases, the key stakeholders directly involved in the process provide important input into the recommendations for making changes or for using a different approach in the future.

Enablers and Enhancers. When there is success, the obvious question is, "How can we repeat this or even improve on this in the future?" The answer to this question is also found at Level 3. Identifying the factors that contribute directly to the success of the project is critical because those same items can be used to replicate the process to produce specific results in the future and to enhance results. When key stakeholders identify those issues, it helps make the project successful and provides an important case history of what is necessary for success.

Rewards Those Who Are Most Effective. Measuring application and implementation allows the client and HR staff to reward those who are doing the best job of applying the processes and implementing the HR project. Measures taken at this level provide clear evidence of various efforts and roles, providing an excellent basis for performance review or special recognition. This often has a reinforcing value for keeping the project on track and communicating a strong message for future improvements.

Key Issues

When implementing a process to measure application and implementation of HR solutions, several key issues should be addressed. These are very similar to the Level 1 (reaction/satisfaction) issues. A few issues may differ slightly due to the post-project time frame for this type of data.

Areas of Coverage. To a large degree the areas of coverage for this process parallel the same areas in measuring reaction and satisfaction as identified in Chapter 3. However, because of the follow-up time frame, the other additional issues become opportunities to measure success. In addition, the perspective of the follow-up is changed to post-program rather than the predictive nature of some of the issues in Level 1. The areas of coverage are fully detailed in the section on using questionnaires to measure application and implementation. Here, the detailed issues can serve as a guide for finding the areas of coverage for all types of data collection methods at this level.

Sources. The sources of data mirror those identified under the heading "Measuring Reaction and Satisfaction," in Chapter 3. Essentially, all key stakeholders are candidates for sources of data. Perhaps the most important source is those who are actually involved in the application and implementation. It may involve the entire team, or team leaders charged with the responsibility of implementation.

Timing. The timing of data collection can vary significantly. because this is a follow-up, the key issue is determining the best time for a post-program evaluation. The challenge is to analyze the nature and scope of the application and implementation and determine the earliest time that a trend and pattern will evolve. This occurs when the application of skills becomes routine and the implementation is making significant progress. This is a judgment call. The important point is to go in as early as possible so that potential adjustments can still be made but, at the same time, wait until there is significant change in behavior for the implementation to be observed and measured. In HR projects spanning a considerable length of time in terms of complete implementation, several measures may be taken at three- to six-month intervals. This gives successive input in terms of implementation progress and clearly shows the extent of improvement, using effective measures at well-timed intervals, and identifies the issues that are standing in the way of a successful implementation.

Responsibilities. Measuring application and implementation may involve the responsibility and work of others. Because this time period follows the HR initiative's completion, an important issue may surface in terms of who is responsible for this follow up. There is a range of possibilities, from HR staff to the client staff, as well as the possibility of an external, independent third party. This matter should be addressed in the planning stage so that there is no misunderstanding as to the distribution of responsibilities. More importantly, those who are responsible should fully understand the nature and scope of their responsibility and what is necessary to collect the data. Additional information on responsibilities is covered in a later chapter.

Using Questionnaires to Measure Application and Implementation

Questionnaires have become a mainstream data collection tool for measuring application and implementation because of their flexibility, low cost, and ease of administration. The issues involved in questionnaire design discussed in Chapter 3 apply equally to questionnaire development for measuring follow-up application and implementation. This section will be limited to the specific content issues of follow-up questionnaires.

One of the most difficult tasks is to determine specific issues that need to be addressed on a follow-up questionnaire. Although the content items on a follow-up questionnaire can be the same as questionnaires used in measuring reaction and satisfaction, the following content items are more desirable for capturing application, implementation, and impact information (Levels 3 and 4 data). Figure 4-1 presents a questionnaire used in a follow-up evaluation of an HR initiative on a stress management program.

The evaluation was designed to capture the ROI, with the primary method of data collection being the follow-up questionnaire. This example will be used to illustrate many of the issues involving potential content items for a follow-up questionnaire.

National Bank operates in a strong competitive environment. Following the acquisition of many smaller banks, the workload expanded, systems and processes had to be consolidated, and market share was a continuing strategic issue. Employees at the main branch worked long hours facing tight deadlines and customer demands; there seemed to be no end in sight. The branch management initiated a project to help relieve the tension. Management recognized that a stressful situation existed and a stress management program was implemented to help meet the needs of the employees. Management recognized that the program would not only help employees to manage stress, but it should also help the bank to achieve strategic goals. All branch employees were involved in the program.

Six months after the program was implemented, an evaluation was planned. Each branch in the network had a scorecard that tracked performance through several measures such as new accounts, total deposits, and growth by specific products. All product lines were monitored. All branch employees provided input on the questionnaire shown in Figure 4-1. Most of the data from the questionnaire covered application and implementation, while some involved impact measures. This type of feedback helps HR staff know which parts of the initiative are most effective and useful.

Progress with Objectives. Sometimes it is helpful to assess progress made with the objectives of the project in the follow-up evaluation as illustrated by question one in Figure 4-1. Although this issue is usually assessed during the initiative, it is sometimes helpful to revisit the objectives after the participants have had an opportunity to implement the project.

Action-Plan Implementation. If an action plan is required in the initiative, the questionnaire should reference the plan and determine the extent to which it has been implemented. If the action-plan requirement is very low-key, perhaps only one question on

(text continued on page 115)

Stress Management for Intact Work Teams
Follow-Up Impact Questionnaire

Check one: ☐ Team Member   ☐ Team Leader/Manager

1. Listed below are the objectives of the stress management program. After reflecting on this program, please indicate the degree of success in meeting the objectives.

OBJECTIVES	Failed	Limited Success	Generally Successful	Completely Successful
PERSONAL				
☐ Identify sources of stress in work, personal, and family worlds				
☐ Apply coping strategies to manage stressful situations				
☐ Understand to what degree stress is hampering your health and performance				
☐ Take steps to enhance personal health and overall performance				
☐ Access internal and external resources to help reach personal goals				
GROUP				
☐ Identify sources of stress for group				
☐ Identify sources of distress and satisfaction				
☐ Apply skills to manage and reduce stress in work group				
☐ Develop action plan to improve work group effectiveness				
☐ Improve effectiveness and efficiency measures for work group				

Figure 4-1.

2. Did you develop and implement a 21-day action plan?

Yes ☐   No ☐

If yes, please describe the success of the plan. If not, explain why.

_____

_____

3. Please rate, on a scale of 1-5, the relevance of each of the program elements to your job, with (1) indicating no relevance, and (5) indicating very relevant.

_____ StressMap® Instrument   _____ Action Planning

_____ Group Discussion   _____ Program Content

4. Have you used the reference materials since you participated in the program?

Yes ☐   No ☐

Please explain.

_____

_____

5. Please indicate the degree of success in applying the following skills and behaviors as a result of your participation in the stress management program.

	1	2	3	4	5	
	No Success	Little Success	Some Success	Significant Success	Very Much Success	No Opportunity to Use Skills
a) Selecting con-tainable behavior for change						
b) Identifying measures of behavior						
c) Taking full responsibility for your actions						

Figure 4-1. Continued.

	1	2	3	4	5	
	No Success	Little Success	Some Success	Significant Success	Very Much Success	No Opportunity to Use Skills
d) Selecting a buddy to help you change behavior						
e) Identifying and removing barriers to changing behavior						
f) Staying on track with the 21-day action plan						
g) Applying coping strategies to manage stressful situations						
h) Using control effectively						
i) Knowing when to let go						
j) Responding effectively to conflict						
k) Creating a positive climate						
l) Acknowledging a complaint properly						
m) Reframing problems						
n) Using stress talk strategies						

Figure 4-1. Continued.

6. Indicate the types of relationships where you have used the skills.

☐ _____ Coworkers

☐ _____ Manager or supervisor

☐ _____ Company employee in another function

☐ _____ Spouse

☐ _____ Child

☐ _____ Friend

☐ _____ Other: (list) _____

PERSONAL CHANGES

7. What has changed about your on-the-job behavior as a result of this program? (positive attitude, fewer conflicts, better organized, fewer outbursts of anger, etc.)

_____

_____

_____

8. Recognizing the changes in your own behavior and perceptions, please identify any specific personal accomplishments/improvements that you can link to this program (time savings, project completion, fewer mistakes, etc.).

_____

_____

_____

Figure 4-1. Continued.

9. What specific value in U.S. dollars can be attributed to the above accomplishments/ improvements? Use first-year values only. Although this is a difficult question, try to think of specific ways in which the above improvements can be converted to monetary units. Use one year of data. Along with the monetary value, please indicate the basis of your calculation. $ _____

Basis.

_____

_____

_____

10. Other factors often influence improvements in performance. Please indicate the percent of the above improvement that is related directly to this program. ____%

11. What level of confidence do you place in the above estimations? (0% = No Confidence, 100% = Certainty) ____%

Please explain.

_____

_____

_____

GROUP CHANGES

---

12. What has changed about your work group as a result of your group's participation in this program? (interactions, cooperation, commitment, problem solving, creativity, etc.)

_____

_____

_____

Figure 4-1. Continued.

13. Please identify any specific group accomplishments/improvements that you can link to the program (project completion, response times, innovative approaches).

_____

_____

_____

14. What specific value in U.S. dollars can be attributed to the above accomplishments/improvements? Use first-year values only. Although this is a difficult question, try to think of specific ways in which the above improvements can be converted to monetary units. Use one year of values. Along with the monetary value, please indicate the basis of your calculation. $ _____

Basis.

_____

_____

_____

15. Other factors often influence improvements in performance. Please indicate the percent of the above improvement that is related directly to this program. _____%

16. What level of confidence do you place on the above estimations? (0% = No Confidence, 100% = Certainty) _____%

Please explain.

_____

_____

_____

Figure 4-1. Continued.

17. Do you think this program represented a good investment for the company?

Yes ☐   No ☐

Please explain.

_____

_____

_____

18. For each of the areas below, indicate the extent to which you think this program has influenced these measures in your work group.

	No Influence	Some Influence	Moderate Influence	Significant Influence	Very Much Influence
a) Productivity					
b) Efficiency					
c) Quality					
d) Response Time					
e) Cost Control					
f) Customer Service					
g) Customer Satisfaction					
h) Employee Turnover					

Figure 4-1. Continued.

i) Absenteeism

_____

j) Employee Satisfaction

_____

k) Healthcare Costs

_____

l) Safety and Health Costs

_____

Please cite specific examples or provide more details.

_____

_____

_____

19. Please rate the success of the HR staff during the implementation
    and support of this project.
    Use the following scale:

    1. No success
    2. Limited success
    3. Moderately successful
    4. Generally successful
    5. Very successful

Team Characteristic	1	2	3	4	5
Capability	☐	☐	☐	☐	☐
Motivation	☐	☐	☐	☐	☐
Cooperation	☐	☐	☐	☐	☐
Support for team	☐	☐	☐	☐	☐
Training for team	☐	☐	☐	☐	☐
Communication	☐	☐	☐	☐	☐

Figure 4-1. Continued.

20. What barriers, if any, have you encountered that have prevented you from using skills or knowledge gained in this program? Please explain.

_____

_____

_____

21. What has helped this project be successful? Please explain.

_____

_____

_____

22. Which of the following best describes the actions of your manager during the stress management program?

☐ Very little discussion or reference to the program

☐ Casual mention of program with few specifics

☐ Discussed details of program in terms of content, issues, concerns, etc.

☐ Discussed how the program could be applied to work group

☐ Set goals for changes/improvements

☐ Provided ongoing feedback on the action plan

☐ Provided encouragement and support to help change behavior

☐ Other

(comments) . . . _____

_____

23. Could other solutions have been effective in meeting this need?

Yes ☐   No ☐

Please explain.

_____

_____

Figure 4-1. Continued.

24. What specific suggestions do you have for improving the stress management program? Please specify.

☐ Content _____

☐ Duration _____

☐ Presentation _____

☐ Other _____

25. Other comments:

_____

_____

_____

Figure 4-1. Continued.

(text continued from page 105)

the follow-up questionnaire will be devoted to the action plan, as illustrated in question two in Figure 4-1. If the action plan is quite comprehensive and contains an abundance of Levels 3 and 4 data, then the questionnaire takes a secondary role, and most of the data collection process will focus directly on the status of the completed action plan. The action-planning process is described later in this chapter.

Relevance of the HR Initiative. Although the relevance of the HR initiative is often assessed during the project, as Level 1 data, it is sometimes helpful to assess the relevance to various aspects of the program after application and implementation. This feedback helps program designers know which parts of the program were actually useful on the job, providing lasting value. Question three in Figure 4-1 shows one approach to this issue.

Use of Job-Related Materials. If participants are provided with job aids and references to use on the job, then it may be helpful to determine the extent to which these materials have been used. This is particularly helpful when operation manuals, reference

books, and job aids have been distributed and explained in the
HR program and are expected to be used on the job. Question
four in Figure 4-1 focuses on this issue.

Knowledge/Skill Use. Perhaps one of the most important questions on the follow-up questionnaire focuses on the application
of skills and knowledge. As shown in question five in Figure 4-1,
the specific skills and knowledge areas are listed, with the question framed around the amount of change since the initiative was
implemented. This is the recommended approach when there are
no pre-program data. If pre-program data have been collected,
it is more appropriate to compare post-program assessments with
pre-program assessments using the same type of question. A more
detailed variation of this question is to list each skill and indicate
the frequency of use. For many skills, it is important to experience frequent use quickly after the skills are acquired so that the
skills become internalized.

Changes with Work. Sometimes it is helpful to determine what
specific activities or processes have changed about participants'
work as a result of the program. Question six establishes a
framework to determine which relationships were affected by
application of the stress management program. Question six is
unique to this situation. As question seven in Figure 4-1 illustrates, the participants explore how their skill applications (listed
previously) have actually changed their work habits (in this case,
the behavior change caused by managing stress is the issue).

Improvements/Accomplishments. Question eight in Figure 4-1
begins a series of four impact questions that are appropriate for
most follow-up questionnaires. The first question in the series
seeks specific accomplishments and improvements that are directly
linked to the HR program. This question focuses on specific,
measurable successes that can be easily identified by the participants. Because this is an open-ended question, it can be helpful
to provide examples that indicate the nature and range of responses
requested. However, examples can also limit the responses.

Monetary Impact. Perhaps the most difficult question, number
nine in Figure 4-1, asks participants to provide monetary values

for the improvements identified in question seven. Although these are business impact data, it may be helpful to collect them here. Only the first-year improvement is sought. Participants are asked to specify net improvements so that the actual monetary values will represent gains from the HR program. An important part of the question is the basis for calculation, where participants specify the steps taken to develop the annual net value and the assumptions made in the analysis. It is important for the basis to be completed with enough detail to understand the process.

Improvements Linked with HR Program. The next question in the series of impact questions, number ten in Figure 4-1, isolates the effects of the HR program. Participants indicate the percentage of the improvement that is directly related to the initiative. As an alternative, the various factors that have influenced the results may be listed. Participants are then asked to allocate a percentage to each factor.

Note that questions twelve through sixteen in Figure 4-1 are the same as questions seven through eleven, but tailored for a group setting. Because of the nature of stress, the questionnaire needed to address both personal and group situations.

Confidence Level. To adjust for the uncertainty of the data provided in the impact questions, participants are asked to provide a level of confidence for each estimation. This confidence factor is expressed as a percentage with a range of zero to 100 percent, as shown in question eleven in Figure 4-1. This input adjusts the participant estimates to account for their uncertainty. This conservative approach adds credibility to the estimation process.

Investment Perception. The participants' perception of the value of the HR initiative is useful information. As illustrated in Question 17 in Figure 4-1, participants are asked if they believe the project to be a good investment. An option for this question is to present the actual cost of the HR initiative so that participants can respond more accurately. Also, the question can be divided into two parts: one reflecting the investment of money by the organization and the other an investment in the participants' time in the project. The perceived value is an indicator that the HR processes are being implemented.

Linkage with Output Measures. Sometimes it is helpful to determine the degree to which the initiative has influenced certain output measures. As shown in Question 18 in Figure 4-1, participants are often asked to indicate the degree to which they think certain measures have been influenced by the initiative. However, when this issue is uncertain, listing potential business performance measures known to have been influenced and asking participants to indicate which measures they believe have been influenced will identify the measures most influenced by the initiative.

Success of HR Team. Sometimes it is helpful to solicit input about the working relationship between the HR staff and the participants. Question 19 in Figure 4-1 asks participants to indicate the degree to which the HR staff is successful in implementing and supporting the project. This information is helpful in making adjustments in future projects.

Barriers. Several barriers can influence the successful application of an HR project. Question 20 in Figure 4-1 seeks the identification of these barriers. As an alternative, the perceived barriers are listed and participants check all that apply. Still another variation is to list the barriers with a range of responses, indicating the extent to which the barrier inhibited results.

Enablers. Just as important as barriers are the enablers—those issues, events, or situations that have enabled the project to be successful. The same options are available with this question as in the question on barriers. Question 21 in Figure 4-1 addresses this issue.

Management Support. Management support is critical to the successful application of newly acquired skills. At least one question should be included in the questionnaire on the degree of management support. Sometimes this question is structured so that various descriptions of management support are detailed, and participants check the one that applies to their situation. Question 22 in Figure 4-1 is an example of such a question.

Appropriateness of Solution. A recommended process or program in an HR project is usually only one of many potential solutions to a performance problem. If the initial analysis and needs assessment is faulty or if there are alternative approaches to meeting the desired business need, another solution may achieve the same or greater success. The participant is asked to identify alternative solutions that could have been effective in obtaining the same or similar results. Question 23 in Figure 4-1 represents this type of question. The HR staff can use this information to help improve processes and understand the use of alternative approaches.

Suggestions for Improvement. Participants are asked to provide suggestions for improving any part of the initiative or process. As illustrated in Question 24 in Figure 4-1, the open-ended structure is intended to solicit qualitative responses to be used to make improvements.

Other Comments. A final step is to seek other comments about a project. This provides an opportunity to offer additional intangible benefits, present concerns, or suggest issues that will need to be addressed in the future. Question 25 in Figure 4-1 is such a question.

Improving the Response Rate for Questionnaires and Surveys

Given the wide range of potential issues to explore in a follow-up questionnaire or survey, asking all of the questions can cause the response rate to be reduced considerably. The challenge, therefore, is to approach questionnaire and survey design and administration for maximum response rate. This is a critical issue when the questionnaire is a key data collection activity and much of the evaluation hinges on the questionnaire results. The following actions can be taken to increase response rate. Although the term *questionnaire* is used, the same rules apply to surveys.

Provide Advance Communication. If appropriate and feasible, program participants and other stakeholders should receive advance communications about the plans for the questionnaire or survey. This minimizes some of the resistance to the process. It provides an opportunity to explain in more detail the circumstances surrounding the evaluation, and positions the evaluation as an integral part of the HR program—not as an add-on activity that someone initiated three months after the implementation.

Communicate the Purpose. Stakeholders should understand the reason for the questionnaire, including who or what initiated this specific evaluation. They should know if the evaluation is part of a systematic process or a special request for this HR program only.

Explain Who Will See the Data. It is important for respondents to know who will see the data and the results of the questionnaire. If the questionnaire is anonymous, it should clearly be communicated to participants what steps will be taken to ensure anonymity. If senior executives will see the combined results of the study, the respondents should know it.

Describe the Data Integration Process. The respondents should understand how the questionnaire results will be combined with other data, if available. Often the questionnaire is only one of the data collection methods used. Participants should know how the data are weighted and integrated into the entire impact study, as well as interim results.

Keep the Questionnaire as Simple as Possible. A simple questionnaire does not always provide the full scope of data necessary for a comprehensive analysis. However, the simplified approach should always be kept in mind when questions are developed and the total scope of the questionnaire is finalized. Every effort should be made to keep it as simple and brief as possible.

Simplify the Response Process. To the extent possible, it should be easy to respond to the questionnaire. If appropriate, a self-addressed stamped envelope should be included. Perhaps e-mail could be used for responses, if it is easier. In still other situations, a response box is provided near the work station.

Use Local Management Support. Management involvement at the local level is critical to response-rate success. Managers can distribute the questionnaires themselves, make reference to the questionnaire in staff meetings, follow up to see if questionnaires have been completed, and generally show support for completing the questionnaire. This direct supervisor support will prompt many participants to respond with usable data.

Let the Participants Know They Are Part of the Sample. For large HR initiatives, a sampling process may be used. When that is the case, participants should know they are part of a carefully selected sample and that their input will be used to make decisions regarding a much larger target audience. This action often appeals to a sense of responsibility for participants to provide usable, accurate data for the questionnaire.

Consider Incentives. A variety of incentives can be offered, and they usually fall into three categories. First, an incentive is provided in exchange for the completed questionnaire. For example, if participants return the questionnaire personally or through the mail, they will receive a small gift, such as a T-shirt or mug. If identity is an issue, a neutral third party can provide the incentive. In the second category, the incentive is provided to make participants feel guilty about not responding. Examples are a dollar bill clipped to the questionnaire or a pen enclosed in the envelope. Participants are asked to "take the dollar, buy a cup of coffee, and fill out the questionnaire." A third group of incentives is designed to obtain a quick response. This approach is based on the assumption that a quick response will ensure a greater response rate. If an individual puts off completing the questionnaire, the odds of completing it diminish considerably. The initial group of participants may receive a more expensive gift or they may be part of a drawing for an incentive. For example, in one program, the first twenty-five returned questionnaires were placed in a drawing for a $400 gift certificate. The next twenty-five were added to the first twenty-five in the next drawing. The longer a participant waits, the lower the odds of winning.

Have an Executive Sign the Introductory Letter. Participants are always interested in who sent the letter with the questionnaire. For maximum effectiveness, a senior executive who is responsible for a major area where the participants work should sign the letter. Employees may be more willing to respond to a senior executive when compared with situations where a member of the HR implementation team signs a letter.

Use Follow-up Reminders. A follow-up reminder should be sent a week after the questionnaire is received and another sent two weeks later. Depending on the questionnaire and the situation, these times can be adjusted. In some situations, a third follow-up is recommended. Sometimes the follow-up is sent in a different media. For example, a questionnaire may be sent through regular mail, whereas the first follow-up reminder is from the immediate supervisor and a second follow-up is sent via e-mail.

Send a Copy of the Results to the Participants. Even if it is an abbreviated report, participants should see the results of the questionnaire. More importantly, participants should understand that they will receive a copy of the impact study when they are asked to provide the data. This promise will often increase the response rate, as some individuals want to see the results of the entire group along with their particular input.

Estimate the Length of Time to Complete the Questionnaire. Respondents often have a concern about the time it may take to complete the questionnaire. A very lengthy questionnaire may quickly turn off the participants and cause it to be discarded. Sometimes, lengthy questionnaires can be completed quickly because many of them have forced-choice questions or statements that make it easy to respond. However, the number of pages may frighten the respondent. Therefore, it is helpful to indicate the estimated length of time needed to complete the questionnaire— perhaps in the letter itself or at least noted in the communications. This provides extra information so that respondents can decide if they are willing to invest the required amount of time into the process. A word of caution is necessary, though: the amount of time must be realistic. Purposely underestimating it can do more harm than good.

Show the Timing of the Planned Steps. Sometimes the respondents want to know more detail regarding when they can see the results or when the results will be presented to particular groups.

It is recommended that a timeline be presented, showing when different phases of the process will be completed (for example, when the data will be analyzed, when the data will be presented to different groups, and when the results will be returned to the participants in a summary report). This timetable provides some assurance that the process is well-organized and professional, and that the length of time to receive a data summary will not be too long. Another word of caution: the timetable must be followed to maintain the confidence and trust of the individuals.

Give Materials a Professional Appearance. While it should not be an issue in most organizations, unfortunately, there are too many cases when a questionnaire is not developed properly, does not appear professional, or is not easy to follow and understand. The participants must gain respect for the process and for the organization. To do this, a sense of professionalism must be integrated throughout data collection, particularly in the appearance and accuracy of the materials. Sloppy questionnaires will usually command sloppy responses, or no response at all.

Explain the Questionnaire During the Implementation. Sometimes it is helpful to explain to the participants and other key stakeholders that they will be required or asked to provide certain types of data. When this is feasible, questionnaires should be reviewed question by question so that the participants understand the purpose, the issues, and how to respond. This will only take ten to fifteen minutes but can increase the response rate, enhance the quality and quantity of data, and clarify any confusion that may exist on key issues.

Collect Data Anonymously. Participants are more likely to provide frank and candid feedback if their names are not on the questionnaire, particularly when the program is going astray or is off target. Anonymous input is desired whenever possible and whenever the groups are large enough to protect anonymity. When this is the case, every effort should be made to protect the anonymous input, and explanations should be provided regarding how the data are analyzed, minimizing the demographic makeup of respondents so that the individuals cannot be identified in the analysis.

Collectively, these items help boost response rates of follow-up questionnaires. Using all of these strategies can result in a 50 to 70 percent response rate, even with lengthy questionnaires that might take thirty minutes to complete.

Using Interviews to Measure Application and Implementation

Another helpful collection method is the interview, although it is not used as frequently as questionnaires. Interviews can be conducted by the HR implementation staff, the client staff, or a third party. Interviews can secure data not available in performance records or data difficult to obtain through written responses or observations. Also, interviews can uncover success stories that can be useful in communicating evaluation results. Program participants may be reluctant to describe their results in a questionnaire but will volunteer the information to a skillful interviewer using probing techniques. The interview is versatile and appropriate application data (Level 3) as well as reaction and satisfaction data. A major disadvantage of the interview is that it is time consuming. It also requires training or preparing interviewers to ensure that the process is consistent.

Types of Interviews. Interviews usually fall into two basic types: structured and unstructured. A structured interview is much like a questionnaire. Specific questions are asked with little room to deviate from the desired responses. The primary advantages of the structured interview over the questionnaire are that the interview process can ensure the questionnaire is completed and that the interviewer understands the responses supplied by the participant.

The unstructured interview permits probing for additional information. This type of interview uses a few general questions, which can lead to more detailed information as important data are uncovered. The interviewer must be skilled in the probing process. Typical probing questions are:

- ☐ Can you explain that in more detail?
- ☐ Can you give me an example of what you are saying?
- ☐ Can you explain the difficulty that you say you encountered?

Interview Guidelines. The design steps for interviews are similar to those of the questionnaire. A brief summary of key issues with interviews is outlined here.

Develop Questions to Be Asked. Once a decision has been made about the type of interview, specific questions need to be developed. Questions should be brief, precise, and designed for easy response.

Test Out the Interview. The interview should be tested on a small number of participants. If possible, the interviews should be conducted as part of the early stages of the program. The responses should be analyzed and the interview revised, if necessary.

Train the Interviewers. The interviewer should have appropriate skills, including active listening, the ability to form probing questions, and the ability to collect and summarize information into a meaningful form.

Provide Clear Instructions. The participant should understand the purpose of the interview and know what will be done with the information. Expectations, conditions, and rules of the interview should be thoroughly discussed. For example, the participant should know if statements will be kept confidential. If the participant is nervous during an interview and develops signs of anxiety, he or she should be made to feel at ease.

Administer Interviews with a Plan in Mind. As with other evaluation instruments, interviews need to be conducted according to a predetermined plan. The timing of the interview, the person who conducts the interview, and the location of the interview are all issues that become relevant when developing an interview plan. For a large number of stakeholders, a sampling plan may be necessary to save time and reduce the evaluation cost.

Using Focus Groups to Measure Application and Implementation

An extension of the interview, focus groups are particularly helpful when in-depth feedback is needed. The focus group involves a small group discussion conducted by an experienced facilitator. It is designed to solicit qualitative judgments on a planned topic or issue. Group members are all required to provide their input, as individual input builds on group input.

When compared to questionnaires, surveys, or interviews, the focus group strategy has several advantages. The basic premise of using focus groups is that when quality judgments are subjective, several individual judgments are better than one. The group process, where participants often motivate one another, is an effective method for generating new ideas and hypotheses. It is inexpensive and can be quickly planned and conducted. Its flexibility makes it possible to explore an HR initiative's unexpected outcomes or applications.

Applications for Evaluation. The focus group is particularly helpful when qualitative information is needed about the success of an HR program. For example, the focus group can be used in the following situations:

☐ To evaluate reactions to specific procedures, tasks, schedules, or other components of an initiative
☐ To assess the overall effectiveness of the initiative as perceived by the participants immediately following the implementation
☐ To assess the potential impact of the initiative

Essentially, focus groups are helpful when evaluation information is needed but cannot be collected adequately with simple, quantitative methods.

Guidelines. While there are no set rules on how to use focus groups for evaluation, the following guidelines should be helpful:

Ensure that Management and the Client Embrace Focus Groups. Because this is a relatively new process for evaluation, it might be unknown to some management groups. Managers need to understand focus groups and their advantages. This should raise their level of confidence in the information obtained from group sessions.

Plan Topics, Questions, and Strategy Carefully. As with any evaluation instrument, planning is the key. The specific topics, questions, and issues to be discussed must be carefully planned and sequenced. This enhances the comparison of results from one group to another and ensures that the group process is effective and stays on track.

Keep the Group Size Small. While there is no magical group size, a range of six to twelve seems appropriate for most focus group applications. A group has to be large enough to ensure different points of view but small enough to give every participant a chance to talk freely and exchange comments.

Ensure a Representative Sample of the Target Population. It is important for groups to be stratified appropriately so that participants represent the target population. The group should be homogeneous in experience, rank, and influence in the organization.

Insist on Facilitators with Appropriate Expertise. The success of a focus group rests with the facilitator, who must be skilled in the focus group process. Facilitators must know how to control aggressive members of the group and diffuse the input from those who want to dominate the group. Also, facilitators must be able to create an environment in which participants feel comfortable to offer comments freely and openly. Consequently, some organizations use external facilitators.

In summary, the focus group is an inexpensive and quick way to determine the strengths and weaknesses of initiatives. However, for a complete evaluation, focus group information should be combined with data from other instruments.

Observing Participants on the Job to Measure Application and Implementation

Another potentially useful data collection method is observing participants on the job and recording any changes in behavior and specific actions taken. This technique is particularly useful when it is important to know precisely how the participants are using new skills, knowledge, tasks, procedures, or systems. Participant observation is often used in sales and sales support projects. The observer may be a member of the HR staff, the participant's supervisor, a member of a peer group, or an external resource. The most common observer, and probably the most practical, is a member of the HR staff.

Guidelines for Effective Observation. Observation is often misused or misapplied to evaluation situations, forcing some to abandon the process. The effectiveness of observation can be improved with the following guidelines.

Observers Must Be Fully Prepared. Observers must fully understand what information is needed and what skills are covered in the initiative. They must be prepared for the assignment and provided a chance to practice observation skills.

The Observations Should Be Systematic. The observation process must be planned so that it is executed effectively without any surprises. The individuals observed should know in advance about the observation and why they are being observed, unless the observation is planned to be invisible. In this case, the individuals are monitored unknowingly. The timing of observations should be a part of the plan. There are right times to observe a participant, and there are wrong times. If a participant is observed when work situations are not normal (for example, in a crisis), the data collected may be useless.

Planning a systematic observation is important. Several steps are necessary to accomplish a successful observation:

1. Determine what behavior will be observed.
2. Prepare the forms for the observer's use.
3. Select the observers.
4. Prepare a schedule of observations.
5. Prepare observers to observe properly.
6. Inform participants of the planned observation, providing explanations.
7. Conduct the observations.
8. Summarize the observation data.

The Observers Should Know How to Interpret and Report What They See. Observations involve judgment decisions. The observer must analyze which behaviors are being displayed and what actions are being taken by the participants. Observers should know how to summarize behavior and report results in a meaningful manner.

The Observer's Influence Should Be Minimized. Except for "mystery" or "planted" observers and electronic observations, it is impossible to completely isolate the overall effect of an observer. Participants will display the behavior they think is appropriate, performing at their best. The presence of the observer must be minimized. To the extent possible, the observer should blend into the work environment.

Select Observers Carefully. Observers are usually independent of the participants. They are typically members of the HR staff. The independent observer is usually more skilled at recording behavior and making interpretations of behavior and is usually unbiased in these interpretations. Using an independent observer reduces the need for HR staff to prepare observers and relieves the operating department or division of the responsibility. On the other hand, the independent observer has the appearance of an outsider, and participants may resent this kind of observer. Sometimes it is more feasible to recruit observers from outside the organization. Another advantage this approach has is the ability to neutralize the prejudicial feelings entering the decisions.

Observation Methods. Five methods of observation are suggested and are appropriate depending on the circumstances surrounding the type of information needed. Each method is briefly described below.

Behavior Checklist and Codes. A behavior checklist is useful for recording the presence, absence, frequency, or duration of a participant's behavior as it occurs. A checklist does not provide information on the quality, intensity, or possible circumstances surrounding the behavior observed. The checklist is useful, though, because an observer can identify exactly which behaviors should or should not occur. Measuring the duration of a behavior may be more difficult and requires a stopwatch and a place on the form to record time intervals. This factor is usually not as important when compared with whether or not a particular behavior was observed and how often. The number of behaviors listed in the checklist should be small and listed in a logical sequence if they normally occur in a sequence. A variation of this approach involves coding behaviors on a form. Although this method is useful when there are many behaviors, it is more time consuming because a code is entered that identifies a specific behavior instead of checking an item.

Delayed Report Method. With a delayed report method, the observer does not use any forms or written materials during the observation. The information is either recorded after the observation is completed or at particular time intervals during an observation. The observer tries to reconstruct what has been witnessed during the observation period. The advantage of this approach is that the observer is not as noticeable, and there are no forms being completed or notes being taken during the observation. The observer becomes more a part of the situation and less of a distraction. An obvious disadvantage is that the information written may not be as accurate and reliable as the information collected at the time it occurred. A variation of this approach is the 360° feedback process in which surveys are completed on other individuals based on observations within a specific time frame.

Video Recording. A video camera records behavior in every detail. However, this intrusion may be awkward and cumbersome, and the participants may be unnecessarily nervous or self-conscious while they are being videotaped. If the camera is concealed, the privacy of the participant may be invaded. Because of this, video recording of on-the-job behavior is not frequently used.

Audio Monitoring. Monitoring conversations of participants who are using the skills taught in the HR initiative is an effective observation technique. For example, in a large communication company's telemarketing department, sales representatives were prepared to sell equipment by telephone. To determine if employees were using the skills and procedures properly, telephone conversations were monitored on a randomly selected basis. Although this approach may stir some controversy, it is an effective way to determine if skills are being applied consistently and effectively.

For it to work smoothly, it must be fully explained and the rules clearly communicated.

Computer Monitoring. For employees who work regularly with a keyboard, computer monitoring is becoming an effective way to "observe" participants as they perform job tasks. The computer monitors times, sequence of steps, use of routines, and other activities to determine if the participant is performing the work according to the guidelines of the HR program. As technology continues to be a significant part of the workplace, computer monitoring holds much promise. This is particularly helpful for application and implementation data.

Using Action Plans and Follow-Up Assignments to Measure Application and Implementation

In some cases, follow-up assignments can develop implementation and application data. In a typical follow-up assignment, the participant is asked to meet a goal or complete a particular task or project by a set date. A summary of the results of the completed assignments provides further evidence of the success of the HR program and actual implementation of new skills and knowledge gained.

The action plan is the most common type of follow-up assignment process and is fully described in this section. With this approach, participants are required to develop action plans as part of the HR program. Action plans contain detailed steps to accomplish specific objectives related to the program. The process is one of the most effective ways to enhance support for an HR project and build the ownership needed for the successful application and implementation of the project.

The plan is typically prepared on a printed form, such as the one shown in Figure 4-2. The action plan shows what is to be done, by whom, and the date by which the objectives should be accomplished. The action-plan approach is a straightforward, easy-to-use method for determining how participants will change their behavior on the job and achieve success with the HR program. The approach produces data that answer such questions as:

ACTION PLAN

Page _____ of _____

Name: _____ HR Staff Signature _____ Follow-Up Date _____

Objective: _____ Evaluation Period _____ to _____

Action Steps	Expected Consequences	Target Date	Responsibility
1.			
2.			
3.			
4.			
5.			
6.			
7.			
8.			

Comments: _____
_____
_____

Figure 4-2.

☐ What on-the-job improvements have been realized since the program was implemented?
☐ Are the improvements linked to the program?
☐ What may have prevented participants from accomplishing specific action items?

With this information, HR staff can decide if the project should be modified and in what ways, if it is not too late. Collectively, the HR staff and client can assess the findings to evaluate the success of the program.

Developing the Action Plan. The development of the action plan requires two major tasks: determining the areas for action and writing the action items. Both tasks should be completed during the HR program and, at the same time, be related to on-the-job activities. A list of areas for action can be developed with the help of HR staff. The list may include an area needing improvement or representing an opportunity for increased performance. Examples of typical questions that should be answered before determining the areas for action are listed below:

☐ How much time will this action take?
☐ Are the skills for accomplishing this action item available?
☐ Who has the authority to implement the action plan?
☐ Will this action have an effect on other individuals?
☐ Are there any organizational constraints for accomplishing this action item?

Usually, it is more difficult to write specific action items than it is to identify the action areas. The most important characteristic of an action item is that it is written so that everyone involved will know when it occurs. One way to help achieve this goal is to use specific action verbs and set deadlines for completion of each action item. Some examples of action items are:

☐ Implement the new customer contract software by (date).
☐ Identify and secure a new customer account by (date).
☐ Handle every piece of paper only once to improve my personal time management by (date).
☐ Probe my customers directly about a particular problem by (date).

If appropriate, each action item should indicate other individuals or resources necessary for completion of the action item. Planned behavior changes should be observable. It should be obvious to the HR program participant and others when the change takes place. Action plans, as used in this context, do not require the prior approval or input from the participant's supervisor although, as in any case, supervisor support may be helpful.

Using Action Plans Successfully. The action-plan process can be an integral part of the HR program and is not necessarily considered an add-on or optional activity. To gain maximum effectiveness from action plans to collect data for evaluation, the following steps should be implemented.

Communicate the Action-Plan Requirement Early. One of the most negative reactions to action plans is the surprise factor often inherent in the way the process is introduced. When participants realize they must develop a detailed action plan, there is often immediate, built-in resistance. Communicating to participants in advance, when the process is shown to be an integral part of the HR program, will often minimize resistance. When participants fully realize the benefits before they attend the first session, they take the process more seriously and usually perform extra steps to ensure its success.

Describe the Action Planning Process at the Outset of the Project. At the first meeting, action plan requirements are discussed, including an outline of the purpose of the process, why it is necessary, and the basic requirements during and after the HR initiative. Some HR staff members furnish a separate notepad for program participants to collect ideas and useful techniques for their action plans. This is a productive way to focus more attention on the process.

Teach the Action Planning Process. An important prerequisite for action planning success is an understanding of how it works and how specific action plans are developed. A portion of the HR program time is allocated to teaching participants how to develop plans. In this session, the requirements are outlined, special forms and procedures are discussed, and a positive example is distributed and reviewed. Sometimes an entire half-day module is allocated to this process so that participants will fully understand and use it. Any available support tools, such as key measures, charts, graphs, suggested topics, and sample calculations, should be used in this session to help facilitate the plan's development.

Allow Time to Develop the Plan. When action plans are used to collect data for project evaluation, it is important to allow participants to develop plans during the HR program. Sometimes it is helpful to have participants work in teams so they can share ideas as they develop specific plans. In these sessions, HR staff often monitor the progress of individuals or teams to keep the process on track and to answer questions.

Have HR Staff Members Approve Action Plans. It is essential for the action plan to be related to HR program objectives and, at the same time, represent an important accomplishment for the organization when it is completed. It is easy for participants to stray from the intent and purpose of action planning and not give it the attention it deserves. Consequently, it is helpful to have the HR staff member actually sign off on the action plan, ensuring that the plan reflects all of the requirements and is appropriate for the HR initiative. In some cases, a space is provided for the HR staff member signature on the action-plan document.

Ask Participants to Isolate the Effects of the HR Program. Although the action plan is initiated because of the HR program, the actual improvements reported on the action plan may be influenced by other factors. Thus, the action planning process should not take full credit for the improvement. For example, an action plan to reduce product defects could take only partial credit for an improvement because of the other variables that will usually affect the defect rate. Although there are several ways to isolate the effects of an HR program, participant estimation is usually more appropriate in the action-planning process. Consequently, the participants are asked to estimate the percentage of the improvement actually related to a particular HR program. This question can be asked on the action plan form or on a follow-up questionnaire.

Require Action Plans to Be Presented to the Group, If Possible.
There is no better way to secure commitment and ownership of
the action-planning process than to have a participant describe
his or her action plan in front of fellow participants. Presenting
the action plan helps ensure that the process is thoroughly
developed and will be implemented on the job. If the number of
participants is too large for individual presentations, perhaps the
group can be divided into teams, and one participant can be
selected from the team. Under these circumstances, the team will
usually select the best action plan for presentation to the group.

Explain the Follow-up Mechanism. Participants must have a clear
understanding of the timing of the action plan, implementation,
and follow up. The method in which data will be collected,
analyzed, and reported should be openly discussed. Five options
are common:

1. The group is convened to discuss progress on the plans.
2. Participants meet with their immediate managers and discuss
   the success of the plan. A copy is forwarded to the HR staff.
3. A meeting is held with the evaluator, the participant, and
   the participant's manager to discuss the plan and the information it contains.
4. Participants send the plan to the evaluator and it is discussed in a conference call.
5. Participants send the plan directly to the HR staff with no
   meetings or discussions. This is the most common option.

Although there are other ways to collect the data, it is important
to select a mechanism that fits the culture and constraints of
the organization.

Collect Action Plans at Predetermined Follow-up Times. Because
it is critical to have an excellent response rate, several steps may
be necessary to ensure that action plans are completed and the
data are returned to the appropriate individual or group for
analysis. Some organizations use follow-up reminders by mail or
e-mail. Others call participants to check progress. Still others offer
assistance in developing the final plan. These steps may require
additional resources, which must be weighed against the impor-

tance of having more data. When the action-plan process is implemented as outlined in this chapter, the response rates will normally be very high—in the 50 to 80 percent range. Usually, participants will see the importance of the process and will develop their plans in detail during the HR initiative.

Summarize and Report the Data. If developed properly, each action plan should result in improvements. Also, each individual has indicated the percentage of improvement directly related to the HR program either on the action plan or the questionnaire. The data must be tabulated, summarized, and reported in a way that shows success with application and implementation.

Advantages/Disadvantages of Action Plans. Although there are many advantages to using action plans, there are at least two concerns:

1. The process relies on direct input from the HR program participant, usually with no assurance of anonymity. As such, the information can sometimes be biased and unreliable.
2. Action plans can be time consuming for the participant and, if the participant's manager is not involved in the process, there may be a tendency for the participant not to complete the assignment.

As this section has illustrated, the action-plan approach has many inherent advantages. Action plans are simple and easy to administer; are easily understood by participants; are suitable in a wide variety of HR initiatives; are appropriate for all types of data; are able to measure reaction, learning, behavior changes, and results; and may be used with or without other evaluation methods.

Because of the tremendous flexibility and versatility of the process and the conservative adjustments that can be made in analysis, action plans have become important data collection tools for HR program evaluation.

Using Performance Contracts to Measure Application and Implementation

The performance contract is essentially a slight variation of the action-planning process. Based on the principle of mutual goal setting, a performance contract is a written agreement between a participant and the participant's manager. The participant agrees to improve performance in an area of mutual concern related to the HR program. The agreement is in the form of a project to be completed or a goal to be accomplished soon after the HR initiative is complete. The agreement spells out what is to be accomplished, at what time, and with what results.

Although the steps can vary according to the specific kind of contract and the organization, a common sequence of events follows:

1. The employee (participant) becomes involved in the HR program.
2. The participant and manager mutually agree on a subject for improvement related to the HR program ("What's in it for me?").
3. Specific, measurable goals are set.
4. The participant is involved in the initiative when the contract is discussed, and plans are developed to accomplish the goals.
5. After the HR program, the participant works on the contract against a specific deadline.
6. The participant reports the results of the effort to the manager.
7. The manager and participant document the results and forward a copy to the HR staff along with appropriate comments.
8. The individuals mutually select the subject or action to be taken or performance to be improved prior to the initiative.

The process of selecting the area for improvement is similar to the process used in the action-planning process. The topic can cover one or more of the following areas:

☐ Routine performance—includes specific improvements in routine performance measures, such as production, efficiency, and error rates
☐ Problem solving—focuses on specific problems, such as an unexpected increase in accidents, a decrease in efficiency, or a loss of morale
☐ Innovative or creative applications—includes initiating changes or improvements in work practices, methods, procedures, techniques, and processes

☐ Personal development—involves learning new information or acquiring new skills to increase individual effectiveness

The topic selected should be stated in terms of one or more objectives. The objectives should state what is to be accomplished when the contract is complete. The objectives should be:

☐ written
☐ understandable by all involved
☐ challenging (requiring an unusual effort to achieve)
☐ achievable (something that can be accomplished)
☐ largely under the control of the participant
☐ measurable and dated

The details required to accomplish the contract objectives are developed following the guidelines for action plans presented earlier. Also, the methods for analyzing data and reporting progress are essentially the same, as with the action-planning process.

Shortcut Ways to Measure Application and Implementation

Measuring application and implementation is a critical issue for most HR programs or initiatives. It would be hard to understand the success of the project unless there was some indication as to how well the stakeholders are using the process. Although this section presented a variety of techniques to measure application and implementation, ranging from questionnaires to observation to action plans, a simplified approach for low-key, inexpensive projects is to use a simple questionnaire. The questionnaire presented in Figure 4-1 is very detailed around a complex project. A much more simplified questionnaire addressing five or six key issues would be sufficient for small-scale projects. The areas that should be targeted are actual changes in:

☐ Work and skills applied
☐ Specific implementation issues
☐ Degree of success of implementation
☐ Problems encountered in implementation
☐ Issues that supported the project

These are the core issues that must be addressed.

Another option is to combine data collected on reaction and satisfaction with the data on application and implementation. These are related issues, and a questionnaire combining the key issues on topics presented in this chapter and in Chapter 3 may be sufficient. The important point is to collect data in the simplest way to see how well the project worked.

Capturing Business Impact Data

This section focuses directly on tracking business performance measures. Some HR staff members—and clients—regard business impact data as the most important type because of their connection to business unit success. Also, less-than-desired results in business measures are what translate into a business need that ultimately initiate the HR programs. This section covers the types of business impact data and the specific processes needed to generate the measures within an HR program. Coverage begins with monitoring the record-keeping systems and moving to action plans and the use of questionnaires. These three processes account for most of the opportunities for collecting these important and critical data.

Why Measure Business Impact?

Although there are several obvious reasons for measuring impact, four particular issues support the rationale for collecting business impact data related to an HR program or initiative.

Higher-Level Data. Following the assumption that higher-level data create more value for the client, the business impact measures in a five-level framework offer more valuable data. They are the data considered to be the consequence of the application and implementation of an HR program. They often represent the bottom-line measures that are positively influenced when a program is successful.

A Business Driver for HR Programs. For most HR programs, the business impact data represent the initial drivers for the program. It is the problem of deterioration or less-than-desired performance, or the opportunity for improvement of a business measure that often leads to an HR initiative. If the business needs defined by business measures are the drivers for a project, then the key measure for evaluating the project is the business impact. The extent to which measures actually have changed is the key determinant of the success of the project.

Payoff with Clients. Business impact data often reflect key payoff measures from the perspective of the client (internal and/or external). These are the measures often desired by the client and that the client wants to see changed or improved. They often represent hard, indisputable facts that reflect performance critical to the business and operating unit level of the organization.

Easy to Measure. One unique feature about business impact data is that they are often very easy to measure. Hard and soft data measures at this level often reflect key measures that are found in plentiful numbers throughout an organization. It is not unusual for an organization to have hundreds or even thousands of measures reflecting specific business impact items. The challenge is to connect the HR program objectives to the appropriate business measures. This is more easily accomplished at the beginning of the HR initiative due to the availability and ease with which many of the data items can be located.

Types of Data

The fundamental premise for evaluating an HR initiative is to collect data directly related to the objectives of the project. HR staff members are sometimes concerned that appropriate data are not available in the organization. Fortunately, this is not the case. The data needed to evaluate HR programs are already collected in a vast majority of settings. The confusion sometimes stems from the types of outcomes planned for HR programs. Often, the program focuses on skill and behavioral outcomes reflecting what participants will be able to do after the project is completed. The outcomes of some HR programs are easy to observe and evaluate. It is easy to measure the speed and quality of a new team-based assembly line, for instance. However, behavioral outcomes associated with change management are not nearly as obvious or measurable.

Demonstrating that a manager is an effective change agent is much more difficult than demonstrating that an assembly line operation is maintaining quality and quantity standards.

To help focus on the desired measures, a distinction is made in two general categories of data: hard data and soft data. Hard data are the primary measurements of improvement, presented through rational, undisputed facts that are easily gathered. They are the most desirable type of data to collect. The ultimate criteria for measuring the effectiveness of management rest on hard data items, such as productivity, profitability, cost control, and quality control.

Hard data are:

- [ ] easy to measure and quantify
- [ ] relatively easy to convert to monetary values
- [ ] objectively based
- [ ] common measures of organizational performance
- [ ] credible with management

Because changes in these data may lag behind changes in the organization by many months, it is highly recommended to supplement these measures with interim assessments of measures of soft data, such as attitude, motivation, satisfaction, and skill usage. Although an HR program designed to enhance competencies or manage change should have an ultimate impact on hard data items, it may be more efficiently measured by soft data items. Soft data are more difficult to collect and analyze but are used when hard data are unavailable.

Soft data are:

- [ ] sometimes difficult to measure or quantify directly
- [ ] difficult to convert to monetary values
- [ ] subjectively based, in many cases
- [ ] less credible as a performance measurement
- [ ] usually behaviorally oriented

Hard. Hard data can be grouped into four categories (or sub-divisions) as shown in Figure 4-3. These categories—output, quality, cost, and time—are typical performance measures in

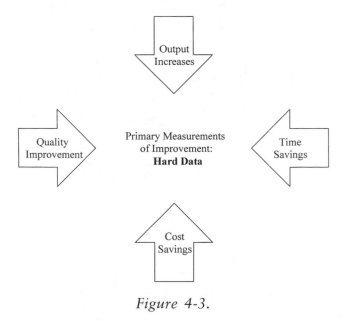

Figure 4-3.

almost every organization. When they are unavailable, the basic approach is to convert soft data to one of the four basic categories.

Output. Probably the most visible hard data results achieved from HR programs are those involving improvements in the output of the work unit. Every organization, regardless of type, has basic measurements of work output, appearing in various forms as outlined in Table 4-1. Since these factors are monitored by organizations, changes can be easily measured by comparing before- and after-work output.

Quality. One of the most significant hard data results is quality. Every organization is concerned with quality, and processes are usually in place to measure and monitor quality. Many HR programs are designed to improve quality, and the results can be easily documented using a variety of quality improvement measurements as illustrated in Table 4-1.

Cost. Another significant hard data results area is improvement in costs. Many HR programs that produce a direct cost savings

Table 4-1
Examples of Hard Data

Output	Quality	Costs	Time
Units produced	Scrap	Budget variances	Cycle time
Tons manufactured	Waste	Unit costs	Response time for complaint
Items assembled	Rejects	Cost by account	Equipment downtime
Items sold	Error rates	Variable costs	Overtime
Sales	Rework	Fixed costs	Average delay time
Forms processed	Shortages	Overhead costs	Time to project completion
Loans approved	Product defects	Operating costs	Processing time
Inventory turnover	Deviation from standard	Delay costs	Supervisory time
Patients visited	Product failures	Penalties/fines	Training time
Applications processed	Inventory adjustments	Project cost savings	Meeting time
Students graduated	Percentage of tasks	Accident costs	Repair time
Tasks completed	completed properly	Program costs	Efficiency (time-based)
Productivity	Number of accidents	Sales expense	Work stoppages
Work backlog	Customer complaints	Administrative costs	Order response time
Incentive bonus		Average cost reduction	Late reporting
Shipments			Lost time days
New accounts			
generated			

can easily show a bottom-line contribution. A few examples of the types of costs are shown in Table 4-1. There can be as many cost items as there are accounts in a cost-accounting system. In addition, costs can be combined to develop any number of combinations needed for evaluation.

Time. The fourth hard data category area is time. Easy to measure and just as critical as cost and quality, time savings may mean a project is completed faster than was planned, a new product was introduced earlier, or the time to repair equipment was reduced. The savings translate into additional output or lower operating costs. Examples of time savings generated by HR programs are shown in Table 4-1.

The distinction between these four groups of hard data is sometimes unclear, since there are overlap factors to consider. For example, accident costs may be listed under the cost category, the number of accidents listed under quality, and the lost-time days due to an accident listed under the time category. The rationale? Accidents represent a cost that can easily be determined. Accidents are usually caused by someone making a mistake and are often a reflection of the quality of employee efforts. Days lost on the job represent time lost to the organization or an incentive bonus may be listed as output, since the amount of bonus is usually tied directly to the output of an employee or group of employees. However, the bonus is usually presented in cash, which represents a cost to the organization. The distinction between the different subdivisions is not as important as the awareness of the vast number of measurements in these four areas.

Soft Data. There are times when hard, rational numbers just do not exist. When this is the case, soft data may be meaningful in evaluating HR programs. Table 4-2 shows common types of soft data, categorized or subdivided into six areas: work habits, climate, new skills, development, satisfaction, and initiative. There may be other ways to divide soft data into categories. Because of the many types of soft data, the possibilities are almost limitless.

Work Habits. Employee work habits are critical to the success of a work group. Dysfunctional work habits can lead to an unproductive and ineffective work group, while productive work

Table 4-2
Examples of Soft Data

Work Habits	Customer Service
Absenteeism	Customer complaints
Tardiness	Customer satisfaction
Visits to the dispensary	Customer dissatisfaction
First-aid treatments	Customer impressions
Violations of safety rules	Customer loyalty
Number of communication	Customer retention
breakdowns	Customer value
Excessive breaks	Lost customers

Work Climate/Satisfaction	Employee Development
Number of grievances	Number of promotions
Number of discrimination charges	Number of pay increases
Employee complaints	Number of training programs
Litigation	attended
Job satisfaction	Requests for transfer
Organizational commitment	Performance appraisal ratings
Employee turnover	Increases in job effectiveness

Attitude Shifts	Initiative/Innovation
Employee loyalty	Implementation of new ideas
Increased confidence	Successful completion of projects
	Number of suggestions
	implemented
	Setting goals and objectives
	New products and services
	developed
	New patents and copyrights

habits can boost the output and morale of the group. The most common and easily documented unproductive work habits include absenteeism and tardiness. These can be tied to cost much easier than other types of soft data. Some HR programs, such as absenteeism reduction, are designed to improve the work habits of employees. In most organizations, measurement systems are in place to record employee work habit problems such as absenteeism, tardiness, and visits to the infirmary. In other situations, the work habits may have to be documented by the employee's supervisor.

Work Climate/Satisfaction. The climate of the work group is important in team effectiveness. Grievances, discrimination charges, complaints, and job dissatisfaction are often linked to the work climate. The result: less efficiency, less output, unionization drives, and possibly employee resignations. Many HR programs are designed to improve work climate.

HR programs are also frequently designed to improve satisfaction with work, environment, or customers. Reactions to these measures provide additional evidence of success of the program.

Customer Service. One of the most important soft data areas is the customer service category. Measuring the extent of customer satisfaction and dissatisfaction is critical to developing the desired customer loyalty and retention.

Employee Development. Another important type of soft data is employee development. Promotions, transfers, pay increases, and performance ratings are typical data that indicate improvement in this area. In the case of managers/supervisors, measures focus on the extent to which they provide developmental opportunities for their employees.

Attitude Shifts. A fifth type of soft data comes in the form of attitude shifts. Employee loyalty and increased confidence are typical measures of shifts in attitude.

Initiative and Innovation. The final category of soft data is initiative. In some HR programs, participants are encouraged to try new ideas and techniques. The extent to which employees accomplish their goals is additional evidence of the success of the program. Also, the employees' initiative to generate ideas and submit suggestions is further indication that improvement has occurred. New product and service developments and new inventions, patents and copyrights are important innovation measures.

As with hard data, these subdivisions have some overlap. Some items listed under one category could appropriately be listed in another. For instance, consider employee loyalty. Loyalty is related both to the feelings and attitudes of an employee, as well as his or her work habits. An employee exhibits loyalty through attitudes and feelings in the following situations:

☐ balancing the organization's goals with personal goals
☐ purchasing the company's products rather than those of a competitor

On the other hand, loyalty may surface in these work habits of an employee:

☐ returns to work promptly after break
☐ studies job information on his or her own time
☐ takes work home when necessary to finish the job

Soft Data Versus Hard Data. The preference of hard data in the evaluation of HR programs does not dilute the value of soft data. Soft data are essential for a complete evaluation of HR programs. A project's total success may rest on soft data measurements. For example, in a project to reduce turnover at a fast-food restaurant, four key measures of success were identified: employee turnover, interview-to-hire ratios, participants' performance evaluations, and reduced litigation.

Most HR programs use a combination of hard and soft data items in the evaluation. A comprehensive evaluation uses several hard data and soft data measurements. For example, an HR program in the maintenance department of one organization yeilded the following measures of success:

☐ reduction of costs associated with specific maintenance activities
☐ improvement in production equipment and processes
☐ changes in maintenance responsibilities and procedures
☐ improvement in training of maintenance employees
☐ changes in organization and staffing

These changes included both hard data (production and costs) and soft data (changes in procedures, and changes in the organization). Soft data are usually best used when evaluating behavior and skill outcomes. For example, in building core competencies, which has proven to be a very effective strategy for many organizations, the evaluation of behavioral and skill outcomes relies almost entirely on soft data.

The important point is that there is a place for both hard- and soft-data evaluations. A comprehensive HR program will use both types of data. Some initiatives will rely on soft data as primary measures, while others will rely on hard data as primary measures. Hard data are preferred because of their distinct advantages and level of credibility.

Other Data Categories. In addition to classifying data as hard and soft, it is sometimes helpful to explain other ways to classify or categorize data. As shown in Figure 4-4, data can be categorized at several different levels. As the figure illustrates, some data are considered strategic and are linked to the corporate level of an organization. Other data are more operational at the business unit level. Still others are considered more tactical in nature and scope and are used at the operating level.

Examples of data categorized at the strategic level include financial, people-oriented, or internal versus external. At the business unit level, classifications such as output, quality, time, cost, job satisfaction, and customer satisfaction are critical categories. At the tactical level, the categories are more plentiful and include items such as productivity, efficiency, cost control, quality, time, attitudes, and individual and team performance. The important point is not the concern about the classification of data but an awareness of the vast array of data available. Regardless of what they are called, these data are a consequence measure of HR program success. These measures are captured throughout an organization and used for a variety of purposes. The challenge

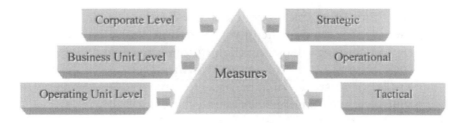

Figure 4-4.

is to find the data items connected directly to the HR program. Ideally, this would be accomplished on the front end of the process so that the data are linked with the initial analysis. If not, it would be a process of trying to identify the appropriate measures for the output of the HR program.

Monitoring Business Performance Data

Data are available in every organization to measure business performance. Monitoring performance data enables management to measure performance in terms of output, quality, costs, time, job satisfaction, and customer satisfaction. In determining the source of data in the evaluation, the first consideration should be existing databases and reports. In most organizations, performance data suitable for measuring improvement resulting from an HR program are available. If not, additional record-keeping systems will have to be developed for measurement and analysis. At this point, the question of economics surfaces. Is it economical to develop the record-keeping systems necessary to evaluate HR programs? If the costs are greater than the expected return for the entire program, then it is pointless to develop those systems.

Using Current Measures. If existing performance measures are available, specific guidelines are recommended to ensure that the measurement system is easily developed.

Identify Appropriate Measures. Existing performance measures should be thoroughly researched to identify those related to the proposed objectives of the HR program. Frequently, an organization will have several performance measures related to the same item. For example, the efficiency of a production unit can be measured in several ways, some of which are outlined below:

- ☐ the number of units produced per hour
- ☐ the number of on-schedule production units
- ☐ the percentage of use of the equipment
- ☐ the percentage of equipment downtime
- ☐ the labor cost per unit of production
- ☐ the overtime required per unit of production
- ☐ total unit cost

Each of these, in its own way, measures the efficiency of the production unit. All related measures should be reviewed to determine those most relevant to the HR program.

Convert Current Measures to Usable Ones. Occasionally, existing performance measures are integrated with other data, and it may be difficult to keep them isolated from unrelated data. In this situation, all existing related measures should be extracted and tabulated again to be more appropriate for comparison in the evaluation. At times, conversion factors may be necessary. For example, the average number of new sales orders per month may be presented regularly in the performance measures for the sales department. In addition, the sales costs per sales representative are also presented. However, in the evaluation of an HR program, the average cost per new sale is needed. The average number of new sales orders and the sales lost per sales representative are required to develop the data necessary for comparison.

Developing New Measures. In some cases, data are not available for the information needed to measure the effectiveness of an HR program. The HR staff must work with the client to develop record-keeping systems, if economically feasible. In one organization, a turnover problem with new professional staff prompted an HR initiative. To help ensure success of the project, several measures were planned, including early turnover defined as the percentage of employees who left the company in the first six months of employment. Initially this measure was not available. Once the program was implemented, the organization began collecting early turnover figures for comparison. Several questions regarding this issue should be addressed:

- ☐ Which department will develop the measurement system?
- ☐ Who will record and monitor the data?
- ☐ Where will it be recorded?
- ☐ Will forms be used?

These questions will usually involve other departments or a management decision that extends beyond the scope of the HR staff. Often the administration department, operations, or the information technology unit will be instrumental in helping determine whether new measures are needed and, if so, how they will be developed.

Using Action Plans to Develop Business Impact Data

An earlier section showed how action plans can capture Level 3 data to measure application and implementation. The action plan can also be a very useful tool for capturing business impact data. The basic design principles and the issues involved in developing and administering action plans are the same for business impact data as they are for application and implementation. However, a few issues unique to business impact and ROI are presented here. The following steps are recommended when an action plan is developed and implemented to capture business impact data and convert the data to monetary values.

Have Each Participant Set Goals and Targets. As shown in Figure 4-5, an action plan can be developed with a direct focus on business impact data. The plan presented in this figure requires participants to develop an overall objective for the plan, which is usually the primary objective of the HR solution. In some cases, there may be more than one objective, which requires additional action plans. In addition to the objective, the improvement measure and the current levels of performance are identified. This information requires the participant to anticipate the application and implementation of the HR program and set goals for specific performances that can be realized.

The action plan is completed during the HR program, often with the input, assistance, and facilitation of the HR staff. The HR staff members actually approve the plan, indicating that it meets the particular requirements of being very Specific, Measurable, Achievable, Realistic, and Time-based (SMART). The plan can actually be developed in a one- to two-hour time frame and often begins with action steps related to the implementation of the HR solution. These action steps are actually Level 3 activities that detail the application and implementation of the HR solution. All of these steps build support for, and are linked to, business impact measures.

ACTION PLAN

Name: _____ HR Staff Signature _____ Follow-Up Date _____
Objective: _____ Evaluation Period _____ to _____
Improvement Measure: _____ Current Performance _____ Target Performance _____

Action Steps	Analysis
1. _____	A. What is the unit of measure? _____
2. _____	B. What is the value (cost) of one unit? $ _____
3. _____	C. How did you arrive at this value? _____
4. _____	
5. _____	
6. _____	D. How much did the measure change during the evaluation period? (monthly value) _____
7. _____	E. What percent of this change was actually caused by this program? _____ %
Intangible Benefits: _____	F. What level of confidence do you place on the above information? (100%=Certainty and 0%=No Confidence) _____ %

Comments: _____

Figure 4-5.

Define the Unit of Measure. The next important issue is to define the actual unit of measure. In some cases, more than one measure may be used and will subsequently be contained in additional action plans. The unit of measure is necessary to break the process down into the simplest steps so that the ultimate value of the program can be determined. The unit can be output data, such as an additional unit manufactured or additional hotel room rented, or it can be sales and marketing data such as additional sales units, dollars earned, or a one percent increase in market share. In terms of quality, the unit can be one reject, error, or defect. Time-based units are usually measured in minutes, hours, days, or weeks. Other units are specific to their particular type of data, such as one grievance, complaint, or absence. The important point is to break them down into the simplest terms possible.

Require Participants to Assign Monetary Values for Each Improvement. During the HR program, participants are asked to determine, calculate, or estimate the monetary value for each improvement outlined in the plan. The unit value is determined using standard values, expert input, external databases, or estimates. The process used in arriving at the value is described in the action plan. When the actual improvement occurs, participants will use these values to capture the annual monetary benefits of the plan. For this step to be effective, it is helpful to see examples of common ways in which values can be assigned to the actual data.

Participants Implement the Action Plan. Participants implement the action plan during the HR program implementation, which often lasts for weeks or months following the initiative. Upon completion, a major portion if not all of the project is slated for implementation. The participants implement action-plan steps and the subsequent results are achieved.

Participants Estimate Improvements. At the end of the specified follow-up period—usually three months, six months, nine months, or one year—the participants indicate the specific improvements made, sometimes expressed as a monthly amount. This determines the actual amount of change that has been observed, measured, or recorded. It is important for the participants to understand the necessity for accuracy as data are recorded. In most cases only the changes are recorded, as those amounts are needed to calculate the actual value of the program. In other cases, before and after data may be recorded, allowing the research to calculate the actual differences.

Ask Participants to Isolate the Effects of the HR Initiative. Although the action plan is initiated because of the HR initiative, the actual improvements reported on the action plan may be influenced by other factors. Thus, the action planning process initiated in the HR program should not take full credit for the improvement. For example, an action plan to reduce employee turnover in a division could take only partial credit for an improvement because of the other variables that affect the turnover rate. While there are several ways to isolate the effects of an HR initiative, participant estimation is usually most appropriate in the action-planning process. Consequently, program participants are asked to estimate the percentage of the improvement actually related to this particular program. This question can be asked on the action plan form or in a follow-up questionnaire.

Ask Participants to Provide a Confidence Level for Estimates. Because the process to convert data to monetary values may not be exact and the amount of the improvement actually related to the program may not be precise, participants are asked to indicate their level of confidence in those two values, collectively. On a scale of zero to 100 percent, where zero percent means the values are completely false and 100 percent means the estimates represent certainty, this value provides participants a mechanism for expressing their uneasiness with their ability to be exact with the process.

Collect Action Plans at Specified Time Intervals. An excellent response rate is essential, so several steps may be necessary to ensure that the action plans are completed and returned. Usually participants will see the importance of the process and will develop their plans in detail before leaving the program. Some organizations use follow-up reminders by mail or e-mail. Others call HR program participants to check progress. Still others offer assistance in developing the final plan. These steps may require additional resources, which must be weighed against the importance of having more data.

Summarize the Data and Calculate the ROI. If developed properly, each action plan should have annualized monetary values associated with improvements. Also, each individual should have indicated the percentage of the improvement directly related to the program. Finally, participants should have provided a confidence percentage to reflect their uncertainty with the process and the subjective nature of some of the data that may be provided.

Because this process involves estimates, it may not appear to be accurate. Several adjustments during the analysis make the process very credible and more accurate. The following adjustments are made:

Step 1: For those participants who do not provide data, it is assumed that they had no improvement to report. This is a very conservative approach.

Step 2: Each value is checked for realism, usability, and feasibility. Extreme values are discarded and omitted from the analysis.

Step 3: Because the improvement is annualized, it is assumed the program had no improvement after the first year for short-term projects. Some programs add value in years two and three.

Step 4: The improvement from Step 3 is then adjusted with the confidence level, multiplying it by the confidence percentage. The confidence level is actually an error percentage suggested by the participants. For example, a participant indicating 80 percent confidence with the process is reflecting a 20 percent error possibility. In a $10,000 estimate with an 80 percent confidence factor, the participant is suggesting that the value can be in the range of $8,000 to $12,000. To be conservative, the lower number is used. Thus, the confidence factor is multiplied times the amount of improvement.

Step 5: The new values are then adjusted by the percentage of the improvement related directly to the program using straight multiplication. This isolates the effects of the HR initiative.

The monetary values determined in these five steps are totaled to arrive at a total program benefit. Because these values are already annualized, the total of these benefits becomes the annual benefits for the program. This value is placed in the numerator of the ROI formula to calculate the ROI.

Case Application. The impact of the action plan process is impressive. In a medium-sized manufacturing facility, an HR program was implemented for an operations division in a metals company. Some of the areas addressed were productivity improvement, scrap reduction, absenteeism, turnover, grievances, and safety. These areas were analyzed thoroughly, and supervisors implemented improvements in each area. Supervisors were required to develop action plans for improvement and report the results in a follow-up six months after the program. In this situation, the improvement measures were predetermined by the needs assessment. The following results were documented from a pilot group:

☐ The department unit hour was increased from 65 to 75. This is a basic measure of productivity, where a unit hour of 60 is considered to be average and acceptable work.
☐ Scrap was reduced from 11 percent to 7.4 percent.
☐ Absenteeism was reduced from 7 percent to 3.25 percent.
☐ The annual turnover rate was drastically reduced from 30 percent to 5 percent.
☐ Grievances were reduced by 80 percent.
☐ Lost-time accidents were reduced by 95 percent.

These results were achieved by supervisors applying and implementing the HR solutions and reporting the results of action plans. Although these results are impressive, three additional steps are needed to develop the ultimate evaluation, the return on investment. First, the amount of improvement actually linked to the program must be determined. In this situation, supervisors estimated the percentage of the improvement directly linked to the program. For example, while the absenteeism improvement showed an overall decrease of 3.75 percent, the supervisors collectively estimated that only 46 percent of the absenteeism reduction was actually linked to the HR program. Thus, a 3.75

percent absenteeism reduction actually becomes 1.725 percent. This figure can be adjusted further by factoring in a confidence level (provided by supervisors when they supplied the estimate). In this example, supervisors were 84 percent confident in their allocation of the absenteeism improvement. This adjustment means that 1.725 percent then becomes 1.45 percent when adjusted for the 84 percent confidence level (1.725 × .84 = 1.45%). These two adjustments isolate the effects of the HR program on the output variable and are fully described in Chapter 5.

The second step to develop the ROI is to convert the data to monetary values. In the same example, the value for a single absence must be determined and used to calculate the annual benefit of the improvement. There are at least ten ways to place values on data, and they are fully described in Chapter 6. In this example, supervisors developed an estimated value of one absence, a value that was used previously in several applications in which the cost of absenteeism was needed. Thus, the total number of absences avoided was calculated and multiplied by the value of one absence to obtain the program's annual impact on absenteeism reduction. This process shows clearly the economic value of the program on that specific output variable. These two steps, isolating the effects of initiative and converting data to monetary values, are performed for each of the six improvement variables, and the total value represents the annual economic benefit of the program.

The third step necessary to move to an ROI is to develop the fully loaded costs of the program. In this step, the costs related to the needs assessment and program development are prorated. All direct HR program costs are captured, along with the cost of participants' salaries and benefits while they were actually involved in the HR initiative. The fully loaded cost for all participants reflects the total investment in this program for the group. This process is fully explained in Chapter 7. With these three additional steps, the ROI can be calculated using formulas described earlier in this book (net benefits divided by costs). In this example, total annual benefits directly attributed to the program after converting all six improvement items to monetary units were $775,000. The fully loaded costs for the HR program were developed to be $65,000. Thus, the ROI becomes as follows:

$$\text{ROI} = \frac{\text{Net Program Benefits}}{\text{Program Costs}} = \frac{\$775,000 - \$65,000}{\$65,000} \times 100 = 1{,}092\%$$

This impressive ROI has credibility because of the conservative adjustments made to the data. Without these three additional steps, the target audience may be left wondering how much of the results were actually linked to the program and if the benefits exceeded the costs to the degree reflected in the ROI.

The action-planning process is a very useful way to collect business impact data. Use of the process has several inherent advantages. Most of the data are taken directly from participants and often have the credibility needed in the analysis. Also, much of the responsibility for the analysis and evaluation is shifted to the participants as they tackle three of the most critical parts of the process. In effect, they collect data, show improvements, isolate the effects of the HR initiative, and convert data to monetary values. This enables the evaluation to be conducted with limited resources and shifts much of the actual involvement to those who are actually applying and implementing the HR program.

Using Questionnaires to Collect Business Impact Measures

As described earlier, the questionnaire is one of the most versatile data collection tools and can be appropriate for Levels 1, 2, 3, and 4 data. In the previous section, a questionnaire example is presented in which not only Level 3 application and implementation data are collected, but business impact data are developed as well. Some of the issues discussed there apply equally in collecting business impact data. Essentially, the design principles and the content issues are the same except that questionnaires developed for a business impact evaluation will contain additional questions to capture those data items.

Key Impact Questions. Figure 4-6 shows a series of key impact questions that can be added to a questionnaire to capture business impact data. Although there are a variety of ways to collect this category of data, these simple questions can be powerful if participants are committed to providing this type of information.

1. What has changed about you or your work as a result of your participation in this project? (Specific behavior change, action items, new projects, etc.)

    _____

    _____

    _____

2. Please identify any specific accomplishments/improvements that you can link to the project. (Job performance, project completion, response times, etc.).

    _____

    _____

    _____

3. What specific annualized value in U.S. dollars can be attributed to the above accomplishments/improvements? Use first-year values only. While this is a difficult question, try to think of specific ways in which the above improvements can be converted to monetary units. Along with the monetary value, please indicate the basis of your calculation. $____

    Basis:

    _____

    _____

    _____

4. Other factors often influence improvements in performance. Please indicate the percentage of the above improvement that is related directly to this project. ____%.

    Please explain.

    _____

    _____

    _____

Figure 4-6.

5. Do you think this program represented a good investment for the company?

Yes ☐   No ☐

Please explain.

_____

_____

_____

6. What level of confidence do you place on the above estimations? (0% = No Confidence, 100% = Certainty) ____%

_____

_____

_____

Figure 4-6. Continued.

To ensure an appropriate response, the strategies outlined in Chapter 3, under the heading "Improving the Response Rate for Questionnaires and Surveys," apply equally to follow-up questionnaires where business impact data are collected. These questions must be thoroughly explained and if possible even reviewed prior to actually achieving the accomplishments outlined in the questionnaire. The first impact question provides participants with the opportunity to detail specifically what has changed about their work as a result of the HR program. These are actually application data, but they set the stage for collecting the business impact data.

Question two focuses directly on business impact data but is expressed in general terms to allow flexibility for participant responses. If the responses need to follow a narrowly focused set of possibilities, the question can be more narrowly worded.

Question three focuses on the actual monetary values. Although this may only be necessary if an ROI analysis is planned, it is sometimes helpful to see the impact of the particular change in business measures expressed in monetary terms. Participants are asked not only to supply the values, but to provide an annual improvement as well. Most importantly, they are asked to provide an explanation of how they arrived at these values. This brings additional credibility to the responses and is important in making the decision to use the data.

Question four focuses on isolating the effects of the HR initiative on business impact measures. In almost every setting, other factors will influence the output measures, so it is important to try to determine how much of the improvement is actually related to the HR initiative. This question attempts to do that by asking participants to provide a percentage of the improvement related to the HR initiative.

Question five simply asks participants their opinion as to whether or not the program was a good investment for the company. While this information cannot be used in the analysis, it provides supporting evidence of success—or the lack thereof.

Finally, in question six, the level of confidence is captured using the scale of zero to 100 percent. This confidence is spread over all of the questions and can be used to provide additional supporting evidence around the data gathered in the previous question. Also, the confidence value can be used to adjust the data. This will be explored later.

These simple questions can make the data collection instrument powerful and can identify significant improvements in the business impact area.

There are different approaches and different ways to explore the issues surrounding data collection. The most important issue is that the proper climate be established for participants to provide the data.

ROI Analysis. Although there are several approaches to data analysis, the recommended steps to calculate the ROI are briefly described here. The calculations are based on the responses from the series of impact questions. The following five adjustments are made to the data to ensure that they are credible and accurate:

1. The participants who do not complete the questionnaire or provide usable data on the impact questions are assumed to have no improvement.
2. Extreme and unrealistic data items are omitted.
3. Only annualized values are used, as requested in the responses.

4. The values are adjusted to reflect the confidence level of participants.
5. The values are adjusted for the amount of the improvement related directly to the program.

These five adjustments create a very credible value that is usually considered to be an understatement of the benefits.

SELECTING THE APPROPRIATE METHOD FOR EACH LEVEL

This chapter and the previous one presented several methods to capture data. Collectively, they offer a wide range of opportunities for collecting data in a variety of situations. Eight specific issues should be considered when deciding which method is appropriate for a situation. These should be considered when selecting data collection methods for other evaluation levels as well.

Type of Data. Perhaps one of the most important issues to consider when selecting the method is the type of data to be collected. Some methods are more appropriate for Level 4, while others are best for Level 3. Table 4-3 shows the most appropriate types of data for specific methods of Levels 3 and 4 data collection. Follow-up surveys, observations, interviews, and focus groups are best suited for Level 3 data, sometimes exclusively. Performance monitoring, action planning, and questionnaires can easily capture Level 4 data.

Participants' Time for Data Input. Another important factor in selecting the data collection method is the amount of time participants must spend with data collection and evaluation systems. Time requirements should always be minimized, and the method should be positioned so that it is a value-added activity (that is, the participants understand that this activity is something valuable so they will not resist). This requirement often means that sampling is used to keep the total participant time to a minimum. Some methods, such as performance monitoring, require no participant time, while others, such as interviews and focus groups, require a significant investment in time.

Table 4-3
Collecting Follow-Up Data

Data-Collection Method	Level 3	Level 4
Follow-up surveys	✓	
Follow-up questionnaires	✓	✓
Observation on the job	✓	
Interviews with participants	✓	
Follow-up focus groups	✓	
Action planning	✓	✓
Performance contracting	✓	✓
Business performance monitoring		✓

Supervisory Time for Data Input. The time that a participant's direct supervisor must allocate to data collection is another important issue in the method selection. This time requirement should always be minimized. Some methods, such as performance contracting, may require much involvement from the supervisor before and after the program. Other methods, such as questionnaires administered directly to participants, may not require any supervisor time.

Cost of Method. Cost is always a consideration when selecting the method. Some data collection methods are more expensive than others. For example, interviews and observations are very expensive. Surveys, questionnaires, and performance monitoring are usually inexpensive.

Disruption of Normal Work Activities. Another key issue in selecting the appropriate method—and perhaps the one that generates the most concern with managers—is the amount of disruption the data collection will create. Routine work processes should be disrupted as little as possible. Some data collection techniques, such as performance monitoring, require very little time and distraction from normal activities. Questionnaires generally do not disrupt the work environment and can often be completed in only a few minutes, or even after normal work hours. On the other extreme, some items such as observations and interviews may be too disruptive to the work unit.

Accuracy of Method. The accuracy of the technique is another factor to consider when selecting the method. Some data collection methods are more accurate than others. For example, performance monitoring is usually very accurate, whereas questionnaires can be distorted and unreliable. If actual on-the-job behavior must be captured, observation is clearly one of the most accurate methods.

Utility of an Additional Method. Because there are many different methods to collect data, it is tempting to use too many data collection methods. Multiple data collection methods add to the time and costs of the evaluation and may result in very little additional value. Utility refers to the added value of the use of an additional data collection method. As more than one method is used, this question should always be addressed. Does the value obtained from the additional data warrant the extra time and expense of the method? If the answer is no, the additional method should not be implemented.

Cultural Bias for Data Collection Method. The culture or philosophy of the organization can dictate which data collection methods are used. For example, some organizations are accustomed to using questionnaires and find the process fits in well with their culture. Some organizations will not use observation because their culture does not support the potential invasion of privacy often associated with it.

SHORTCUT WAYS TO CAPTURE BUSINESS IMPACT DATA

While this chapter has explored several different ways to capture business impact data, there are some ways the process can be simplified when the projects are small in scope or inexpensive to develop and deliver.

Revisit Initial Needs. In the ideal situation, the business needs are the drivers for the project. If possible, the initial needs will be revisited to see which specific measures need to change as a result of the HR initiative. These are the measures that should be examined for changes. This can be an extremely simple process if the project is developed as it should be. If not, other approaches may be necessary.

Monitor Business Performance Measures. For most HR initiatives, even those small in scope, it is possible to monitor the business measures that are linked or perceived to be linked to the projects. These are usually well known, discussed in conjunction with the project, and readily available in operating units and business units throughout the organization. Only those measures perceived to be directly linked to the program should be examined, and some caution should be taken not to overextend the project by examining measures that may be only casually linked to the HR initiative.

Build It into the Process. As described in one of the examples in this chapter, it is a relatively easy task to build data collection and part of the analysis into the project. With this approach, the participants provide the data, isolate the effects of the HR initiative on those data, and covert the data to monetary values. The remaining steps for the ROI process are simply the additional steps for capturing the costs, detailing the intangibles, actually developing the ROI calculations, and, of course, presenting the entire report. By building data collection and some analysis into the process and gaining the necessary commitments from participants, it is possible for an HR implementation team to generate the required business data that are directly connected to the project with very little cost and effort.

If Questionnaires Are Used, Consider Business Impact Data. If a detailed follow-up questionnaire is used to capture data for application and implementation, a few additional questions can be added to capture business impact. The key impact questions contained in Figure 4-6 are simple questions that can usually be addressed by many professional employees. They can be included in the questionnaire with little additional effort, and the analysis is not very time consuming. The results can be eye-opening, far-reaching data that not only show value but also identify several issues pertinent to the HR initiative. Collectively, these are shortcut ways to ensure that business impact data are collected with minimum effort. It is important and almost essential that business data be collected if they are linked to the HR program. After all, this is the type of data that most clients desire and are expecting from the project.

CONCLUSION

After describing the types of data that reflect application in the work setting and business impact, this chapter provides an overview of several data collection approaches that can be used to capture application and business data—critical issues in determining the success of the project. These essential measures determine not only the success achieved, but areas where improvement is needed and areas where the success can be replicated in the future. A variety of techniques are available, ranging from observation to questionnaires to action plans to performance monitoring, but the method chosen must match the scope of the project. Complicated projects require a comprehensive approach that measures all of the issues involved in application and implementation. Simple projects can take a less formal approach and collect data only from a questionnaire. The credibility of data will always be an issue when this level of data is collected and analyzed. Several strategies are offered to enhance the credibility of data analysis.

CHAPTER 5

Isolating the Effects of an HR Program

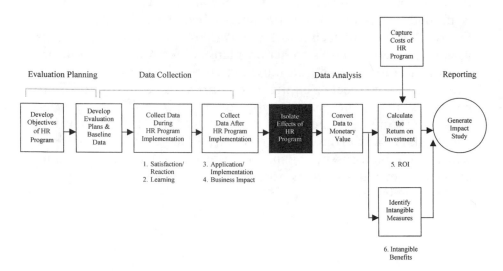

The following situation is repeated often. A significant increase in performance is noted after a major human resource program or initiative is conducted, and the two events appear to be linked. A key manager asks, "How much of this improvement was caused by the HR program?" When this potentially embarrassing question is asked, it is rarely answered with any degree of accuracy and credibility. Although the change in performance may be linked to the HR program, other factors probably contributed to the improvement as well. This chapter explores ten useful strategies to isolate the effects of HR programs and initiatives. These strategies are used in some of the best organizations as they attempt to measure the return on investment of HR programs.

Portions of this chapter were first published in one of the HR field's leading publications [1].

PRELIMINARY ISSUES

The cause and effect relationship between the initiation of an HR program and the actual benefits of the implementation can be confusing and difficult to prove but can be accomplished with an acceptable degree of accuracy. The challenge is to develop one or more specific strategies to isolate the effects of the program early in the process, usually as part of an evaluation plan. Up-front attention ensures that appropriate strategies will be used with minimum costs and time commitments.

Chain of Impact

Before presenting the strategies, it is helpful to examine the chain of impact implied in the different levels of evaluation. As an example, suppose a new performance management process is implemented in an organization. Measurable results achieved from the program should be derived from the application of skills/knowledge and attitude on the job for a specified period of time after the program has been implemented. This on-the-job application of the HR program is referred to as Level 3 in the five evaluation levels described in Chapter 1 and reported elsewhere [2]. The desired results from those administering the process (supervisors and managers) may differ from the results expected from the rest of the workforce. Supervisors and managers may be expected to administer the process effectively, to be better coaches, and to present a supportive attitude about the process. Others may be expected to perform better because expectations and performance/development plans are more clearly defined by the new process. Continuing with this logic, successful application of the performance management process on the job should stem from supervisors learning new skills and approaches or acquiring new knowledge in the training program that introduces the process, which is measured as a Level 2 evaluation. Therefore, for a business results improvement (Level 4 evaluation), this chain of impact implies that measurable on-the-job applications are realized (Level 3 evaluation) and new knowledge and skills are learned (Level 2 evaluation). Without this preliminary evidence, it is difficult to isolate the effects of the HR program. In other words, if there is no learning or application of the process on the job, it is virtually impossible to conclude that any performance improvements were caused by the program. This chain of impact requirement with the different levels of evaluation is supported in the literature [3]. From a practical standpoint, this issue requires data collection at four levels for an ROI calculation. If data are collected for business results, data should also be collected for other levels of evaluation to ensure that the program helped produce the business results. Although this requirement is a prerequisite to isolating the effects of implementation of the performance management process, it does not prove that there was a direct connection nor does it pinpoint how much of the improvement was caused by the new process. It merely shows that without improvements at previous levels, it is difficult to make a connection between the ultimate outcome and the new performance management process.

Identifying Other Factors

As a first step in isolating HR's impact on performance, all the key factors that may have contributed to the performance improvement should be identified. This step communicates to interested parties that other factors may have influenced the results, underscoring that the new program implemented by HR is not the sole source of improvement. Consequently, the credit for improvement is shared with several possible variables and sources, an approach that is likely to gain the respect of management.

Several potential sources identify major influencing variables. If the program is designed on request, the client may be able to identify factors that will influence the output variable. The client will usually be aware of other initiatives or programs that may impact the output.

Those who implement or use HR programs are usually aware of other influences that may cause performance improvement. After all, it is the impact of their collective efforts that is being monitored and measured. In many situations, they witness previous movements in the performance measures and pinpoint the reasons for changes.

HR analysts, developers, and program administrators are another source for identifying variables that have an impact on results. The needs analysis will usually uncover these influencing variables.

In some situations, participants' supervisors may be able to identify variables that influence the performance improvement. This is particularly useful when the affected population is composed of non-exempt employees (operatives) who may not be fully aware of all the variables that can influence performance.

Finally, middle and top managers may be able to identify other influences based on their experience and knowledge of the situation. Perhaps they have monitored, examined, and analyzed the variables previously. The authority positions of these individuals often increase the credibility of the data.

Taking time to focus attention on variables that may have influenced performance brings additional accuracy and credibility to the process. It moves beyond the scenario in which results are presented with no mention of other influences, a situation that often destroys the credibility of an HR impact report. It also provides a foundation for some of the strategies described in this book by identifying the variables that must be isolated to show the effects of HR programs, processes, and initiatives. A word of caution is appropriate here. Halting the process after this step would leave many unknowns about actual program impact and might leave a negative impression with management because this step may have identified variables that management did not previously consider. Therefore, it is recommended that the HR staff go beyond this initial step and use one or more of the ten strategies that isolate the impact of the HR initiative.

THE TEN STRATEGIES

The remainder of this chapter describes in detail the ten strategies to isolate the effects of an HR program. Not all strategies are appropriate for every program. The final section of the chapter discussses the use of the strategies and provides factors to consider when deciding which strategy is most appropriate.

Use of Control Groups

The most accurate approach to isolate the impact of an HR initiative is the use of control groups in an experimental design process [4]. This approach involves the use of an experimental group that receives the HR program and a control group that does not. The composition of both groups should be as identical as possible, and if feasible, the selection of participants for each group should be on a random basis. When this is possible and both groups are subjected to the same environmental influences, the difference in the performance of the two groups can be attributed to the HR program/initiative.

As illustrated in Figure 5-1, the control group and the experimental group do not necessarily have pre-program measurements. Measurements are taken after the program implementation, and the difference in the performance of the two groups shows the amount of improvement that is directly related to the HR program.

Control group arrangements appear in many settings. A review cited a Federal Express company's ROI analysis, which used control groups, as a good example of the state of the art in measuring ROI [5]. The study focused on twenty employees who went through an intense, redesigned two-week training program soon after being hired to drive company vans. Their performance was compared with a control group of twenty other new hires whose managers were told to do no more or less on-the-job training than they normally would do. Performance was tracked for the two groups for ninety days in categories such as accidents, injuries, time-card errors, and domestic airbill errors. The ten performance categories were assigned dollar values by experts from engineering, finance, and other groups. The program demonstrated that the performance of the highly trained employees was superior (resulting in a 24 percent return on investment) to that of the group that did not receive the upgraded training.

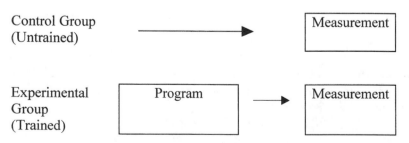

Figure 5-1. Post-test only, control group design.

One caution to keep in mind is that the use of control groups may create an image that the HR staff is creating a laboratory setting, which can cause a problem for some executives. To avoid this stigma, some organizations run a pilot program using pilot participants as the experimental group and not informing the non-participating control group. Another example illustrates this approach. An international pipe and fittings manufacturing company developed an improved incentive plan for its customer service engineers who sell directly to the customer [6]. The incentive program was designed to improve engineers' performance and to produce higher levels of sales. Previously, the incentive plan was not structured well, and engineers and their managers had complained about the plan features and design. The manager of compensation was convinced that the new incentive plan would significantly increase sales. Senior management was skeptical and wanted proof, a familiar scenario. The program was pilot-tested with a group of thirty sales engineers in Europe. In another country, another group of thirty sales engineers with similar individual and market characteristics served as a control group and were not aware of the new incentive plan. Prior to implementing the new plan, performance was measured using average daily sales (sales divided by number of days) for ninety days for each of the two groups. After implementation of the new plan, the average daily sales were recorded for another ninety days. A significant difference in the sales of the two groups emerged, and because the groups were almost identical and were subjected to the same environmental influences, it was concluded that the sales differences were a result of the new incentive plan and not other factors. In this setting, pilot testing allowed the use of a control group without the publicity and potential criticism that is typical using control groups.

The control group process does have some inherent problems that may make it difficult to apply in practice. The first major problem is the selection of the groups. From a practical perspective it is virtually impossible to have identical control and experimental groups. Dozens of factors can affect employee performance, some of them individual and others contextual. To address the issue on a practical basis, it is best to select two or three variables that will have the greatest influence on performance. For example, in an interactive selling skills program in a retail store chain, three groups were trained, and their performances were compared with three similar groups, which were the control groups. The selection of the particular groups was based on three variables store executives thought would influence performance most from one store to another: actual market area, store size, and customer traffic. Although other factors could influence performance, these three variables were used to make the selection.

Another problem is contamination, which can develop when people participating in the program/initiative actually inform or teach others who are in the control group. Sometimes the reverse situation occurs when members of the control group model the behavior from the group implementing the change. In either case, the experiment becomes contaminated as the influence is passed on to the control group. This can be minimized by ensuring that control groups and experimental groups are at different locations, have different shifts, or are on different floors in the same building. When this is not possible, sometimes it is helpful to explain to both groups that one group will implement a new program now and another will implement it at a later date. Also, it may be helpful to appeal to the sense of responsibility of those being informed and ask them not to share the information or skills with others.

A third problem occurs when the different groups function under different environmental influences. Because they may be in different locations, the groups may have different environmental influences. This was a major concern in the implementation of the new incentive plan mentioned previously. Sometimes the selection of the groups can help prevent this problem from occurring. Also, using more groups than necessary and discarding those with some environmental differences is another tactic.

A fourth problem with using control groups is that doing so may appear too research-oriented for most business organizations. For example, executives may not want to take the time to experiment before proceeding with a program, or they may not want to withhold a program from any group just to measure the impact of an experimental program. Because of this concern, some HR practitioners do not entertain the idea of using control groups. When the process is used, however, some organizations conduct it with pilot participants as the experimental group and non-participants as the control group. Under this arrangement, the control group is not informed of its control group status.

Because this is an effective approach for isolating the impact of an initiative, it should be considered as a strategy when a major ROI impact study is planned. In these situations it is important for the program impact to be isolated to a high level of accuracy; the primary advantage of the control group process is accuracy.

Trendline Analysis

Another useful technique for approximating the impact of human resource programs or initiatives is trendline analysis. With this approach, a trendline is drawn, using previous performance as a base and extending the trend into the future. When an HR program is implemented, actual performance is compared with the trendline. Any improvement of performance beyond what the trendline predicted can then be reasonably attributed to the HR program. Although this is not an exact process, it provides a reasonable estimation of the impact of the program.

Figure 5-2 shows an example of this trendline analysis taken from a shipping department of a large distribution company. The percent reflects the level of actual shipments compared with scheduled shipments. Data are presented before and after an HR process improvement program that was conducted in July. As

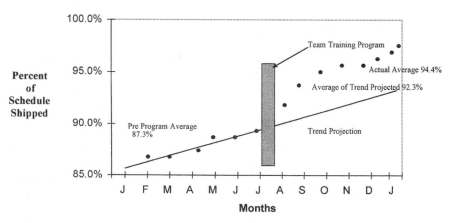

Figure 5-2. Trendline analysis example.

shown in the figure, there was an upward trend on the data prior to conducting the HR program. Although the program apparently had a dramatic effect on shipment productivity, the trendline shows that improvement would have continued anyway, based on the trend that had been previously established. It is tempting to measure the improvement by comparing the average six-months shipments prior to the program (87.3 percent) to the average of six months after the program (94.4 percent) yielding a 6.9 percent difference However, a more accurate comparison is the six-month average after the program compared with the trendline (92.3 percent). In this example, the difference is 2.1 percent. Using this more modest measure increases the accuracy and credibility of the process to isolate the impact of the program.

A primary disadvantage of this trendline approach is that it is not always accurate. The use of this approach assumes that the events that influenced the performance variable prior to the program are still in place after the program, except for the implementation of the training program (that is, the trends that were established prior to training will continue in the same relative direction). Also, it assumes that no new influences entered the situation at the time training was conducted and during the data collection time period. This may not always be the case.

The primary advantage of this approach is that it is simple and inexpensive. If historical data are available, a trendline can quickly be drawn and differences estimated. Although not exact, it does provide a quick assessment of the impact of HR programs.

Forecasting Methods

A more analytical approach to trendline analysis is forecasting methods that predict a change in performance variables. This approach represents a mathematical interpretation of the trendline analysis discussed above when other variables entered the situation at the time of the human resource program or initiative. A linear model, in the form of $y = ax + b$, is appropriate when only one other variable influences the output performance, and that relationship is characterized by a straight line. Instead of drawing the straight line, a linear equation is developed, which calculates a value of the anticipated performance improvement.

An example will help explain the application of this process. A large bank implemented a new screening and selection employment system for recently hired sales associates [7]. The new system was designed to enhance the caliber of associates hired and to match characteristics and traits to the job requirements. The outcome was expected to be an increase in sales volume for each new sales associate when compared with the average sales of existing salespeople. An important measure of the program's success was the sales-per-employee calculation six months after the selection system implementation compared with the same measure prior to the implementation. The average daily sales per employee prior to implementation, using a one-month average, was $1,100 (rounded to the nearest $100). Six months after the implementation, the average daily sales per employee was $1,500. Two related questions must be answered: Is the difference in these two values attributable to the implementation of the new screening and selection system? Did other factors influence the actual sales level?

After reviewing potential influencing factors with several store executives, only one factor, the level of advertising, appeared to have changed significantly during the period under consideration. When reviewing the previous sales data per employee and the level of advertising, a direct relationship appeared to exist. As expected, when advertising expenditures were increased, the sales per employee increased proportionately.

Using the historical values to develop a simple linear model yielded the following relationship between advertising and sales: $y = 140 + 40x$, where y is the daily sales per employee and x is the level of advertising expenditures per week (divided by 1,000). This equation was developed by the marketing department using the method of least squares to derive a mathematical relationship between two variables. This is a routine option on some calculators and is included in many software packages.

The level of weekly advertising expenditures in the month preceding implementation of the new selection system was $24,000, and the level of expenditures in the sixth month after implementation was $30,000. Assuming that the other factors possibly influencing sales were insignificant, the store executives determined the impact of the advertising by plugging in the new advertising expenditure amount, 30, for x and calculating the daily sales, which yields $1,340.

Thus, the new sales level caused by the increase in advertising was $1,340, as shown in Figure 5-3. Because the new actual value is $1,500, then $160 (i.e., $1,500 – $1,340) must be attributed to the screening and selection system. Figure 5-4 shows graphically the effect of both the training and advertising.

A major disadvantage with this approach occurs when many variables enter the process. The complexity multiplies, and the use of sophisticated statistical packages for multiple variable analysis is necessary. Even then, a good fit of the data to the

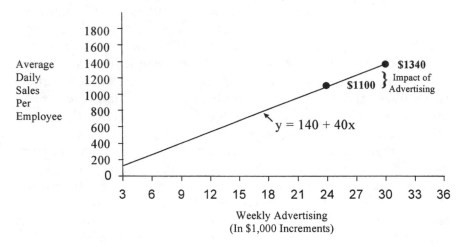

Figure 5-3. Forecasting daily sales based on advertising.

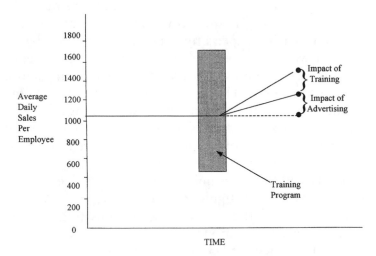

Figure 5-4. Isolating the impact of HR programs.

model may not be possible. Unfortunately, some organizations have not developed mathematical relationships for output variables as a function of one or more inputs. Without them, the forecasting method is difficult to use.

The primary advantage of this process is that it can accurately predict business performance measures without the implementation of HR initiatives, if appropriate data and models are available. The presentation of specific methods is beyond the scope of this book and is contained in other works [8].

Participant Estimates

An easily implemented method to isolate the impact of human resource programs and initiatives is to obtain information directly from program participants. The effectiveness of this approach rests on the assumption that the affected population is capable of determining or estimating how much of a performance improvement is related to the HR program. Because their actions may have produced the improvement, employees involved in the initiative may have very accurate input about the issue. They should know how much of the change was caused by their participation in a program, followed by their application of the new policy, procedure, process, or skill. Although an estimate, this value will usually have considerable credibility with management because participants are at the center of the change or improvement. Participant estimation is obtained by asking the following series of questions after describing the improvement:

Typical Questions to Determine Business Impact

1. What percent of this improvement can be attributed to the application of skills/techniques/knowledge gained in the program?
2. What is the basis for this estimation?
3. What confidence do you have in this estimate, expressed as a percent?
4. What other factors contributed to this improvement in performance?
5. What other individuals or groups could estimate this percentage or determine the amount?

Table 5-1 illustrates this approach with an example of one participant's estimations.

Participants who do not provide information about these questions are excluded from the analysis. Also, erroneous, incomplete, and extreme information should be discarded before analysis. To be conservative, the confidence percentage can be factored into the values. The confidence percentage is actually a reflection of the error in the estimate. Thus, an 80 percent confidence level equates to a potential error range of ± 20 percent. With this approach, the level of confidence is multiplied by the estimate using the lower side of the range. In the example, the participant allocates 50 percent of the improvement to the new HR incentive plan but is only 70 percent confident about this estimate. The confidence percentage is multiplied by the estimate to develop a usable incentive plan factor value of 35 percent. This adjusted percentage is then multiplied by the actual amount of the improvement (post-program minus pre-program value) to isolate the portion attributed to the HR incentive plan. The adjusted improvement is now ready for conversion to monetary values and, ultimately, is used in the return on investment.

Perhaps an illustration of this process can reveal its effectiveness and acceptability. In a large global organization, the impact of a leadership development program for new managers was being assessed. Because the decision to calculate the impact of the

Table 5-1
Example of a Participant's Estimation

Factor That Influenced Improvement	Percent of Improvement Caused By This Factor	Confidence Expressed As a Percent
1. Implementation of Incentive Plan	50%	70%
2. Change in Procedures	10%	80%
3. Adjustment in Standards	10%	50%
4. Redesign of Office Space	20%	90%
5. Increased Management Attention	10%	50%
6. Other	___%	___%
Total	100%	

program was made after the program had been conducted, the control group arrangement was not feasible as a method to isolate the effects of training. Also, before the program was implemented, no specified Level 4 (business results) data were identified that were linked to the program. Consequently, it was difficult to use trendline analysis. Participants' estimates proved to be the most useful way to estimate the impact. In a detailed follow-up questionnaire, participants were asked a variety of questions regarding the job applications of what was learned from the program. As part of the program, the individuals were asked to develop action plans and implement them, although no specific follow-up plan was needed. The following series of impact questions provided evaluators with estimations of the impact:

Impact Questions

1. How have you and your job changed as the result of participating in this program? (skills and knowledge application)
2. What is the impact of these changes in your work unit? (specific measures)
3. What is the annual value of this change or improvement in your work unit? (Although this is difficult, please make every effort to estimate this value.)
4. What is the basis for the estimate provided above? (Please indicate the assumptions you made and the specific calculations you performed to arrive at the value.)
5. What confidence do you place in the estimate above? (100% = Certainty, 0% = No Confidence)
6. Recognizing that many factors influence output results in addition to the HR program in which you participated, please estimate the percent of the improvement that is directly related to this program. (It may be helpful to first identify all the other factors and then provide an estimate of this factor.)

Although this series of questions is challenging, when set up properly and presented to participants in an appropriate way, it can be very effective for collecting impact data. Table 5-2 shows a sample of the calculations from these questions for this particular program.

Although this is an estimate, this approach does have considerable accuracy and credibility. Five adjustments are effectively employed with this approach to reflect a conservative approach:

1. The individuals who do not respond to the questionnaire or provide usable data on the questionnaire are assumed to have no improvements. This is probably an overstatement because some individuals will have improvements but will not report them on the questionnaire.
2. Extreme data and incomplete, unrealistic, and unsupported claims are omitted from the analysis, although they may be included in the intangible benefits.
3. Because only annualized values are used, it is assumed that there are no benefits from the program after the first year of implementation. In reality, a leadership development program should be expected to add value for several years after implementation. This may also be true of some HR programs.
4. The confidence level, expressed as a percent, is multiplied by the improvement value to reduce the amount of the improvement by the potential error.
5. The improvement amount is adjusted by the amount directly related to the HR program, expressed as a percent.

When presented to senior management, the results of this particular impact study were perceived to be an understatement of the program's success. The data and the process were considered credible and accurate.

As an added enhancement to this method, management may be asked to review and approve the estimates from participants. For example, in an HR program involving the performance management skills program for Yellow Freight Systems, a large trucking company, participants estimated the amount of savings that should be attributed to the program [9]. A sample of these estimates is shown in Table 5-3. Managers at the next two levels above participants reviewed and approved the estimates. Thus, the managers actually confirmed participants' estimates.

Table 5-2

Sample of Input from Participants in a Leadership Program for New Managers

Participant	Annual Improvement Value	Basis for Value	Confidence	Isolation Factor	Adjusted Value
11	$36,000	Improvement in efficiency of group. $3,000 month × 12 (Group Estimate)	85%	50%	$15,300
42	90,000	Turnover reduction. Two turnover statistics per year. Base salary × 1.5 = 45,000	90%	40%	32,400
74	24,000	Improvement in customer response time. (8 hours to 6 hours). Estimated value: $2,000/month	60%	55%	7,920
55	$2,000	5% improvement in my effectiveness ($40,500 × 5%)	75%	50%	750
96	$10,000	Absenteeism reduction (50 absences per year × $200)	85%	75%	6,375
117	$8,090	Team project completed 10 days ahead of schedule. Annual salaries $210,500 = $809 per day × 10 days	90%	45%	3,279
118	159,000	Under budget for the year by this amount	100%	30%	47,700

Table 5-3
Sample of Results from Performance Management Skills

Terminal in Division I	Improvement	Percentage of Improvement Attributed to Performance Management Skills	Dollar Value*
A	To reduce high cost per bill caused by poor planning on pickup and delivery and low sales, manager installed job models and feedback systems, coached supervisors and drivers, and praised all employees for improved performance. Cost per bill decreased an average of $1.30.	25%	$6,928(C)
B	In new terminal with cost per bill running high, manager installed job models and used coaching and rewards for supervisory, administrative, and sales staff. Terminal's profits increased from $43,253 to $49,024.	10%	27,680(R)
C	Terminal had low bill count and high cost per bill. Manager installed job models and feedback systems, and used interpersonal skills. Cost per bill decreased an average of $1.79, over same period before the program.	5%	800(C)
D	Terminal had low bill count, which contributed	25%	9,856(C)

to a high cost per bill.
Manager installed job
models and feedback
systems, and used rewards
and coaching with office
staff, supervisors, and
sales representatives. Cost
per bill decreased an
average of $0.92; number
of bills increased from
7,765 to 9,405 per month.

E	Terminal had low bill count and high cost per bill. Manager installed job models and had his sales manager and operations manager install job models, also. All managers used rewards, coaching, and interpersonal skills. Cost per bill decreased from $22.49 to $21.00; number of bills increased from 11,716 to 12,974 per month.	50%	56,060(C)
F	Terminal had rising cost per bill with a fluctuating bill count. Manager used job models and feedback reports. Cost per bill decreased from $17.13 to $15.46; number of bills rose from 6,160 to 7,357 per month.	10%	5,754(C)

(R) indicates a revenue gain; (C) indicates decreased costs.

This process has some disadvantages. It is an estimate, and consequently, it does not have the accuracy desired by some HR managers. Also, the input data may be unreliable because some participants are incapable of providing these types of estimates. They might not be aware of exactly which factors contributed to the results.

Several advantages make this strategy attractive. It is a simple process, easily understood by most participants and by others who review evaluation data. It is inexpensive, takes little time and analysis, and thus results in an efficient addition to the evaluation process. Estimates originate from a credible source—the individuals who actually produced the improvement.

The advantages seem to offset the disadvantages. Isolating the effects of human resource programs and initiatives will never be precise. However, the participants' estimate may be accurate enough for most clients and management groups. The process is appropriate when the participants are managers, supervisors, team leaders, sales associates, engineers, and other professional and technical employees.

Supervisor Estimates

In lieu of, or in addition to, participant estimates, the participants' supervisors may be asked to provide the extent of HR's role in influencing organization improvement. In some settings, participants' supervisors may be more familiar with the other influential factors. Consequently, they may be better equipped to provide estimates of impact. The recommended questions to ask supervisors, after describing the improvement caused by the participants, are:

Typical Questions to Ask Supervisors

1. What percent of the improvement in performance measures of the participant resulted from the HR program?
2. What is the basis for this estimate?
3. What is your confidence in this estimate, expressed as a percentage?
4. What other factors could have contributed to this success?
5. Please list the factors with the estimates in the table provided.
6. What other individuals or groups would know about this improvement and could estimate this percentage?

These questions are essentially the same ones described in the participant's questionnaire. Supervisor estimates should be analyzed in the same manner as participant estimates. To be more conservative, actual estimates may be adjusted by the confidence percentage. When participants' estimates have also been collected, the decision of which estimate to use becomes an issue. If there is some compelling reason to think one estimate is more credible than the other, then the more credible one should be used. The most conservative approach is to use the lowest value and include an appropriate explanation. Another potential option is to recognize that each source has its own unique perspective and that an average of the two is appropriate, placing an equal weight on each input. If feasible, it is recommended that inputs be obtained from both participants and supervisors.

An example will illustrate the process for both participant estimates and supervisor estimates. A restaurant chain implemented an HR program on performance management for manager trainees. The program was expected to teach participants how to establish measurable goals for employees, provide performance feedback, measure progress toward goals, and take action to ensure that goals are met. During the program, each manager trainee developed an action plan for improvement, using the skills taught in the program. As part of the program, managers learned how to convert measurable improvements into an economic value for the restaurant. The action plan could focus on any improvement area as long as it was accompanied by skills acquired in the program and was converted to either cost savings or restaurant profits. Some of the improvement areas were inventory, food spoilage, cash shortages, employee turnover, absenteeism, and productivity.

As part of the follow-up evaluation, each action plan was thoroughly documented showing results in quantitative terms, which were converted to monetary values. Realizing that other factors could have influenced the improvement, manager trainees were asked to estimate the percent of improvement that resulted from the application of the skills acquired during the program. Each manager trainee was asked to be conservative with the estimates. The annual monetary value for each improvement for each participant was calculated. Independently, restaurant managers (immediate supervisors) were asked to estimate, for each manager trainee, what percentage of improvement came from the action plan, which should be attributed to the performance management program. The managers (in this case the restaurant managers, who were closely involved in the action planning process for this program) usually are aware of factors that influence costs and profits and usually know how much of an improvement is traceable to the HR program. The results are shown in Table 5-4.

The estimate of HR's impact can be calculated using the conservative approach of selecting the lower value. As an alternative, the average value of the two can be used. The conservative approach yields an overall improvement of $78,905, whereas the average of the two percentages yields a value of $83,721. Participant 5 did not submit a completed action plan and was discarded from the analysis, although the costs are still included in the ROI calculation.

Another interesting observation emerges from this type of analysis. When the average of the three largest participant improvements is compared with the average of the three smallest values, important information is revealed about the potential for return on investment (in this case, $21,667 compared with $1,947, before adjustments). If all the participants focused on high-impact improvements, a substantially higher ROI could have been achieved. This can be helpful information for the management group, whose support is often critical to the success of programs. Although an impressive ROI is refreshing, a potentially much greater ROI is outstanding.

This approach has the same disadvantages as participant estimates. It is subjective and, consequently, may be viewed with skepticism by senior management. Also, supervisors may be reluctant to participate or may be incapable of providing accurate impact estimates. In some cases they may not know about other factors that contributed to the improvement.

The advantages of this approach are similar to the advantages of participant estimation. It is simple and inexpensive and enjoys an acceptable degree of credibility because it comes directly from the supervisors of those individuals involved in the implementation of the HR program. When combined with participant estimation, the credibility is enhanced considerably. Also, when factored by the level of confidence, its value further increases.

Table 5-4
Estimates of Training Impact from Participants and Supervisors

Participant	Improvement (Dollar Value)	Basis	Percent Estimate from Manager Trainees	Percent Estimate from Store Managers	Conservative Integration	Average Value Integration
1	$5,500	Labor Savings	50%	50%	$2,750	$3,025
2	15,000	Turnover	50%	40%	6,000	6,750
3	9,300	Absenteeism	55%	75%	6,045	6,510
4	2,100	Shortages	90%	80%	1,680	1,785
5	0		—	—	—	—
6	29,000	Turnover	40%	50%	11,600	13,050
7	2,241	Inventory	70%	100%	1,569	1,905
8	3,621	Procedures	100%	90%	3,259	3,440
9	21,000	Turnover	75%	70%	14,700	15,225
10	1,500	Food Spoilage	100%	100%	1,500	1,500
11	15,000	Labor Savings	80%	70%	10,500	11,250
12	6,310	Accidents	70%	75%	4,417	4,575
13	14,500	Absenteeism	80%	75%	11,600	11,238
14	3,650	Productivity	100%	90%	3,285	3,468
Total	$128,722				$78,905	$83,721

Management Estimates

In some cases, upper management may estimate the percent of improvement that should be attributed to the HR program. For example, in Litton Guidance and Control Systems, the results from a self-directed team process were adjusted by management [10]. After considering additional factors—such as technology, procedures, and process changes—that could have contributed to the improvement, management then applied a subjective factor, in this case 60 percent, to represent the portion of the results that should be attributed to the self-directed team process designed by HR. The 60 percent factor was developed in a meeting with top managers and therefore had the benefit of group ownership. Although this process is very subjective, the input is received from the individuals who often provide or approve funding for HR programs. Sometimes their level of comfort with the process is the most important consideration.

Customer Input

Another helpful approach in some narrowly focused situations is to solicit input about the impact of HR initiatives directly from customers. In these situations, customers are asked why they chose a particular product or service, or to explain how their reaction to the product or service has been influenced by individuals applying skills and abilities influenced by an HR program. This strategy focuses directly on what the improvement program is often designed to improve. For example, after a teller training program was conducted after a bank merger, market research data showed that the percentage of customers who were dissatisfied with teller knowledge had been reduced by 5 percent when compared with market survey data before training [11]. Because teller knowledge was increased by training, the 5 percent reduction of dissatisfied customers was directly attributable to the training program.

In another example, the HR department of a large telecommunication company developed and implemented a knowledge management program for HR staff members, focusing on internal customer engagements. As internal customers used HR's services, they benefited from the HR staff's greater knowledge of the core business, understanding of issues, and turnaround time to define and recommend HR solutions. A follow-up survey administered by HR revealed significant improvements in the relationship with the HR staff and their internal customer. Knowledge about the "core business" and "turnaround time" were ranked very high as reasons for improved service by HR. Customers' survey responses to the HR staff's level of knowledge and related questions provided evidence of the improved service attributed to the knowledge management program.

Expert Estimation

External or internal experts can sometimes estimate the portion of results that can be attributed to human resource programs. When using this strategy, experts must be carefully selected based on their knowledge of the process, program, and situation. For example, an expert in quality in the electric utility industry might be able to provide estimates of how much change in a quality measure can be attributed to the HR component of a TQM program and how much can be attributed to other factors in the implementation of a TQM program.

An example will illustrate this process. A well-respected quality manager of a large southeastern utility used a control group arrangement when implementing a TQM initiative. The HR component included team restructuring and training. Six months after the TQM implementation, the control group results determined that the HR component generated a 12 percent increase in quality, caused by less waste and rework. Given this value, implementation should result in a 12 percent improvement in another electric utility with a similar target audience involving the same job functions and type of HR program. Although the situation can vary considerably, this is an approximate value to use in comparison. If more than 12 percent was achieved, the additional amount could be caused by a factor other than the HR program. Experts, consultants, or researchers are usually available for almost any field. They can bring their experience with similar situations into the analysis.

This approach does have disadvantages. It can be inaccurate unless the program and setting in which the estimate is made is very similar to the program in question. Also, this approach may lose credibility because the estimates come from external sources and may not necessarily involve those who are close to the process.

This process has an advantage in that its credibility often reflects the reputation of the expert or independent consultant. It is a quick source of input from a reputable expert or independent consultant. Sometimes top management will place more confidence in external experts than its own internal staff.

Subordinate Input of HR Program Impact

In some situations, the subordinates of managers and supervisors being trained or being asked to support and implement a new policy/procedure will provide input concerning the extent of impact. Although they will not usually be able to estimate how much of an improvement can be attributed to the HR program or a policy change, they can provide input in terms of what other factors might have contributed to the improvement. This approach is appropriate in programs in which leaders, supervisors, and managers are implementing work unit changes or in which they are the conduit for implementation of HR policy and procedures. Improvements are realized through the supervisors' use of the new skills or actions regarding a policy/procedure. Each supervisor's employees provide input about changes that have occurred since the HR program was implemented or since the HR policy/procedure was implemented. They help determine the extent to which other factors have changed in addition to supervisor behavior.

Subordinate input is usually obtained through surveys or interviews. When the survey results show significant changes in supervisor behavior after implementation of an HR program or policy and no significant change in the general work climate, the improvement in work performance, therefore, must be attributed to the changes in supervisor behavior because other factors remained constant.

An example illustrates this process. In a human resource program designed to improve performance of work units through enhancing supervisory skills, significant results were obtained at CIGNA, a large insurance company [12]. After the HR program was conducted, action plans were developed, and the supervisors reported significant improvements in the performance of their work units. To isolate the impact of the HR program, pre and post survey data were taken with the employees to determine the extent of changes in supervisor behavior and the general climate. The survey consisted of 36 Likert-type, five-point scale items that were used to create seven different indices. Six of these indices measured the supervisor's behavior, and the seventh measured general organizational climate for which the supervisor was not necessarily responsible. The survey results showed significant differences in supervisor behavior before and after HR program implementation. The results did not, however, show a significant change in the general climate. Therefore, the improvement in work performance was attributed to the changes in supervisor behavior because other factors appeared to remain constant.

This approach has some disadvantages. Data from subordinates are subjective and may be questionable because of the possibility for biased input. Also, in some cases the subordinates may have difficulty determining changes in the work climate. This approach does offer a useful way to isolate the impact of the program from other influences. In some cases, subordinates are aware of the factors that caused changes in their work units, and they can provide input about the magnitude or quantity of these changes. When combined with other methods that isolate impact, this process has increased credibility.

Calculating the Impact of Other Factors

Although not appropriate in all cases, in some situations it may be feasible to calculate the impact of factors (other than HR initiatives) that influenced the improvement and then conclude that the HR program is credited with the remaining portion. In this approach, HR takes credit for improvement that cannot be attributed to other factors.

An example will help explain the approach. In a consumer lending program for a large bank, a significant increase in consumer loan volume was generated after an incentive plan was installed for consumer loan officers. Part of the increase in volume was attributed to the incentive plan, and the remaining was caused by the influence of other factors operating during the same time period. Two other factors were identified by the evaluator: A loan officer's production improved with time, and falling interest rates caused an increase in consumer volume.

In regard to the first factor, as loan officers make loans, their confidence improves. They use consumer lending policy manuals and gain knowledge and expertise through trial and error. The amount of this factor was estimated by using input from several internal experts in the marketing department.

For the second factor, industry sources were used to estimate the relationship between increased consumer loan volume and falling interest rates. These two estimates together accounted for a certain percent of increased consumer loan volume. The remaining improvement was attributed to the HR incentive plan.

This method is appropriate when the other factors are easily identified and the appropriate mechanisms are in place to calculate their impact on the improvement. In some cases it is just as difficult to estimate the impact of other factors as it is for the impact of the HR program/initiative, leaving this approach less advantageous. This process can be very credible if the method used to isolate the impact of other factors is credible.

USING THE STRATEGIES

With ten strategies available that isolate the impact of HR programs, selecting the most appropriate strategies for the specific program can be difficult. Some strategies are simple and inexpensive, while others are more time consuming and costly. When attempting to make the selection decision, several factors should be considered:

- ☐ feasibility of the strategy
- ☐ accuracy provided with the strategy
- ☐ credibility of the strategy with the target audience
- ☐ specific cost to implement the strategy
- ☐ the amount of disruption in normal work activities as the strategy is implemented
- ☐ participant, staff, and management time needed for a particular strategy to be successful

Multiple strategies or multiple sources for data input should be considered because two sources are usually better than one. When multiple sources are used, a conservative method is recommended to combine the inputs. A conservative approach builds acceptance. The target audience should always be provided with explanations of the process and the various subjective factors involved. Multiple sources allow an organization to experiment with different strategies and build confidence with a particular strategy. For example, if management is concerned about the accuracy of participants' estimates, a combination of a control group arrangement and participants' estimates could be attempted to check the accuracy of the estimation process.

It is not unusual for the ROI of HR initiatives to be extremely large. Even when a portion of the improvement is allocated to other factors, the numbers are still impressive in many situations. The audience should understand that, although every effort is made to isolate the impact, it is still a figure that is not precise and may contain error. It represents the best estimate of the impact given the constraints, conditions, and resources available. Chances are it is more accurate than other types of analyses regularly used in other functions within the organization.

CONCLUSION

This chapter presented a variety of strategies that isolate the effects of HR programs. The strategies represent the most effective approaches to address this issue and are used by some of the most progressive organizations. Too often, results are reported and linked with HR programs without any attempt to isolate the portion of results that can be attributed to HR. If the HR function is to continue to improve its professional image as well as to meet its responsibility for obtaining results, this issue must be addressed early in the process.

REFERENCES

1. Phillips, J. J. "Was It the Training?" *Training and Development*, March 1996, pp. 28–32.
2. Phillips, J. "Return on Investment—Beyond the Four Levels." *Academy of HRD 1995 Conference Proceedings*. E. Holton (Ed.), 1995.
3. Alliger, G. M., and Janak, E. A. "Kirkpatrick's Levels of Training Criteria: Thirty Years Later." *Personnel Psychology*, Vol. 42, 1989, pp. 331–342.
4. Pine, J., and Tingley, J. C. "ROI of Soft Skills Training." *Training*, February 1993, pp. 55–66.

5. Hassett, J. "Simplifying ROI." *Training*, September 1992, p. 54.
6. This brief example is taken from a case in which the company preferred not to be identified.
7. This brief example is taken from a very complicated case. Some of the values have been changed, and the case has been simplified to enhance the understanding of this process.
8. For additional information, see: Makridakis, S. *Forecasting Methods for Management*, 5th ed. New York: Wiley, 1989.
9. Zigon, J. "Performance Management Training," in *In Action: Measuring Return on Investment, Vol. 1*. Phillips, J. J. (Ed.) Alexandria, Va.: American Society for Training and Development, 1994, pp. 253–270.
10. Graham, M., Bishop, K., and Birdsong, R. "Self-Directed Work Teams," in *In Action: Measuring Return on Investment, Vol. 1*. Phillips, J. J. (Ed.) Alexandria, Va.: American Society for Training and Development, 1994, pp. 105–122.
11. Rust, R. T., Zahorik, A. J., and Keiningham, T. L. *Return on Quality: Measuring the Financial Impact of Your Company's Quest for Quality*. Chicago: Probus Publishers, 1994.
12. Kirkpatrick, D. L. "The Bottom Line: CIGNA Corporation." *Evaluating Training Programs*. San Francisco: Berrett-Koehler, 1994, pp. 190–206.

CHAPTER 6

Converting Data to Monetary Value

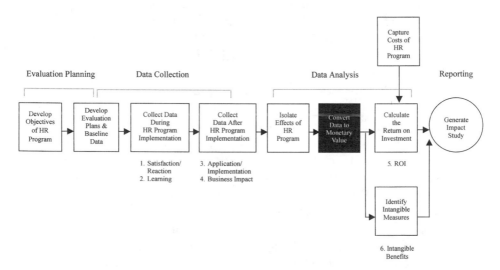

Traditionally, impact studies concludes with a tabulation of business results, which is a Level 4 evaluation. In those situations, the program is considered successful if it produced improvements such as quality enhancements, reduced absenteeism, or improved customer satisfaction. Although these results are important, it is more insightful to compare the monetary value of the results with the cost of the HR program. This evaluation is the ultimate level in the five-level evaluation framework presented in Chapter 1. This chapter shows how leading organizations are moving beyond tabulating business results to converting data to monetary value, a necessary step to calculate a return on investment (Level 5).

Chapter 1 presented the process of calculating the ROI, Chapter 2 focused on the initial analysis and on planning the evaluation, and Chapters 3 and 4 outlined the methods used to collect data. Chapter 5 described a variety of strategies to isolate the effects of HR programs from other factors. This chapter presents a variety of techniques to convert data to monetary benefits.

PRELIMINARY ISSUES

Sorting Hard and Soft Data

After collecting performance data, many organizations find it helpful to divide data into hard and soft categories as explained in Chapter 4. Hard data are the traditional measures of organizational performance because they are objective, easy to measure, and easy to convert to monetary values. Hard data are often very common measures, achieve high credibility with management, and are available in every type of organization.

Hard data represent the output, quality, cost, and time, of work-related processes. Almost every department or unit will have hard data performance measures. For example, a government office approving applications for work visas in a foreign country will have these four measures among its overall performance measurement: the number of applications processed (output), the time it takes to process and approve an application (time), cost per application processed (cost), and the number of errors made processing applications (quality). Ideally, HR programs for employees in this office should be linked to one or more hard data measures.

Because many HR programs are designed to influence soft variables, soft data are needed in evaluation. Soft data are usually subjective, sometimes difficult to measure, almost always difficult to convert to monetary values, and behaviorally oriented. When compared with hard data, soft data usually have less credibility as a performance measure. Soft data items can be grouped into several categories as illustrated in Chapter 4.

General Steps to Convert Data

Before describing the specific strategies to convert hard and soft data to monetary values, this section summarizes the general steps used to convert data in each strategy. These steps should be followed for each data conversion.

Focus on a unit of measure. First, identify a unit of improvement. For output data, the unit of measure is the item produced, service provided, or sale consummated. Time measures vary and include items such as the time to complete a project, cycle time, and customer response time. The unit is usually expressed as minutes, hours, or days. Quality is a common measure, and the unit may be one error, reject, defect, or rework item. Soft data measures vary, and the unit of improvement may include items such as a grievance, an absence, an employee turnover statistic, or a one-point change in the customer satisfaction index.

Determine a value for each unit. Place a value (V) on the unit identified in the first step. For measures of production, quality, cost, and time, the process is relatively easy. Most organizations have records or reports reflecting the value of items such as one unit of production or the cost of a defect. Soft data are more difficult to convert to a value because the cost of one absence, one grievance, or a one-point change in the employee attitude survey is often difficult to pinpoint. The ten strategies in this chapter provide an array of techniques to make this conversion. When more than one value is available, either the most credible or the lowest, most conservative value should be used.

Calculate the change in performance data. Calculate the change in output data after the effects of the HR program have been isolated from other influences. The change (ΔP) is the performance improvement, measured as hard or soft data, that is directly attributable to an HR program. The value may represent the performance improvement for an individual, a team, a group, or several groups of participants.

Determine an annual amount for the change. Annualize the ΔP value to develop a total change in the performance data for one year. This procedure has become a standard approach with many organizations that wish to capture the total benefits of an HR program. Although the benefits may not be realized at the same level for an entire year, some programs will continue to produce benefits beyond one year. Therefore, using one year of benefits is considered a conservative approach.

Calculate the total value of the improvement. Develop the total value of improvement by multiplying the annual performance change (ΔP) by the unit value (V) for the complete group in question. For example, if one group of participants for a program is being evaluated, the total value will include total improvement for all participants in the group. This value for annual program benefits is then compared with the cost of the program, usually through the return on investment formula presented in Chapter 1.

STRATEGIES FOR CONVERTING DATA TO MONETARY VALUES

An example taken from a grievance reduction program at a manufacturing plant describes the five-step process of converting data to monetary values. This program was developed and implemented after a needs assessment revealed that a lack of cooperation between management and labor leadership was causing an excessive number of grievances. Thus, the actual number of grievances resolved at Step 2 in the grievance process was selected as an output measure. Table 6-1 shows the steps taken to assign a monetary value to the data for a total program impact of $546,000.

Ten strategies are available to convert data to monetary values. Some strategies are appropriate for a specific type of data or data category, and other strategies can be used with virtually any type of data. The HR staff's challenge is to select the particular strategy that best matches the type of data and situation. The ten strategies are presented next, beginning with the first three, which apply to hard data. The remaining seven are listed beginning with the most credible approach to convert soft data.

CONVERTING OUTPUT DATA TO CONTRIBUTION

When an HR program has produced a change in output, the value of the increased output can usually be determined from the organization's accounting or operating records. For organizations operating on a profit basis, this value is usually the marginal profit contribution of an additional unit of production or unit of service provided. For example, HR partnered with a production team of a major appliance manufacturer and was able to boost production of small refrigerators with a series of comprehensive HR programs. The unit of improvement, therefore, was the profit margin of one refrigerator. In organizations that are performance- rather

Table 6-1
An Example to Illustrate Steps to Convert Data to Monetary Values

---

Setting: Grievance Reduction Program in a Manufacturing Plant

---

Step 1 **Focus on a Unit of Improvement**

The unit of improvement chosen was one grievance that reached Step 2 in the four-step grievance resolution process.

Step 2 **Determine a Value of Each Unit**

Using internal experts, the labor relations staff, the cost of an average grievance was estimated to be $6,500 when considering time and direct costs (V = $6,500).

Step 3 **Calculate the Change in Performance Data**

Six months after the program was completed, total grievances reaching Step 2 declined by ten per month. Supervisors determined that seven of the ten grievance reductions related to the program (supervisor estimates used here to isolate the effects of the HR program).

Step 4 **Determine an Annual Amount for the Change**

Using the six-month value (seven per month) yields an annual improvement of eighty-four ($\Delta P = 84$).

Step 5 **Calculate the Annual Value of the Improvement**

Annual Value = ΔP times V
= 84 times $6,500
= $546,000

---

than profit-driven, this value is usually reflected in the savings accumulated when an additional unit of output is realized for the same input requirements. For example, a visa section of a government office processed an additional visa application at no additional cost. Thus, an increase in output translated into a cost savings equal to the unit cost of processing a visa.

The formulas and calculations used to measure this contribution depend on the organization and its records. Most organizations have this type of data readily available for performance monitoring and goal setting. Managers often use marginal cost statements and sensitivity analyses to pinpoint the value associated with changes in output. If the data are not available, the HR staff must initiate or coordinate the development of appropriate values.

In one case involving a commercial bank, a sales seminar conducted for consumer loan officers resulted in additional consumer loan volume (output) [1]. To measure the return on investment in the program, it was necessary to calculate the value (profit contribution) of one additional consumer loan. This was a relatively easy item to calculate from the bank's records. As shown in Table 6-2, several components went into this calculation.

The first step was to determine the yield, which was available from bank records. Next, the average spread between the cost of funds and the yield received on the loan was calculated. For example, the bank could obtain funds from depositors at 5.5 percent on average, including the cost of operating the branches. The direct costs of making the loan, such as salaries of employees directly involved in consumer lending and advertising costs for consumer loans, had to be subtracted from this difference. Historically, these direct costs amounted to 0.82 percent of the loan value. To cover overhead costs for other corporate functions, an additional 1.61 percent was subtracted from the value. The remaining 1.82 percent of the average loan value represented the bank's profit margin on a loan.

Table 6-2
Loan Profitability Analysis

Profit Component	Unit Value
Average loan size	$15,500
Average loan yield	9.75%
Average cost of funds (including branch costs)	5.50%
Direct costs for consumer lending	0.82%
Corporate overhead	1.61%
Net Profit Per Loan	1.82%

CALCULATING THE COST OF QUALITY

Quality is a critical issue, and its cost is an important measure in most manufacturing and service firms. Because many HR programs are designed to improve quality, the HR staff must place a value on the improvement in certain quality measures. For some quality measures, the task is easy. For example, if quality is measured with a defect rate, the value of the improvement is the cost to repair or replace the product. The most obvious cost of poor quality is the scrap or waste generated by mistakes. Defective products, spoiled raw materials, and discarded paperwork all result from poor quality. This scrap and waste translates directly into a monetary value. For example, in a production environment, the cost of a defective product is the total cost incurred to the point when the mistake is identified minus the salvage value.

Employee mistakes and errors can cause expensive rework. The most costly rework occurs when a product is delivered to a customer and must be returned for correction. The cost of rework includes both labor and direct costs [2]. In some organizations, the cost of rework can be as much as 35 percent of operating costs. In one example of an HR program involving problem solving and team building for dispatchers in an oil company, a measure of rework was the number of pullouts [3]. A pullout occurred when a delivery truck could not fill an order for fuel at a service station. The truck returned to the terminal for an adjustment to the order. The average cost of the pullout was developed by tabulating the cost of a sample of actual pullouts. The cost elements included driver time involved, the cost of the truck, the cost of terminal use, and an estimate of administrative costs.

Perhaps the costliest element of poor quality is customer and client dissatisfaction. In some cases, serious mistakes can result in lost business. Customer dissatisfaction is difficult to quantify, and attempts to arrive at a monetary value may be impossible using direct methods. Usually the judgment and expertise of sales, marketing, or quality managers are the best sources by which to try to measure the impact of dissatisfaction. A growing number of quality experts now measure customer and client dissatisfaction with market surveys [4]. However, other strategies discussed in this chapter may be more appropriate to measure the cost of customer dissatisfaction.

CONVERTING EMPLOYEE TIME

Reduction in employee time is a common objective of HR programs. In a team environment, a program could enable the team to perform tasks in a shorter time frame or with fewer people. On an individual basis, time management workshops are designed to help professional, sales, supervisory, and managerial employees save time in performing daily tasks. The value of the time saved is an important measure of the program's success, and this conversion is a relatively easy process.

The most obvious time savings come from labor reduction costs in performing work. The monetary savings are found by multiplying the hours saved times the labor cost per hour. For example, after attending a time-management training program called Priority Manager, participants estimated that each participant saves an average of seventy-four minutes per day, worth $31.25 per day or $7,500 per year [5]. This time savings was based on the average salary plus benefits for the typical participant.

The average wage with a percent added for employee benefits will suffice for most calculations. However, employee time may be worth more. For example, additional costs of maintaining an employee (office space, furniture, telephone, utilities, computers, secretarial support, and other overhead expenses) could be included in the average labor cost. Thus, the average wage rate may quickly escalate to a large number. However, the conservative approach is to use the salary plus employee benefits.

In addition to the labor cost per hour, other benefits can result from a time savings. These include improved service, avoidance of penalties for late projects, and the creation of additional opportunities for profit. These values can be estimated using other methods discussed in this chapter.

A word of caution is in order when the time savings are developed. Time savings are only realized when the amount of time saved translates into a cost reduction or profit contribution. If an HR program results in a savings in manager time, a monetary value is realized only if the manager used the additional time in a productive way. If a team-based program generates a new process that eliminates several hours of work each day, the organization will realize actual savings only if there is a cost savings from a reduction in employees or a reduction in overtime pay. Therefore, an important preliminary step in developing time savings is to determine if the organization will realize a "true" savings.

HISTORICAL COSTS

Sometimes historical records contain the value of a measure in and reflect the cost (or value) of a unit of improvement. This strategy involves identifying the appropriate records and tabulating the actual cost components for the item in question. For example, a large construction firm implemented a safety awareness program to improve safety performance. The program improved several safety-related performance measures, ranging from OSHA fines to total worker compensation costs. Examining the company's records using one year of data, the HR staff calculated the average cost for each safety measure.

Historical data are usually available for most hard data. Unfortunately, this is generally not true for soft data, and therefore other strategies, explained in this chapter, must be employed to convert the soft data to monetary values.

INTERNAL AND EXTERNAL EXPERTS' INPUT

When faced with converting soft data items for which historical records are not available, it might be feasible to consider using input from people who are experts in the processes that are influenced by the HR solution. With this approach, internal experts provide the cost (or value) of one unit of improvement. Those individuals who have knowledge of the situation as well as the respect of the management group often make the best prospects for expert input. These experts must understand the processes and be willing to provide estimates, as well as the assumptions used in arriving at the estimates. When requesting input from these individuals, it is best to explain the full scope of what is needed, providing as many specifics as possible. Most experts have their own methodology to develop this value. For example, when a quality network workshop was conducted to analyze ways to reduce downtime for pattern changes in an automotive engine casting plant, the downtime was reduced from fourteen minutes to eleven minutes. The HR team conducting the workshop used the chief financial officer (CFO) as an internal expert to place a value on downtime. The CFO used his own methodology to provide a value of $223.75 for each minute of downtime. This can be a very credible number because the value is probably also used for other reporting situations.

An example will help clarify this approach. In one manufacturing plant, a team-building program was designed to reduce the number of grievances filed at Step 2. (This is the step in which the grievance is recorded in writing and becomes a measurable soft data item.) Except for the actual cost of settlements and direct external costs, the company had no records of the total costs of grievances (that is, there were no data regarding the time required to resolve a grievance). Therefore, an estimate was needed from an expert. The manager of labor relations, who had credibility with senior management and thorough knowledge of the grievance process, provided an estimate of the cost. He based his estimate on the average settlement when a grievance was lost; the direct costs related to the grievances (arbitration, legal fees, printing, research); the estimated amount of supervisory, staff, and employee time associated with the grievance; and a factor for reduced morale. This internal estimate, although not a precise figure, was appropriate for this analysis and had adequate credibility with management.

When internal experts are not available, external experts are sought. External experts must be selected based on their experience with the unit of measure. Fortunately, many experts are available who work directly with important measures such as employee attitudes, customer satisfaction, turnover, absenteeism, and grievances. They are often willing to provide estimates of the cost (or value) of these items. Because the credibility of the value is directly related to his or her reputation, the credibility and reputation of the expert are critical.

VALUES FROM EXTERNAL DATABASES

For some soft data items, it may be appropriate to use estimates of the cost (or value) of one unit based on the research of others. This strategy taps external databases that contain studies and research projects focusing on the cost of data items. Fortunately, many databases are available that report cost studies of a variety of data items related to HR programs. Data are available regarding the cost of turnover, absenteeism, grievances, accidents, and even customer satisfaction. The difficulty lies in finding a database with studies or research efforts for a situation similar to the program under evaluation. Ideally, the data would come from a similar setting in the same industry, but that is not always possible. Sometimes data about all industries or organizations would be sufficient, perhaps with an adjustment to fit the industry under consideration.

An example illustrates the use of this process. An HR program was designed to reduce turnover of branch managers in a financial services company [6]. To complete the evaluation and calculate the ROI, the cost of turnover was needed. To develop the turnover value internally, several costs would have to be identified, including the cost of recruiting, employment processing, orientation, training new managers, lost productivity while a new manager is trained, quality problems, scheduling difficulties, and customer satisfaction problems. Additional costs include regional manager time to work with the turnover issues and, in some cases, exit costs of litigation, severance, and unemployment. Obviously, these costs are significant. HR managers may not have the time to calculate the cost of turnover, particularly when it is needed for a one-time event such as evaluating a training program. In this example, turnover cost studies in the same industry placed the value at about $1\frac{1}{2}$ times the average annual salaries of the employees. Most turnover cost studies report the cost of turnover as a multiple of annual base salaries. In this example, management decided to be conservative and adjusted the value downward to equal the average annual base salary of branch managers.

PARTICIPANT ESTIMATES

In some situations, program participants estimate the value of a soft data improvement. This strategy is appropriate when participants can provide estimates of the cost (or value) of the unit of measure improved by implementation of the HR program. When using this approach, participants should receive clear instructions, along with examples of the type of information needed. The advantage of this approach is that the individuals closest to the improvement often can provide the most reliable estimates of its value.

An example illustrates this process. An absenteeism reduction program including policies and practices was implemented for a group of supervisors. The program/process was designed to lower the absenteeism rate of the employees in their work units. Successful application of the policies and practices was expected to result in a reduction in absenteeism. To calculate the ROI for the program, it was necessary to determine the average value of one absence in the company. As is the case with most organizations, historical records for the cost of absenteeism were not available. Experts were not available, and external studies were sparse for this particular industry. Consequently, supervisors (program participants) were asked to estimate the cost of an absence. In a group-interview format, each participant was asked to recall the last time an employee in his or her work group was unexpectedly absent and to describe what was necessary to compensate for the absence. Because the impact of an absence varies considerably from one employee to another within the same work unit, the group listened to all explanations. After reflecting on what must be done when an employee is absent, each supervisor was asked to provide an estimate of the average cost of an absence in the company. During such a process, some supervisors will likely feel reluctant to provide estimates, but with prodding and encouragement they will usually provide a value. The values are then averaged for the group, and the result is the cost of an absence to be used in evaluating the HR program in question. Although this cost is an estimate, it is probably more accurate than data from external studies, calculations using internal records, or estimates from experts. And because it comes from supervisors who deal with the issue daily, it usually has credibility with senior management.

Supervisor Estimates

In some situations, participants may be incapable of placing a value on the improvement. Their work may be so far removed from the output of the process that they cannot reliably provide estimates. In these cases, the team leaders, supervisors, or managers of participants may be capable of providing estimates. Consequently, they may be asked to provide a value for a unit of improvement linked to the program. For example, a training program for customer service representatives was designed to reduce customer complaints. Application of the skills and knowledge learned from the program resulted in a reduction in complaints, but the value of a single customer complaint was needed to determine the value of improvement. Although customer service representatives had knowledge of some issues surrounding customer complaints, they were not well versed in the full impact, so their supervisors were asked to provide a value.

In other situations, supervisors are asked to review and approve participants' estimates. For example, an HR program for terminal managers at Yellow Freight Systems involved the implementation of both a new performance appraisal process and training [7]. After the program was completed, participants estimated the value of their improvements that were directly related to their participation in the program and the use of the new process. Their immediate managers then reviewed the estimates, as well as the process the participants used to arrive at the estimates. Supervisors could either confirm, adjust, or discard the values provided by the participants.

SENIOR MANAGER ESTIMATES

In some situations senior management provides estimates of the value of data. With this approach, senior managers interested in the process or program are asked to place a value on the improvement based on their perception of its worth. This approach is used when calculating the value is very difficult or when other sources of estimation are unavailable or unreliable. An example illustrates this strategy. A hospital chain was attempting to improve customer satisfaction with several HR interventions including internal policy changes related to performance standards and a customer service training program for all employees. The program was designed to improve customer service and thus improve the external customer satisfaction index. To determine the value of the program, a value for a unit of improvement (one point on the index) was needed. Because senior managers had deep interest in improving the index, they were asked to provide input regarding the value of one unit. In a regular staff meeting, each senior manager and hospital administrator was asked to describe what it means for a hospital when the index increases. After some discussion, each individual was asked to provide an estimate of the monetary value gained when the index moves one point. Although initially reluctant to provide the information, with some encouragement the managers and administrators furnished values, which were then averaged. This resulted in an estimate of the worth of one unit of improvement, which was used as a basis of calculating the benefit of the program. Although this process is subjective, it does have the benefit of ownership from senior executives, the same executives who approved the program budget.

HR STAFF ESTIMATES

The final strategy for converting data to monetary values is to use HR staff estimates. Using all the available information and experience, the staff members most familiar with the situation provide estimates of the value. For example, an international oil company created a dispatcher attendance program designed to reduce dispatcher absenteeism, along with other performance problems. The HR staff estimated the cost of an absence to be $200 [8]. This value was then used in calculating the savings for the reduction of absenteeism after implementation for the dispatchers. Although the staff may be capable of providing accurate estimates, this approach may be perceived as biased. It should be used only when other approaches are not available.

SELECTING THE APPROPRIATE STRATEGY

With so many strategies available, the challenge is to select one or more strategies appropriate for the situation. The following guidelines can help determine the proper selection.

Use the strategy appropriate for the type of data. Some strategies are designed specifically for hard data, while others are more appropriate for soft data. Consequently, the actual type of data will often dictate the strategy. Hard data, while always preferred, are not always available. Soft data are often required and thus must be addressed with the strategies appropriate for soft data.

Move from most accurate to least accurate strategies. The first three strategies in this chapter apply to hard data and should be used with the appropriate measure. The next seven strategies apply to soft data. The seven strategies beginning with "Historical Costs" are presented in order of accuracy and credibility, beginning with the most accurate and credible. Working down the list, each of the seven strategies should be considered for its feasibility in the situation. The strategy with the most accuracy is recommended, if it is feasible in the situation.

Consider availability and convenience when selecting strategy. Sometimes the availability of a particular source of data will drive the selection. In other situations, the convenience of a technique may be an important factor in selecting the strategy.

When seeking estimates, use the source who has the broadest perspective on the issue. The person providing an estimate must be knowledgeable of the processes and the issues surrounding the value of the data.

Use multiple strategies when feasible. Sometimes it helps to have more than one strategy for obtaining a value for the data. When multiple sources are available, more than one source should be used as a comparison or to provide another perspective. When multiple sources are used, the data must be integrated using a convenient decision rule such as the lowest value. This is preferred because of the conservative nature of the lowest value.

Minimize the amount of time required to select and implement the appropriate strategy. As with other processes, it is important to keep the amount of time invested as low as possible so that the total time and effort for the ROI does not become excessive. Some strategies can be implemented with less time than others can. Too much time at this step can dampen an otherwise enthusiastic attitude about the process.

Accuracy and Credibility of Data

The Credibility Problem

The strategies presented in this chapter assume that each data item collected and linked with HR programs can be converted to a monetary value. Although estimates can be developed using one or more strategies, the process of converting data to monetary values may lose credibility with the target audience, who may doubt its use in analysis. Very subjective data, such as a change in employee morale or a reduction in the number of employee conflicts, are difficult to convert to monetary values. The key question for this determination is this: Could these results be presented to senior management with confidence? If the process does not meet this credibility test, the data should not be converted to monetary values and instead should be listed as an intangible benefit. Other data, particularly hard data items, could be used in the ROI calculation, leaving the very subjective data as intangible improvements.

The accuracy of data and the credibility of the conversion process are important concerns. HR professionals sometimes avoid converting data because of these issues. They feel more comfortable reporting that an HR program reduced absenteeism from 6 percent to 4 percent without attempting to place a value on the improvement. They assume that each person receiving the information will place a value on the absenteeism reduction. Unfortunately, the target audience may know little about the cost of absenteeism and will usually underestimate the actual value of the improvement. Consequently, some attempt should be made to include this conversion in the ROI analysis.

How the Credibility of Data Is Influenced

When ROI data are presented to selected target audiences, credibility will be an issue. The following factors will influence the degree to which the target audience believes the data.

Reputation of the source of data. The actual source of the data represents the first credibility issue. How credible is the individual or groups providing the data? Do they understand the issues? Are they knowledgeable of all the processes? The target audience often places more credibility on data obtained from people who are closest to the source of the actual improvement or change.

Reputation of the source of the study. The target audience scrutinizes the reputation of the individual, group, or organization presenting the data. Does this source have a history of providing accurate reports? Is the source unbiased with its analyses? Is it fair in its presentation of the data? Answers to these and other questions will form an impression about the reputation.

Motives of the evaluators. Do the individuals presenting the data have an ax to grind? Do they have a personal interest in creating a favorable or unfavorable result? These issues will cause the target audience to examine the motives of those who conducted the study.

Methodology of the study. The audience will want to know specifically how the research was conducted. How were the calculations made? What steps were followed? What processes were used? A lack of information about the methodology will cause the audience to become suspicious of the results.

Assumptions made in the analysis. In many ROI studies, assumptions are made, and then calculations and conclusions are based on these assumptions. What are the assumptions? Are they standard? How do they compare with other assumptions in other studies? How do they compare with assumptions made by other business units or parts of the organization? When assumptions are omitted, the audience will substitute their own often-unfavorable assumptions.

Realism of the outcome data. Impressive ROI values could cause problems. When outcomes appear unrealistic, the target audience may have difficulty believing them. Huge claims often fall on deaf ears, causing reports to be thrown away before they are reviewed.

Types of data. Members of the target audience usually prefer hard data. They are seeking business performance data tied to output, quality, costs, and time. These measures are usually easily understood and closely related to organizational performance. Conversely, soft data are sometimes viewed suspiciously from the outset because many senior executives are concerned about the data's soft nature and limitations on the analysis.

Scope of analysis. Is the scope of the analysis narrow? Does it involve just one group or all the employees in the organization? Limiting the study to a small group, or series of groups, of employees makes the process more accurate.

Collectively, these factors influence the credibility of an ROI impact study and provide a framework from which to develop the ROI report. Thus, when considering each of the issues, the following key points are suggested for an ROI impact study:

☐ Use the most credible and reliable source for estimates.

☐ Present the material in an unbiased, objective way.

☐ Fully explain the methodology used throughout the process, preferably on a step-by-step basis.

☐ Define the assumptions made in the analysis, and compare them with assumptions made in other similar studies.

☐ Consider factoring or adjusting output values when they appear unrealistic.

☐ Use hard data when possible and combine with soft data if available.

☐ Keep the scope of the analysis narrow. Conduct the impact with one or more groups of participants in the program, instead of all participants or all employees.

Making Adjustments

Two potential adjustments should be considered before finalizing the monetary value. In some organizations in which soft data are used and values are derived with imprecise methods, senior management is sometimes offered the opportunity to review and approve the data. Because of the subjective nature of this process, management may factor (reduce) the data so that the final results are more credible. In one example, senior managers at Litton Industries adjusted the value for the benefits derived from the implementation of self-directed teams [9].

The other adjustment concerns the time value of money. Because an investment in a program is made within one time period and the return is realized in a later time period, a few organizations adjust the program benefits to reflect the time value of money, using discounted cash flow techniques. The actual monetary benefits of the program are adjusted for the time period during which costs are incurred and benefits are realized (the return). The amount of this adjustment, however, is usually small compared with the typical benefits realized from HR programs.

CONCLUSION

In conclusion, organizations are attempting to be more aggressive when defining the monetary benefits of HR programs and processes. Progressive HR managers are no longer satisfied with reporting business performance results from HR interventions. Instead, they are taking additional steps to convert business results data to monetary values and compare those values with the program's cost, thereby obtaining an ultimate level of evaluation—the return on investment. This chapter presented ten strategies to convert business results to monetary values, offering an array of techniques to fit any situation and program.

REFERENCES

1. Phillips, J. J. "Measuring ROI in an Established Program," in *In Action: Measuring Return on Investment, Vol. 1*. J. J. Phillips (Ed.) Alexandria, Va.: American Society for Training and Development, 1994, pp. 187–198.
2. Seimke, R. "Cost of Quality: You Can Measure It." *Training*, August 1990, pp. 62–63.
3. Payne, Rebecca. "Improving Customer Service Skills," in *In Action: Measuring Return on Investment, Vol. 1*. J. J. Phillips (Ed.) Alexandria, Va.: American Society for Training and Development, 1994, pp. 169–186.
4. Rust, R. T., Zahorik, A. J., and Keiningham, T. L. *Return on Quality: Measuring the Financial Impact of Your Company's Quest for Quality*. Chicago: Probus Publishers, 1994.
5. Stamp, D. *The Workplace of the 21st Century*. Bellevue, Wash.: Priority Management Systems, 1992.
6. Schoeppel, Cynthia. "Turning Down Manager Turnover," in *In Action: Measuring Return on Investment, Vol. 1*. J. J. Phillips (Ed.) Alexandria, Va.: American Society for Training and Development, 1994, pp. 213–222.
7. Zigon, J. "Performance Management Training," in *In Action: Measuring Return on Investment, Vol. 1* J. J. Phillips (Ed.) Alexandria, Va.: American Society for Training and Development, 1994, pp. 253–270.
8. Payne, Rebecca. "Improving Customer Service Skills," in *In Action: Measuring Return on Investment, Vol. 1* J. J. Phillips (Ed.) Alexandria, Va.: American Society for Training and Development, 1994, pp. 169–186.
9. Graham, M., Bishop, K., and Birdsong, R. "Self-Directed Work Teams," in *In Action: Measuring Return on Investment, Vol. 1*. J. J. Phillips (Ed.) Alexandria, Va.: American Society for Training and Development, 1994, pp. 105–122.

CHAPTER 7

Monitoring the Cost of Human Resource Programs

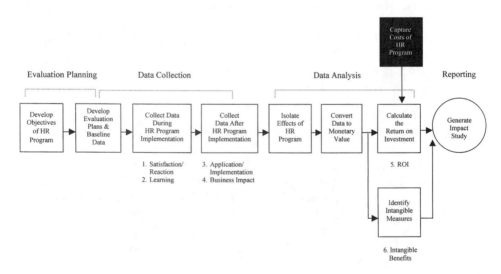

| Evaluation Planning | | Data Collection | | | Data Analysis | | | Reporting |

Capture Costs of HR Program

| Develop Objectives of HR Program | Develop Evaluation Plans & Baseline Data | Collect Data During HR Program Implementation | Collect Data After HR Program Implementation | Isolate Effects of HR Program | Convert Data to Monetary Value | Calculate the Return on Investment | Generate Impact Study |

1. Satisfaction/ Reaction
2. Learning

3. Application/ Implementation
4. Business Impact

5. ROI

Identify Intangible Measures

6. Intangible Benefits

Tabulating program costs is an essential step in developing the ROI calculation because this step produces the denominator in the ROI formula. Paying attention to costs is just as important as paying attention to benefits. In practice, however, costs are often more easily captured than benefits. This chapter explores the costs accumulation and tabulation steps, outlining the specific costs that should be captured and some economical ways in which they can be developed.

216

Cost Strategies

Importance of Costs

Capturing costs presents a challenge because the figures must be accurate, reliable, and realistic. Although most organizations develop costs with much more ease than developing the economic value of the benefits, the true cost of an HR program often eludes even some of the best organizations. Although the figure for the total HR direct budget usually can be easily developed, the difficulty comes when attempting to determine the specific costs of a program, including the indirect costs related to it. To develop a realistic ROI, costs must be accurate and credible. Otherwise, the painstaking difficulty and attention to the program benefits will be wasted because of inadequate or inaccurate costs.

Pressure to Disclose All Costs

Today there is more pressure than ever before to report all HR program costs, or what are referred to as fully loaded costs. This takes the cost profile beyond the direct cost of HR programs and includes the time participants take part in implementation meetings, information meetings, and training, including their benefits and other overhead. For years, management has realized that HR programs have many indirect costs. Now management is asking for an accounting of these costs. Perhaps a situation that recently developed in state government best illustrates this point. The state auditor audited the management controls of a large state agency. A portion of the audit focused on HR program costs. The following comments come from the auditor's report:

Costs tracked at the program level focus on direct or "hard" costs and largely ignore the cost of time spent participating in or supporting the HR program. The costs of participant time to prepare for and attend necessary sessions are not tracked. For one series of programs, including such costs raised the total program cost dramatically. The agency stated that the total two-year costs for the specific program was about $600,000. This figure generally includes only direct costs and, as such, is substantially below the costs of the time spent by staff in preparing for and attending the program. When accounting for prework and attendance, the figure comes to a total of $1.39 million. If the statewide average of 45.5% for fringe benefits is considered, the total indirect cost of staff time to prepare for and attend the program becomes $2 million. Finally, if the agency's direct costs of $600,000 are added to the $2 million total indirect cost just noted, the total becomes over $2.6 million. Among other factors that would drive actual total costs higher still are:

☐ cost of travel, meals, and lodging for participants;
☐ allocated salaries and fringes of staff providing administrative and logistic support; and
☐ opportunity costs of productivity lost by staff in doing prework and attending the program.

Failure to consider all indirect or "soft" costs may expose the agency to non-compliance with the Fair Labor Standards Act (FLSA), particularly as the program expands through the organization. Since FLSA requires that such staff be directly compensated for overtime, it is no longer appropriate for the agency to ask employees to complete prework on their own time. Continuing to handle such overtime work this way may also encourage false overtime reporting, skew overtime data, and/or increase the amount of uncompensated overtime.

Numerous barriers exist to agency efforts at determining "How much does the program cost?":

☐ Cost systems tend to hide administrative, support, internal, and other indirect or "soft" costs.
☐ Costs generally are monitored at the division level rather than at the level of individual programs or activities.
☐ Cost information required by activity-based cost systems is not being generated.

As this case vividly demonstrates, the cost of the program is much more than direct expenditures, and management expects the HR department to include fully loaded costs in their reports.

Fully Loaded Costs

To take the conservative approach to calculating the ROI, it is recommended that HR costs be fully loaded. With this approach, all costs that can be identified and linked to a particular program are included. The philosophy is simple: When in doubt regarding the denominator, put it in (that is, if it is questionable whether a cost should be included, it is recommended that the cost be included, even if the cost guidelines for the organization do not require it). When an ROI is calculated and reported to target audiences, the process should withstand even the closest scrutiny in terms of its accuracy and credibility. The only way to meet this test is to ensure that all costs are included. Of course, from a realistic viewpoint, if the controller or chief financial officer insists on not using certain costs, then it is best to leave them out.

The Danger of Costs Without Benefits

It is dangerous to communicate the costs of an HR program to management without presenting the resulting benefits. Unfortunately, many organizations have fallen into this trap for years. Because they can easily collect costs, they present these costs to management in all types of ingenious ways, such as cost of the program, cost per employee, and cost per development hour. Although these may be helpful for efficiency comparisons, presenting the costs without benefits may create trouble.

When most executives review HR costs, a logical question comes to mind: What benefit did the organization receive from the program? This is a typical management reaction, particularly when management perceives that costs are very high. For example, in one organization, all the costs associated with its executive leadership programs were tabulated and reported to the senior managers to let them know the total investment in these programs. The total figure exceeded the perceived value, and the top management group immediately requested a summary of benefits derived from these programs. This reaction initiated a review of the programs, with the conclusion that leadership development produced little, if any, economic benefits. Consequently, the programs were drastically reduced and revised.

Although this may be an extreme example, it shows the danger of presenting only half the equation. Because of this danger, some organizations have developed a policy of not communicating HR cost data unless the benefits can be captured and presented along with the costs. Even if the benefit data are subjective and intangible, they are included with the cost data. This helps to keep balance regarding these two issues.

Policies and Guidelines

Organizations may find it helpful to detail their philosophy and policy on costs by issuing a set of guidelines for the HR staff members and others who monitor and report costs. Cost guidelines detail specifically what costs are included with HR programs and how the data are captured, analyzed, and reported. Cost guidelines can range from a 1-page document in small organizations to a 100-page manual in a large, complex organization. The simpler approach is better. When fully developed, the finance and accounting staff should review the cost guidelines. The final document serves as the guiding force in collecting, monitoring, and reporting costs. Then, when an ROI is calculated and reported, costs are included in summary form, and the cost guidelines are referenced in a footnote or attached as an appendix.

Typical Cost Categories

The most important task in defining tasks is to define which specific costs should be included in a tabulation of the program costs. This task involves decisions that will be made by the HR staff and usually approved by management. If appropriate, the finance and accounting staff may need to approve the list. Table 7-1 shows the recommended cost categories for a fully loaded, conservative approach to estimating costs. Each category is described below.

Prorated vs. Direct Costs

Usually all costs related to a program are captured and expensed to that program. However, three categories are usually prorated over several components of the same program. Needs analysis, design and development, and acquisition are all significant costs that should be prorated over the life of the program. With a conservative approach, the life of the program should be very short. Some organizations will consider one year of operation for the program; others may consider two or three years. If some ques-

Table 7-1
Program Cost Categories

Cost Item	Prorated	Expensed
Analysis Costs	✓	
Development/Acquisition Costs	✓	
Implementation Costs		✓
☐ Salaries/Benefits—Facilitators		✓
☐ Salaries/Benefits—Coordination		✓
☐ Program Materials and Fees		✓
☐ Travel/Lodging/Meals		✓
☐ Facilities for Meetings/Training		✓
☐ Participants' Salaries/Benefits		✓
☐ Participant Replacement Costs (if applicable)		✓
☐ Lost Production (explain basis)		✓
Operating Costs		✓
☐ Salaries/Benefits—Participants and Facilitators		✓
☐ Salaries/Benefits—Program Coordination	✓	✓
☐ Salaries/Benefits—Program Manager	✓	✓
☐ Supplies, Materials, Equipment, Facilities		✓
☐ Travel/Lodging/Meals		✓
☐ Outside Services	✓	✓
Evaluation	✓	✓
General Overhead Allocation	✓	

tion exists about the specific time period to be used in the proration formula, the finance and accounting staff should be consulted.

A brief example will illustrate the proration of development costs. In a large utility company, an employee safety program was developed and implemented because of a series of accidents during the past several months. The program included changes in the procedure to put caution tags on dangerous equipment during outages. The program was developed at a cost of $195,000 and was expected to have a three-year life cycle before it needed updating. The revision costs at the end of the three years were estimated to be about one-half of the original development costs, or $97,500. The program would be conducted with forty-two groups in a three-year period, with an ROI calculation planned for one specific group. Because the program would have one-half its residual value at the end of three years, one-half of the cost should be written off for this three-year period. Thus, the $97,500, representing half the development costs, would be spread over the forty-two groups as a prorated development cost. Thus, an ROI for one group would have a development cost of $2,321 included in the cost profile.

Benefits Factor

When presenting participant salaries and salaries of staff associated with programs, the benefits factor should be included. This number is usually well known in the organization and is used in other costing formulas. It represents the cost of all employee benefits expressed as a percent of base salaries. In some organizations this value is as high as 50 to 60 percent. In others, it may be as low as 25 to 30 percent. The average in the USA is 38 percent [1].

MAJOR COST CATEGORIES

Analysis Costs

One of the most often overlooked cost categories is the cost of conducting an analysis of needs. In some programs this cost is zero because the program is conducted without an analysis. However, as more organizations focus increased attention on needs analysis, this item will become a more significant cost in the future. All costs associated with the analysis should be captured to the fullest extent possible. These costs include the time staff members spend conducting the analysis, direct fees and expenses for external consultants who conduct the analysis, and internal services and supplies used in the analysis. The total costs are usually prorated over the life of the program. Depending on the type and nature of the program, the program life should be kept to a reasonable number, in the one- to three-year time frame. Of course the exception would be exceedingly expensive programs that are not expected to change significantly for several years.

Development/Acquisition Costs

One of the more significant cost categories is the cost of designing and developing the program. This cost includes internal HR staff time in both design and development, as well as the purchase of supplies, videos, CD-ROMs, and other materials directly related to the program. It also includes the use of external vendors. As with analysis costs, design and development costs are usually prorated, perhaps using the same time frame. One to three years is recommended unless the program is not expected to change for many years and the costs are significant.

In lieu of development costs, many organizations purchase programs to use directly or in a modified format. The acquisition costs for these programs include the purchase price of the materials, fees to vendors, licensing agreements, and other costs associated with the right to implement the program. These acquisition costs should be prorated using the same rationale above; one to three years should be sufficient. If the program needs modification or if some additional development is required, these costs should be included as development costs. In practice, many programs have both acquisition costs and development costs.

Implementation Costs

Often, the largest segment of costs is associated with delivery. This cost segment includes five major categories.

Salaries of facilitators and coordinators. The salaries of facilitators or program coordinators should be included. If a coordinator is involved in more than one program, the appropriate time should be allocated to the specific program. If external facilitators are used, all charges should be included for the portion of the program and time frame being evaluated. The important issue is to capture all the direct time of internal employees or external consultants who work directly with the program. The benefits factor should be included each time direct labor costs are involved. This factor is a widely accepted value, usually generated by the finance and accounting staff and in the 30 to 40 percent range.

Program materials and fees. Specific program materials such as guidelines, job aids, software, notebooks, textbooks, case studies, exercises, and participant workbooks should be included in the delivery costs, along with license fees, user fees, and royalty payments if any.

Travel, lodging, and meals. Direct travel for participants, facilitators, or coordinators should be included. Lodging and meals are included for participants during travel, as well as meals during the meeting or program. Refreshments should also be included.

Facilities. The direct cost of the facilities for meetings or learning sessions should be included. For external programs, this is the direct charge from the hotel or conference center. If the program is implemented in-house, the conference room represents a cost for the organization, and the cost should be estimated and included even if it is not the practice to include facilities' cost in other reports.

Participants' salaries and benefits. The salaries plus employee benefits of participants represent an expense that should be included. For situations in which the program has already been implemented, these costs can be estimated using average or midpoint values for salaries in typical job classifications. When a program is targeted for an ROI calculation, participants can provide their salaries directly and in a confidential manner.

If a replacement employee must substitute for an employee who is attending meetings on HR issues, and if this cost exceeds the value of the salary and benefits already captured, then the excess cost must also be calculated. For example, here's how to calculate the excess cost if four employees staff a casting operation in a pipe manufacturing facility and then one of the four leaves the premises to attend a meeting related to an HR program or to serve on an HR task force. The pipe manufacturing facility in this example has determined that the casting operation can continue to operate at three-quarters staffing for only one day. So if the one casting employee, who earns $40 per hour, attends a two-day HR task force meeting, on the second day an employee from another shift will need to substitute for the absent employee. If the replacement employee earns overtime wages of $60 per hour, the replacement cost captured should be $20 per hour ($60 minus $40) times the eight-hour shift, yielding a replacement cost of $160. Because the salary and benefits for the employee attending the meeting have already been captured, it is only necessary to capture the added cost (the overtime pay) of the replacement employee. The replacement employee is turning out the same product at the same productivity level as the employee who is attending the meeting, so no loss of output occurs.

Using the same example above, if the crew cannot produce 100 percent output on the first day because of the three-quarters staffing level, then the cost of lost production must also be included as an HR program cost, with an appropriate explanation.

Operating Costs

Costs to operate and maintain the HR program must be captured on a continuing basis. These include ongoing salaries and benefits of the program manager/coordinator, as well as the cost of office supplies, materials, program expenses, and technology support. Other costs are treated similarly to implementation costs.

Also, if long-term ongoing operating costs exist for a program, then these costs may need to be expressed on an annual basis. When appropriate, these costs may be prorated on a per-year basis so that they can be used to develop an ROI. For example, if an HR program is being evaluated to determine program benefits realized from March 1 to August 31, then the annual operating cost would need to be prorated to capture six months of operating costs.

Evaluation Costs

Usually the total evaluation cost is included in the program costs to compute the fully loaded cost. ROI costs include the cost of developing the evaluation strategy, designing instruments, collecting data, analyzing data, and preparing and distributing reports. Cost categories include time, materials, purchased instruments, and surveys. A case can be made to prorate the evaluation costs over several programs instead of charging the total amount as an expense. For example, if twenty-five sessions of an HR program are conducted in a three-year period and one group is selected for an ROI calculation, then the ROI costs could logically be prorated over the twenty-five sessions. This is because the results of the ROI analysis should reflect the success of the other programs and will perhaps result in changes that will influence the other programs as well.

Overhead

A final charge is the cost of overhead, which includes the additional costs in the HR function not directly related to a particular program or implementation. The overhead category represents any HR department cost not considered in the above calculations. Typical items include the cost of administrative support; departmental office expenses such as utilities, space, telephones, computers, and copy machines; salaries of HR managers; and other fixed costs. Some organizations obtain an estimate for allocation by dividing the total overhead by the number of program implementation days for the year. This becomes a standard value to use in calculations.

COST ACCUMULATION AND ESTIMATION

There are two basic ways to classify HR costs. One is accomplished by assigning the expenditure a description, such as labor, materials, supplies, travel, and so forth. These are called expense account classifications. The other is accomplished by assigning categories in the HR process or function, such as program development, implementation, and evaluation. An effective system monitors costs by account categories (shown in Table 7-2) according to the description of those accounts but also includes a method for accumulating costs by the HR process/functional category. Many systems stop short of this second step. Although the first grouping sufficiently gives the total program cost, it does not allow for a useful comparison with other programs or indicate areas in which costs might be excessive by relative comparisons.

Cost Classification Matrix

Costs are accumulated under both of the above classifications. The two classifications are obviously related, and the relationship depends on the organization. For instance, the specific costs that compose the analysis part of a program may vary substantially with the organization.

An important part of the classification process is to define the kinds of costs, in the account classification system, that normally apply to the process/functional categories. The matrix shown in Table 7-2 represents the categories for accumulating all HR-related

Table 7-2
Cost Classification Matrix

Expense Account Classification	Process/Functional Categories				
	Analysis	Development/ Acquisition	Implementation	Operating	Evaluation
00 Salaries and Benefits—HR Staff	X	X	X	X	X
01 Salaries and Benefits—Other Staff Members	X	X			
02 Salaries and Benefits—Participants			X	X	X
03 Meals, Travel, and Incidental Expenses—HR Staff	X	X	X	X	X
04 Meals, Travel, and Accommodations—Participants			X	X	X
05 Office Supplies and Expenses	X	X		X	X
06 Program Materials and Supplies		X	X	X	
07 Printing	X	X	X	X	X
08 Outside Services	X	X	X	X	X
09 Equipment Expense Allocation	X	X	X	X	X
10 Equipment—Rental		X	X	X	
11 Equipment—Maintenance			X	X	
12 Registration Fees	X			X	
13 Facilities Expense Allocation			X	X	
14 Facilities Rental		X	X		
15 General Overhead Allocation	X	X	X	X	X
16 Other Miscellaneous Expenses	X	X	X	X	X

costs in the organization. Those costs that normally are a part of a certain process/functional category have an X beside them in the matrix, indicating that particular category. Each member of the HR staff should know how to charge expenses properly (for example, expenses for equipment that is rented to use in the development and implementation of a specific program). In this example, should all or part of the cost be charged to development? Or to implementation? More than likely the cost will be allocated in proportion to the extent the item was used for each category.

Cost Accumulation

With expense account classifications clearly defined and the process/functional categories determined, it is easy to track costs for individual programs. This is accomplished by using special account numbers and project numbers. The example that follows illustrates the use of these numbers.

A project number is a three-digit number representing a specific HR program. For example:

Employee Concerns Program	112
Gainsharing Program	215
Statistical Quality Control	418
Valuing Diversity	791

Numbers are also assigned to the process/functional categories shown in Table 7-2. Using the example presented earlier, the following numbers are assigned:

Analysis	1
Development/Acquisition	2
Implementation	3
Operating	4
Evaluation	5

Using the two-digit numbers assigned to account classifications in Table 7-2, an accounting system is complete. For example, if workbooks are reproduced to give to participants in the valuing diversity workshop, the appropriate charge number for that reproduction is 07-3-791. The first two digits denote the account classification, the next digit the process/functional category, and the last three digits the project number. This system enables rapid accumulation and monitoring of HR costs. Total costs can be presented by:

☐ HR program (valuing diversity)
☐ Process/functional categories (implementation)
☐ Expense account classification (printing)

Cost Estimation

The previous sections covered procedures for classifying and monitoring costs related to HR programs. It is important to monitor and compare ongoing costs with the budget or with projected costs. However, a significant reason for tracking costs is to predict the cost of future programs. Usually this goal is accomplished through a formal cost estimation method unique to the organization.

Some organizations use cost estimating worksheets to arrive at the total cost for a proposed program. Figure 7-1 shows an example of cost estimating worksheets that are used to calculate analysis, development, implementation, operating, and evaluation costs. The worksheets contain a few formulas that make it easier to estimate the cost. In addition to these worksheets, current charge rates for services, supplies, and salaries should be available for computational purposes. These data become outdated quickly and are usually prepared periodically as a supplement.

The most appropriate basis for predicting costs is to analyze the previous costs by tracking the actual costs incurred in all phases of a program, from analysis to evaluation. This way, it is possible to see how much is being spent on programs and how much is being spent in the different categories. Until adequate cost data are available, it is necessary to use the detailed analysis in the worksheets for cost estimation.

(text continued on page 232)

Analysis Costs	Total
Salaries and Employee Benefits—HR Staff (No. of People × Avg. Salary × Employee Benefits Factor × No. of Hours on Project)	_____
Meals, Travel, and Incidental Expenses	_____
Office Supplies and Expenses	_____
Printing	_____
Outside Services	_____
Equipment Expenses	_____
Registration Fees	_____
General Overhead Allocation	_____
Other Miscellaneous Expenses	_____
Total Analysis Cost	=======

Development/Acquisition Costs

		Total
Salaries and Employee Benefits (No. of People × Avg. Salary × Employee Benefits Factor × No. of Hours on Project)		_____
Meals, Travel, and Incidental Expenses		_____
Office Supplies and Expenses		_____
Program Materials and Supplies		_____
Film	_____	
Videotape	_____	
Audiotapes	_____	
35mm Slides	_____	
CD-ROMs	_____	
Software	_____	
Overhead Transparencies	_____	
Artwork	_____	
Manuals and Materials	_____	
Other	_____	
Printing		_____
Outside Services		_____
Equipment Expense		_____
General Overhead Allocation		_____
Other Miscellaneous Expenses		_____
Total Development/Acquisition Costs		=======

Figure 7-1. Cost estimating worksheets.

Implementation Costs	Total
Participant Costs	_____
Salaries and Employee Benefits (No. of Participants × Avg. Salary × Employee Benefits Factor × Hours or Days of Captive Time)	_____
Meals, Travel, and Accommodations (No. of Participants × Avg. Daily Expenses × Days of Captive Time)	_____
Program Materials and Supplies	_____
Participant Replacement Costs (if applicable)	_____
Lost Production (if applicable; explain basis)	_____
Program Manager/Coordinator/Facilitator Costs	_____
Salaries and Benefits _____	
Meals, Travel, and Incidental Expenses _____	
Outside Services _____	
Facilities Expense Allocation	_____
Equipment Expense	_____
Other Miscellaneous Expenses	_____
Total Delivery Costs	========
Operating Costs	
Participant Costs	_____
Salaries and Employee Benefits (No. of Participants × Avg. Salary × Employee Benefits Factor × Hrs. or Days of Time Utilizing the Program)	_____
Meals, Travel, and Accommodations (No. of Participants × Avg. Daily Expenses × Days of Captive Time)	_____
Program Materials and Supplies	_____
Participant Replacement Costs (if applicable)	_____
Lost Production (if applicable; explain basis)	_____
Program Manager/Coordinator Costs	_____
Salaries and Benefits _____	
Meals, Travel, and Incidental Expenses _____	
Outside Services _____	
Facility Costs	_____
Facilities Rental	_____

Figure 7-1. Continued.

Facilities Expense Allocation   _____

Equipment Expense   _____

Other Miscellaneous Expenses   _____

    Total Operating Costs   ══════

Evaluation Costs	Total

Salaries and Employee Benefits—HR Staff
  (No. of People × Avg. Salary × Employee
  Benefits Factor × No. of Hours on Project)   _____

Meals, Travel, and Incidental Expenses   _____

Participant Costs   _____

Office Supplies and Expenses   _____

Printing   _____

Outside Services   _____

Equipment Expense   _____

Other Miscellaneous Expenses   _____

    Total Evaluation Costs   ══════

General Overhead Expense   ══════

TOTAL PROGRAM COSTS   ══════

Figure 7-1. Continued.

(text continued from page 229)

SUMMARY

Costs are important and should be fully loaded in the ROI calculation. From a practical standpoint, including some of the costs may be optional—based on the organization's guidelines and philosophy. However, because of the scrutiny involved in ROI calculations, it is recommended that all costs be included, even if doing so goes beyond the requirements of the company policy.

REFERENCE

1. Annual Employee Benefits Report. *Nations Business*, January 1996, p. 28.

CHAPTER 8

Calculating the Actual Return on Investment

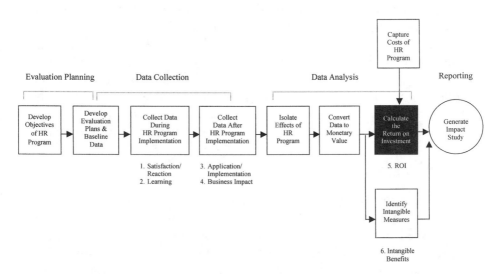

Evaluation Planning | Data Collection | Data Analysis | Reporting

Capture Costs of HR Program

| Develop Objectives of HR Program | Develop Evaluation Plans & Baseline Data | Collect Data During HR Program Implementation | Collect Data After HR Program Implementation | Isolate Effects of HR Program | Convert Data to Monetary Value | Calculate the Return on Investment | Generate Impact Study |

1. Satisfaction/ Reaction
2. Learning

3. Application/ Implementation
4. Business Impact

5. ROI

Identify Intangible Measures

6. Intangible Benefits

The monetary values for program benefits, developed in Chapter 6, are combined with program cost data, developed in Chapter 7, to calculate the return on investment. This chapter explores several approaches for developing the return on investment, describing the various techniques, processes, and issues involved. Before presenting the formulas for ROI calculation, the chapter describes a few basic issues. An adequate understanding of these issues is necessary to complete this major step in the ROI process.

BASIC ISSUES

Definitions

The phrase *return on investment in HR* is often misused, sometimes intentionally. In some situations, a broad definition for ROI includes any benefit from the program. In these situations, ROI is a vague concept in which even subjective data linked to a program are included in the concept of the return. In this book, the return on investment has a more precise meaning and represents an actual value developed by comparing program costs with benefits. The two most common measures are the benefit/cost ratio and the ROI formula. Both are presented along with other approaches that calculate the return.

For many years, HR practitioners and researchers have sought to calculate the actual return on the investment for HR programs and initiatives. If HR programs are considered an investment, not an expense, then it is appropriate to place the HR investment in the same funding mechanism as other investments, such as the investment in equipment and facilities. Although these other investments differ quite a bit, management often views them in the same way. Thus, it is critical to the success of the HR field to develop specific values that reflect the return on the investment.

Annualized Values

All the formulas presented in this chapter use annualized values so that the first-year impact of the program investment is developed. Using annual values is becoming a generally accepted practice for developing the ROI in many organizations. This approach is a conservative way to develop the ROI, because many short-term HR programs add value in the second or third year. For long-term HR programs, annualized values are inappropriate, and longer time frames need to be used. For example, in an ROI analysis of a program to send employees to the USA to obtain MBA degrees, a Singapore-based company used a seven-year time frame. The program required two years for degree completion and then a five-year impact, with post-program data used to develop the ROI. However, for most programs that last anywhere from one day to one month, first-year values are appropriate.

When selecting the approach to measure ROI, it is important to communicate to the target audience the formula used and the assumptions made to arrive at the decision to use the formula. This action can prevent misunderstandings and confusion surrounding how the ROI value was actually developed. Although this chapter describes several approaches, two stand out as the preferred methods: the benefit/cost ratio and the basic ROI formula. These two approaches are described next, along with brief coverage of the other approaches.

BENEFIT/COST RATIO

One of the earliest methods for evaluating HR investments is the benefit/cost ratio (BCR). This method compares the benefits of the HR program with the program's costs, in a ratio. In formula form, the ratio is:

$$BCR = \frac{Program\ Benefits}{Program\ Costs}$$

In simple terms, the BCR compares the annual economic benefits of the program with the cost of the program. A BCR value of one means that the benefits equal the costs. A BCR of two, usually written as 2:1, indicates that each dollar spent on the program returned two dollars as benefits.

The following example illustrates the use of the benefit/cost ratio. An electric and gas utility implemented an applied behavior management program designed for managers and supervisors [1]. In a follow-up evaluation, action planning and business performance monitoring were used to capture benefits. The first-year payoff for the program equaled $1,077,750. The total fully loaded implementation costs were $215,500. Thus, the ratio was:

$$BCR = \frac{\$1,077,750}{\$215,500} = 5:1$$

Every one dollar invested in this program returned five dollars in benefits.

The principal advantage of using this approach is that it avoids traditional financial measures so that no confusion results when comparing HR investments with other investments in the company. Investments in plants, equipment, or subsidiaries, for example, are not usually evaluated with the benefit/cost method. Some HR executives prefer not to use the same method (BCR) to compare the return on HR investments with the return on other investments. Consequently, the ROI for HR stands alone as a unique type of evaluation.

Unfortunately, no standards exist as to what constitutes an acceptable benefit/cost ratio. A standard should be established within an organization, perhaps even for a specific type of program. However, a 1:1 ratio is unacceptable for most programs, and some organizations require a 1.25:1 ratio, where 1.25 times the cost of the program is the benefit.

ROI FORMULA

Perhaps the most appropriate formula for evaluating HR investments is net program benefits divided by cost. The ratio is usually expressed as a percent when the fractional values are multiplied by 100. In formula form, the ROI becomes:

$$ROI(\%) = \frac{\text{Net Program Benefits}}{\text{Program Costs}} \times 100$$

Net benefits are program benefits minus program costs. The ROI value is related to the BCR by a factor of one. For example, a BCR of 2.45 is the same as an ROI value of 145 percent. This formula is essentially the same as ROI in other types of investments. For example, when a firm builds a new plant, the ROI is found by dividing annual earnings by the investment. The annual earnings are comparable to net benefits (annual benefits minus the cost). The investment is comparable to program costs, which represent the investment in the program.

An ROI for an HR investment of 50 percent means that the costs were recovered and an additional 50 percent of the costs were reported as "earnings." For example, a cost of $100 requires earnings of $150 in order to bring a 50 percent return.

$$ROI(\%) = \frac{\$150 - \$100}{\$100} \times 100 = 50\%$$

An HR investment of 150 percent indicates that the costs were recovered and an additional 1.5 multiplied by the costs was captured as "earnings." An example illustrates the ROI calculation. Magnavox Electronics Systems Company conducted an eighteen-week literacy program for entry-level electrical and mechanical assemblers [2]. The results of the program were impressive. Productivity and quality alone yielded an annual value of $321,600. The total fully loaded costs for the program were $38,233. Thus, the return on investment became:

$$ROI(\%) = \frac{\$321,600 - \$38,233}{\$38,233} \times 100 = 741\%$$

For each dollar invested, Magnavox received 7.4 dollars in return after the cost of the program had been recovered.

Using the ROI formula essentially places HR investments on a level playing field with other investments using the same formula and similar concepts. Key management and financial executives who regularly use ROI with other investments can easily understand the ROI calculation.

Although no generally accepted standards exist, some organizations establish a minimum requirement or hurdle rate for an ROI in an HR program. Some organizations set an ROI minimum of 25 percent. This target value usually exceeds the percentage required for other types of investments. The rationale: The ROI process for HR is still relatively new and often involves some subjective input, including estimations. Because of that, a higher standard is required or suggested, with 25 percent being the desired figure for these organizations.

BCR/ROI Case Application

Background Information

Retail Merchandise Company (RMC)—a large, national store chain located in most major USA markets—attempted to boost sales by conducting an interactive selling skills program for sales associates. The program, developed and delivered by an outside vendor, represented a response to a clearly defined need to increase the level of interaction between the sales associate and the customer. The program consisted of two days of skills training followed by three weeks of on-the-job application of the skills. The third day of the program was used for follow-up and additional training. Three groups, representing the electronics departments of three stores, initially received the training, as a pilot implementation. A total of four participated.

ROI Analysis

Post-program data collection was accomplished using three methods. First, the average weekly sales of each associate was monitored (business performance monitoring of output data). Second, a follow-up questionnaire was distributed three months after the associates completed the training to determine Level 3 success (actual application of the skills on the job). Third, Level 3 data were solicited in a follow-up session, which was conducted on the third day. In this session, participants disclosed their success (or lack of success) with the application of new skills. They also discussed techniques to overcome the barriers to program implementation.

This program used a control group to isolate the effects of training. Three additional store locations were identified (control group) and compared with the three groups in the pilot training (experimental group). The variables of store size, store location, and customer traffic levels were used to match the two groups so that they could be as identical as possible. The method to convert data to monetary values is a direct profit contribution of the increased output. The actual profit obtained from an additional one dollar of sales was readily available and used in the calculation.

BCR and ROI Calculations

Although the program was evaluated at all five levels, this study focused on the Level 5 calculation. Levels 1, 2, and 3 data either met or exceeded expectations. Table 8-1 shows the Level

Table 8-1
Level 4 Data: Average Weekly Post-Training Sales

Weeks After Training	Trained Group	Control Group
1	$9,723	$9,698
2	9,978	9,720
3	10,424	9,812
13	13,690	11,572
14	11,491	9,683
15	11,044	10,092
Average for Weeks 13, 14, and 15	$12,075	$10,449

4 data, the average weekly sales of both groups after the training. For convenience and at the request of management, a three-month follow-up period was used. Management wanted to implement the program at other locations if it appeared successful in this first three months of operation. Three months may be premature to determine the total impact of the program, but it often becomes a convenient time period for evaluation. Sales data for the first three weeks after training are shown in Table 8-1, along with data for the last three weeks of the evaluation period (weeks 13, 14, and 15). The data show what appears to be a significant difference in the two values.

Two steps are required to move from the Level 4 data to Level 5. Step 1 calls for Level 4 data to be converted to monetary values. Because sales is the Level 4 data being converted here, in this instance the sales data must be converted to profit contribution as noted below. Step 2 requires the cost of the program to be tabulated. Table 8-2 shows the annualized program benefits. The total benefit was $71,760. Of the total forty-eight participants, forty-six still remained in the same jobs for which they received training at the end of the three months. To be conservative, the other two participants' potential improvements were removed from the calculation. The profit contribution at the store

Table 8-2
Annualized Program Benefits

46 of 48 participants remained in same jobs after 3 months	
Average Weekly Sales Trained Groups	$12,075
Average Weekly Sales Untrained Groups	$10,449
Increase	$1,626
Profit Contribution 2%	$32.50
Total Weekly Improvement (32.50 × 46)	$1,495
Total Annual Benefits ($1,495 × 48 Weeks)	**$71,760**

level, obtained directly from the accounting department, was 2 percent. For every one dollar of additional sales attributed to the program, only two cents would be considered the added value. At the corporate level, the number was even smaller, about 1.2 percent. As in this example, first-year values are usually used to reflect the total impact of the program. Ideally, if new skills are acquired, as indicated in the Level 3 evaluation, some value for the use of those skills should be added in year two and perhaps even year three. However, for short-term programs, only first-year values are used, requiring the investment to have an acceptable return in a one-year time period. This completes Step 1, converting benefits to monetary values.

Table 8-3 shows the cost summary for this program. Costs are fully loaded, including data for all forty-eight participants. Because a vendor conducted the program, there are no direct development costs. The facilitation fee actually covers the pro-rated development costs, as well as the delivery costs. The participants' salaries plus a 35 percent factor for employee benefits were included in the costs. Facilities costs were included, although the company does not normally capture the costs when internal facilities are used, as was the case with this program. The estimated cost for the coordination and evaluation was also included. The total cost was $32,984. Thus, the benefit/cost ratio became:

$$\text{BCR} = \frac{\$71,760}{\$32,984} = 2.2:1$$

Table 8-3
Cost Summary

48 participants, spread across 3 sessions	
Facilitation Fees: 3 sessions @ $3,750 each	$11,250
Program Materials: 48 @ $35/participant	1,680
Meals/Refreshments: 3 days @ $28/participant/day	4,032
Facilities: 9 days @ $120/day	1,080
Participant Salaries Plus Benefits (35%)	12,442
Coordination/Evaluation	2,500
Total Costs	**$32,984**

and the return on investment became:

$$\text{ROI}(\%) = \frac{\$71,760 - \$32,984}{\$32,984} \times 100 = 118\%$$

Thus, the program had an excellent return on investment in its initial trial run after three months of on-the-job application of the skills.

OTHER ROI MEASURES

In addition to the traditional ROI formula previously described, several other measures are occasionally used under the general term *return on investment*. These measures are designed primarily for evaluating other types of financial measures, but sometimes they work their way into HR evaluations.

Payback Period

The payback period is a common method for evaluating capital expenditures. With this approach, the annual cash proceeds (savings) produced by an investment are equated to the original cash outlay required by the investment to arrive at some multiple of cash proceeds equal to the original investment. Measurement is usually in terms of years and months. For example, if the cost savings generated by an HR program remain constant each year, the payback period is determined by dividing the total original cash investment (development costs, outside program purchases, etc.) by the amount of the expected annual or actual savings. The savings represent the net savings after the program expenses are subtracted. To illustrate this calculation, assume that an initial program cost is $100,000 with a three-year useful life. The annual net savings from the program is expected to be $40,000. Thus, the payback period becomes:

$$\text{Payback Period} = \frac{\text{Total Investment}}{\text{Annual Savings}} = \frac{100,000}{40,000} = 2.5 \text{ years}$$

The program will "pay back" the original investment in 2.5 years.

The payback period is simple to use but has the limitation of ignoring the time value of money. It has not enjoyed widespread use in evaluating HR investments.

Discounted Cash Flow

Discounted cash flow is a method of evaluating investment opportunities in which certain values are assigned to the timing of the proceeds from the investment. The assumption, based on interest rates, is that a dollar earned today is more valuable than a dollar earned a year from now.

There are several ways of using the discounted cash flow concept to evaluate capital expenditures. The most popular one is probably the net present value of an investment. This approach compares the savings, year by year, with the outflow of cash required by the investment. The expected savings received each year is discounted by selected interest rates. The outflow of cash is also discounted by the same interest rate. If the present value of the savings should exceed the present value of the outlays after discounting at a common interest rate, management usually views the investment as acceptable. The discounted cash flow method has the advantage of ranking investments, but it becomes difficult to calculate.

Internal Rate of Return

The internal rate of return (IRR) method determines the interest rate required to make the present value of the cash flow equal zero. It represents the maximum rate of interest that could be paid if all project funds were borrowed and the organization had to break even on the projects. The IRR considers the time value of money and is unaffected by the scale of the project. It can be used to rank alternatives and to make accept/reject decisions when a minimum rate of return is specified. A major weakness of the IRR method is that it assumes all returns are reinvested at the same internal rate of return. This can make an investment alternative with a high rate of return look even better than it really is and a project with a low rate of return look even worse. In practice, the IRR is rarely used to evaluate HR investments.

UTILITY ANALYSIS

Another interesting approach for developing the HR payoff is utility analysis. Utility is a function of the duration of an HR program's effect on employees' performance, the number of employees affected, the validity of the HR program, the value of the job for which HR initiative was provided, and the total program cost.

Utility analysis measures the economic contribution of a program according to how much effect the program had in identifying and modifying behavior, hence the future service contribution of employees. Schmidt, Hunter, and Pearlman derived the following formula for assessing the dollar value of a training program [3]:

$$\Delta U = T \times N \times dt \times Sdy - N \times C$$

where ΔU = Monetary value of the training program
   T = Duration in number of years of a training program's effect on performance
   N = Number of employees trained
   dt = True difference in job performance between the average trained and the average untrained employee in units of standard deviation

Sdy = Standard deviation of job performance of the untrained
        group in dollars
C = Cost of training per employee

Of all the factors in this formula, the true difference in job
performance (dt) and the value of the target job (Sdy) are the
most difficult to develop. The validity of the HR program is
determined by noting the performance differences between trained
and untrained employees. The simplest method for obtaining this
information is to have supervisors rate the performance of both
groups. Supervisors and experts estimate the value of the target
job, Sdy.

Utility analysis is based totally on estimations. Because of the
subjective nature of this approach, it has not achieved widespread
acceptance by HR professionals as a practical tool for evaluating
the return on HR investments.

Consequences of Not Providing an HR Solution

Another method to determine the return on HR solutions is
to withhold the solution and calculate the consequences. For some
organizations, withholding an HR solution produces serious
consequences. A company's inability to perform adequately might
mean that it is unable to take on additional business or that it
may lose existing business because of an untrained work force
or an inadequate compensation system. Also, HR programs can
help avoid serious operational problems (accidents) and non-
compliance issues (EEO violations). This particular method of
calculating the return on HR investments has received recent
attention and involves the following steps:

- ☐ Establish that a potential problem, loss, or opportunity exists.
- ☐ Isolate the problems that lack of performance may create,
  such as noncompliance issues, loss of business, or the
  inability to take on additional business.
- ☐ Develop an estimate of the potential value of the problem,
  loss, or opportunity.
- ☐ If other factors are involved, determine the impact of each
  factor on the loss of income.

☐ Estimate the total cost of an HR solution using the techniques outlined in Chapter 7.

☐ Compare benefits with costs.

This approach has some disadvantages. The potential loss of income can be highly subjective and difficult to measure. Also, it may be difficult to isolate the factors involved and to determine their weight relative to lost income. Because of these concerns, this approach to evaluating the return on HR investments is limited.

ROI Issues

ROI Complexity

As discussed in Chapter 1, developing the return on investment in HR is a complex issue. The approach presented in this book is to take the complex process and simplify it by breaking it into small steps so it is understandable and acceptable to a variety of audiences. Figure 8-1 illustrates the complexity of this process.

This book has presented the ten most common ways to collect post-program data, ten ways to isolate the effects of HR programs on business performance measures, and ten ways to convert data into monetary values. In essence, there are 1,000 possible ways to evaluate an HR program, as shown in Figure 8-1. This fact alone is often enough to cause some of the most eager individuals to avoid the ROI process. However, when each step is taken separately and issues are addressed for a particular topic, the decisions are made incrementally all the way through the process. This helps to reduce a complex process to a more simplified and manageable effort. Figure 8-1 underscores an important advantage of this process. With so many different ways to tackle these three critical issues, the ROI process can be applied to almost any type of program in any setting.

Cautions When Using ROI

Because of the complexity and sensitivity of the ROI process, caution is needed when developing, calculating, and communicating the return on investment. The implementation of the ROI

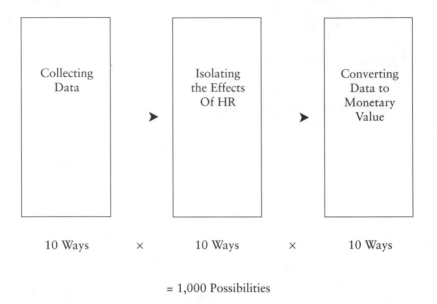

Figure 8-1. ROI complexity. The number of possibilities increase the complexity.

process is a critical goal of many HR departments. A few issues, described next, should be addressed to keep the process from going astray.

The ROI process should be developed for programs for which a needs assessment/analysis has been conducted. Because of the evaluation problems that can develop when there is not a clear needs assessment, the ROI should be conducted only with programs that have had a comprehensive needs assessment, preferably with Levels 3 and 4 data. However, practical considerations and management requests may prohibit this suggested requirement.

The ROI analysis should always include one or more strategies for isolating the effects of the HR program. Because of the importance of accounting for the influence of other factors, this step in the process must not be ignored. Too often, an excellent study, from what appears to be a remarkably successful HR effort, is perceived as worthless because there was no attempt to account for other factors. Omission of this step seriously diminishes the credibility of the study.

When making estimates, use the most reliable and credible sources. Because estimates are critical to any type of analysis, they will usually be an important part of the ROI process. When used, they should be developed properly and obtained from the most reliable and credible sources, those individuals who best understand the overall situation and can provide the most accurate estimation.

Take a conservative approach when developing both benefits and costs. Conservatism in ROI analysis builds accuracy and credibility. What matters most is how the target audience perceives the value of the data. A conservative approach is always recommended for both the numerator of the ROI formula (benefits) and the denominator (program costs).

Use caution when comparing the ROI in HR with other financial returns. There are many ways to calculate the return on funds invested or assets employed. The ROI is just one of them. Although the calculation for ROI in HR uses the same basic formula as in other investment evaluations, the target group may not fully understand it. Its calculation method and its meaning should be clearly communicated. More importantly, it should be accepted by management as an appropriate measure for HR program evaluation.

Involve management in developing the return. Management ultimately decides whether an ROI value is acceptable. To the extent possible, management should be involved in setting the parameters for calculations and establishing targets by which HR programs are considered acceptable within the organization.

Approach sensitive and controversial issues with caution. Occasionally, sensitive and controversial issues will surface when discussing an ROI value. It is best to avoid debates about what is measurable and what is not measurable unless clear evidence exists regarding the issue in question. Also, some programs are so fundamental to the survival of the organization that any attempt to measure them is unnecessary. For example, a program designed to improve customer service in a customer-focused company may escape the scrutiny of an ROI evaluation because of the assumption that if the program is well designed, it will improve customer service.

Teach others the methods for calculating the return. Each time an ROI is calculated, the HR manager should use the opportunity to educate other managers and colleagues in the organization. Even if such a task does not fall under their areas of responsibility,

these individuals will see the value of this approach to HR evaluation. Also, when possible, each project should serve as a case
study to educate the HR staff about specific techniques and methods.

Do not boast about a high return. It is not unusual to generate
what appears to be an extremely high return on investment for
an HR program. Several examples in this book have illustrated
the possibilities. An HR manager who boasts about a high rate
of return opens the door to potential criticism from others unless
the calculation is based on indisputable facts.

Do not try to use ROI for every program. Some programs are
difficult to quantify, and an ROI calculation may not be feasible
for them. Other methods of presenting the benefits may be more
appropriate. HR executives are encouraged to set targets for the
percent of programs in which ROIs are developed. Also, specific
criteria should be established to guide selection of programs for
ROI analysis.

CONCLUSION

After the HR program benefits are collected and converted to
monetary values and the program costs are developed in a fully
loaded profile, the ROI calculation becomes a simple step. It is
just a matter of plugging the values into the appropriate formula.
This chapter has presented the two approaches most often used
for calculating the return: the ROI formula and the benefit/cost
ratio. Several other alternatives were presented briefly but are not
widely used to determine the return on HR solutions.

REFERENCES

1. Wescott, R. "Applied Behavior Management Training," in *In
   Action: Measuring Return on Investment, Vol. 1.* J. Phillips (Ed.)
   Alexandria, Va.: American Society for Training and Development,
   1994, pp. 235–252.
2. Ford, D. "Three Rs in the Workplace," in *In Action: Measuring
   Return on Investment, Vol. 1.* J. Phillips (Ed.) Alexandria, Va.:
   American Society for Training and Development, 1994, pp. 85–104.
3. Schmidt, F. L., Hunter, J. E., and Pearlman, K. "Assessing the
   Economic Impact of Personnel Programs on Workforce Productivity."
   Personnel Psychology, Vol. 35, 1982, pp. 333–347.

CHAPTER 9

Identifying Intangible Measures

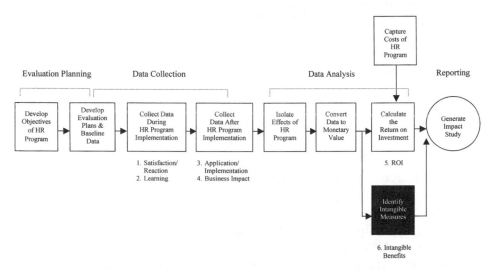

Intangible measures are the benefits or detriments, directly linked to the HR program, that are not converted to monetary values. Although in many cases these programs can be converted, for various reasons it has been decided not to convert them. These measures are often monitored after the HR program has been implemented, and although not converted to monetary values, they are still important in the evaluation process. Although the range of intangible measures has almost no limit, this chapter describes the more common variables often linked with HR programs. Here is a list of typical intangible variables connected to such programs:

- ☐ Attitude survey data
- ☐ Organizational commitment
- ☐ Climate survey data
- ☐ Employee complaints
- ☐ Grievances
- ☐ Discrimination complaints
- ☐ Stress reduction
- ☐ Employee turnover
- ☐ Employee absenteeism
- ☐ Employee tardiness
- ☐ Employee transfers
- ☐ Customer satisfaction survey data
- ☐ Customer complaints
- ☐ Customer response time
- ☐ Teamwork
- ☐ Cooperation
- ☐ Conflict
- ☐ Decisiveness
- ☐ Communication
- ☐ Employee satisfaction

KEY ISSUES

Importance of Intangible Measures

Not all measures can or should be converted to monetary values. By design, some are captured and reported as intangible measures. Although intangibles may not be perceived to be as valuable as the measures converted to monetary values, intangible measures are critical to the overall evaluation process [1]. In some programs, intangible or nonmonetary benefits can be more important than monetary or tangible measures. Consequently, these measures should be monitored and reported as part of the overall evaluation. In practice, every HR program, regardless of its nature, scope, and content, will have intangible measures associated with it [2]. The challenge is to efficiently identify and report them.

Identification of Measures

Intangible measures can be identified in several ways, at different stages in the process. First, they can be uncovered early in the process, during the needs assessment/analysis. Once identified, the intangible data are planned for collection as part of the overall data collection strategy. For example, an employee complaint resolution program may have several hard data measures linked to the program. During the needs assessment/analysis, an intangible measure—employee satisfaction—may also be identified and then monitored, with no plans to convert it to a monetary value. Thus, from the beginning, the measure of employee satisfaction is destined to be a nonmonetary benefit reported along with the ROI results.

A second way to identify an intangible benefit is to discuss the impact of the HR program with clients or sponsors. Clients can usually identify intangible measures that they expect the program to influence. For example, a college recruiting program was implemented in a large multinational company, and an ROI analysis was planned. Program designers, recruiters, HR managers, and senior executives identified potential intangible measures that they perceived were influenced by the program.

Third, an intangible measure can be identified during an attempt to convert the data to monetary values. If the process used to convert a set of data to monetary values cannot be completed without compromising credibility, the measure should be reported as an intangible benefit. For example, in an HR quality program, customer satisfaction was identified early in the process as one of the measures of success. A conversion to monetary values was attempted. However, the process of assigning a value to the data lost credibility; therefore, customer satisfaction was reported as an intangible benefit.

Last, an intangible measure can be identified during a follow-up evaluation. In such a situation, the measure—although not expected or anticipated in the initial program design—surfaces on a questionnaire, in an interview, or during a focus group. Questions are often asked about other improvements linked to the HR programs. Several intangible measures are usually provided, and no attempts are planned to place a value on the actual measure. For example, during the evaluation of a customer-service training program, participants were asked specifically what had improved about their work areas and their relationships with customers, as a result of applying the skills they acquired in the program. The participants provided more than a dozen intangible measures that managers perceived to be linked directly to the program.

Analysis

For most intangible data, no specific analysis is planned. Some evaluators report that previous attempts to convert intangible data to monetary units resulted in aborting the entire process; thus no further data analysis was conducted. Some cases may call for attempts to isolate the effects of an HR program by using one or more of the methods outlined in Chapter 5. This step is necessary when a need exists to know the specific amount of change in the intangible measure that is linked to the program. In many cases, the intangible data reflect improvement. However, neither the precise amount of the improvement nor the amount of improvement related directly to the HR program is clearly identified. Because the value of these data is not placed in the ROI calculation, intangible measures are not normally used to justify additional HR initiatives or continuation of existing programs. Consequently, a detailed analysis is not needed. Intangible benefits are viewed as supporting evidence of a program's success and are presented as qualitative data.

EMPLOYEE SATISFACTION

Employee satisfaction is perhaps one of the most important intangible measures. Almost any program will improve job satisfaction if the participants, participants' managers, participants' customers, or peer group members perceive the program to be successful. This section describes some of the most influential employee satisfaction measures.

Attitude Survey Data

Many organizations conduct attitude surveys, which reflect the degree to which employees feel satisfied with the organization, their jobs, their supervisors, their coworkers, and a host of other issues. Employee job satisfaction is closely correlated with absenteeism and turnover, both of which are linked with some HR programs. Some attitude survey items focus on issues directly related to HR programs, such as satisfaction with the quality of leadership of managers and supervisors. Attitude survey data are usually linked to HR program results when specific issues on the survey relate to the program. For example, when a new pay plan was implemented for all employees at a television station, the annual attitude survey contained five questions directly tied to perceptions and attitudes influenced by the new plan.

Because attitude surveys are usually taken annually, the results may not be in sync with the timing of the program implementation. When job satisfaction is one of the program objectives, some organizations conduct surveys at a prescribed time frame after the HR program is implemented and design the survey instrument around issues related to the HR program. This approach, however, can be expensive.

Organizational Commitment

Measuring organizational commitment is perhaps a more important method for understanding the motivational state of employees. Similar to attitude surveys, organizational commitment instruments reflect the degree to which employees align with company goals, values, philosophy, and practices. High levels of organizational commitment often correlate with high levels of productivity and performance; therefore, organizational commitment is an important intangible measure. Changes in survey data may reflect the success of the HR program in improving organizational commitment. The difficulty with this intangible measure is that it is not routinely measured in organizations.

Climate Survey Data

Some organizations conduct climate surveys, which reflect work climate changes such as variances in communication, openness, trust, and quality of feedback. Climate surveys are similar to attitude surveys but are more general and often focus on a range of workplace issues and environmental enablers and inhibitors. Climate surveys conducted before and after the implementation of an HR program may reflect the extent to which the HR program changes these intangible measures.

Employee Complaints

Some organizations record and report specific employee complaints. A reduction of employee complaints sometimes directly relates to HR programs, such as a team-building program. Consequently, the level of complaints is used as a measure of the program's success and is sometimes reported as an intangible measure.

Grievances

In both union and non-union organizations, grievances often reflect the level of dissatisfaction or disenchantment with a variety of factors in the organization. Sometimes, HR programs, such as labor management cooperation, are designed to reduce an excessive number of grievances. An improvement in the grievance level reflects the success of the HR program. This measure may be converted to a monetary value; however, it also may be reported as an intangible measure.

Discrimination Complaints

Employee dissatisfaction shows up in different types of discrimination complaints, ranging from informal complaints to external charges and even litigation. New HR policies and programs may be designed to prevent complaints or to reduce the current level of complaint activity. The result of the policies and programs, in terms of complaint reduction, sometimes is not converted to monetary values because of the various assumptions and estimations involved in the process. When this is the case, these measures are reported as intangible program benefits.

Stress Reduction

Occasionally, HR programs reduce work-related stress by showing participants how to improve the way they accomplish their jobs, accomplish more in a workday, and relieve tension and anxiety. The subsequent reduction in stress may be directly linked to the HR program.

EMPLOYEE WITHDRAWAL

When job satisfaction deteriorates to the point at which employees withdraw from work or the organization, either permanently or temporarily, disaster can result. Several employee withdrawal measures are monitored and are often linked to performance improvement programs. Additional information about employee withdrawal measures outlined in this section can be found in other resources, including *Accountability in Human Resource Management* by Jack J. Phillips [3].

Employee Turnover

Perhaps the most critical employee withdrawal variable is employee turnover. An extremely costly variable, turnover can have devastating consequences on organizations when it is excessive. Redesign of employee benefits, addition of new benefits, and many supervisor and team leader programs are designed to reduce employee turnover. In many situations, turnover is actually converted to monetary values, using one of the methods described in Chapter 6. However, because of the multitude of costs and assumptions involved in developing the value, some organizations prefer not to convert turnover to a monetary value. When this is the case, turnover should be reported as an intangible benefit, reflecting the success of the HR initiatives.

Employee Absenteeism

Absenteeism is another disruptive and costly variable. Many HR programs are designed to reduce absenteeism, and the impact of HR programs on absenteeism can usually be pinpointed by an evaluation impact study. Although the cost of absenteeism can be developed, sometimes the conversion process does not hold enough credibility for some audiences, and consequently, absenteeism changes are reported as intangible benefits.

Employee Tardiness

Many organizations actually monitor tardiness, especially with the use of electronic and computerized time reporting. Tardiness, an irritating work habit problem, can cause inefficiencies and delays. A few HR programs are designed to reduce it. Tardiness is very difficult to convert to a monetary value. Consequently, when tardiness is presented as an improvement influenced by an HR program, it is listed as an intangible benefit.

Employee Transfers

A unique way for employees to withdraw is to request a transfer to another section, department, or division of the organization. Requests for transfers often reflect dissatisfaction with a variety of issues, including management, policies, and practices in the organization. HR programs are sometimes designed to reduce or remove the unpleasant environmental influences that cause dissatisfaction. In these situations, requests for transfers are monitored and reported as an intangible benefit of an HR program. Usually no attempt is made to assign monetary values to transfers.

CUSTOMER SERVICE

Because of the importance of building and improving customer service, a variety of measures are often monitored and reported as a payoff of HR programs. Customer-service programs can directly influence these measures. Because of the difficulty of placing values on them, customer service measures are not usually converted to monetary values and are reported as intangible benefits. This section describes several measures.

Customer Satisfaction Survey Data

One of the most important measures is actual survey data showing the degree to which customers are pleased with the products and services. These survey values, reported as absolute data or as an index, represent important data against which to measure the success of customer service programs. Although techniques are available to convert survey data to monetary values in most situations, the conversion is rarely attempted. Consequently, customer service improvements are usually reported as intangible benefits.

Customer Complaints

Most organizations monitor customer complaints. Each complaint is recorded along with the disposition and the time required to resolve the complaint, as well as specific costs associated with the complaint resolution. Organizations sometimes design programs to reduce the number of customer complaints. Because assigning an accurate monetary value to a customer complaint is difficult, the measure usually becomes a very important intangible benefit.

Customer Response Time

Providing prompt customer service is a critical issue in most organizations. Consequently, the time it takes to respond to specific customer service requests or problems is recorded and monitored. Response time reduction is sometimes an objective of HR programs; however, the reduction is not usually converted to monetary values. Thus, customer response time becomes an important intangible benefit.

Other Customer Responses

A variety of other types of customer responses can be tracked, such as creativity of customer response, responsiveness to cost and pricing issues, customer loyalty, and other important issues customers may specify or require. Monitoring these variables can provide more evidence of the HR program's results when the program influences particular variables. And because of the difficulty of assigning values to the items, they are usually reported as intangible measures.

TEAM EFFECTIVENESS MEASURES

A variety of measures are often monitored to reflect how well teams work. Although the output of teams and the quality of their work are often measured as hard data and converted to monetary values, other interpersonal measures may be monitored and reported separately. This section represents a few of these measures.

Teamwork

Sometimes organizations survey team members before and after a program to see if the level of teamwork increases as a result of the program. The monetary value of increased teamwork is rarely developed, and consequently, it is reported as an intangible benefit.

Cooperation

The success of a team often depends on the cooperative spirit of team members. Some instruments measure the level of cooperation before and after team structures are implemented. Because of the difficulty of converting this measure to a monetary value, it is always reported as an intangible benefit.

Conflict

In team environments, the level of conflict is often measured. A reduction in conflict may reflect the success of the introduction of teams into the workplace. In most situations, a monetary value is not placed on conflict reduction, and it is reported as an intangible benefit.

Decisiveness

Teams make decisions, and the timing of the decision-making process often becomes an issue. Consequently, decisiveness is sometimes measured in terms of the speed at which decisions are made. Survey measures may reflect the team's perception or, in some cases, may monitor how quickly decisions are made. Some programs are expected to influence the decision-making process, and improvements are usually reported as intangible benefits.

Communication

A variety of communication instruments reflect the quality and quantity of communication within a team. Changes in communication skills, or perceptions of skills, driven by an HR program are not usually converted to monetary values and are reported as an intangible benefit.

Other Team Measures

Although the previously listed measures are common, many other potential measures are available to reflect the performance and functioning of teams. Table 9-1 shows a report of the intangible measures after an organization had undertaken a team-building

Table 9-1

A Sample of Intangible Measures of Team Effectiveness

Item	# of Responses	Point Range	Total Points	Point Average	Rank (By Average)
Clearly states mission/goals	7	4-6	34	4.9	4
Operates creatively	7	3-7	37	5.3	2
Focuses on results	7	4-5	31	4.3	6
Clarifies roles and responsibilities	7	2-6	34	4.9	4
Is well organized	7	4-6	36	5.1	3
Builds upon individual strengths	7	5-7	41	5.9	1
Supports leadership/each other	7	4-6	37	5.3	2
Develops team climate	5	3-5	21	4.2	7
Resolves disagreements	6	2-5	20	3.3	9
Communicates openly	7	2-4	21	3.0	10
Makes objective decisions	7	3-6	33	4.7	5
Evaluates its own effectiveness	7	2-4	24	3.4	8

Source: Bader, G. E., Bloom, A. E., and Chang, R. Y. Measuring Team Performance. Irvine, Calif.: Richard Chang Associates, 1994.

program. These measures, obtained as part of a survey process, show the possibilities for reflecting team success.

CONCLUSION

A variety of available intangible measures reflect the success of HR programs. Although they may not be perceived to be as valuable as specific monetary measures, they are an important part of an overall evaluation. Intangible measures should be identified, explored, examined, and monitored for changes when they are linked to the HR program. Collectively, they add an interesting dimension to the overall program results, because most, if not all, programs have unique intangible measures associated with them. Although this chapter covered some of the most common intangibles, the coverage was not meant to be complete. The number of intangible measures has almost no limit.

REFERENCES

1. Denzin, N. K., and Lincoln, Y. S. (Eds.) *Handbook of Qualitative Research*. Thousand Oaks, Calif.: Sage Publications, 1994.
2. Gummesson, E. *Qualitative Methods and Management Research* (rev. ed.). Thousand Oaks, Calif.: Sage Publications, 1991.
3. Phillips, Jack J. *Accountability in Human Resource Management*. Houston: Gulf Publishing, 1996.
4. Bader, G. E., Bloom, A. E., and Chang, R. Y. *Measuring Team Performance*. Irvine, Calif.: Richard Chang Associates, 1994.

CHAPTER 10

Communicating Results

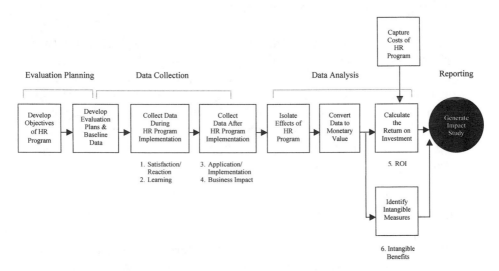

With data in hand, what's next? Should the data be used to modify the program, change the process, show the contribution, justify new programs, gain additional support, or build goodwill? How should the data be presented? The worst course of action is to do nothing. Communicating results is as important as achieving results. Achieving results without communicating them is like planting seeds and failing to fertilize and cultivate the seedlings—the yield simply won't be as great. This chapter provides useful information to help present evaluation data to the various audiences using both oral and written reporting methods.

WHY BE CONCERNED ABOUT COMMUNICATING RESULTS?

Communicating results is a critical issue in HR programs. While it is important to communicate achieved results to interested stakeholders once the initiative is complete, it is also important to communicate throughout the process. Constant communication ensures that information is flowing so adjustments can be made and so that all stakeholders are aware of the success and issues surrounding the program. There are at least five key reasons for being concerned about communication in an HR program.

Measurement and Evaluation Mean Nothing Without Communication

As Mark Twain once said, "Collecting data is like collecting garbage—pretty soon we will have to do something with it." If success is measured and evaluation data are collected, they mean nothing unless the findings are communicated promptly to the appropriate audiences so they will be aware of what is occurring and can take action if necessary. Communication allows a full loop to be made from the program results to necessary actions based on those results.

Communication Is Necessary to Make Improvements

Because information is collected at different points during the process, the communication or feedback to the various groups that will take action is the only way adjustments can be made. Thus, the quality and timeliness of communication become critical issues for making necessary adjustments or improvements. Even after the program is completed, communication is necessary to make sure the target audience fully understands the results achieved and how the results could either be enhanced in future programs or in the current program, if it is still operational. Communication is the key to making these important adjustments at all phases of the program.

Communication Is Necessary to Explain Contributions

The contribution of the HR program surrounding the six major types of measures is a confusing issue at best. The different target audiences will need a thorough explanation of the results. A communication strategy including techniques, media, and the overall process will determine the extent to which they understand the contribution. Communicating results, particularly with business impact and ROI, can quickly become confusing for even the most sophisticated target audiences. Communication must be planned and implemented with the goal of making sure the audiences understand the full contribution.

Communication Is a Sensitive Issue

Communication is one of those important issues that can cause major problems. Because the results of an initiative can be closely linked to the political issues in an organization, communication can upset some individuals while pleasing others. If certain individuals do not receive the information or it is delivered inconsistently from one group to another, problems can quickly surface. Not only is it an understanding issue, it is also a fairness, quality, and political correctness issue to make sure communication is properly constructed and effectively delivered to all key individuals who need the information.

A Variety of Target Audiences Need Different Information

Because there are so many potential target audiences for receiving communication about the success of an HR initiative, it is important for the communication to be tailored directly to their needs. A varied audience will command varied needs. Planning and effort are necessary to make sure the audience receives all of the information it needs, in the proper format, and at the proper time. A single report for all audiences may not be appropriate. The scope, size, media, and even the actual information of different types and different levels will vary significantly from one group to another, making the target audience the key to determining the appropriate communication process.

Collectively, these reasons make communication a critical issue, although it is often overlooked or underestimated in HR programs. This chapter builds on this important issue and shows a variety of techniques for accomplishing all types of communication for various target audiences.

PRINCIPLES OF COMMUNICATING RESULTS

The skills required to communicate results effectively are almost as delicate and sophisticated as those needed to obtain results. The style is as important as the substance. Regardless of the message, audience, or medium, a few general principles apply and are explored next.

Communication Must Be Timely

Usually, HR results should be communicated as soon as they are known. From a practical standpoint, it may be best to delay the communication until a convenient time, such as the publication of the next client newsletter or the next general management meeting. Questions about timing must be answered. Is the audience ready for the results in light of other things that may have happened? Is it expecting results? When is the best time for having the maximum effect on the audience? Are there circumstances that dictate a change in the timing of the communication?

Communication Should Be Targeted to Specific Audiences

Communication will be more effective if it is designed for a particular group. The message should be specifically tailored to the interests, needs, and expectations of the target audience.

The results of an HR program are used in this chapter and reflect outcomes at all levels, including the six types of data developed in this book. Some of the data are developed earlier in the program and communicated during the program. Other data are collected after the program's implementation and communicated in a follow-up study. Thus, the results, in their broadest sense, may involve early feedback in qualitative terms to ROI values in varying quantitative terms.

Media Should Be Carefully Selected

For particular groups, some media may be more effective than others. Face-to-face meetings may be better than special bulletins. A memo distributed exclusively to top management may be more effective than the company newsletter. The proper method of communication can help improve the effectiveness of the process.

Communication Should Be Unbiased and Modest

It is important to separate fact from fiction and accurate statements from opinions. Various audiences may accept communication from HR staff members with skepticism, anticipating biased opinions. Boastful statements sometimes turn off recipients, and most of the content is lost. Observable, believable facts carry far more weight than extreme or sensational claims. Although such claims may get audience attention, they often detract from the importance of the results.

Communication Must Be Consistent

The timing and content of the communication should be consistent with past practices. A special communication at an unusual time during the HR initiative may provoke suspicion. Also, if a particular group, such as top management, regularly receives communication on HR outcomes, it should continue receiving communication—even if the results are not positive. If some results are omitted, it might leave the impression that only positive results are reported.

Testimonials Are More Effective Coming from Individuals the Audience Respects

Opinions are strongly influenced by others, particularly those who are respected and trusted. Testimonials about HR results, when solicited from individuals respected by others in the organization, can influence the effectiveness of the message. This respect may be related to leadership ability, position, special skills, or knowledge. A testimonial from an individual who commands little respect and is regarded as a substandard performer can have a negative impact on the message.

The Audience's Opinion of the HR Department Will Influence the Communication Strategy

Opinions are difficult to change, and a negative opinion of the HR staff members may not change with the mere presentation of facts. However, the presentation of facts alone may strengthen the opinions held by those who already agree with the HR results. It helps reinforce their position and provides a defense in discussions with others. An HR department with a high level of credibility and respect may have a relatively easy time communicating results. Low credibility can create problems when trying to be persuasive. The reputation of the department's credibility is an important consideration in developing the overall strategy.

These general principles are important to the overall success of the communication effort. They should serve as a checklist for the HR team when disseminating program results.

A MODEL FOR COMMUNICATING RESULTS

The process of communicating program results must be systematic, timely, and well-planned, as illustrated in the model in Figure 10-1. The model represents seven components of the communication process that should normally occur in the sequence shown.

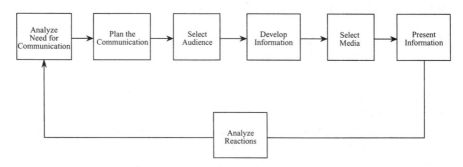

Figure 10-1.

The first step is one of the most important and consists of an analysis of the need to communicate results from an HR program. Possibly, a lack of support for the HR effort was identified, and perhaps the need for making changes to or continuing to fund the program was uncovered. There may be a need to restore confidence or build credibility for the HR program. Regardless of the triggering events, an important first step is to outline the specific reasons for communicating the results of the program.

The second step focuses on a plan for communication. Planning is very important and usually involves three types of plans rather than an overall plan for communicating results in all types of HR programs. The first plan includes numerous issues to be addressed in all communication about the program. The second plan covers the communication around the program, detailing exactly what will be communicated, when, and to which groups. The third plan covers communicating specific types of data, such as the results at the end in terms of an impact study.

The third step involves selecting the target audiences for communication. Audiences range from top management to past participants, all of which have their own special communication needs. All groups should be considered in the communication strategy. An artfully crafted, targeted communication may be necessary to win the approval of a specific group.

The fourth step involves developing written material to explain program results. This can include a wide variety of possibilities, from a brief summary of the results to a detailed research report on the evaluation effort. Usually, a complete report is developed, and then selected parts or summaries from the report are used for different media.

Selecting the medium is the fifth step. Some groups respond more favorably to certain methods of communication. A variety of approaches, both oral and written, are available to the HR professional.

Information is presented in the sixth step. The product is delivered with the utmost care, confidence, and professionalism.

The last step, but not the least significant, is analyzing reactions to the communications. Positive reactions, negative reactions, and a lack of comments are all indicators of how well the information was received and understood. An informational but unscientific analysis may be appropriate for many situations. Tuning in to the reaction of a specific group may often suffice. For an extensive and more involved communication effort, a formal and structured feedback process may be necessary. Reactions could trigger an adjustment to the communication of the same program results or provide input to make adjustments for future program communications.

This communications model is not intended to make the process complicated. Rather, it is a process to ensure clear, accurate information is provided to the appropriate audiences. More than one audience usually receives the results of an HR initiative, and each audience has its own unique needs. Each of the components in the model should be given consideration, if only informally, before the communications strategy is developed. Otherwise, the full impact of the effort may be diminished. The various steps in the model are amplified in the remainder of this chapter.

Analyzing the Need for Communication

Because there may be other reasons for communicating results, a list should be tailored to the organization and adjusted as necessary. The reasons for communicating HR results depend on the specific program, the setting, and the unique needs. The most common reasons are:

☐ *To secure approval for the HR program and allocate resources of time and money.* The initial communication presents a proposal, projected ROI, or other data intended to secure the program approval. This communication may not have much data but rather anticipates what is to come.

☐ *To gain support for the initiative and its objectives.* It is important to have support from a variety of groups. This communication is intended to build the necessary support to make the initiative work successfully.

☐ *To secure agreement on the issues, solutions, and resources.* As the program begins, it is important for all those directly involved to have some agreement and understanding of the important elements and requirements surrounding the program.

☐ To *build credibility for the HR department, its techniques, and the finished products.* It is important early in the process to make sure that those involved understand the approach and reputation of the HR department, and, based on the approach taken, the commitments made by all parties.

☐ To *reinforce the processes used in the HR initiative.* It is important for key managers to support the initiative and reinforce the various processes used in the HR program. This communication is designed to enhance those processes.

☐ To *drive action for improvement in the HR program.* This early communication is designed as a process improvement tool to effect changes and improvements as the needs are uncovered and suggestions are made by various individuals.

☐ To *prepare participants for the HR program.* It is necessary for those most directly involved in the program, the participants, to be prepared for assignments, roles, and responsibilities that will be required of them as they bring success to the initiative.

☐ To *enhance results throughout the initiative and the quality of future feedback.* This communication is designed to show the status of the program and to influence decisions, seek support, or communicate events and expectations to the key stakeholders. In addition, it will enhance both the quality and quantity of information as stakeholders see the feedback cycle in action.

☐ To *show the complete results of the HR initiative.* This is perhaps the most important communication, where all of the results involving all six types of measures are communicated to the appropriate individuals so they have a full understanding of the success or shortcomings of the program.

☐ To *underscore the importance of measuring results.* Some individuals need to understand the importance of measurement and evaluation and see the need for having important data on different measures.

☐ To *explain techniques used to measure results.* Several individuals on the client team and support staff need to understand the techniques used in measuring results. In some cases, these techniques may be transferred internally to use with other programs. In short, these individuals need to understand the soundness and theoretical framework of the process used.

☐ *To stimulate desire in participants to be involved in the program.* Ideally, HR participants want to be involved in the initiative. This communication is designed to pique their interest in the program, the assignment, and their importance to the program.

☐ *To stimulate interest in the HR department's products.* From an HR department perspective, some communications are designed to create interest in all of the products and services based on the results obtained by the current product or process.

☐ *To demonstrate accountability for client expenditures.* It is important for a broad group to understand the need for accountability and the approach of the HR department or staff members. This ensures accountability for expenditures on the program.

☐ *To market future HR initiatives.* From an HR department perspective, it is important to build a database of successful programs to use in convincing others that the HR process can add value.

Because there may be other reasons for communicating results, the list should be tailored to the individual organization.

Planning the Communication

Any type of successful activity must be carefully planned for it to produce the maximum results. This is a critical part of communicating the results of HR initiatives. The actual planning of the communications is important to ensure that each audience receives the proper information at the right time and that appropriate actions are taken. Three separate issues are important in planning the communication of results, as presented next.

Communication Policy Issues. In examining the complete HR process, policy issues need to be developed around the communication of results. These range from providing feedback during an initiative to communicating the ROI from an impact study. Policy issues rest with both the client and the HR department. Internally, the client group may want to develop the policy around communication results as part of an overall policy on HR initiatives. From the HR department standpoint, the policy may be developed as part of the overall results-based approach to HR initiatives. Seven different areas will need some attention as the policies are developed:

1. **What will actually be communicated?** It is important to detail the types of information communicated throughout the HR program—not only the six types of data from the ROI process model but the overall progress with HR may be a topic of communication as well.
2. **When will the data be communicated?** With communications, timing is critical. If adjustments in the program need to be made, the information should be communicated quickly so that swift actions can be taken.
3. **How will the information be communicated?** This shows the preferences toward particular types of communication media. For example, some organizations prefer to have written documents sent out as reports, while others prefer face-to-face-meetings, and still others want electronic communications used as much as possible.
4. **The location for communication.** Some prefer that the communication take place close to the HR program, others prefer client offices, and still others prefer the HR department's facilities. The location can be an important issue in terms of convenience and perception.
5. **Who will communicate the information?** Will the HR group, an independent person, or an individual involved on the client team communicate the information? The person communicating must have credibility so that the information is believable.
6. **The target audience.** Identify specific target audiences that should always receive information and others that will receive information when appropriate.

7. **The specific actions that are required or desired.** When information is presented, in some cases no action is needed; in others, changes are desired and sometimes even required.

Collectively these seven issues frame the policy around communication as a whole.

Planning the Communication Around the Entire Program. When a program is approved, the communication plan is usually developed. This details how specific information is developed and communicated to various groups and the expected actions. In addition, this plan details how the overall results will be communicated, the time frames for communication, and the appropriate groups to receive information. The client and HR department need to agree on the extent of detail in the plan.

Communicating an Impact Study. The third issue is a plan aimed at presenting the results of an impact study. This occurs when a major HR initiative is completed and the overall, detailed results are known. One of the major issues is who should receive the results and in what form. This is more specialized than the plan for the entire program because it involves the final study from the program. Table 10-1 shows the communication plan for a major team-based HR initiative that had a stress-reduction solution. Teams were experiencing high levels of stress and, through a variety of activities and job changes, stress began to diminish among the teams. The same process was made available to other teams who were experiencing similar symptoms.

Five different communication pieces were developed for different audiences. The complete report was an ROI impact study, a seventy-five-page report that served as the historical document for the program. It went to the client, the HR staff and the particular manager of each of the teams involved in the studies. An executive summary, a much smaller document, went to some of the higher-level executives. A general interest overview and summary without the ROI calculation went to the participants. A general-interest article was developed for company publications, and a brochure was developed to show the success of the HR

Table 10-1
HR Program Communication Plan

Communication Document	Communication Target(s)	Distribution Method
Complete Report with Appendices (75 pages)	☐ Client Team ☐ HR Staff ☐ Intact Team Manager	Distribute and Discuss in a Special Meeting
Executive Summary (8 pages)	☐ Senior Management in the Business Units ☐ Senior Corporate Management	Distribute and Discuss in a Routine Meeting
General Interest Overview and Summary without the Actual ROI Calculation (10 pages)	☐ Participants	Mail with Letter
General Interest Article (1 page)	☐ All Employees	Publish in Company Publication
Brochure Highlighting Program, Objectives, and Specific Results	☐ Team Leaders with an Interest in the Project ☐ Other Clients	Include with Other Marketing Materials

program. That brochure was used in marketing the same process internally to other teams and served as additional marketing material for the HR department. This detailed plan may be part of the overall plan for the HR program but may be fine-tuned during the actual process.

Collectively, these three types of plans underscore the importance of organizing the communication strategy for a particular HR initiative or the overall HR process in an organization.

Selecting the Audience for Communications

When approaching a particular audience, the following questions should be asked about each potential group:

- ☐ Are they interested in the initiative?
- ☐ Do they really want to receive the information?
- ☐ Has someone already made a commitment to them regarding communication?
- ☐ Is the timing right for this audience?
- ☐ Are they familiar with the initiative?
- ☐ How do they prefer to have results communicated?
- ☐ Do they know the HR staff members?
- ☐ Are they likely to find the results threatening?
- ☐ Which medium will be most convincing to this group?

For each target audience, three actions are needed:

1. To the greatest extent possible, the HR staff should know and understand the target audience.
2. The HR staff should find out what information is needed and why. Each group will have its own needs relative to the information desired. Some want detailed information while others want brief information. Rely on the input from others to determine audience needs.
3. The HR staff should try to understand audience bias. Each will have a particular bias or opinion. Some will quickly support the results, whereas others may be against them or be neutral. The staff should be empathetic and try to understand differing views. With this understanding, communi-

cations can be tailored to each group. This is especially critical when the potential exists for the audience to react negatively to the results.

The potential target audiences to receive information about HR results are varied in terms of job levels and responsibilities. Determining which groups will receive a particular communication piece deserves careful thought, as problems can arise when a particular group receives inappropriate information or when another is omitted altogether. A sound basis for proper audience selection is to analyze the reason for communication, as discussed in an earlier section. Table 10-2 shows common target audiences and the basis for selecting the audience.

Perhaps the most important audience is the client or client team. This group (or individual) initiates the program, reviews data, selects the HR team, and weighs the final assessment of the effectiveness of the program. Another important target audience is the top management group. This group is responsible for allocating resources to the HR initiative and needs information to help justify expenditures and gauge the effectiveness of the efforts.

Selected groups of managers (or all managers) are also important target audiences. Management's support and involvement in the HR process and the department's credibility are important to success. Effectively communicating program results to management can increase both support and credibility.

Communicating with the participants' team leaders or immediate managers is essential. In many cases, they must encourage participants to implement the program. Also, they often support and reinforce the objectives of the program. An appropriate return on investment improves the commitment to HR interventions and provides credibility for the HR staff.

Occasionally, results are communicated to encourage participation in the program. This is especially true for those programs offered on a volunteer basis. The potential participants are important targets for communicating results.

HR program participants need feedback on the overall success of the effort. Some individuals may not have been as successful as others in achieving the desired results. Communicating the

Table 10-2
Common Target Audiences

Reason for Communication	Primary Target Audiences
To Secure Approval for the Initiative	Client, Top Executives
To Gain Support for the Initiative	Immediate Managers, Team Leaders
To Secure Agreement with the Issues	Participants, Team Leaders
To Build Credibility for the HR Department	Top Executives
To Enhance Reinforcement of the Processes	Immediate Managers
To Drive Action for Improvement	HR Staff Members
To Prepare Participants for the Program	Team Leaders
To Enhance Results and Quality of Future Feedback	Participants
To Show the Complete Results of the Initiative	Client Team
To Underscore the Importance of Measuring Results	Client, HR Staff Members
To Explain Techniques Used to Measure Results	Client, Support Staff
To Create Desire for a Participant to Be Involved	Team Leaders
To Stimulate Interest in the HR Department's Products	Top Executives
To Demonstrate Accountability for Client Expenditures	All Employees
To Market Future HR Programs	Prospective Clients

results adds additional pressure to effectively implement the program and improve results for the future. For those achieving excellent results, the communication will serve as a reinforcement of the HR initiative. Communicating results to program participants is often overlooked, with the assumption that since the program is over, they do not need to be informed of its success.

The HR staff must receive information about program results. Whether for small programs where staff members receive a program update, or for larger programs where a complete team is involved, those who design, develop, facilitate, and implement the program must be given information about its effectiveness. Evaluation information is necessary so adjustments can be made if the program is not as effective as it could be.

The support staff should receive detailed information about the process to measure results. This group provides support services to the HR team, usually in the department where the program is conducted.

Company employees and stockholders may be less likely targets. General-interest news stories may increase employee respect. Goodwill and positive attitudes toward the organization may also be byproducts of communicating program results. Stockholders, on the other hand, are more interested in the return on their investment.

While Table 10-2 shows the most common target audiences, there can be others in a particular organization. For instance, management or employees can be subdivided into different departments, divisions, or even subsidiaries of the organization. The number of audiences can be large in a complex organization. At a minimum, four target audiences are always recommended: a senior management group, the participants' immediate manager or team leader, the program participants, and the HR staff.

Developing the Information: The Impact Study

The type of formal evaluation report depends on the extent of detailed information presented to the various target audiences. Brief summaries of program results with appropriate charts may be sufficient for some communication efforts. In other situations, particularly with significant HR interventions requiring extensive funding, the amount of detail in the evaluation report is more crucial. A complete and comprehensive impact study report may be necessary. This report can then be used as the basis of information for specific audiences and various media. The report may contain the following sections.

Management/Executive Summary. The management summary is a brief overview of the entire report, explaining the basis for the evaluation and the significant conclusions and recommendations. It is designed for individuals who are too busy to read a detailed report. It is usually written last but appears first in the report for easy access.

Background Information. The background information provides a general description of the program. If applicable, the needs assessment that led to the implementation of the program is summarized. The solution is fully described, including the events that led to the HR initiative. Other specific items necessary to provide a full description of the program are included. The extent of detailed information depends on the amount of information the audience needs.

Objectives. The objectives for both the program and the actual solutions are outlined. Sometimes they are the same but may be separate. The report details the particular objectives of the study itself so that the reader clearly understands desired accomplishments for the program or initiative. In addition, if there were specific HR solutions implemented during this process, they are detailed here, as these are the issues or objectives from which the different types or levels of data will be collected.

Evaluation Strategy/Methodology. The evaluation strategy outlines all the components that make up the total evaluation process. Several components of the results-based model and the ROI process presented in this book are discussed in this section of the report. The specific purposes of evaluation are outlined, and the evaluation design and methodology are explained. The instruments used in data collection are also described and presented as exhibits. Any unusual issues in the evaluation design are discussed. Finally, other useful information related to the design, timing, and execution of the evaluation is included.

Data Collection and Analysis. This section explains the methods used to collect data, as outlined in Chapters 3 and 4. The data collected are usually presented in the report in summary form. Next, the methods used to analyze data are presented with interpretations.

Program Costs. Program costs are presented in this section. A summary of the costs by category is included. For example, analysis, development, implementation, and evaluation costs are recommended categories for cost presentation. The assumptions made in developing and classifying costs are discussed in this section of the report.

Reaction and Satisfaction. This section details the data collected from key stakeholders, particularly the participants involved in the process, to measure the reaction to the HR program and a level of satisfaction with various issues and parts of the process. Other input from the client group is also included to show the level of satisfaction.

Learning. This section shows a brief summary of the formal and informal methods for measuring learning. It explains how participants have learned new processes, skills, tasks, procedures, and practices from the HR program.

Application and Implementation. This section shows how the program was actually implemented and the success with the application of new skills and knowledge. Implementation issues are addressed, including any major success and/or lack of success.

Business Impact. This section shows the actual business impact measures representing the business needs that initially drove the program. This shows the extent to which performance has changed during the implementation of the HR initiative.

Return on Investment. This section actually shows the ROI calculation along with the benefits/cost ratio. It compares the value with what was expected and provides an interpretation of the actual calculation.

Intangible Measures. This section shows the various intangible measures directly linked to the HR initiative. Intangibles are those measures not converted to monetary values or included in the actual ROI calculation.

Barriers and Enablers. The various problems and obstacles affecting the success of the program are detailed and presented as barriers to implementation. Also, those factors or influences that had a positive effect on the program are included as enablers. Together, they provide tremendous insight into what can hinder or enhance programs in the future.

Conclusions and Recommendations. This section presents conclusions based on all the results. If appropriate, brief explanations are presented on how each conclusion was reached. A list of recommendations or changes in the program, if appropriate, is provided with brief explanations for each recommendation. It is important that the conclusions and recommendations are consistent with one another and with the findings described in the previous section.

These components make up the major parts of a complete evaluation report.

Developing the Report. Table 10-3 shows the table of contents from a typical evaluation report for an ROI evaluation. This specific study was conducted for a large financial institution and involved an ROI analysis on an HR program for commercial banking. The typical report provides background information, explains the processes used and, most importantly, presents the results.

While this report is an effective, professional way to present ROI data, several cautions need to be followed. Because this document reports the success of an HR initiative involving a group of employees, complete credit for the success must go to the participants and their immediate leaders. Their performance generated the success. Another important caution is to avoid boasting about results. Although the ROI process may be accurate and credible, it still may have some subjective issues. Huge claims of success can quickly turn off an audience and interfere with the delivery of the desired message.

Table 10-3
Format of an Impact Study Report

☐ General Information
  • Background
  • Objectives of Study
☐ Methodology for Impact Study
  • Levels of Evaluation
  • ROI Process
  • Collecting Data
  • Isolating the Effects of HR
  • Converting Data to Monetary Values
☐ Data Analysis Issues
☐ Costs
☐ Results: General Information
  • Response Profile
  • Success with Objectives
☐ Results: Reaction and Satisfaction
  • Data Sources
  • Data Summary
  • Key Issues
☐ Results: Learning
  • Data Sources
  • Data Summary
  • Key Issues
☐ Results: Application and Implementation
  • Data Sources
  • Data Summary
  • Key Issues
☐ Results: Business Impact
  • General Comments
  • Linkage with Business Measures
  • Key Issues
☐ Results: ROI and Its Meaning
☐ Results: Intangible Measures
☐ Barriers and Enablers
  • Barriers
  • Enablers
☐ Conclusions and Recommendations
  • Conclusions
  • Recommendations
☐ Exhibits

A final caution concerns the structure of the report. The methodology should be clearly explained, along with assumptions made in the analysis. The reader should readily see how the values were developed and how the specific steps were followed to make the process more conservative, credible, and accurate. Detailed statistical analyses should be placed in the appendix.

Selecting the Communication Media

There are many options available to communicate program results. In addition to the impact study report, the most frequently used media are meetings, interim and progress reports, the organization's publications, and case studies.

Meetings. Meetings are fertile opportunities for communicating program results, if used properly. All organizations have a variety of meetings and, in each, the proper context and HR results are an important part. A few examples illustrate the variety of meetings.

Staff Meetings. Throughout the chain of command, staff meetings are held to review progress, discuss current problems, and distribute information. These meetings can be an excellent forum for discussing the results achieved in an HR initiative when it relates to the group's activities. Program results can be sent to executives for use in staff meetings, or a member of the HR team can attend the meeting to make the presentation.

Manager Meetings. Regular meetings with the first-level management group are quite common. Typically, items are discussed that will possibly help their work units. A discussion of an HR program and the subsequent results can be integrated into the regular meeting format.

Panel Discussions. Although not common in all organizations, panel discussions can be very helpful in showing how a problem was solved. A typical panel might include two or more managers or team leaders discussing their approach to a solution of a problem common to other areas. A successful discussion based on the results of a recent program can provide convincing data to other managers.

Best Practices Meetings. Some organizations have best practices meetings or video conferences to discuss recent successes and best practices. This is an excellent opportunity to learn and share methodologies and results.

Business Update Meetings. A few organizations have initiated a periodic meeting for all members of management, in which the CEO reviews progress and discusses plans for the coming year. A few highlights of HR program results can be integrated into the CEO's speech, showing top executive interest, commitment, and support. HR results are mentioned along with operating profit, new facilities and equipment, new company acquisitions, and next year's sales forecast.

Whenever a management group convenes in significant numbers, evaluate the appropriateness of communicating HR program results.

Interim and Progress Reports. Although usually limited to large-scale initiatives, a highly visible way to communicate results is through interim and routine memos and reports. Published or disseminated via computer intranet on a periodic basis, they usually have several purposes:

☐ To inform management about the status of the program
☐ To communicate the interim results achieved in the HR initiative
☐ To activate needed changes and improvements

A more subtle reason for the report is to gain additional support and commitment from the management group and to keep the program intact. This report is produced by the HR staff and distributed to a select group of managers in the organization. Format and scope vary considerably. Common topics are presented here.

Schedule of Activities. A schedule of planned steps/activities should be an integral part of this report. A brief description should be presented.

Reactions from Program Participants. A brief summary of reaction evaluations may be appropriate to report initial success. Also, brief interviews with participants might be included.

Program Results. A key focus of this report is the results achieved from the HR program. Significant results that can be documented should be presented in an easily understood format. The method(s) of evaluation should be briefly outlined, along with the measurement data.

Support Team Member Spotlight. A section that features a key support team member can be very useful. Emphasis is placed on the member's efforts and involvement in HR activity. Statements or interview comments may be useful.

Change in Responsibility. Occasionally, people involved in planning, developing, implementing, or evaluating the program are reassigned, transferred, or promoted. It is important to communicate how these changes affect responsibilities and the program.

Participant Spotlight. A section that highlights a member of the client team can focus additional attention on results. This is an opportunity to recognize outstanding participants responsible for excellent results with the program and bring attention to unusual achievements.

   While the previous list may not be suited for every report, it represents topics that should be presented to the management group. When produced in a professional manner, the report can improve management support and commitment to the effort.

The Organization's Publications and Standard Communication Tools. To reach a wide audience, the HR department can use in-house publications. Whether a newsletter, magazine, newspaper, or electronic file, these types of media usually reach all employees. The information can be quite effective if communicated appropriately. The scope should be limited to general interest articles, announcements, and interviews. Following are types of issues that should be covered in these publications.

Program Results. Results communicated through these types of media must be significant enough to arouse general interest. For example, a story with the headline, "Safety program helps produce one million hours without a lost-time accident," will catch the attention of many people because they may have participated in the program and can appreciate the significance of the results. Reports on the accomplishments of a group of participants may not create interest unless the audience relates to the accomplishments.

For many HR initiatives, results are achieved weeks or even months after the program is completed. Participants need reinforcement from many sources. If results are communicated to a general audience, including the participant's subordinates or peers, there is additional pressure to continue the program or similar ones in the future.

Building Interest. Stories about participants involved in an HR initiative and the results they achieve create a favorable image. Employees are made aware that the company is investing time and money to improve performance and prepare for the future. This type of story provides information about programs that employees otherwise may not have known about and sometimes creates a desire to participate if given the opportunity.

Participant Recognition. General audience communication can bring recognition to program participants, particularly those who excel in some aspect of the program. When participants deliver unusual performance, public recognition can enhance their self-esteem.

Human Interest Stories. Many human interest stories can come out of HR initiatives. A rigorous program with difficult requirements can provide the basis for an interesting story about participants who implement the program.

In one organization, the editor of the company newsletter participated in a demanding HR program and wrote a stimulating article about what it was like to be a participant. The article gave the reader a tour of the entire program and its effectiveness in terms of the results achieved. It was an interesting and effective way to communicate about a challenging activity.

The benefits are many and the opportunities endless for HR professionals to use in-house publications and company-wide intranets to let others know about the success of programs.

E-mail and Electronic Media. Internal and external Web pages on the Internet, company-wide intranets, and e-mail are excellent vehicles for releasing results, promoting ideas, and informing employees and other target groups of HR results. E-mail, in particular, provides a virtually instantaneous means with which to communicate and solicit response from large numbers of people.

Program Brochures and Pamphlets. A brochure might be appropriate for programs conducted on a continuing basis, where participants have produced excellent results. It should be attractive and present a complete description of the program, with a major section devoted to results obtained with previous participants, if available. Measurable results and reactions from participants, or even direct quotes from individuals, could add spice to an otherwise dull brochure.

Case Studies. Case studies represent an effective way to communicate the results of an HR initiative. Consequently, it is recommended that a few programs be developed in a case format. A typical case study describes the situation, provides appropriate background information (including the events that led to the initiative), presents the techniques and strategies used to develop the study, and highlights the key issues in the program. Case studies tell an interesting story of how the evaluation was developed and the problems and concerns identified along the way.

Case studies have many useful applications in an organization. First, they can be used in group discussions, where interested individuals can react to the material, offer different perspectives, and draw conclusions about approaches or techniques. Second, the case study can serve as a self-teaching guide for individuals trying to understand how evaluations are developed and used in the organization. Finally, case studies provide appropriate recognition for those involved in the actual case. More importantly, they recognize the participants who achieved the results, as well as the managers who allowed the participants to be involved in the program. The case study format has become one of the most effective ways to learn about program evaluation.

A Case Example. The various methods for communicating results can be creatively combined to fit any situation. Here is an effective example using three approaches: a case study, management meetings, and a brochure.

The production division of a manufacturing company had achieved outstanding results through an HR initiative involving processes and work flow. The results were in the form of key bottom-line measures, such as lost-time accidents, grievances, scrap rate, and unit hour. The unit hour was a basic measure of individual productivity.

These results were achieved through the efforts of the supervisors applying and implementing several HR solutions. This fact was discretely mentioned at the beginning of a presentation made by two of the supervisors. In a panel discussion format with a moderator, the two supervisors outlined the accuracy of the results. This was presented in a question-and-answer session during a monthly meeting for all supervisors. The supervisors mentioned that the results were linked to the HR program.

The comments were published in a brochure and distributed to all supervisors through their department managers. The title of the publication is "Getting Results: A Success Story." On the inside cover, specific results are detailed, along with additional information on the program. A close-up photograph of each supervisor, taken during the panel discussion, is included on this page. The next two pages present a summary of the techniques used to secure the results. The brochure was used in staff meetings as a discussion guide to cover the points from the panel discussion. Top executives were also sent copies. In addition, the discussion was videotaped and used in subsequent interventions as a model of application for workplace changes to improve performance. The brochure also served as a handout.

The communication effort was a success. All levels of management had favorable responses and top executives asked the HR department to implement similar programs in other areas.

Communicating the Information

Perhaps the biggest challenge of communication is the actual delivery of the message. This can be accomplished in a variety of ways and settings based on the actual target audience and the media selected for the message. Three particular approaches deserve additional coverage. The first approach is providing insight into how to provide feedback throughout the HR program to make sure information flows so changes can be made. The second is presenting an impact study to a senior management team. This may be one of the most challenging tasks for the HR department. The third is communicating regularly and routinely with the executive management group. Each of these three approaches is explored in more detail.

Providing Feedback. One of the most important reasons for collecting reaction, satisfaction, and learning data is to provide feedback so adjustments or changes can be made throughout the HR program. In most HR initiatives, data are routinely collected and quickly communicated to a variety of groups. Table 10-4 shows a feedback action plan designed to provide information to several feedback audiences using a variety of media.

As the plan shows, data are collected during the program at four specific time intervals and communicated back to at least four audiences—and sometimes six. Some of these feedback sessions result in identifying specific actions that need to be taken. This process becomes comprehensive and needs to be managed in a very proactive way. The following steps are recommended for providing feedback and managing the feedback process. Many of the steps and issues follow the recommendations of Peter Block in his successful book, *Flawless Consulting*.

1. *Communicate quickly.* Whether it is good news or bad news, it is important to let individuals involved in the program have the information as soon as possible. The

recommended time for providing feedback is usually a matter of days and certainly no longer than a week or two after the results are known.

2. *Simplify the data.* Condense data into an understandable, concise presentation. This is not the format for detailed explanations and analysis.

3. *Examine the role of the HR team and the client in the feedback situation.* Sometimes the HR team is the judge, and sometimes the HR team is the jury, prosecutor, defendant, or witness. On the other hand, sometimes the client is the judge, jury, prosecutor, defendant, or witness. It is important to examine the respective roles in terms of reactions to the data and the actions that need to be taken.

4. *Use negative data in a constructive way.* Some of the data will show that things are not going so well, and the fault may rest with the HR department or the client. In either case, the story basically changes from "Let's look at the success we've made" to "Now we know which areas to change."

5. *Use positive data in a cautious way.* Positive data can be misleading, and if they are communicated too enthusiastically, they may create expectations beyond what may materialize later. Positive data should be presented in a cautious way— almost in a discounting mode.

6. *Choose the language of the meeting and communication very carefully.* Use language that is descriptive, focused, specific, short, and simple. Avoid language that is too judgmental, macro, stereotypical, lengthy, or complex.

7. *Ask the client for reactions to the data.* After all, the client is the No. 1 customer, and the client's reaction is critical since it is most important that the client is pleased with the program.

8. *Ask the client for recommendations.* The client may have some good recommendations of what needs to be changed to keep a program on track or put it back on track if it derails.

9. *Use support and confrontation carefully.* These two issues are not mutually exclusive. There may be times when support and confrontation are needed for the same group. The client may need support and yet be confronted for

Table 10-4
Feedback Action Plan

Data Collection Item	Timing	Feedback Audience	Media	Timing of Feedback	Action Required
1. Pre-project Survey ☐ Climate/ Environment ☐ Issue Identification	Beginning of the Program	Client Team Participants	Meeting	One Week	None
		Team Leaders	Survey Summary	Two Weeks	None
		HR Staff	Survey Summary	Two Weeks	Communicate Feedback
			Meeting	One Week	Adjust Approach
2. Implementation Survey ☐ Reaction to Plans ☐ Issue Identification	Beginning of Actual Implementation	Client Team Participants	Meeting	One Week	None
		Team Leaders	Survey Summary	Two Weeks	None
		HR Staff	Survey Summary	Two Weeks	Communicate Feedback
			Meeting	One Week	Adjust Approach
					Comments

Client Team	Meeting	One Week	None
3. Implementation Reaction Survey/Interviews □ Reaction to Solution □ Suggested Changes One Month into Implementation			
Participants	Study Summary	Two Weeks	None
Support Staff	Study Summary	Two Weeks	Support Changes
Team Leaders	Study Summary	Two Weeks	Support Changes
Immediate Managers	Study Summary	Three Weeks	Adjust Approach
HR Staff	Study Summary	Three Days	
	Meeting		

Client Team	Meeting	One Week	Comments
4. Implementation Feedback Questionnaire □ Reaction (Satisfaction) □ Barriers □ Projected Success End of Implementation			
Participants	Study Summary	Two Weeks	None
Support Staff	Study Summary	Two Weeks	None
Team Leaders	Study Summary	Two Weeks	Support Changes
Immediate Managers	Study Summary	Three Weeks	Support Changes
HR Staff	Study Summary	Three Days	Adjust Approach
	Meeting		

lack of improvement or sponsorship. The HR team may be confronted on the problem areas that are developed but may need support as well.

10. *React and act on the data.* Weigh the different alternatives and possibilities to arrive at the adjustments and changes that will be necessary.

11. *Secure agreement from all key stakeholders.* This is essential to make sure everyone is willing to make adjustments and changes that seem necessary.

12. *Keep the feedback process short.* Don't let it become bogged down in long, drawn-out meetings or lengthy documents. If this occurs, stakeholders will avoid the process instead of being willing to participate in the future.

Following these twelve steps will help move the program forward and provide important feedback, often ensuring that adjustments are supported and made.

Presenting Impact Study Data to Senior Management. Perhaps one of the most challenging and stressful communications is presenting an impact study to the senior management team, which also serves as the client in an HR program. The challenge is convincing this highly skeptical and critical group that outstanding results have been achieved (assuming they have), in a reasonable time frame, addressing the salient points, and making sure the managers understand the process. Two particular issues can create challenges. First, if the results are impressive, it may be difficult to make the managers believe the data. On the other extreme, if the data are negative, it will be a challenge to make sure managers don't overreact to the negative results and look for someone to blame. Following are guidelines that can help make sure this process is planned and executed properly:

☐ Plan a face-to-face meeting with senior team members for the first one or two major impact studies. If they are unfamiliar with the complete ROI process, a face-to-face meeting is necessary to make sure they understand the process. The good news is that they will probably attend the meeting because they have not seen ROI data developed for this type of program. The bad news is that it takes a lot of time, usually one to two hours for this presentation.

☐ After a group has had a face-to-face meeting with a couple of presentations, an executive summary may suffice. At this point they understand the process, so a shortened version may be appropriate.

☐ After the target audience is familiar with the process, a brief version may be necessary, which will involve a one- to two-page summary with charts and graphs showing all six types of measures.

☐ In making the initial presentation, the results should not be distributed beforehand or even during the session but saved until the end of the session. This will allow enough time to present the process and react to it before the target audience sees the actual ROI number.

☐ Present the process step by step, showing how the data were collected, when they were collected, who provided the data, how the data were isolated from other influences, and how they were converted to monetary values. The various assumptions, adjustments, and conservative approaches are presented along with the total cost of the initiative. The costs are fully loaded so that the target audience will begin to buy into the process of developing the actual ROI.

☐ When the data are actually presented, the results are presented step-by-step, starting with Level 1, moving through Level 5, and ending with the intangibles. This allows the audience to see the reaction and satisfaction, learning, application and implementation, business impact, and ROI. After some discussion about the meaning of the ROI, the intangible measures are presented. Allocate time to each level as appropriate for the audience. This helps overcome the potentially negative reactions to a very positive or negative ROI.

☐ Show the consequences of additional accuracy if it is an issue. The tradeoff for more accuracy and validity often means more expense. Address this issue whenever necessary, agreeing to add more data if required.

☐ Collect concerns, reactions, and issues for the process and make adjustments accordingly for the next presentation.

Collectively, these steps will help prepare for and present one of the most critical meetings in the human resources ROI process.

Communicating with Executive Management and Clients. No group is more important than top executives when it comes to communicating HR results. In many situations, this group is also the client. Improving communications with this group requires developing an overall strategy, which may include all or part of the actions outlined next.

Strengthen the Relationship with Executives. An informal and productive relationship should be established between the HR group responsible for the program and the top executive at the location where the program is taking place. Each should feel comfortable discussing needs and program results. One approach is to establish frequent, informal meetings with the executive to review problems with current programs and discuss other performance problems/opportunities in the organization. Frank and open discussions can provide the executive with insight not possible from any other source. Also, it can be very helpful to the HR group in determining the direction of the initiative.

Show How HR Programs Have Helped Solve Major Problems. While hard results from recent programs are comforting to an executive, solutions to immediate problems may be more convincing. This is an excellent opportunity to discuss a possible future initiative.

Distribute Memos About Program Results. When an initiative has achieved significant results, make appropriate top executives aware of them. This can easily be done with a brief memo or summary outlining what the program was supposed to accomplish, when it was implemented, who was involved, and the results achieved. This should be presented in a for-your-information format that consists of facts rather than opinions. A full report may be presented later.

All significant communications about HR programs, plans, activities, and results should include the executive group. Frequent information from the HR programs, as long as it is not boastful, can reinforce credibility and accomplishments.

Ask the Executive to Be Involved in the Review. An effective way to enhance commitment from top executives is to ask them to serve on an HR review committee. A review committee provides input and advice to the HR staff about a variety of issues, including needs, problems with the present program, and program evaluation issues. This committee can be helpful in letting executives know what the programs are achieving.

Conduct an HR Review. An HR review meeting is an effective way to communicate results to top executives. While this review can be conducted more frequently, an annual basis is common. The primary purpose is to show top management what has been accomplished with HR and what is planned for the future. It can last from two hours to two days depending on the scope of the meeting and the amount of HR activity. This meeting is best suited for situations in which there are long-term programs, long-term relationships, and/or multiple programs with the same firm. A typical agenda for this review meeting is shown in Table 10-5.

This meeting may be the single most important event on the HR department's calendar during the year. It must be planned carefully, timely, well-executed, and controlled to accomplish its purpose. This approach has been used in many organizations, and the reaction has been extremely favorable. Executive managers want to know what the organization is accomplishing, what results have been achieved and, most of all, they want to have input on the decisions for new programs.

Analyzing Reactions to Communication

The best indicator of how effectively the results of an HR program have been communicated is the level of commitment and support from the management group. The allocation of requested resources and strong commitment from top management are tangible evidence of management's perception of the results. In addition to this macro-level reaction, there are a few techniques HR professionals can use to measure the effectiveness of their communication efforts.

Whenever results are communicated, the reaction of the target audiences can be monitored. These reactions may include non-verbal gestures, oral remarks, written comments, or indirect

Table 10-5
Annual HR Review Agenda

Time	Annual Review Meeting Topic
8:00 a.m.	Review of HR for the past year
8:30	Evaluation strategy for each program and the results achieved
9:30	Significant deviations from the expected results (both positive and negative)
10:00	Break
10:15	Basis for determining needs for the next year
10:30	Anticipated programs for the coming year (secure support and approval)
10:45	Proposed evaluation strategy and potential payoffs
11:00	Problem areas in the HR process (lack of support, where management involvement is needed, or other potential problems that can be corrected by executive management)
11:30	Concerns of executive management
Noon	Adjourn

actions that reveal how the communication was received. Usually, when results are presented in a meeting, the presenter will have some indication of how the results were received by the group. The interest and attitudes of the audience can usually be quickly evaluated.

During the presentation, questions may be asked or, in some cases, the information is challenged. In addition, a tabulation of these challenges and questions can be useful in evaluating the type of information to include in future communications. Positive comments about the results are certainly desired and, when they are made—formally or informally—they should also be noted and tabulated.

HR staff meetings are an excellent arena for discussing the reaction to communicating results. Comments can come from many sources depending on the particular target audiences. Input from different members of the staff can be summarized to help judge the overall effectiveness.

When major program results are communicated, a feedback questionnaire may be used for an entire audience or a sample of the audience. The purpose of this questionnaire is to determine the extent to which the audience understood and/or believed the information presented. This is practical only when the effectiveness of the communication has a significant impact on the future actions of the HR department.

Another approach is to survey the management group to determine its perceptions of the results. Specific questions should be asked about results. What does the management group know about the results? How believable are the results? What additional information is desired about the program? This type of survey can help provide guidance in communicating results.

The purpose of analyzing reactions is to make adjustments in the communication process—if adjustments are necessary. Although the reactions may involve intuitive assessments, a more sophisticated analysis will provide more accurate information to make these adjustments. The net result should be a more effective communication process.

Shortcut Ways to Provide Feedback and Communicate with Clients

Although this chapter has presented a full array of possibilities for all types of programs, a simplified and shortcut approach may be appropriate for small-scale projects and inexpensive HR initiatives. The following five issues can be addressed with minimal time.

1. Planning can be very simple and occupy only one block in the evaluation planning document. It is helpful to reach an agreement as to who will see the data and when they will receive the data.

2. Feedback during a program should be simplified using a questionnaire, followed by a brief meeting to communicate the results. This is almost informal but should address as many of the issues outlined in this chapter as possible. Most importantly, it should be kept simple and should lead to action if it is needed.

3. An impact study should be developed showing the actual success of the program, preferably with all six types of data. If certain types of data have been omitted, the impact study should be developed with the data that are available, following the appropriate areas or topics contained in an impact study, as outlined in this chapter.

4. The impact study results should be presented in a face-to-face meeting with the clients and perhaps with the executive group if they are not the same group. This is usually a meeting that will be easy to schedule and necessary from the perspectives of both the client and the HR team. A one-hour meeting can show the results of the program and respond to various issues. Using suggestions for conducting this meeting, as outlined in this chapter, would be helpful in this situation.

5. Keep impact study data for marketing purposes. From the perspective of the HR department, these are excellent marketing data that can be used in a generic way to convince others that the HR program is successful. From the client's perspective, this is a historical document that leaves a permanent record of success and can be used as a reference in the future. When communicating results from past studies, client confidentiality and protection of sensitive information should be honored.

FINAL THOUGHTS

This chapter presented the final step in the results-based approach to HR accountability, as shown in the ROI model. Communicating results is a crucial step in the overall evaluation process. If this step is not taken seriously, the full impact of the results will not be realized. The chapter began with general principles for communicating program results. A communications model was presented, which can serve as a guide for any significant communication effort. The various target audiences were discussed and, because of its importance, emphasis was placed on the executive group. A suggested format for a detailed evaluation report was also provided. Much of the remainder of the chapter included a detailed presentation of the most commonly used media for communicating program results, including meetings, client publications and electronic media. Numerous examples illustrated these concepts.

PART III

Important Issues with ROI Implementation

CHAPTER 11

Forecasting the ROI

Sometimes it is confusing to know when it is appropriate to develop the ROI, what types of data to collect, and what level of evaluation is most appropriate for an ROI calculation. The traditional and recommended approach, described in the previous chapters, is to base ROI calculations strictly on business results obtained from the HR program or initiative. Business performance measures (Level 4 data) are easily converted to monetary values, which is necessary for an ROI calculation. Sometimes these measures are not available, and it appears that an ROI calculation is out of the question. This chapter will illustrate that ROI calculations are possible at various times, including before the project is initiated.

Why Forecast ROI?

Although calculating ROI based on post-project data is the most accurate way to assess and develop an ROI calculation, sometimes it is important to know the actual forecast before the final results are tabulated. Forecasting during the project, or even before the project is pursued in some cases, is an important issue when critical reasons drive the need for a forecasted ROI.

To reduce uncertainty. Whenever uncertainty can be reduced in a project, doing so benefits the client. In a perfect world, the client would like to know the expected payoff from any business decision. Realistically, forecasting the exact payoff may not be possible, and from a practical standpoint, it may not be feasible. Still, there remains the desire to take the uncertainty out of the equation and to act on the best data available. This sometimes pushes the project to a forecasted ROI before any resources are expended. Some managers will simply not budge without a pre-project forecast. They need some measure of expected success before allocating any resources to the project.

Because the cost of a project is too expensive without some data. In some cases even a pilot project is not practical until some analysis has been conducted to examine the potential ROI. For example, if the HR program involves a significant amount of resources in the design, development, and delivery, a client may not want to expend the resources even for a pilot group unless there is some assurance of a likelihood of success with a positive ROI. Although there may be some tradeoffs with a lower profile and lower-cost pilot program, the pre-program ROI nevertheless becomes an important issue in these situations, prompting some clients to stand firm until an ROI forecast is produced.

To compare with post data. Whenever there is a plan to collect data about the success of the HR program regarding application, implementation, impact, and ROI, it helps to compare actual results with pre-project expectations. In an ideal world, if forecasted ROI should have a defined relationship with the actual ROI, they should be very similar, or at least one should lead to the other with some adjustments. One of the important reasons for forecasting ROI is to see how well the forecast holds up under scrutiny of the post-project analysis.

To save costs. Several cost saving issues prompt the ROI forecast. First, the forecast itself often costs very little because it involves estimations and many different assumptions. Second, if the forecast itself becomes a reliable predictor of the post-project analysis, then the forecasted ROI might substitute for the actual ROI—at least with some adjustments. This could save costs on the post-project analysis. Finally, the forecasted ROI data might be used for comparisons in other areas for other types of HR programs. Thus, the forecasted ROI might have some potential transfer benefit to specific projects.

To comply with policy. More and more organizations are developing policy statements and, in the case of government agencies, sometimes even passing laws to require a forecasted ROI before undertaking major projects. For example, any project costing more than $300,000 must have a forecasted ROI before the organization can approve it. In a government outside the United States, vendors can receive partial payments on a project if the ROI forecast is positive and likely to enhance the organization. This formal policy is becoming a frequent reason for developing the ROI forecast.

Collectively, these five reasons are causing many organizations to look at pre-program forecast, or at least a projection during the program, so that the client and the HR team will have some estimate of the expected payoff.

THE TRADEOFFS OF FORECASTING

The actual ROI can be developed at different times and at different levels. Unfortunately, the ease, convenience, and low cost involved in capturing a forecasted ROI has its tradeoff in accuracy and credibility. As Figure 11-1 shows, there are five distinct time intervals during a project when the ROI can actually be developed. This figure shows the relationship of each level of evaluation with credibility, accuracy, cost, and difficulty. These levels and time intervals are as follows:

a. A **pre-project forecast** can be developed using estimates of the impact of the program. This approach lacks accuracy, but it is also the least expensive and least difficult ROI to calculate. There is value in developing the ROI on a pre-project basis, and the next section discusses this.

b. **Reaction and satisfaction data** can be developed and extended to determine an anticipated impact including the ROI. In this case, participants actually anticipate and project the impact as the HR program is applied and implemented and as it influences specific business measures. Although the accuracy and credibility increase from the pre-project basis, this approach still lacks the credibility and accuracy desired for most situations.

c. **Learning data** in some projects can be used to forecast the actual ROI. This approach applies only when formal testing has shown a relationship between acquiring certain skills or knowledge and subsequent performance. When this correlation is available (it is usually developed to validate the test), test data can be used to forecast subsequent performance.

ROI with:	Data Collection Timing (relative to project)	Credibility	Accuracy	Cost to Develop	Difficult
Pre-project Forecast	Before Project	Not Very Credible	Not Very Accurate	Inexpensive	Not Difficult
Reaction and Satisfaction Data	During Project				
Learning Data	During Project				
Application and Implementation	After Project				
Business Impact Data	After Project	Very Credible	Very Accurate	Expensive	Very Difficult

Figure 11-1. ROI at different times and levels.

The performance can then be converted to monetary impact, and the ROI can be developed. This has less potential as an evaluation tool because of the lack of situations for which a predictive validation can be developed.

d. In some situations in which frequency of application and actual use of skills are critical, the **application and implementation** of these skills can be converted to a value, using employee compensation as a basis. This is particularly helpful in situations in which competencies are being developed and values are being placed on improving competencies, even when there is no immediate increase in pay.

e. Finally, the ROI can be developed from **business impact data** converted directly to monetary values and compared with the cost of the program. This post-project evaluation is the basis for most of the ROI calculations in this book and has been the principal approach used in previous chapters. It is the preferred approach, but because of the pressures already outlined above, it is appropriate to examine ROI calculations at other times and at levels other than Level 4. This chapter provides a detailed view of pre-project evaluation and the ROI calculations based on reaction. To a lesser degree, this chapter also addresses the ROI calculations developed from learning and application data.

PRE-PROJECT ROI FORECASTING

Perhaps one of the most useful steps in convincing a client that an HR initiative is beneficial is to forecast the project. The process closely parallels the post-project analysis except the extent of the impact must be estimated along with the forecasted cost.

Basic model. Figure 11-2 shows the basic model for capturing the necessary data for a pre-program forecast. This model is basically a modification of the post-program ROI model except that data and the program's influence are projected instead of being collected during different time frames. In place of the data collection is an estimation of the change in impact data expected to be influenced by the HR initiative. Isolating the effects of the project becomes a non-issue as the estimate of output takes the isolation factor into consideration. For example, when a person is asked to indicate how much of the particular improvement can

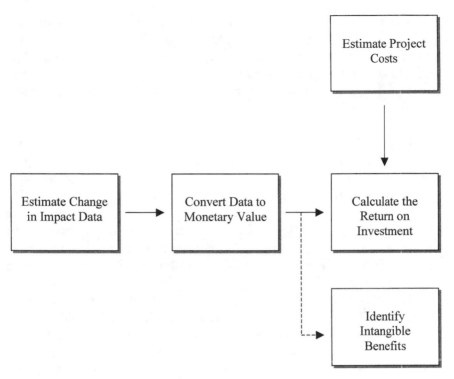

Figure 11-2. Pre-PRO ROI forecast model.

be driven by the HR program/initiative, the extent of isolation factor is already taken into consideration. The HR initiative is the only factor under consideration. The other factors have been inherently isolated in the estimation process. The method to covert data to monetary values is exactly the same because the data items examined on a pre- and post-program analysis should be the same. Estimating the project's cost should be an easy step because cost can easily be anticipated based on previous projects, using reasonable assumptions about the current HR initiative. The anticipated intangibles are merely speculation in forecasting but reliably indicate which measures may be influenced in addition to those included in the ROI calculations. The formula used to calculate the ROI is the same as in the post analysis. The amount of monetary value from the data conversion, which is based on the estimate of change, is included as the numerator, while the estimated cost of the HR initiative is inserted into the denominator. The projected benefit/cost analysis can be developed along with the actual ROI. The steps to develop the process are detailed next.

Steps to develop the actual ROI. This section presents the detailed steps to develop the pre-project ROI forecast in simplified form:

1. Develop the Levels 3 and 4 objectives using as many specifics as possible. This should come from the initial needs analysis and assessment. These objectives detail what would actually change in the work setting and identify which measures would actually be influenced. If this is not known, then this places the entire forecasting process in jeopardy. There must be some assessment of what measures will change as a result of the HR initiative, and someone must be able to estimate the likely extent of this change.

2. Estimate or forecast the monthly improvement in the business impact data. This is considered to be the amount of influence directly related to the program and is denoted by ΔP.

3. Convert the business impact data to monetary values using one or more of the methods described in Chapter 6. These are the same techniques used in a post-project analysis, and this value is denoted by V.

4. Develop the estimated annual impact for each measure. In essence, this is the first-year improvement resulting from the HR initiative, showing the value contributed for each measure. In formula form this is $\Delta P \times V \times 12$.

5. Factor additional years into the analysis if a project will have a significant useful life beyond the first year. When this is the case, these values may need to be factored to reflect a diminished benefit for subsequent years. The client or owner of the process should give some indication as to the amount of the reduction and the values developed for years two, three, and so on. It helps to be conservative by using the smallest number possible.

6. Estimate the fully loaded HR program cost. Using all the cost categories contained in Chapter 7, the fully loaded cost should be estimated and projected for the duration of the HR program impact. If program benefits are included beyond year one, be sure to include the costs for these

additional years as well. Again, the calculation would include all direct and indirect costs.

7. Calculate the forecasted ROI using the total projected benefits, and calculate the estimated cost using the standard ROI formula.
8. Use sensitivity analysis to develop several potential ROI values with different levels of improvement (ΔP). When more than one measure is changing, the analysis would perhaps be performed using a spreadsheet showing different possible scenarios for output and the subsequent ROI for each.
9. Identify the potential intangible benefits by using input from those most knowledgeable of the situation. These potential intangible benefits are only anticipated and are based on assumptions from previous experience with this type of HR initiative.
10. Communicate the ROI projection and anticipated intangibles with much care and caution. The target audience must clearly understand that this is based on several assumptions (clearly defined) and that values are the best possible estimates. However, there is much room for error.

These ten steps enable an individual or team to forecast the ROI. The most difficult part of the process is the initial estimate of performance improvement. Several sources of data are available for this purpose, as described next.

Forecasting/estimating performance improvement. Several sources of input are available when attempting to estimate the actual performance improvement that an HR program will influence. These six important considerations should be explored:

1. Experience in the organization gained from previous or similar HR programs can form the basis of the estimate. Adapting that breadth of experience can be an important factor because comparisons are rarely, if ever, exact.
2. HR project team members may have experience with similar projects in other organizations or in other situations. The experience of the designers, developers, and implementers in the HR project will pay off as they reflect on their experiences with other organizations.

3. External experts who have worked in the field or tackled similar projects in other organizations can provide input. These may be other HR professionals, HR suppliers, designers, or others who have earned reputations for knowing about this type of process in this type of situation.

4. Estimates can be obtained from a subject matter expert (SME) in the organization. This individual is well acquainted with the internal processes that the HR initiative seeks to alter, modify, or improve. SMEs may also be quite knowledgeable about the various factors that influence one or more of the specific impact measures. Internal SMEs often serve in critical functions and sometimes are the most favored resource for obtaining estimates.

5. Estimates can be obtained directly from the client or sponsor for the project. This is the individual who makes the ultimate purchasing decision and provides data or input about the anticipated change in a measure that is linked to the HR program. This influential position makes this person an extremely credible source.

6. Individuals who are directly involved in the HR initiative and have been targeted as the participants (target population) are sometimes in a position to know how much a particular type of HR initiative can change or improve a measure. These individuals understand the processes, procedures, and particular performance measurements being influenced. Their close proximity to the situation makes them a very credible source and sometimes the most accurate source of projecting or estimating the amount of change.

Collectively, these sources provide an appropriate array of possibilities to help estimate the value of an improvement. As the weakest link in the ROI forecasting process, this step deserves the most attention. The target managers who are interested in forecasted ROI should understand where the estimates came from and who made them. More importantly, they must see the source as credible; otherwise the forecasted ROI has no credibility.

Case example. It is helpful to illustrate how a forecasted ROI can be developed using some of the processes explained here. A global financial services company was interested in purchasing a customer contact management software program to enable its sales-relationship managers to keep track of routine correspondence and communication with customers. The needs assessment indicated a need for this type of capability. Training was a major consideration for the end users, and a training consultant from HR's corporate training function was assigned to the project team along with members from the sales and information technology functions. An assignment of the designated project team would involve further detailing the exact needs, selecting the appropriate software package, and implementing the software and training along with appropriate job aids as necessary. However, before pursuing the project and purchasing software, a forecasted ROI was developed. By following the steps above, it was determined that the implementation of this project would influence four business impact measures as follows:

1. Increased sales to existing customers
2. A reduction in customer complaints regarding missed deadlines, late responses, and failure to complete transactions
3. A reduction in the response time to customer inquiries and requests
4. Increased customer satisfaction evidenced by composite survey index scores

With comprehensive customer contact management software, the sales-relationship managers should benefit from quick and effective customer communication and have easy access to customer databases. The software should also provide the functionality to develop calendars and to-do lists. They should further benefit from features such as built-in contact management, calendar sharing, and an Internet-ready tool. To determine the extent to which the four measures would change with appropriate training and implementation, input was derived from four sources:

1. Internal software developers who are experts in various software applications provided input about affected changes in each of the measures.
2. The sales-relationship managers provided input in terms of expected changes in the variables if the software was used regularly.
3. The client funding the project provided input about what could be expected when the capability of software was properly used.

4. Finally, a survey of software developers provided some input.

All the input represents estimates, and the actual results may differ significantly. However, the client was interested in a forecast based on a very limited analysis but strengthened with the best expert opinions available. After some discussion of the availability of data and after examining the techniques to convert data to monetary values, the following conclusions were reached:

1. The increase in sales could easily be converted to monetary values, as the margin for this particular project is applied directly.
2. The cost of a customer complaint could be based on a discounted internal value currently in use, thus providing a generally accepted cost of a complaint.
3. The actual customer response time is not tracked accurately nor is the value for this measure readily available. It was anticipated that this would be an intangible benefit.
4. There is no generally accepted monetary value for increasing customer satisfaction, so the impact on customer satisfaction would be listed as a potential intangible.

After reviewing the possible scenarios, it was determined that there could be a range of possibilities for increasing sales and reducing complaints. The sales increase should be in the range of 3 to 9 percent. Thus, three scenarios were developed, using 3 percent, 6 percent, and 9 percent as the projected increases in sales. In terms of the actual number of complaints, the ROI calculation was developed for a single division of the organization. Complaints were in the range of ten to thirty monthly. Three scenarios were developed for the reduction in the number of actual complaints, using a reduction of ten, twenty, and thirty in the ROI calculation.

The increase in sales was easily converted to monetary values using the margin rates. The reduction in customer complaints was easily converted using the discounted value for a customer complaint. The cost for the project could easily be estimated based on input from those who examined the situation very briefly. The total cost was developed to include software and equipment, development costs, materials, facilitators, facilities for meetings, lost time for learning activities, and coordination and evaluation. This fully loaded projected cost when compared with the benefits yielded in a range of expected ROI values. Table 11-1 shows the matrix of the nine possible scenarios using payoffs on the two measures. The ROI values range from a low of 60 percent ROI to a high of 180 percent. With these projected values, the decision to move forward was a relatively easy one because all the worst-case scenarios were very positive, and the best case was approximately three times that value. As this example illustrates, the process needs to be kept simple, using the best and most credible sources available to quickly arrive at estimates of the process. Recognizing that these are estimates, the advantages are simplicity and low cost. These factors should be considered when developing the processes.

Forecasting with a pilot program. Although the steps listed above provide a process for estimating the ROI when a pilot program is not conducted, the much more favored approach is to develop a small-scale pilot project and develop the ROI based on post-program data. This scenario involves the following five steps:

1. As in the previous process, develop Levels 3 and 4 objectives.
2. Initiate the project on a very small-scale sample as a pilot project without all the bells and whistles. Keep the cost extremely low, but keep the fundamentals of the project intact.

Table 11-1
Expected ROI Values for Different Outputs

Potential Sales Increase Existing Customers (%)	Potential Compliant Reduction (Monthly Reduction)	Expected ROI (%)
3	10	60
3	20	90
3	30	120
6	10	90
6	20	120
6	30	150
9	10	120
9	20	150
9	30	180

3. Conduct the program by fully implementing it with one or more of the typical groups of individuals who can benefit from the program.
4. Develop the ROI using the ROI process model for post-program analysis. In essence, this is the model used in the previous chapters.
5. Finally, make the decision to implement throughout the organization based on the results of the pilot project.

This provides a much more accurate approach to developing data based on a pilot program, withholding the full implementation until results can be concluded from the pilot study. In this scenario, data can be developed involving all the six types of measures outlined in this book.

FORECASTING ROI WITH REACTION DATA

When a reaction evaluation includes planned applications from an HR initiative, these important data can ultimately be used in ROI calculations. With questions concerning how participants plan to use what they have learned and what results they expect to achieve, higher-level evaluation information can be developed. The questions presented in Table 11-2 illustrate how this type of data is collected with an end-of-program implementation questionnaire. Participants are asked to state specifically how they plan to apply the HR program and the results they expect to achieve. They are asked to convert their accomplishments to an annual monetary value and to show the basis for developing the values. Participants can adjust their responses with a level of confidence to make the data more credible and to allow them to reflect their uneasiness with the process.

When tabulating data, evaluators multiply the confidence level by the annual monetary value, which results in a more conservative estimate for use in the data analysis. For example, if a participant estimated that the monetary impact of the HR program would be $10,000 but was only 50 percent confident, a $5,000 value would be used in the calculations.

To develop a summary of the expected benefits, the evaluator takes several steps. First, any data that are incomplete, unusable, extreme, or unrealistic are discarded. Next, an adjustment is made

Table 11-2
Important Questions to Ask on Feedback Questionnaires

Planned Improvements

☐ As a result of this HR initiative what specific actions will you attempt as you apply what you have learned?

1. _____

2. _____

3. _____

☐ Please indicate what specific measures, outcomes, or projects will change as a result of your actions.

1. _____

2. _____

3. _____

☐ As a result of the anticipated changes in the above, please estimate (in monetary values) the benefits to your organization over a period of one year. _____

☐ What is the basis of this estimate?

_____

_____

☐ What confidence, expressed as a percentage, can you put in your estimate? (0% = No Confidence; 100% = Certainty) _____%

---

to the estimate for the confidence level, as previously described. Individual data items are then totaled. Finally, as an optional step, the total value is adjusted, again by a factor that reflects the subjectivity of the process and the possibility that participants will not achieve the results they anticipate. This adjustment factor can be determined by the project team. In one organization, the benefits are divided by two to develop a number to use in the equation. Finally, the ROI is calculated using the net benefits from the HR program divided by the HR program costs. This value, in essence, becomes the expected return on investment, after the confidence adjustment for accuracy and the adjustment for subjectivity.

This process can be best described using an actual case. M&H Engineering and Construction Company designs and builds large commercial projects such as plants, paper mills, and municipal water systems. Safety is always a critical issue at M&H and usually commands much management attention. To improve the current level of safety performance, a safety improvement program was initiated for project engineers and construction superintendents. The program focused on safety leadership, safety planning, safety inspection, safety meetings, accident investigation, safety policy and procedures, safety standards, and workers' compensation. After completing this project, engineers and superintendents were expected to improve the safety performance of their specific construction projects. A dozen safety performance measures used in the company were discussed and analyzed during the program. At the end of the program roll-out, participants completed a comprehensive Level 1 reaction feedback questionnaire. The questionnaire probed into specific action items planned as a result of this program and asked participants to project estimated monetary values of their planned improvements. In addition, participants explained the basis for the improvements and estimates, and placed a confidence level on their estimates. Table 11-3 presents data provided by the first group of participants. Only eighteen of the twenty-four participants supplied data, (experience has shown that approximately 50 to 70 percent of participants will provide usable data for this series of questions). The total cost of the HR program, including participants' salaries, was $29,000. Prorated development costs were included in this cost figure.

The monetary value of the planned improvements is extremely high, reflecting the participants' optimism and enthusiasm at the end of an effective HR program during which specific actions are planned. As a first step in the analysis, extreme data items are omitted. Data such as millions, unlimited, and $4 million are discarded, and each remaining value is multiplied by the confidence value and totaled. This adjustment is a way of reducing

Table 11-3
Level 1 Data for ROI Calculations

Participant No.	Estimated Value	Basis	Confidence Level
1	$80,000	Reduction in Accidents	90%
2	90,000	OSHA Reportable Injuries	80%
3	50,000	Accident Reduction	100%
4	10,000	First Aid Visits/Visits to Doctor	100%
5	50,000	Reduction in Lost Time Injuries	95%
6	Millions	Total Accident Cost	100%
7	75,000	Workers' Compensation	80%
8	7,500	OSHA Citations	75%
9	50,000	Reduction in Accidents	100%
10	30,000	Workers' Compensation	80%
11	150,000	Reduction in Total Accident Costs	90%
12	20,000	OSHA Fines/Citations	70%
13	40,000	Accident Reductions	100%
14	4,000,000	Total Cost of Safety	95%
15	65,000	Total Workers' Compensation	50%
16	Unlimited	Accidents	100%
17	45,000	Injuries	90%
18	2,000	Visits to Doctor	100%

very subjective estimates. The resulting tabulations yielded a total improvement of $655,125. Because of the subjectivity of the process, the values were adjusted again by a factor of two, an arbitrary number suggested by the principal HR safety consultant, and supported by the management group. This "adjusted" value is $327,563, or $328,000 with rounding. The projected ROI, based on the end-of-program feedback questionnaire given at the program's conclusion but before actual job application, is as follows:

$$\text{ROI} = \frac{\$328,000 - \$29,000}{\$29,000} \times 100 = 1,031\%$$

The HR safety consultant communicated these projected values to the CEO but cautioned that the data were very subjective, although they had been twice adjusted downward. The safety consultant also emphasized that the forecasted results were generated by the participants in the program, who should be aware of what they could accomplish. In addition, she mentioned that a follow-up was planned to determine the results that were actually delivered by the group.

A word of caution is in order when using Level 1 ROI data. These calculations are highly subjective and may not reflect the extent to which participants will apply what they have learned to achieve results. A variety of influences in the work environment can enhance or inhibit the participants' attainment of performance goals. Having high expectations at the end of the HR program roll-out is no guarantee that those expectations will be met. Disappointments are documented regularly in HR programs throughout the world and are reported in research findings.

Although this process is subjective and possibly unreliable, it does have some usefulness. First, if an evaluation must stop at this level, this approach provides more insight into the value of the program than the data from typical reaction questionnaires. Managers will usually find these data more useful than a report stating that "40 percent of participants rated the HR program above average." Unfortunately, there is evidence that a high percentage of evaluations stop at this first level of evaluation. Reporting Level 1 ROI data is a more useful indication of the potential impact of the HR program than the alternative, which is to report attitudes and feelings about the HR program and about those who designed, administered, or implemented it.

Second, these data can form a basis for comparison of different projects of the same type of intervention (for example, safety). If one HR program forecasts an ROI of 300 percent whereas another projects 30 percent, then it appears the first program may be more effective than the other. The participants in the first program have more confidence in the planned application of the HR program.

Third, collecting this type of data focuses increased attention on program outcomes. Participants involved in the intervention will understand that specific behavior change is expected, and this influences results for the organization. This issue becomes clear to participants as they anticipate results and convert them to monetary values. Even if this projected improvement is ignored, the exercise is productive because of the important message sent to participants.

Fourth, if a follow-up is planned to pinpoint post-program results, the data collected in the Level 1 evaluation can be helpful for comparison. This data collection helps participants plan the implementation of what they have learned. Incidentally, when a follow-up is planned, participants are more conservative with these projected estimates.

The calculation of the ROI at Level 1 is increasing, and some organizations have based many of their ROI calculations on Level 1 data. Although these calculations may be very subjective, they do add value, particularly if they are included as part of a comprehensive evaluation system.

FORECASTING ROI WITH LEARNING DATA

Testing for changes in skills and knowledge in a program is a common technique for Level 2 evaluation. In many situations, participants are required to demonstrate their knowledge or skills at the end of the program, and their performance is expressed as a numerical value. When this type of test is developed, it must be reliable and valid. A reliable test is one that is stable over time and produces consistent results. A valid test is one that measures what it purports to measure. Because a test should reflect the content of the HR program, successful mastery of content should be related to improved job performance. Consequently, there should be a relationship between test scores and subsequent on-the-job performance. Figure 11-3 illustrates the potential relationship between test scores and job performance in a perfect correlation. This relationship, expressed as a correlation coefficient, is a measure of validity of the test.

This testing situation provides an excellent opportunity for an ROI calculation with Level 2 data using test results. When there is a statistically significant relationship between test scores and on-the-job performance, and the performance can be converted to monetary units, then it is possible to use test scores to estimate the ROI from the program, using the following six steps:

1. Ensure that the program content reflects desired on-the-job performance.
2. Develop an end-of-program test that reflects program content.
3. Establish a statistical relationship between test data and output performance of participants.
4. Predict performance levels of each participant with given test scores.
5. Convert performance data to monetary values.
6. Compare total predicted value of program with the program costs.

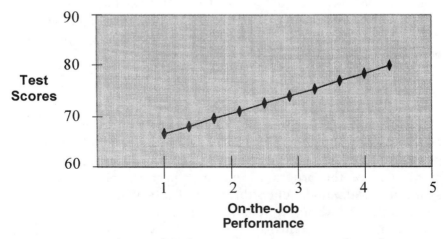

Figure 11-3. Relationship between test scores and performance.

This approach has its best application when significant learning is taking place or when the project or program focuses almost entirely on developing learning solutions. The absence of validated tests are problematic in this issue because the instruments cannot be used to project actual performance unless there have been some steps to ensure the validity.

An example will illustrate this approach. Consumer Products Marketing (CPM) is the marketing division of a large consumer products company. Sales representatives for CPM make frequent sales calls to large retail food and drug companies with the objective of increasing sales and market share of CPM products. Sales representatives must ensure that retailers understand the advantages of CPM products, provide adequate display space for its products, and assist in promotional and advertising efforts.

CPM has developed a strong sales culture and recruits highly capable individuals for sales representative assignments. A program was initiated to develop new sales representatives. Newly recruited sales representatives rotated through different divisions of the company in a two-month assignment to learn where and how the products were made and their features and benefits, as well as specific product marketing strategies. This initial assignment culminated with an intensive, one-week professional marketing program, which focused on sales techniques, marketing strategies, and customer service skills. At the end of the one-week assignment, participants completed a comprehensive exam, which reflected the knowledge and skills learned in the program. As part of the exam, participants analyzed specific customer service and sales situations and decided on specific actions. Also, the test covered product features, policies, and marketing practices.

To validate the test, CPM developed a correlation between test scores and actual on-the-job performance measured by sales volumes, sales growth, and market shares for sales representatives. The correlation was statistically significant with each variable. As a quick way of calculating the expected ROI for the program, CPM estimated output levels for each item using the test scores and then converted them to monetary values and calculated the ROI.

As with the previous ROI estimate with end-of-program questionnaires, some cautions are in order. This is a forecast of the ROI and not the actual value. Although participants may acquire the skills and knowledge from a program, there is no guarantee that they will apply the techniques and processes successfully and that the results will be achieved. This process assumes that the current group of participants has the same relationship to output performance as previous groups. It ignores a variety of environmental influences, which can alter the situation. And finally, the process requires calculating the initial correlation coefficient, which may be difficult to develop for many tests.

Although this approach develops an estimate based on historical relationships, it can be useful in a comprehensive evaluation strategy, and it has several advantages. First, if post-program evaluations (Level 4) are not planned, this process will yield more information about the projected value of the program than could be obtained from the raw test scores. This process represents an expected return on investment based on the historical relationships involved. Second, by developing individual ROI measurements and communicating them to participants, the process has reinforcement potential. It communicates to participants that increased sales and market share are expected through the applications of what was learned in the program. Third, this process can have considerable credibility with management and can preclude expensive follow-ups and post-program monitoring. If these relationships are statistically sound, the estimate should have credibility with the target population as well.

FORECASTING ROI WITH APPLICATION OF SKILLS AND COMPETENCIES

In almost every HR project, participants are expected to change their on-the-job behaviors by applying new behavior from the HR initiative. On-the-job applications are critical to HR program success, particularly with the focus on competencies. Although the use of the skills on the job is no guarantee that results will follow, it is an underlying assumption for most programs that if the knowledge and skills are applied, then results will follow. A few organizations attempt to take this process a step further and measure the value of on-the-job behavior change and calculate the ROI. In these situations, estimates are taken from individual participants, their supervisors, the management group, or experts in the field. The following steps are used to develop the ROI:

☐ Develop competencies for the target job.
☐ Indicate the percentage of job success that is represented by the competencies included in the HR program.
☐ Determine the monetary values of competencies, using salaries and employee benefits of participants.
☐ Compute the worth of pre- and post-program skill levels.
☐ Subtract post-program values from pre-program values.
☐ Compare the total added benefits with the program costs.

An example will help illustrate one technique to measure the value of on-the-job applications. With the help of HR professionals, the United States government redesigned its Introduction to Supervision course, a five-day learning solution for newly appointed supervisors. The HR program focused on eight competencies:

1. Role and responsibilities of the supervisor
2. Communication
3. Planning, assigning, controlling, and evaluating work
4. Ethics
5. Leadership
6. Analyzing performance problems
7. Customer service
8. Managing diversity

The immediate managers of the new supervisors indicated that these eight competencies accounted for 81 percent of first-level supervisors' jobs. For the target group being evaluated, the average annual salary plus benefits for the newly appointed supervisors was $42,202. Thus, multiplying this figure by the amount of job success accounted for by the competencies (81 percent), yielded a dollar value of $34,184 per participant. If a person was performing successfully in these eight competencies for one year, the value to the agency would be $34,184. Of course, this assumed that employees were paid an amount equal to their contribution when they were fully competent.

Using a scale of 0 to 9, managers rated the skills for each of the competencies before the program was conducted. The average level of skills required to be successful in the job was determined to be 6.44. The average skill rating, prior to the program, was

4.96, which represented 77 percent of the 6.44 (that is, participants were performing at 77 percent of the level necessary to be successful in the competencies). After the program, the average skill rating was 5.59, representing 87 percent of the level necessary for success.

Monetary values were assigned based on the participants' salaries. Performance at the required level was worth $34,184. At a 77 percent proficiency level, the new supervisors were performing at a contribution value of $26,322. After the application of the learning, this value reached 87 percent, representing a contribution value of $29,740. The difference in these values, $3,418, represents the gain per participant attributable to the program. The program cost was $1,368 per participant. Thus, the ROI is:

$$\text{ROI} = \frac{\$3,418 - \$1,368}{\$1,368} = \frac{2,050}{1,368} \times 100 = 150\%$$

As with other estimates, a word of caution is in order. These results are subjective because the rating systems used are subjective and may not necessarily reflect an accurate assessment of the value of the program. Also, because an HR program is usually implemented to help the organization achieve its objectives, some managers insist on tangible changes in hard data, such as quantity, quality, cost, and time. For them, Level 3 evaluation is not always a good substitute for Level 4 data, if they are available.

Although this process is subjective, it has several useful advantages. First, if there are no plans to track the actual impact of the program in terms of specific measurable business results (Level 4), then this approach represents a credible substitute. In many HR programs, particularly skill-building programs for supervisors, it is difficult to identify tangible changes on the job. Therefore, alternate approaches to determine the worth of HR programs are needed. Second, this approach results in data that are usually credible with the management group if the group understands how the data are developed and the assumptions behind the data. An important point is that the data for the changes in competence level came from the managers rating their supervisors. In this specific project, the numbers were large enough to make the process statistically significant.

ROI AT LEVEL 4: BUSINESS RESULTS

Most HR programs that develop ROI calculations focus on the business results (Level 4 data) that the program has influenced. These output variables are usually expressed in terms of cost reduction, productivity increases, improved quality, improved customer service, or reduced response times. It is relatively easy to convert them to monetary values for an ROI calculation. Earlier chapters focused on this type of data for ROI calculations, and additional detail is not needed here.

ROI calculations on business results are very credible and reliable if appropriate processes have been used to isolate the effects of the HR program and to accurately convert the results to monetary units. When ROI data are needed, this level of evaluation should always be sought if at all possible. ROI with Level 4 data thus becomes the fifth level of evaluation, the ultimate level of accountability.

SHORTCUT WAYS TO FORECAST ROI

This chapter has presented the techniques for forecasting ROI at four different time frames using four different levels of evaluation data. Two of these techniques would not be useful for simple and inexpensive projects. Forecasting using learning data at Level 2 and forecasting using application data at Level 3 are rare and should be reserved for only large-scale projects involving significant learning events. Validated tests are developed, and other instruments are used to build on the accuracy of the process. There are two useful techniques that may be helpful even for short-term, low-profile, inexpensive projects:

Pre-project/program forecasting. Pre-project forecasting may be necessary and actually desired even if it is not required. Because Level 4 data drive the HR project, business impact measures should be identified up front. Estimating the actual change in these measures is a recommended and highly useful exercise because it begins to show the client and HR professionals the perceived value of the project. This is a fairly simple exercise and was illustrated in a case example earlier in this chapter. It should take no more than one or two days' time to develop a forecast of the project, but it can be extremely valuable in communicating to the client and also providing some clear direction and focus for the program designers and coordinators. The process can be kept simple and credible, and the sources of information can be easy to access.

Forecasting with reaction data. In almost every HR program, reaction data are collected from individuals involved in the program. A worthwhile extension of reaction data is to include several questions that allow those individuals to project the actual success of the project. This was discussed as an option in Chapter 1. Here, it is recommended as an additional simple tool to forecast the actual ROI. This provides some additional insight into the potential worth of the project and alerts the HR staff to potential problems or issues that may need attention as the remaining issues are addressed in the HR initiative. As the information in this chapter illustrated, these questions are simple, and answers can easily be obtained with fifteen to twenty minutes of participants' time. For the process to be successful and usable, the participant must be committed to it. It may be helpful to follow some of the methods of increasing response rate for the various instruments described in this book.

FINAL THOUGHTS

This chapter illustrates that ROI calculations can be developed at different times and at different levels of evaluation, although most HR professionals and clients focus only on Levels 3 and 4 data for ROI calculations. Although post-program data are desired, there are situations in which Level 4 data are not available in a post-program time frame, or when evaluations at that level are not attempted or planned. ROI estimates, developed at Levels 1, 2, and 3, can be useful and helpful to management and the HR staff while at the same time focusing the participants' attention on the economic impact of the HR initiative. Using ROI estimates at Levels 1 and 2 may give a false sense of accuracy. Figure 11-1 shows the relationship of ROI at the different levels. As would be expected, ROI calculations with Level 1 data are the lowest in terms of credibility and accuracy, but they have the advantage of being inexpensive and relatively easy to develop. ROI calculations using Level 4 data are rich in credibility and accuracy but are very expensive and difficult to develop. Although ROI calculations at Level 4 data are preferred, ROI development at other levels is an important part of a comprehensive and systematic evaluation process.

CHAPTER 12

Implementation Issues

The best-designed process model or technique is worthless unless it is integrated efficiently and effectively in the organization. Although the ROI process presented in this book is a step-by-step, methodical, and simplistic procedure, it will fail even in the best organizations if it is not integrated into the mainstream of activity and fully accepted and supported by those who should make it work. This chapter focuses on critical issues involved in implementing the ROI process in the organization.

PLANNING THE IMPLEMENTATION

Few initiatives are effective without proper planning. The ROI process is no exception. As described in Chapter 2, the initial planning and analysis are synonymous with success. Described below are seven key steps in planning for and positioning the ROI process as an essential component of the human resources function.

Identify an ROI Champion

As a first step in the process, one or more individual(s) should be designated as the implementation leader or champion for the process. As in most change efforts, someone must take responsibility for ensuring that the process is implemented successfully. This leader serves as a champion for ROI and is usually the one who understands the process best and sees the vast potential for its contribution. More importantly, this leader must be willing to teach others the process.

The ROI leader has ROI implementation as a full-time responsibility within the HR function. In smaller organizations this would be a part-time responsibility. This role could be titled as the manager of measurement and evaluation, or the responsibility could be assigned to a team with the authority to lead the ROI effort. For example, one company selected five individuals to lead this effort as a team. All five received certification in the ROI process.

Develop the ROI Leader

In preparation to serve as the ROI implementation leader, individuals usually obtain special training that builds specific skills and knowledge in the ROI process. The role of the implementation leader is broad and serves a variety of specialized duties. In some organizations, the implementation leader can take on as many as fourteen roles:

- [ ] Technical expert
- [ ] Cheerleader
- [ ] Consultant
- [ ] Communicator
- [ ] Problem solver
- [ ] Process monitor
- [ ] Initiator
- [ ] Planner
- [ ] Designer
- [ ] Analyst
- [ ] Developer
- [ ] Interpreter
- [ ] Coordinator
- [ ] Teacher

This difficult and challenging assignment needs special training and skill building. In the past only a few programs have been available to help build these skills. Now many such programs exist, some quite comprehensive. One program is designed to certify the individuals who are assuming a leadership role in the implementation of ROI [1]. This certification is built around ten specific skill sets:

(For cards outside the US, please affix a postage stamp)

NO POSTAGE
NECESSARY
IF MAILED
IN THE
UNITED STATES

BUSINESS REPLY MAIL

FIRST-CLASS MAIL   PERMIT NO. 78   WOBURN MA

POSTAGE WILL BE PAID BY ADDRESSEE

DIRECT MAIL DEPARTMENT
BUTTERWORTH-HEINEMANN
225 WILDWOOD AVE
PO BOX 4500
WOBURN MA 01888-9930

Win $100 Worth of Books!

Register online for our FREE e-mail update service or join our mailing list and be entered in our monthly drawing to win $100 worth of books. Visit our website at **www.bh.com** to register and to check out information on our newest releases, complete this postage-paid reply card and return it to us now, or email us at marketing@bhusa.com.

What title have you purchased? _____

_____

How did you hear about it? _____

Where was the purchase made? _____

Name_____

Job Title _____

Institution _____

Address _____

City _____ State _____

Zip/Postcode _____

Country _____

Telephone _____

email _____

❑ Please arrange for me to be kept informed of other books and information services on this and related subjects. This information is being collected on behalf of Reed Elsevier Inc. and may be used to supply information about products by companies within the group.

(FOR OFFICE USE ONLY)

B UTTERWORTH
H EINEMANN

www.bh.com

BRC0700

(For cards outside the US, please affix a postage stamp)

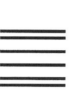

BUSINESS REPLY MAIL

FIRST-CLASS MAIL   PERMIT NO. 78   WOBURN MA

POSTAGE WILL BE PAID BY ADDRESSEE

DIRECT MAIL DEPARTMENT
BUTTERWORTH-HEINEMANN
225 WILDWOOD AVE
PO BOX 4500
WOBURN MA   01888-9930

Win $100 Worth of Books!

Register online for our FREE e-mail update service or join our mailing list and be entered in our monthly drawing to win $100 worth of books. Visit our website at **www.bh.com** to register and to check out information on our newest releases, complete this postage-paid reply card and return it to us now, or email us at marketing@bhusa.com.

What title have you purchased? _____

_____

How did you hear about it? _____

Where was the purchase made? _____

Name _____

Job Title _____

Institution _____

Address _____

City _____ State _____

Zip/Postcode _____

Country _____

Telephone _____

email _____

☐ Please arrange for me to be kept informed of other books and information services on this and related subjects. This information is being collected on behalf of Reed Elsevier Inc. and may be used to supply information about products by companies within the group.

BUTTERWORTH
HEINEMANN

www.bh.com

BRC0700

1. Planning for ROI calculations
2. Collecting evaluation data
3. Isolating the effects of the HR program or initiative
4. Converting data to monetary values
5. Monitoring program costs
6. Analyzing data, including calculating the ROI
7. Presenting evaluation data
8. Implementing the ROI process
9. Providing internal consulting on ROI
10. Teaching others the ROI process

The certification process is quite comprehensive, but such extensive measures may be necessary to build the appropriate skills to address this challenging assignment.

Assign Responsibilities

Defining specific responsibilities is a critical issue because confusion can arise when individuals do not have a clear picture of their specific assignments in the ROI process. Responsibilities apply to two groups. The first is the measurement and evaluation duty of the entire HR staff. Those involved in initiating and implementing programs and initiatives must have some responsibility for measurement and evaluation. These responsibilities include providing input about the design of instruments, planning a specific evaluation, analyzing data, and interpreting the results. Typical responsibilities include:

☐ Ensuring that the needs assessment includes specific business impact measures
☐ Developing specific application objectives (Level 3) and business impact objectives (Level 4) for each program or initiative
☐ Focusing the content of the program on performance improvement, ensuring that exercises, case studies, and skill practices relate to the desired objectives
☐ Keeping participants focused on application and impact objectives
☐ Communicating rationale and reasons for evaluation
☐ Assisting in follow-up activities to capture application and business impact data

☐ Providing technical assistance for data collection, data analysis, and reporting

☐ Designing instruments and plans for data collection and analysis

☐ Presenting evaluation data to a variety of groups

Although it may be inappropriate to involve each member of the staff in all these activities, each individual should have at least one responsibility as part of his or her routine job duties. Assigning responsibilities keeps the ROI process from being disjointed and separate from major HR activities. More importantly, it brings accountability to the initiation of various HR programs.

The second group is the technical support function. Depending on the size of the HR staff, it may be helpful to establish a group of technical experts who provide assistance with the ROI process. When this group is established, it must be clear that the experts are not there to relieve others of evaluation responsibilities but rather to supplement technical expertise. Some firms have found this approach effective. When this type of support is developed, responsibilities revolve around six key areas:

1. Designing data collection instruments
2. Providing assistance for developing an evaluation strategy
3. Analyzing data, including specialized statistical analyses
4. Interpreting results and making specific recommendations
5. Developing an evaluation report or case study to communicate overall results
6. Providing technical support in any phase of the ROI process

Although the HR staff must have specific responsibilities during an evaluation, it is not unusual to require others in support functions to have responsibility for data collection. These and similar responsibilities are defined when a particular evaluation strategy plan is developed and approved.

Develop Evaluation

Establishing specific targets for evaluation levels is an important way to make progress with measurement and evaluation. Targets enable the staff to focus on the improvements needed with specific evaluation levels. During this process, the percent of programs or initiatives planned for evaluation at each level is developed. The first step is to assess the current situation. The number of programs, including repeated segments of a program, is tabulated along with the corresponding level(s) of evaluation currently conducted for each program. Next, the percent of programs being measured at Level 1, reaction and planned action, is calculated. The process is then repeated for each level of the evaluation.

After detailing the current situation, the next step is to determine realistic targets to be met within a specific time frame. Many organizations set annual targets for changes. This process should involve the input of the entire HR staff to ensure the targets are realistic and the staff is committed to the process. If the HR staff does not embrace this process as its own, targets will not be met. The improvement targets must be achievable while, at the same time, challenging and motivating. Table 12-1 shows the targets established for a training function at a manufacturing site for the five levels [2]. Many of the Level 4 evaluations in this organization are taken to ROI. In some organizations, half the Level 4 calculations are taken to Level 5, while in others, every one of them is taken. Table 12-2 shows current percentages and targets for five years in a large multinational company. Table 12-2 shows the gradual improvement of increasing evaluation activity at Levels 3, 4, and 5. Year 0 is the current status in Table 12-2 [3].

Table 12-1
Evaluation Targets for a Training Function
at a Manufacturing Site

Levels	Measures	Percent
Level 1	Reaction, Satisfaction	100%
Level 2	Learning	70%
Level 3	Application	30%
Level 4	Results	20%
Level 5	ROI	10%

Table 12-2

Percentages and Targets for Five Years in a Large
Multinational Company

	Percent of Courses Evaluated at Each Level					
	Year 0	Year 1	Year 2	Year 3	Year 4	Year 5
Reaction and Planned Action	85%	90%	95%	100%	100%	100%
Learning	30%	35%	40%	45%	50%	60%
Job Application	5%	10%	15%	20%	25%	30%
Business Results	2%	4%	5%	9%	12%	15%
ROI	0%	2%	4%	6%	8%	10%

Target setting is a critical component of implementation. It should be completed early in the process with full support of the entire HR staff. Also, if practical and feasible, the targets should have the approval of the key management staff, particularly the senior management team.

Develop a Project Plan for Implementation

An important part of the planning process is to establish timetables for the complete implementation process. This document becomes a master plan for the completion of the different elements presented in this chapter, beginning with assigning responsibilities and concluding with meeting the targets previously described. From a practical basis, this schedule is a project plan for transition from the present situation to a desired future situation. The items on the schedule include, but are not limited to, developing specific ROI projects, building staff skills, developing policy, teaching managers the process, analyzing ROI data, and communicating results. The more detailed the document, the more useful it is. The project plan is a living, long-range document that should be reviewed frequently and adjusted as necessary.

More importantly, it should always be familiar to those who are working with the ROI process. Figure 12-1 shows an ROI implementation project plan for a large petroleum company [3].

Revise/Develop Policies and Procedures

Another key part of planning is revising (or developing) the organization's policy concerning measurement and evaluation for HR programs. The policy statement is designed specifically for the measurement and evaluation process. It is frequently developed

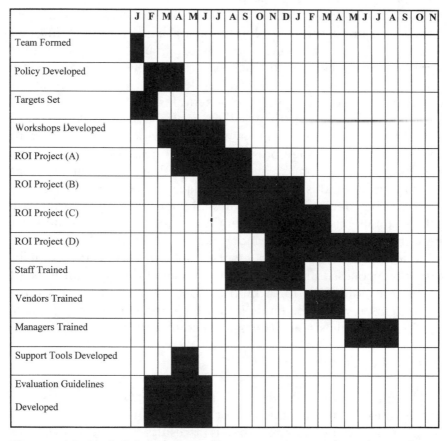

Figure 12-1. ROI implementation project plan for a large petroleum company.

with the input of the HR staff and key managers or clients. Sometimes policy issues are addressed during internal workshops designed to build skills with measurement and evaluation. The policy statement addresses critical issues that will influence the effectiveness of the measurement and evaluation process. Typical topics include adopting the five-level model presented in this book, requiring Levels 3 and 4 objectives in some or all programs, and defining responsibilities for human resources staff. Figure 12-2 shows a sample of topics included in an HR measurement and evaluation policy.

Policy statements are critical because they provide guidance and direction for the staff and for others who work closely with the ROI process. They keep the process clearly focused and enable the group to establish goals for evaluation. Policy statements also provide an opportunity to communicate basic requirements and fundamental accountability issues. More than anything else, they serve as a learning tool to teach others, especially when they are developed in a collaborative and collective way. If policy statements are developed in isolation, excluding ownership of the HR staff and management, they will be ineffective and of little use.

Guidelines for measurement and evaluation are important to show how to use the tools and techniques, guide the design process, provide consistency in the ROI process, ensure that appropriate methods are used, and place the proper emphasis on each of the areas. The guidelines are more technical than are policy statements and often contain detailed procedures showing how the process is actually undertaken and developed. They often include specific forms, instruments, and tools necessary to facilitate the process. Figure 12-3 shows the table of contents of evaluation guidelines for a multinational company. As this table of contents reveals, the guidelines are comprehensive and include significant emphasis on ROI and accountability.

Assess the Climate

The final step in planning the implementation is to assess the organization's current climate for achieving results. One useful tool, presented in the appendix, is a results-based test [4]. This test instrument, or some version of it, can serve as an initial assessment of how the full HR staff, and others whom the staff

1. Purpose
2. Mission
3. Evaluate all programs which will include the following levels:
   a. Reaction and planned action (100%)
   b. Learning (80%)
   c. Application (50%)
   d. Impact (10%)
   e. ROI (5%)
4. Evaluation support group (corporate) will provide assistance and advice in measurement and evaluation, instrument design, data analysis, and evaluation strategy.
5. New programs are developed beginning with needs analysis and ending with communicating results.
6. Data collection instruments must be valid, reliable, economical, and subject to audit by the evaluation support group.
7. Responsibility for HR program results rests with the HR staff, participants, and supervisors of participants.
8. An adequate system for collecting and monitoring HR costs must be in place. All direct costs should be included.
9. At least annually, the management board will review the status and results of HR programs and initiatives. The review will include HR plans, strategies, results, costs, priorities, and concerns.
10. Line management shares in the responsibility for HR program evaluation through follow-up, pre-program commitments, and overall support.
11. External HR consultants must be selected based on previous evaluation. All external HR programs of more than one day in duration will be subjected to evaluation procedures. In addition, the quality of external programs will be assessed by participants.
12. HR program results must be communicated to the appropriate target audience. At a minimum, this includes management (participants' supervisors), participants, and all HR staff.
13. HR staff should be qualified to conduct effective needs-analysis and evaluation.
14. A central database for program development should exist to prevent duplication and should serve as a program resource.
15. Labor union involvement will be included in the total HR plan.

Figure 12-2. Results-based internal HR policy (an example).

Section 1: Policy

1.1   The Need for Accountability
1.2   The Bottom Line: Linking Human Resources with Business Needs
1.3   Results-Based Approach
1.4   Implications
1.5   Communication
1.6   Payoff

Section 2: Responsibilities

2.1   Human Resources Group Responsibilities: Overall
2.2   Human Resources Group Responsibilities: Specifics for Selected Groups
2.3   The Business Unit Responsibilities
2.4   Participant Manager Responsibilities
2.5   Participants' Responsibilities

Section 3: Evaluation Framework

3.1   Purpose of Evaluation
3.2   Levels of Evaluation
3.3   Process Steps for Human Resources Implementation
3.4   Evaluation Model

Section 4: Level 1 Guidelines

4.1   Purpose and Scope
4.2   Areas of Coverage—Standard Form
4.3   Optional Areas of Coverage
4.4   Administrative Issues
4.5   How to Use Level 1 Data

Section 5: Level 2 Guidelines

5.1   Purpose and Scope
5.2   Learning Measurement Issues
5.3   Techniques for Measuring Learning
5.4   Administration
5.5   Using Level 2 Data

Section 6: Level 3 Guidelines

6.1   Purpose and Scope
6.2   Follow-Up Issues
6.3   Types of Follow-Up Techniques
6.4   Administrative Issues
6.5   Using Level 3 Evaluation

Figure 12-3. Evaluation guidelines for a multinational company.

Section 7: Levels 4 and 5 Guidelines

7.1   Purpose and Scope
7.2   Business Impact and ROI Issues
7.3   Monitoring Performance Data
7.4   Extracting Data from Follow-Up Evaluation
7.5   Isolating the Effects of the HR Solution
7.6   Converting Data to Monetary Values
7.7   Developing Costs
7.8   Calculating the ROI
7.9   Identifying Intangible Benefits
7.10   Administrative Issues
7.11   Using Business Impact and ROI Data

Figure 12-3. Continued.

supports, perceive the status of program results. Some organizations take annual assessments to measure progress as the ROI process is implemented. In other organizations, members of the management group answer the questions on the assessment instrument to provide feedback about their perceptions of the effectiveness of HR. The use of an assessment instrument or process provides an excellent understanding of the current status. Then the organization can plan for significant changes, pinpointing particular issues needing support as the ROI process is implemented.

PREPARING THE HR STAFF

One group that often resists the ROI process is the HR staff who determines which programs to implement. These staff members often see evaluation as an unnecessary intrusion into their responsibilities. This section outlines some important issues that must be addressed when preparing the staff for the implementation of ROI.

Involving the Staff

The staff should be involved in all major decisions and issues concerning the process. As policy statements are prepared and evaluation guidelines developed, staff input is absolutely essential. It is difficult for staff members to criticize something they helped design and develop. Using meetings, brainstorming sessions, and task forces, the staff should be involved in every phase of developing the framework and the supporting documents for ROI.

Using ROI as a Learning Tool

One reason the HR staff members may resist the ROI process is that the effectiveness of their programs will be fully exposed, putting their reputations on the line. To overcome this fear of failure, the ROI process should clearly be positioned as a tool for learning and not a tool for evaluating staff performance, at least during its early years of implementation. HR staff members will not be interested in developing a process that will be used against them.

Evaluators can learn as much from failures as successes. If the program is not working, it is best to find out quickly and understand the issues firsthand—not from others. If a program is ineffective and not producing the desired results, its ineffectiveness will eventually be known to clients and/or the management group, if they are not aware of it already. A lack of results will cause managers to become less supportive of HR programs and initiatives. If the weaknesses of programs are identified and adjustments are made quickly, not only will effective programs be developed but the credibility and respect for the function will be enhanced.

Dispelling Myths

Several obstacles to the implementation of the ROI process exist. Some of these are realistic barriers, while others are merely myths that are easily dispelled with further explanation. The most common myths are as follows:

☐ *ROI is too complex for most users.* While there are a few highly complex ROI models out there, many are straightforward and can be easily learned by HR professionals. The process described in this book, for example, is a basic financial formula for accountability that is simple and understandable: earnings divided by investments. "Earnings" equate to net benefits from the HR program, and the "investments" equal the actual costs of the program. Straying from this basic formula can add confusion and create tremendous misunderstanding.

☐ *ROI is expensive and consumes too many critical resources.* The ROI process can become expensive if it is not carefully organized and controlled, and properly implemented. Ten cost-savings approaches to ROI can help reduce cost when an organization is on a shoestring budget [2]. Each of these is discussed throughout this book:

1. Plan for evaluation early in the process.
2. Build evaluation into the HR process.
3. Share the responsibilities for evaluation.
4. Require participants to conduct major steps.
5. Use shortcut methods for major steps.
6. Use sampling to select appropriate programs.
7. Use estimates in the data collection and analysis.
8. Develop internal capability in implementing ROI evaluation.
9. Streamline the reporting process.
10. Use Web-based technology.

☐ *If senior management does not require ROI, there is no need to pursue it.* This idea captures the most innocent bystanders. It is easy to be lulled into providing evaluation and measurement that simply meets the status quo, believing that no pressure means no requirement. The truth is that if senior executives have only seen Level 1 reaction data, they may not be asking for higher-level data because they believe the process that provides this data has not yet been developed. In some cases, HR leaders have convinced top management that programs cannot be evaluated at the ROI level or that the specific impact of an HR program cannot be determined.

Senior managers are beginning to request this type of data. Changes in corporate leadership sometimes initiate important paradigm shifts. New leadership often requires proof of accountability. The process of integrating ROI into an organization takes a good deal of time—about twelve to eighteen months for many organizations. It is not a quick fix, and when senior executives suddenly ask the HR function to produce this kind of data, they may expect the results to be produced quickly. Because of this, HR departments should initiate the ROI measurement process and develop ROI impact studies long before senior management begins asking for ROI data.

☐ *ROI is a passing fad.* Unfortunately, this comment does apply to many of the processes being introduced to organizations today. Accountability for expenditures will always be present, and the ROI provides the ultimate level of accountability. As a tool, ROI has been used for some time. For years, it was used to measure the investment of equipment and new plants. Now it is being used in many other areas. With its rich history, ROI will continue to be used as an important tool in measurement and evaluation.

☐ *ROI measurement produces only one type of data.* This is a common misunderstanding. While the ROI process described in this book shows the costs versus benefits for the HR initiative, it actually serves as a scorecard reporting the following six types of data:

1. Reaction and planned action, showing the reaction of participants to programs and their intentions of plans to use their new knowledge or skills
2. Amount of learning in terms of skills and knowledge or changes in perceptions or behavior
3. Application or implementation of the program or initiative on the job
4. Business impact driven by the application of the program or initiative on the job
5. Return on investment, which shows the cost versus benefits of the initiative
6. Intangible data, representing important data not converted to monetary value

☐ *ROI is not future oriented; it only reflects past performance.* Many evaluation processes are past-oriented and reflect only what has happened with a program. This is the only way to have an accurate assessment of impact. It is possible, though, to adapt ROI measurement to reflect future returns. The challenge is to estimate the actual impact on the measures that will be influenced by a particular program. The rest of the process remains the same. Although this is a novel idea and is a routine request, the accuracy of forecasting is limited in any forecasting model. The consequences can be serious.

☐ *ROI is not a credible process—it is too subjective.* This notion has evolved because some ROI studies involving estimates have been publicized and promoted in literature and conferences. Many ROI studies can and have been conducted without the use of estimates. The problem with estimates often surfaces when attempting to isolate the effects of other factors. Using estimates from the participants is only one of the many different techniques used to isolate the effects of a program. Other techniques involve extremely precise and analytical approaches, such as use of control groups and a trendline analysis.

☐ *ROI measurement is only possible for production and sales.* The fact is ROI often works well in many programs. Many HR programs drive hard data items, such as output, quality, cost, or time. Case after case shows successful application of the ROI process to programs, such as outsourcing and stress management. Additional examples of successful ROI application can be found in compliance programs such as diversity, sexual harassment prevention, and policy implementation. Any type of program or process can be evaluated at the ROI level. Issues occur when ROI is used for programs that should not be evaluated at this level. The ROI process should be reserved for programs that are expensive, that address operational problems and issues related to strategic objectives, or that attract the interest of management in terms of increased accountability.

☐ *ROI is only for manufacturing and service organizations.* Although initial studies appeared in the manufacturing sector, the service sector quickly picked up the ROI process as a useful tool. It then migrated to the nonprofit sector as hospitals and healthcare firms began endorsing and using the process. Next, ROI moved through government sectors around the world and, now, educational institutions are beginning to use the process.

☐ *ROI is appropriate only for large organizations.* While it is true that large organizations with enormous HR budgets have the most interest in ROI, smaller organizations can also use the process, particularly when it is simplified and built into programs. Organizations with as few as 500 people have successfully applied the ROI process, using it as a tool to bring increased accountability and involvement to the human resources function.

☐ *When measuring ROI it is not possible to isolate the influence of other factors*. This is not true. There are at least ten ways to isolate the influence of other factors, and at least one method will work in any given situation. The challenge is to select an appropriate isolation method for the resources and accuracy needed in a particular situation. This false perception probably stems from an unsuccessful attempt at using a control group arrangement—a classic way of isolating the effect of a process, program, or initiative. In practice, a control group does not work in a majority of situations, causing some to abandon the issue of isolating other factors. In reality, there are many other techniques available for isolating factors, and these techniques are gaining credibility for providing accurate, reliable, and valid methods for isolating the effects.

☐ *Because there's no control over what happens after an HR intervention, a process based on measuring on-the-job improvements should not be used*. This idea is fading as organizations face the reality of implementing HR solutions and realize the importance of measuring results. Although the HR function does not have direct control of what happens in the workplace, it does have influence. An HR intervention must be considered within the context of the workplace—the program does not belong to the HR function; rather, it belongs to the organization. Many individuals and groups are involved in programs and, collectively, they have objectives that push expectations beyond the HR organization. These objectives focus on application and impact data that can be collected and used in the ROI analysis.

☐ *There are no standards for the ROI process*. An important problem facing measurement and evaluation is a lack of standardization or consistency. These questions are often asked: "What is a good ROI?" or, "What should be included in the cost so I can compare my data with other data?" or, "When should specific data be included in the ROI value instead of as an intangible?" While the questions are not easily answered, some help is on the way. A professional association called the ROI Network is developing standards for the ROI process, using as its base a group of guiding principles. Also under development is a database that will share thousands of studies so that best practices, patterns, trends, and standards are readily available [5].

These and other obstacles can thwart an otherwise successful implementation. Each must be removed or reduced to help ensure success with the ROI process.

Teaching the Staff

The HR staff will usually possess inadequate skills in measurement and evaluation and thus will need to develop some expertise in the process. Measurement and evaluation does not always constitute a formal part of the preparation to become an HR specialist. Consequently, each staff member must be provided with training on the ROI process to learn how it works, step-by-step. In addition, staff members must know how to develop an evaluation strategy and specific plan, collect and analyze data from the evaluation, and interpret results from data analysis. Sometimes a one- to two-day workshop is needed to build adequate skills and knowledge to understand the process, appreciate what it can do for the organization, see the necessity for it, and participate in a successful implementation. Perhaps the two most useful ROI documents are the data collection plan and ROI analysis plan, discussed in an earlier chapter. These plans show what data will be collected, at what time, and by whom, and how specific analyses will be conducted, including isolating the effects of the program resources and converting data to monetary values. Each staff member should know how to develop, understand, and use these documents.

INITIATING THE ROI PROCESS

The first tangible evidence of the ROI process may be the initiation of the first project for which the ROI is calculated. This section outlines some of the key issues involved in identifying projects and keeping them on track.

Selecting Initial Programs

Selecting a program for ROI analysis is an important and critical issue. Only specific types of programs should be selected for a comprehensive, detailed analysis. Listed below are typical criteria used for identifying programs for analysis. Select programs that—

- ☐ Involve large target audiences
- ☐ Are expected to be viable for a long time
- ☐ Are linked to operational goals and issues
- ☐ Are important to overall strategic objectives
- ☐ Are expensive
- ☐ Have high visibility
- ☐ Have a comprehensive needs assessment

Other considerations when selecting programs for ROI analysis include:

- ☐ The investment of time to implement the program
- ☐ The level of interest in the program by executive management

Using these criteria, or similar criteria, the staff must select the appropriate programs to consider for an ROI project. Ideally, management should concur with, or approve, the criteria.

The next major step is to determine how many projects to undertake initially and in which areas. A small number of initial projects are recommended, perhaps two or three programs. Programs may represent functional areas of HR including compensation, benefits, selection, compliance, training, and labor relations. Programs may also represent initiatives impacting the entire organization, including outsourcing, reengineering, affirmative action, and outplacement. Finally, initiatives that support the HR function from a technical standpoint, such as the implementation of a new HRIS system, may be a candidate for initial ROI implementation. However, caution must be taken when considering such a potentially high-profile project.

The important thing to remember is to select a manageable number of programs to ensure successful implementation of the process.

Reporting Progress

As the projects are developed and the ROI implementation is under way, status meetings should be conducted to report progress and to discuss critical issues with appropriate team members. For example, if a reengineering effort for operations is selected as one of the ROI projects, all the key staff involved in the program should meet regularly to discuss the status of the project. This keeps the project team focused on the critical issues, generates the best ideas to address particular issues and barriers, and builds a knowledge base to implement evaluation in future programs. Sometimes this group is facilitated by an external consultant, an expert in the ROI process. In other cases, the internal ROI leader may facilitate the group.

In essence, these meetings serve three major purposes: reporting progress, learning, and planning. Such a meeting usually begins with a status report for each ROI project, describing what has been accomplished since the previous meeting. Next, the specific barriers and problems encountered are discussed. During the discussions, new issues are interjected in terms of possible tactics, techniques, or tools. Also, the entire group discusses how to remove barriers to success and focuses on suggestions and recommendations for next steps, including developing specific plans. Finally, the next steps are determined.

Establishing Discussion Groups

Because the ROI process is considered difficult to understand and apply, it sometimes helps to establish discussion groups or competency groups designed to enhance the understanding and application of the process. These groups can supplement formal workshops and other training processes and are often quite flexible in their format. An external ROI consultant or the internal ROI leader usually facilitates these groups. In each session a new issue is presented and discussed thoroughly. Concerns about the ROI process are discussed, including how it applies to the organization. The process can be flexible and adjusted to different topics as the needs of the group drive the issues. Ideally, participants of the discussion group have an opportunity to apply, explore, or research the issues between sessions. Assignments such as reviewing a case analysis or reading an article are also appropriate between sessions to continue the development of knowledge and skills associated with the process.

MANAGEMENT TEAM

Perhaps no group is more important to the ROI process than the management team, which must allocate resources and support the human resources programs. In addition, management often provides input and assistance in the ROI process. Specific actions to train and develop the management team should be carefully planned and executed.

A critical issue that must be addressed is the relationship between the staff and key managers. A productive partnership is needed, which requires each party to understand the concerns, problems, and opportunities of the other. Developing this type of relationship is a long-term process that must be deliberately planned and initiated by key HR staff members. Sometimes the decision to commit resources and support for human resource programs is based on the effectiveness of this relationship.

Workshop for Managers

One effective approach to preparing managers for the ROI process is to conduct a workshop for managers. Varying in duration from one-half to two days, a practical workshop shapes critical skills and changes perceptions to enhance the support of the ROI process. Managers leave the workshop with an improved perception of the impact of HR programs and a clearer under-standing of their roles in the process. More importantly, they often have a renewed commitment to making HR programs and initiatives work in their organization.

Because of the critical need for this topic in management training, this workshop should be required for all managers, unless they have previously demonstrated strong support for the HR function. Because of this requirement, it is essential for top executives to support this workshop and, in some cases, take an active role in conducting it. To tailor the program to specific organizational needs, a brief needs assessment may be necessary to determine the specific focus and areas of emphasis for the program.

Target Audiences. Although the target audience for this type of program is usually middle-level managers, the target group may vary with different organizations. In some organizations, the target may be first-level managers, and in others the target may begin with second-level managers. Three important questions help determine the proper audience:

1. Which group has the most direct influence on the HR function?
2. Which management group is causing serious problems by lack of management support?
3. Which group has the need to understand the ROI process so group members can influence the implementation of HR programs?

The answer to these questions is often middle-level managers.

Timing. This workshop should be conducted early in the management development process, before non-supportive habits are delivered. When this program is implemented throughout the organization, it is best to start with higher-level managers and work down the organization. If possible, a version of the program should be a part of a traditional management training program provided to supervisors when they are promoted into managerial positions.

Selling Top Management. Because convincing top management to require this program may be difficult, three approaches should be considered:

1. Discuss and illustrate the consequences of inadequate management support for HR programs. For example, the statistics for wasted time and money are staggering.
2. Show how current support is lacking. An evaluation of an HR program often reveals the barriers to successful implementation. Lack of management support is often the main reason, which brings the issue close to home.
3. Demonstrate how money can be saved and results can be achieved with the ROI process.

The endorsement of the top management group is crucial. In some organizations, top managers actually attend the program to explore firsthand what is involved and what they must do to make the process work. At a minimum, top management should support the program by signing memos that describe the program or by approving policy statements. Top managers should also ask probing questions in their staff meetings from time to time. This will not happen by chance. The HR manager must tactfully coach top executives.

Workshop Content

The program usually covers the topics outlined next. The time allotted for each topic and specific focus depends on the organization, the experience of the managers, the needs of the managers, and the preparation of the management group. The program can be developed in separate modules, creating a situation in which managers can be exempt from certain modules based on their previous knowledge or experience with the topic. This module concept is recommended.

The Overall Importance of HR. Managers need to be convinced that the human resources function is a mainstream responsibility that is gaining importance and influence within organizations. They need to understand the results-based approach of today's progressive HR organization. After completing this module, managers should perceive HR as a critical component in their organization and be able to describe how it contributes to strategic and operational objectives. Data should be presented to show the full scope of HR within the organization. Tangible evidence of top management commitment should be presented in a form such as memos, directives, and policies signed by the CEO or other appropriate top executive. In some organizations, the invitation to attend the program may come from the CEO, a gesture that shows strong top management commitment. Also, external data should be included to illustrate the growth of HR budgets and the increasing importance of the function. A case study showing the linkage between HR and strategy will help demonstrate the importance of key HR initiatives.

The Impact of HR. Too often, managers feel unsure about the success of HR programs. After completing this module, managers will be able to identify the steps to measure the impact of HR programs on important output variables. Reports and studies should be presented showing the impact of key initiatives, using measures such as productivity, quality, cost, response times, and customer satisfaction. Internal evaluation reports, if available, should be presented to managers, showing convincing evidence that the HR function makes a significant difference in the organization. If internal reports are not available, success stories or case studies from other organizations can be used. Part IV in this book provides several case studies in which the impact of HR programs is determined. Managers need to be convinced that HR is a successful, results-based function that exists not only to help with change but also to meet critical organizational goals and objectives.

The HR Process. Managers usually will not support activities or processes that they do not fully understand. After completing this module, managers should be able to describe how the HR process works in their organization and should understand each critical step, from needs assessment to ROI calculation. Managers need to be aware of the effort that goes into developing an HR program and their role in each step of the process. A short case, illustrating all the steps, is helpful in this module. This discussion also reveals various areas of the potential impact of the HR program.

Responsibility for HR. Defining who is responsible for human resources is important to its success. After completing this module, managers should be able to list their specific responsibilities for human resources. Managers must see how they can influence HR programs and the degree of responsibility they must assume in the future. The idea that multiple people should take responsibility for HR should be advocated—this includes managers, participants, participant supervisors, and program leaders/facilitators. Case studies are appropriate in this module to illustrate the consequences when responsibilities are neglected or when managers fail to follow up. Some organizations may revise job descriptions to reflect the HR responsibilities. Other organizations may establish major job-related goals to highlight management responsibility for HR. Overall, this session leaves participants with a clear understanding of how their responsibility is linked to the success of HR programs.

Active Involvement. One of the most important ways to enhance managers' support for HR is to actively involve them in the process. After completing this module, managers will actually commit to one or more ways of active involvement in the future. Table 12-3 shows eleven ways in which managers can be involved, as identified by one company. The information in the table was presented to managers in the workshop. After fully explaining and discussing the areas of involvement, each manager was asked to select one or more ways to be involved in HR in the future. A commitment to at least one involvement role was required.

If used properly, these commitments can provide a rich source of input and assistance from the management group. Workshop participants will offer to be involved in many ways, and HR must follow through with the offers for this involvement. An immediate follow-up on all offers is recommended.

MONITORING PROGRESS AND COMMUNICATING RESULTS

A final part of the implementation process is to monitor overall progress and communicate the results of specific ROI projects. Although it is an often overlooked part of the process, an effective communication plan can help keep the implementation on target and let others know what the ROI process is accomplishing for the organization. Because of the importance of communication, Chapter 10 is dedicated entirely to this topic.

CONCLUSION

In summary, the implementation of the ROI process is a critical part of the process. If not approached in a systematic, logical, and planned way, the ROI process will not become an integral part of the HR function, and consequently the programs will lack accountability. This chapter presented the different elements that must be considered and issues that must be addressed to ensure that implementation is smooth and uneventful. The result will be a complete integration of ROI as a mainstream activity in the ROI process.

Table 12-3
Management Involvement in Human Resources.

The following are areas for present and future involvement in the HR process. Please check your areas of planned involvement.

	In Your Area	Outside Your Area
☐ Attend a program designed for your staff	☐	☐
☐ Provide input for an HR needs analysis	☐	☐
☐ Serve on an HR advisory committee	☐	☐
☐ Provide input for an HR program design	☐	☐
☐ Serve as a subject-matter expert	☐	☐
☐ Serve on a task force to develop a program	☐	☐
☐ Volunteer to evaluate an external HR program	☐	☐
☐ Assist in the selection of a vendor-supplied HR program	☐	☐
☐ Provide reinforcement to your employees as they become involved in HR programs	☐	☐
☐ Coordinate an HR program	☐	☐
☐ Assist in program evaluation or follow-up	☐	☐

REFERENCES

1. *Certification Process for Measuring the Return on Investment in Training and Development Workshop.* Brochure. Birmingham, Ala.: Performance Resources Organization, 1996.
2. Phillips, Patricia Pulliam, and Burkett, Holly. *ROI on a Shoestring.* ASTD Infoline Series. Alexandria, Va.: American Society for Training and Development, 2000.
3. Phillips, J. J. *Return on Investment in Training and Performance Improvement Programs.* Houston, Tex.: Gulf Publishing, 1997.
4. Phillips, J. J. *Accountability in Human Resource Management.* Houston, Tex.: Gulf Publishing, 1996.
5. Phillips, J. J., and Pulliam, Patricia F. "Dispelling the ROI Myths." *Corporate University Review,* May/June 1999, pp. 32–36.

PART IV

Case Applications

CHAPTER 13

Sexual Harassment Prevention*

Healthcare Inc.

By Jack J. Phillips and Dianne Hill

Most organizations have sexual harassment prevention programs, but few are subjected to accountability up to and including a return-on-investment (ROI) analysis. In the setting in this case, a large healthcare chain conducted a sexual harassment prevention workshop involving first-level managers and supervisors. Workshops were followed by meetings with all employees conducted by the same managers and supervisors. In all, seventeen workshops were presented, and the monetary impact was developed. Several unique issues are involved in this case, including the techniques to isolate the effects of training and convert data to monetary values. The analysis used a traditional ROI model and yielded significant and impressive results that surprised the evaluation team and senior managers.

*This case study was previously published in In Action: Measuring Return on Investment, Vol. 2. Jack J. Phillips (Ed.) Alexandria, Va.: American Society for Training and Development, 1997, pp. 17–35.

BACKGROUND

Healthcare Inc. (HI) is a regional provider of a variety of healthcare services through a chain of hospitals, HMOs, and clinics. HI has grown steadily in the last few years and has earned a reputation as an aggressive and financially sound company. HI is publicly owned, with an aggressive management team poised for additional growth.

The healthcare industry in the USA continues to operate in a state of tremendous transformation and transition. The concern about healthcare costs, the threat of additional government regulation, and the implementation of new technology and healthcare delivery systems are radically transforming the healthcare field. HI is attempting to take advantage of these challenges and carve out a significant market share in its regional area of operation.

EVENTS LEADING TO PROGRAM

In the USA, sexual harassment continues to grow as an important and significant employee relations issue. Sexual harassment claims throughout the USA and in the healthcare industry continue to grow, sparked in part by increased public awareness of the issue and the willingness of the victims to report harassment complaints. HI has experienced an increasing number of sexual harassment complaints, with a significant number of them converting to charges and lawsuits. The company record was considered excessive by executives and represented a persistent and irritating problem. In addition, HI was experiencing an unusually high level of turnover, which may have been linked to sexual harassment.

Senior management, concerned about the stigma of continued sexual harassment complaints and the increasing cost of defending the company against claims, instructed the HR vice president to take corrective and preventive action to significantly reduce complaints and ultimately rid the workplace of any signs of harassment. The HR vice president instructed the HRD staff to develop a workshop for employees or managers or both, but only if a lack of understanding and knowledge of the issue existed.

In response to the request, the HRD staff conducted interviews with the entire EEO and affirmative action staff in which the magnitude of the problem and the potential causes were explored. Most of the staff indicated that there seemed to be a significant lack of understanding of the company's policy on sexual harassment and what actually constituted inappropriate or illegal behavior. In addition, the complaints for the last year were examined for issues and patterns. Exit interviews of terminating employees for the last year were reviewed to see if there was a linkage to sexual harassment. Approximately 11 percent of terminating employees identified sexual harassment as a factor in their decision to leave HI. Because of the request to proceed with this program, the HRD staff members did not conduct a full-scale needs assessment. Instead, they augmented the input from the EEO/AA staff with the exit interviews conducted with ten randomly selected first-level supervisors to explore the level of understanding of the policy, inappropriate and illegal behavior, and the perceived causes of the increased complaint activity.

From an analysis of complaints, the typical person accused of sexual harassment was a supervisor and male. The typical victim of harassment was non-supervisory and female. The analysis also revealed that the type of sexual harassment typically experienced at HI was in the category of hostile environment, defined by the EEOC as "an individual making unwelcome sexual advances or other verbal or physical conduct of a sexual nature with the purpose of, or that creates the effect of, unreasonably interfering with an individual's work performance or creating an intimidating, hostile, or offensive working environment." This type of harassment should be minimized by developing a clear understanding of HI's policy regarding harassment and by teaching managers to identify illegal and inappropriate activity. As part of HI's policy, supervisors and managers were required to conduct a limited investigation of informal complaints and to discuss issues as they surfaced.

THE PROGRAM: DESIGN, DEVELOPMENT, AND IMPLEMENTATION

Armed with input from ten interviews and with detailed input from the EEO/AA staff, the major causes of the problem were identified. There was an apparent lack of understanding of (1) the company's sexual harassment policy and (2) what constituted inappropriate and illegal behavior. In addition, there was an apparent insensitivity to the issue. As a result, a one-day sexual harassment prevention workshop was designed for all first- and second-level supervisors and managers. The program had the following objectives. After attending this program, participants should be able to:

- [ ] Understand and administer the company's policy on sexual harassment
- [ ] Identify inappropriate and illegal behavior related to sexual harassment
- [ ] Investigate and discuss sexual harassment issues
- [ ] Conduct a meeting with all direct reports to discuss policy and expected behavior
- [ ] Ensure that the workplace is free from sexual harassment
- [ ] Reduce the number of sexual harassment complaints

Because of the implications of this issue, it was important for the information to be discussed with all employees so that there would not be any misunderstanding about the policy or inappropriate behavior. Consequently, each supervisor was asked to conduct a meeting with his or her direct reports to discuss this topic.

The program design was typical of HI programs, using a combination of purchased and internally developed materials. The one-day program was implemented and conducted during a 45-day period, with 17 sessions involving 655 managers. HR managers and coordinators served as program facilitators.

Why ROI?

HR/HRD programs usually targeted for an ROI calculation are those perceived to be adding significant value to the company, closely linked to the organizational goals and strategic objectives. Then, the ROI calculation is pursued to confirm the added value, and based on the results of the ROI analysis, these programs may be enhanced, redesigned, or eliminated altogether if the ROI is negative. Sexual harassment prevention training is usually different; if the ROI analysis yielded a negative value, the program would not be discontinued. It might be altered for future sessions but only if the behavior changes were not occurring at Level 3.

At HI, this program was chosen for an ROI calculation for two reasons. First, the HR and HRD departments were interested in the accountability of all programs, including sexual harassment programs. Second, a positive ROI would clearly show management that these types of programs, which are preventive in nature, can significantly impact the bottom line when implemented throughout the organization and supported by management.

DATA COLLECTION

Exhibit 13-1 shows the completed data collection plan for the sexual harassment training program. A pre/post-test was administered to measure knowledge of HI's sexual harassment policy and of inappropriate and illegal behavior. The twenty-item questionnaire was evenly split on policy and behavior issues.

To measure the success of program application, three data collection methods were used. First, a meeting record was required of each supervisor and manager to document the actual meeting with employees, recording the time, duration, topics, and participants. Although, this form did not address the quality of the meeting, it provided evidence that the meeting was conducted.

The second data collection method was a survey of the non-supervisory employees, the typical target group for harassment activity. Although the entire team could have been surveyed, it was felt that it was more important to examine behavior change from the perspective of those who were more likely to be victims of harassment. The survey was planned for administration six months after the program was completed. It provided post-program data only and thus each questionnaire had to be worded to capture change since the training was conducted. The fifteen-item survey examined specific behavior changes and environmental changes related to harassment activity, including actions that might be considered inappropriate or offensive. Table 13-1 shows some typical questions.

The third data collection method was a self-assessment questionnaire completed by supervisors and managers. This questionnaire

Exhibit 13-1

Program: ___Preventing Sexual Harassment___ Responsibility: _____ Date: _____

Evaluation Plan: Data Collection

Level	Program Objective(s)	Evaluation Method	Timing	Responsibilities
I Reaction, Satisfaction and Planned Actions	• Obtain a positive reaction to program and materials • Obtain input for suggestions for improving program • Identify planned actions	• Reaction questionnaire	• End of session	• Facilitator
II Learning	• Knowledge of policy on sexual harassment • Knowledge of inappropriate and illegal behavior • Skills to investigate and discuss sexual harassment	• Pre/post-test • Skill practices	• Beginning of session • End of session • During session	• Facilitator
III Job Application	• Administer policy • Conduct meeting with employees • Ensure that workplace is free of sexual harassment	• Self-assessment questionnaire • Complete and submit meeting record • Employee Survey (25% sample)	• 6 months after program • 1 month after program • 6 months after program	• Program evaluator • HRIS staff • Employee communication
IV Business Results	• Reduce internal complaints • Reduce external complaints • Reduce employee turnover	• Performance monitoring • Self-assessment questionnaire	• Monthly for 1 year before and after program • 6 months after program	• Program evaluator

Table 13-1

	Strongly Disagree	Disagree	Neutral	Agree	Strongly Agree
I have noticed less offensive language at work.	☐	☐	☐	☐	☐
I am certain that the company will take swift action against those who are found guilty of sexual harassment.	☐	☐	☐	☐	☐

captured actions, behavior change, and results linked to the program. Although there were a variety of other data collection possibilities, including focus groups, interviews, and third party observation, it was felt that, given the time and cost considerations, these three methods provided sufficient data to capture behavior change and show that the program had succeeded.

Business results measures included several items. Initially, it was planned that internal complaints, lodged formally with the HR division, would be monitored along with external charges filed with various agencies (primarily the EEOC). Because of the lag time between changes in behavior and a reduction in complaints, data would be collected for one year after the program and compared with data from one year before the program to determine specific improvements. Also, as alternative information, litigated complaints would be tracked along with the direct costs, including legal fees, settlements, and losses. In addition, because of the perceived link between a hostile work environment and turnover, annual employee turnover would be examined for the same time period.

ROI Analysis

To develop the ROI calculation, several other issues needed to be addressed to plan for the Level 5 evaluation. The specific method(s) to isolate the effects of the program from other influences would have to be selected and implemented. The various ways in which data are converted to monetary values would need to be pinpointed. Each specific program cost element would have to be identified along with other issues that might influence the reduction in complaints and litigation expenses. Finally, intangible benefits expected from the program needed to be itemized and the communication targets established.

ROI ANALYSIS PLAN

Exhibit 13-2 shows the completed document for the ROI analysis plan. Because of the relatively short time frame required to implement the program and the desire from top management to implement it throughout the organization quickly, a control group arrangement was not feasible. However, because historical data are available for all complaint measures, a trendline analysis was initially planned. Complaint activity would be projected based on twelve months of data prior to the program. Actual performance would be compared with the projected value, and the difference would reflect the actual impact of the program on that measure. In addition to trendline analysis, participants' estimation was planned to compare with trendline data. In this type of situation, supervisors and managers (participants) are asked to indicate the extent to which the program influenced the changes in the number of complaints.

For turnover, trendline analysis could not be used because of the other initiatives implemented to reduce turnover. Thus, a type of forecasting was used in which the percentage of turnover related to sexual harassment is developed for the twelve-month period prior to the program The same percentage is developed for the post-program period.

In regard to converting the data to monetary values, the cost of complaints would be derived both from historical data, when available, and from estimates for other factors, such as the actual time used for harassment complaints. The estimates would be developed with input from the EEO/AA staff. For turnover, industry data would be used because HI had not calculated the actual cost of turnover for any employee groups. The specific cost

Exhibit 13-2

Program: __Preventing Sexual Harassment__   Responsibility: _____   Date: _____

Evaluation Strategy: ROI Analysis

Data Items	Methods of Isolating the Effects of the Program	Methods of Converting Data	Cost Categories	Intangible Benefits	Other Influences/Issues	Communication Targets
Formal internal complaints of sexual harassment	• Trendline Analysis • Participant Estimation	• Historical costs with estimation from EEO/AA staff	• Needs assessment • Program development/ acquisition • Coordination/ Facilitation time	• Job satisfaction • Absenteeism • Stress reduction • Image of HI • Recruiting	• Several initiatives to reduce turnover were implemented during this time period	• All employees (condensed info.) • Senior executives (summary of report with detailed backup)
External complaints of sexual harassment	• Trendline analysis • Participant estimation	• Historical costs with estimation from EEO/AA staff	• Program materials • Food/ refreshments • Facilities • Participant salaries and benefits		• Must not duplicate benefits from both internal and external complaints	• All supervisors and managers (brief report)
Employee turnover	• Forecasting using percent of turnover related to sexual harassment	• External studies within industry	• Evaluation			• All HR/HRD staff (full report)

items, intangible benefits, other influences, and communication targets were all identified and are presented in Exhibit 13-2.

REACTION AND LEARNING DATA

A typical end-of-program questionnaire was used to capture reaction data. Overall, the participants reacted very positively to the program and perceived it to be timely and useful. A composite rating of 4.11 out of a possible 5 was achieved. The vast majority of the participants (93 percent) provided a list of action items planned as a result of the program.

For a Level 2 evaluation, the pre-program test scores averaged 51 and the post-program scores averaged 84, representing a dramatic increase of 65 percent. These results were significant and exceeded the expectations of the program developers. Two important points were underscored with the Level 2 measures. First, the low scores on pre-program testing provided evidence that the program was necessary. The participants did not understand the organization's policy, nor did they recognize what constituted inappropriate and illegal behavior. Second, the dramatic improvement in scores provided assurance that the content of the program was appropriate for both key issues, as the participants learned much about policy and behavior. As part of the Level 2 evaluation, participants were involved in skill practices for issues involving administering policy.

ON-THE-JOB APPLICATION

One of the initial actions required of participants was to conduct a meeting with his/her employees to discuss sexual harassment issues, review HI's policy on sexual harassment, and discuss what constitutes inappropriate and illegal behavior. Handouts and visual aids were provided to each supervisor and manager to assist with the meeting. A meeting record form had to be completed and submitted to the HR department as evidence that the meeting was conducted. The time of the meeting, the duration, the participants by name, and the specific topics covered were noted on the form. Within one month of the program, 82 percent of the participants had completed the meeting record.

Ultimately, 96 percent completed it. Some managers did not conduct meetings because they did not have direct reports.

Six months after the program was conducted, an anonymous survey was conducted with a 25 percent sample of non-supervisory employees. A total of 1,720 surveys were distributed, and 1,100 were returned for a response rate of 64 percent. The survey yielded an average score of 4.1 on a scale of 1 to 5. The rating represents the extent to which the behavior had changed in the six months since the program was conducted. Overall, the survey results indicated that significant behavior change had occurred and the work environment was largely free of harassment.

A follow-up questionnaire was administered directly to all participants six months after the program was conducted. A total of 571 questionnaires were returned, representing a response rate of 87 percent. The questionnaire probed the extent to which program materials were used and specific behavior changes had been realized. In addition, participants estimated the amount of improvement in sexual harassment complaints that was directly attributable to this program. Although the input from participants (managers and supervisors) may be biased, significant changes were reported. In regard to actions completed, 92 percent reported that some actions were completed while 68 percent reported that all actions were completed.

BUSINESS IMPACT

Exhibit 13-3 shows the complaint and turnover data for one year prior to the program and one year after the program. In the six-month follow-up questionnaire, participants were provided the six-month averages from before and after the program and were asked to estimate the percent of improvement actually caused by this program. The average percentages from all participants are included in the right column. The results also show the turnover rate for the non-supervisory employees for the twelve months preceding the program and for the twelve months after the program.

Exhibit 13-4 shows a plot of the formal internal complaints of sexual harassment twelve months prior to the program and twelve months after the program. Prior to the program there was an upward trend of complaints, and senior managers felt this

Exhibit 13-3

Business Performance Measure	One Year Prior to Program	One Year After Program	Factor For Isolating the Effects of Program
Internal Complaints	55	35	74%
External Charges	24	14	62%
Litigated Complaints	10	6	51%
Legal Fees and Expenses	$632,000	$481,000	
Settlement/Losses	$450,000	$125,000	
Total Cost of Sexual Harassment Prevention, Investigation, and Defense*	$1,655,000	$852,000	
Turnover (Non-Supervisory) Annualized	24.2%	19.9%	

*Includes legal fees, settlement/losses, portion of EEO/AA staff assigned to sexual harassment, management time for this activity, printed materials, and miscellaneous expenses.

Exhibit 13-4

Formal Internal Complaints of Sexual Harassment

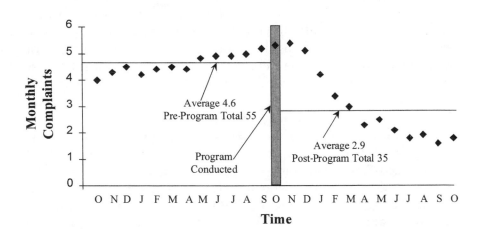

would continue if they took no action to improve the situation. Also, no other initiatives were undertaken to focus attention on sexual harassment. The magnitude of the program, involving seventeen training sessions with 655 managers and meetings with all employees, focused significant attention on the issue. Thus, it was felt that the trendline analysis might be an effective tool for isolating the effects of training.

The turnover rate showed a dramatic improvement during this same time frame. However, because of the serious problem with turnover, other initiatives were undertaken to help reduce the departure rate of employees. Recruiting processes were enhanced, entry-level salaries were increased, and more effective selection techniques were employed during the same time period. All these actions were initiated to develop a better match between the employees and the culture at HI. Thus, the trendline forecast for the turnover rate would be accurate because of the influence of these factors on the turnover rate.

To estimate the percent of turnover reduction directly related to this program, a special version of the forecasting process was considered. During the needs assessment, the exit interview files were reviewed for evidence of sexual harassment as a factor in the decision to leave. In these cases, 11 percent of the actual turnovers had mentioned sexual harassment. Employees are often reluctant to indicate the presence of sexual harassment although this issue may be the reason for their departure. Thus, it was felt that this 11 percent figure was a conservative estimate of the number of terminations related to a hostile work environment. A twelve-month review of exit interviews, on a post-program basis, revealed that only 3 percent of the interviewees mentioned sexual harassment or a hostile work environment as a reason for their departure. Thus, the percent of employees leaving because of sexual harassment dropped from 11 to 3 percent of terminations. The target group for the turnover reduction was non-supervisory employees, which represented an average of 6,844 on a post-program basis and 6,651 on a pre-program basis. For the twelve-month period after the program, the employment levels at HI averaged 7,540, including 655 for the target group for training and 41 senior managers who did not participate directly in the training program. The average non-supervisory salary for the post-program period was $27,850, and for the pre-program period, it was $26,541. Several industry studies on the cost of turnover were briefly discussed, which showed ranges from 110 percent to 150 percent of annual salaries. The evaluation team felt that 75 percent of annual salaries would be a conservative estimate.

PROGRAM COSTS

Program costs are fully loaded and include the cost of the needs assessment ($9,000), design and development ($15,000), and evaluation ($31,000). The needs assessment cost was an estimate based on the direct time and expenses involved in the process. The development costs were low because of the availability of materials for purchase. The evaluation costs include an estimate of all internal and external costs associated with the follow-up evaluation, including the ROI. Participants' salaries and benefits were included although it was not HI's policy to include salaries and benefits as a training expense for a one-day program for supervisors and managers.

Exhibit 13-5 shows the salary profile of participating supervisors and managers. The time necessary for program coordination was estimated along with the time for facilitator preparation and delivery. When considering the average salaries plus benefits for these individuals, a value of $9,600 was estimated. Travel and lodging for coordination and facilitation was a minor factor, estimated at $1,520. Program materials cost $12 per participant, and food and refreshments during the workshop cost $30 per

Exhibit 13-5
Salaries and Benefits of Participants

Management Level	Number Participating in Program	Salary Midpoint Value
7	41	$32,500
8	435	43,600
9	121	54,300
10	58	66,700

Employee benefits costs as a percent of payroll = 39%.
Managers work an average of 47 weeks per year.

participant. The estimated value of the conference rooms used for the program was $150 per day.

MONETARY BENEFITS FROM PROGRAM

Exhibit 13-6 shows the calculation for the monetary benefits from the sexual harassment program. For the reduction of complaints, the value could be based on reducing internal complaints, external charges, or litigated complaints, but not all three. The value for each measure is shown in the exhibit. The values are developed by taking the total cost of sexual harassment prevention, investigation, and defense from Exhibit 13-3 and dividing it by each of these three measures. The total value of the reduction for each measure (indicated in Exhibit 13-3) was developed, leaving the decision of which measure to use. Because of the interest in tracking internal complaints, the evaluation team decided to use it as the unit of improvement in the analysis. Thus, the value of one internal complaint was placed at $24,343. If one complaint could be avoided, HI would save that amount. The lower value is used to be conservative. Another approach is to examine the total cost of sexual harassment, including prevention, investigation, and defense, and use a value equal to the reduction in cost. However, because there is a lag between measures of complaints and actual losses and legal expenses, the reduction illustrated in Exhibit 13-3 may not reflect the actual cost savings.

Although the total improvement is 20 internal complaints, the improvement related directly to the program is 74 percent of that figure, or 14.8 complaints. The 74 percent is an estimate from the supervisors and managers taken directly from the questionnaire, as they were asked to indicate the extent to which the reduction in complaints was related directly to the program. The value of the improvement is $360,276. Exhibit 13-6 shows these calculations.

The value for the turnover reduction was developed in a similar manner. The unit of improvement is one turnover statistic. The 24.2 percent turnover rate represents 1,610 employees who, before the program, left voluntarily or were forced to leave because of performance. According to the exit interviews, 11 percent of those were related to sexual harassment. Thus, 177 terminations were related to sexual harassment. On a post-program basis, the 19.9 percent turnover represents 1,362

Exhibit 13-6
Monetary Benefits from Program

Complaint Reduction

	Pre-Program	Post-Program
Average Cost of Internal Complaint	$30,090	$24,343
Average Cost of External Complaint	$68,958	$60,857
Average Cost of Litigated Complaint	$165,500	$142,000

Unit of Improvement = One Internal Complaint

Value of One Internal Complaint = $24,343

Total Improvement: 55 − 35 = 20

Improvement Related to Program: 20 × 74% = 14.8

Value of Improvement = 14.8 × $24,343 = $360,276

Turnover Reduction

Unit of Improvement = One Turnover Statistic (Termination)

Turnover Pre-Program = 6,651 × 24.2% = 1,610

Turnover, Pre-Program, Related to Hostile Environment:
1,610 × 11% = 177

Turnover, Post-Program: 6,844 × 19.9% = 1,362

Turnover Post-Program Related to Hostile Environment:
1,362 × 3% = 41

Improvement Related to Program: 177 − 41 = 136

Cost of One Turnover: 75% of Annual Salary = $27,850 × .75
= $20,887

Value of Improvement: 136 × $20,887 = $2,840,632

employees. Post-program exit interviews revealed that 3 percent were related to a hostile work environment. Thus, 41 employees left because of the hostile environment. The improvement related directly to the program is 136 terminations, a significant number when the cost of turnover is included. Although there was sufficient evidence to use the annual salary as a cost of turnover, to be conservative the team used 75 percent of the annual salaries, representing $20,887 as a cost of one turnover statistic. Consequently, the 136 yielded a staggering $2,840,632 as the savings generated by the reduction in turnover that was caused by sexual harassment.

Exhibit 13-7 shows the trendline projections for the internal complaint data. The trend, established prior to the program, was projected for the evaluation period. As the projection shows, the impact of the program is even more dramatic than illustrated in the above calculations because of the upward trend of the data. Because the impact is more conservative using the participants' estimates, this figure was used in the analysis. Consequently, the actual calculations represent an understatement of actual performance.

PROGRAM COST

Exhibit 13-8 shows the detail of the program cost categories. Most of the cost items were straightforward and taken from actual cost statements or from estimates given by those closely

Exhibit 13-7
Formal Internal Complaints of Sexual Harassment

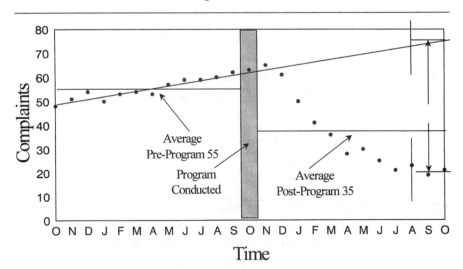

Exhibit 13-8
Program Costs

Needs Assessment (Estimated Cost of Time)	$9,000
Program Development/Acquisition	15,000
Program Coordination/Facilitation Time	9,600
Travel and Lodging for Facilitation and Coordinators	1,520
Program Materials (655 @ $12)	7,860
Food/Refreshments (655 @ $30)	19,650
Facilities (17 @ $150)	2,550
Participant Salaries and Benefits ($130,797 × 1.39)	181,807
Evaluation	31,000
	$277,987

involved in the process. Participants' salaries and benefits were developed using midpoint values for the managers in each classification. The managers' midpoint salary data were converted to a daily rate by dividing by 235 (the number of days actually worked), and this was multiplied by the number of managers at that grade level attending the program. Participants' salaries and benefits greatly overshadow the other cost elements.

ROI Calculation

Exhibit 13-9 shows the benefit/cost ratio and ROI calculations for these values. Benefits based entirely on complaint reduction and turnover reduction are used in the benefit/cost ratio to yield 11.5:1. Thus, for each $1 spent on the program, $11.50 was returned. The ROI calculation, which uses net benefits, shows a return of 1,052 percent, an impressive and staggering amount.

Exhibit 13-9
ROI Calculation

$$BCR = \frac{Benefits}{Costs} = \frac{\$360,276 + \$2,840,632}{\$277,987} = \frac{\$3,200,908}{\$277,987} = 11.5:1$$

$$ROI = \frac{Net\ Benefits}{Costs} = \frac{\$3,200,908 - \$277,987}{\$277,987} = 1,052\%$$

QUESTIONS FOR DISCUSSION

1. Was the needs assessment appropriate for this situation? Please explain.
2. Should this program be evaluated at Levels 4 and 5? If so, what specific measures should be used for Level 4 data?
3. What specific method(s) should be used to isolate the effects of the program?
4. What are the most appropriate ways to convert the Level 4 data to monetary values?
5. Critique the Level 2 and Level 3 results. Was the employee survey necessary? Explain.
6. Which Level 4 complaint measure is most appropriate? Why?
7. Project the trendline for internal complaints and estimate the impact of the program on the number of complaints. Use the average of the last three months for comparison.
8. Is the ROI lower or higher than you expected? Please comment.
9. Do you consider this estimate realistic?
10. How could this process be improved?
11. How would you present these data to management? To all employees?

CHAPTER 14

Competency-Based Pay System

National Crushed Stone Company

By Patricia Pulliam Phillips

Set in an extremely competitive industry, this case shows the impact and return on investment of a competency-based pay system installed in construction aggregate plants. Because the old pay system seemed inefficient and tedious, National Crushed Stone decided to try basing compensation on employees' skills and competencies instead of on the specific jobs performed by employees, as had been done in the past. This case demonstrates how the indisputable data were developed to show the contribution of a new pay scheme and the effects that it had on operations.

BACKGROUND

The crushed stone industry is a very competitive industry in which profit margins are narrow and cost control is everything. Companies in this industry are constantly seeking ways to control costs to gain a competitive advantage in the marketplace. National

Crushed Stone Company is one of the leading firms in the crushed stone industry, with more than 150 locations in several geographic areas. Each crushed stone plant offers a narrowly defined product mix consisting of various sizes of crushed stone used in construction projects such as roads, bridges, and large buildings. National Crushed Stone (NCS) takes pride in its employee relations programs and usually has a stable workforce although turnover is sometimes a problem. A typical plant is staffed with approximately twenty employees and is organized by a plant manager.

COMPETENCY-BASED PAY

Employees perform a variety of jobs from entry-level labor duties to skilled mechanic positions involving equipment repair. Traditionally, employees were assigned to one of twelve different job titles within a plant. Each job had a distinctive pay rate, and employees usually worked in their specific job classifications all day. If they had to work "out of their classification," they were paid at the highest rate. Permanent promotions were rare.

Because the current system seemed too cumbersome and created inefficiencies, the HR manager and the production manager considered the possibility of a skill-based or competency-based pay. With this system, employee pay is based on skills and competencies—not on the particular job the employee is performing at the time. Employees are rewarded with promotions and pay increases for learning new skills required for other jobs. Twelve different pay levels could be replaced with five levels, with larger differentials between the levels.

In theory, this prospect seems attractive. A simplified base pay system would have fewer job classifications, greatly simplifying the plant manager's administrative job. This system should provide an incentive for employees to learn a variety of skills and to receive pay raises quickly. This career advancement element of the system should prevent turnover. In addition, the system should pay off with reduced staffing for the plant and/or a reduction in overtime. A more qualified workforce would mean that fewer employees would be needed to cover all the jobs at the plant. This should reduce in labor costs per ton, if the productivity remains the same or improves.

The attractiveness of the concept would be met with some resistance. Philosophically, plant managers have difficulty with the concept of paying an employee at a higher rate for performing a job that was previously defined at a lower rate. Most believe in paying employees for the jobs they are performing, not for what they are capable of performing. Also, this process would increase the average wage rates in a plant as employees quickly moved to higher job classifications. If the new system was attractive to the employees, the manager might have more requests for promotion than he or she was willing to consider, and requests for training might exceed the ability to provide on-the-job training to build skills. Also, the system might meet with skepticism from the workforce. Although employee relations were good, employees were somewhat skeptical of management actions and, in particular, the implementation of new plans and programs. Altering job classifications was a sensitive area that would be viewed with much skepticism. Employees would have to be convinced that the program was a "win" situation for them.

ROI DRIVERS

The HR manager approached the project in the face of concern about the value of this process. Investments of time would be substantial, and senior management would want some indication of the payoff before pursuing full implementation. The payoff must go beyond the traditional positive feedback from employees and an occasional report showing reduced staffing. It must be subjected to a comprehensive evaluation, up to and including measuring the return on investment (ROI). This way, the HR manager reasoned, senior managers would clearly see the new system as a value-added process that would help them reach their major goals of increased efficiency and greater profits.

It was anticipated that this program would reduce labor cost per ton and reduce employee turnover. In addition, absenteeism was expected to decline, and job satisfaction to improve. While these benefits have been attributed to this concept in other settings, proof is necessary in this setting to convince plant managers to embrace this concept.

Armed with the determination to show the value of the program, the HR manager, with the support of the production manager, pursued the development and implementation of the competency-based system on a pilot basis.

Development and Implementation

The new system was planned for implementation in twelve locations that represented typical plants at NCS. The complete process was developed during a four-month period using the part-time assistance of an external consultant and two internal staff members. Job descriptions were reviewed and rewritten to reflect the skill-based process. During the development, several visits to each location were required as the work was reviewed by plant managers. On some occasions, employees were asked for input as the process was finalized. The new system was completely documented in an administrative manual for plant managers and in a handbook for employees.

Current jobs were slotted into new classifications at each location to show employees how they fit into the scheme. The new system provided only five levels, but with a greater spread between job classifications. A promotion in the new system would be significant, whereas a promotion in the previous system may not have added much actual income for an employee.

The new system was announced to employees in carefully planned meetings. The system was fully described, and handbooks were distributed to present the new structure. Administrative procedures of the system were completely described. Each employee had a private meeting with the manager to discuss how he or she would slot into the new system. More importantly, the manager outlined what would be necessary for promotion. These meetings typically spread over a two-week period after the announcement. A one-day workshop for plant managers of the twelve sites prepared them for implementation. They were provided guidelines to address issues expected to arise as the new process was implemented. The most important challenge for plant managers was to provide training opportunities quickly for those who wanted to move to higher job classifications. In addition, various checks and balances were included to ensure that the integrity of the system was maintained and that employees were not promoted unless they demonstrated an adequate level of competency.

EVALUATION METHODOLOGY

To ensure that the new system received a comprehensive evaluation, a five-level framework for evaluation was undertaken, and the actual calculation of the return on investment was planned. Data would be collected to obtain the reaction from employees (Level 1) and to measure the extent to which they understood the new system (Level 2). In addition, employees' progress would be monitored on the job to determine how the process was being used at each plant (Level 3). Also, specific business measures (Level 4) would be monitored at each plant before and after the program, and compared with a group of similar plants. This control group arrangement involved identifying twelve other crushed stone plants to compare with the twelve destined for implementation. This approach should ensure that the results achieved were directly related to the new system. The actual cost of the system would be compared with the monetary value of the benefits to develop an actual ROI (Level 5). One-year benefits would be obtained and compared with the fully loaded costs. Eventually, second- and third-year benefits would be obtained and analyzed, although the new system was expected to represent a positive return in the first year.

CONTROL GROUP SELECTION

Selecting specific plants to use in a control group represented a challenging issue. Although as many as thirty variables can influence the performance of a crushed stone plant, only a small group of variables can be used, on a practical basis, to select the two groups. The area operations managers of the twelve locations where the system was planned for implementation were asked to identify the top four or five influences (variables) that could impact plant performance. These five variables were:

1. The size of the plant, in terms of annual production
2. The product mix of the plant. Some products required more time to produce and were more abrasive to the equipment.
3. The market, as defined by the construction activity in the local market area

4. The age of the equipment. Older equipment sometimes caused inefficiencies in production. The average equipment age at each plant was a routinely monitored variable.
5. Previous plant productivity.

In addition, two more variables were added. The average wage rate and employee turnover rate of these additional variables should be similar because they were closely related to the perceived payoff of the program. Therefore, seven variables were used to select twelve locations to compare with the twelve locations where the plan would be implemented. Table 14-1 shows the average wage and turnover rate for one year prior to program implementation for both the pilot group and control group.

EVALUATION PLANNING

Planning the evaluation is a key step in measuring the effectiveness of a successful implementation. Detailed planning includes determining the methods for data collection, isolating the effects of the new system, converting data to monetary values, and deciding which costs to capture. The two planning documents used in this analysis are presented as Figures 14-1 and 14-2. Figure 14-1 shows the data collection plan, which includes collecting data for Level 1 (reaction to program), Level 2 (understanding the program), Level 3 (program use), and Level 4 (business impact). The figure also shows the specific data collection methods and the timing for data collection. Responsibilities are also defined. Figure 14-2 presents the plan for the ROI

Table 14-1
Wage and Turnover Data for Both Groups—One
Year Average Before Implementation

	Employee Level	Average Wage	Employee Turnover
Plants with New System	225	$10.28	19%
Plants without New System	231	$10.90	21%

Data Collection Plan

Program: _____ Responsibility: _____ Date: _____

Level	Broad Program Objective(s)	Data Collection Method	Timing of Data Collection	Responsibilities for Data Collection
I Reaction and Satisfaction	• Satisfaction with new system • Acceptance of new system • Commitment to new system	• Questionnaire (2 pages)	• End of initial meeting about new system	• HR representative
II Learning	• Understanding • System Administration • Requirements for advancement	• Objective test: true-false / Multiple choices (15 items)	• End of initial meeting about new system	• HR representative
III Job Application	• Frequency of promotions • Employees at various job levels • Extent of OJT sessions • Individual development plans	• Questionnaire to plant manager • Monitor records	• 1 year after implementation	• HR representative • External consultant
IV Business Results	• Reduce labor cost per ton • Reduce employee turnover • Reduce absenteeism • Improve job satisfaction	• Monitor records • Examine next job satisfaction survey data	• 1 year after implementation	• HR representative • External consultant

Figure 14-1.

ROI Analysis Plan

Program: _____   Responsibility: _____   Date: _____

Data Items	Methods of Isolating the Effects of the Program	Methods of Converting Data	Cost Categories	Intangible Benefits	Other Influences/Issues	Communication Targets
Labor Cost Per Ton	Control Group Arrangement	Direct Conversion—Cost Savings	• Development • Administration • Plant Manager Time • Employee Time • Training/Meetings • Materials • Travel	• Quality • Teamwork • Customer Satisfaction	• Avoid Peak Season, If Possible • No Communication with Control Group	• Employees • Plant Managers • Area Operations Managers • Production Manager • Senior Executives • Other Plant Managers • HR Staff
Employee Turnover	Control Group Arrangement	Industry Data from Study—Adjusted for Company			• Watch for Hawthorne Effect	
Absenteeism	Control Group Arrangement	Estimate from Plant Managers				
Job Satisfaction	Control Group Arrangement	Estimate from Management				

Figure 14-2.

analysis, which includes detailing how the effects of the system will be isolated from other influences and how the data will be converted to monetary values. In addition, the specific cost categories of the program are detailed, along with other important issues concerning the overall evaluation plan.

Results: Reaction and Learning

It was considered important for employees to understand the process and react favorably to it. Although a positive reaction was assumed, employee feedback was obtained in a more formal method using a two-page questionnaire. This was considered necessary because of the potential skepticism from management and the sensitivity of making adjustments to the job classification system. The questionnaire was designed to capture specific reaction in five areas:

1. Satisfaction with the new system and the company
2. Reaction to administrative procedures
3. Specific issues that needed to be addressed
4. Concerns about the new system and administrative processes
5. Potential payoffs for the new system for employees and the local plant

In addition, a simple 15-item objective test, using true/false and multiple choice responses, was administered at the end of the initial meeting to measure understanding of different elements of the plan. A show of hands revealed responses to each question, which were tabulated and then discussed.

For these measures of reaction and learning, the results favorably exceeded expectations in both categories. Employees reacted positively, identified several issues to explore, and expressed few concerns. Test scores averaged 12.6 out of 15, compared with an acceptable average of 10.

Application/Use

For this process to be successfully implemented, it had to be used properly and in a timely manner. Delays in allowing employees to learn new jobs and receive promotions could have resulted in adverse reactions and been counterproductive. Four specific areas were monitored for use:

1. The number and frequency of promotions in the year after program implementation
2. The actual number of employees at each job level during the initial implementation. Specific targets were set for each job level, and actual results were compared with the targets.
3. The number and duration of on-the-job training sessions as employees learned new jobs
4. The number of individual development plans (IDPs) that were prepared as employees made plans to reach certain job levels by certain time frames

Table 14-2 presents a summary of the use of the new system. The number of promotions was tracked with a target of 8 promotions per year per plant, compared with a 3.2 average one year prior to implementation. The actual first year was 11.2. The average job level was 3.6 at the beginning of implementation, and under the new system, a target of 4.0 was established but it actually reached 4.1. Many employees reached the fifth level of job classification. For on-the-job training sessions, the objective was to have at least 3 sessions per week, whereas 3.5 were actually documented. These sessions were defined as a specific time period in which an employee was being trained in a new skill by another employee or supervisor. The time allocated for OJT was anticipated to be 10 hours per week per plant. In actuality, plant managers estimated it to be 12.6 hours per plant. The number of individual development plans was estimated to be 5 per plant. An average of 7.3 was actually generated. In summary, the use of the new system greatly exceeded expectations.

The implementation, however, did not go as smoothly as the previous information suggests. The plant managers provided information using a follow-up questionnaire and estimated times and activity regarding on-the-job training. Although they saw some advantages of the process and the program, they experienced some frustration as employees eagerly wanted to pursue additional training so they could be promoted. Employee requests exceeded the plant managers' ability to provide training, and the managers had to accelerate planned training activity to keep

Table 14-2
Utilization of Plan

	1 Year Prior to New System	At Beginning of Implementation	Objective First Year	Actual First Year
Number of Promotions Per Plant	3.2	—	8.0	11.2
Average Job Level	—	3.6	4.0	4.1
OJT Sessions Per Employee Per Week (estimate)	—	—	3	3.5
Time for OJT Per Week Per Plant (estimate)	—	—	10 hours	12.6 hours
Number of IDPs Per Plant	—	—	5	7.3

employees from growing restless. This accounted for the increase in on-the-job training sessions and the time devoted to the process. The managers felt this additional training time may have caused some inefficiencies although those were not identified.

BUSINESS IMPACT

The most valuable data concerned the changes in business measures directly related to the new system. Table 14-3 shows business impact data presented in terms of employment levels. Ultimately for this process to work, overall employment levels should decrease in a plant where the system has been implemented. As Table 14-3 reveals, a significant reduction occurred in the number of employees in the plants where the system was implemented. Because all plants were subjected to the same environmental influences—such as pricing, sales practice, production processes, and administrative procedures—this difference was considered to be directly attributable to the new system.

As planned, four critical measures were monitored for the ROI calculation: labor cost per ton, employee turnover, absenteeism, and job satisfaction. Table 14-4 shows the experience with the first two variables before and after the system was implemented.

A significant labor cost per ton was realized, along with a significant difference in employee turnover. The values for labor costs per ton and average wage rates represent the average value for the last two months of the year after implementation. Although

Table 14-3
Employment Levels

	Two Months Before Implementation (average)	Last Two Months of Evaluation Period, Months 11 & 12 (average)
Plants with New System	224	203
Plants without New System	233	232

Table 14-4
Business Impact Measures Before and After Implementation

	Turnover 1 Year Prior	Turnover 1 Year After	Labor Costs Per Ton 1 Year Prior	Labor Costs Per Ton 1 Year After	Wage Rate 1 Year Prior	Wage Rate 1 Year After	Production 1 Year After
Plants with New System	19%	11%	76¢	61¢	$10.28	$12.09	12.5M Tons
Plants without New System	21%	20%	82¢	84¢	$10.70	$11.05	13.2M Tons

the average wage rate increased (as shown in Table 14-4), the reduction in the number of employees along with relatively stable production levels yielded a significantly lower labor cost per ton. The labor cost differentials per ton are multiplied by annual production to yield a one-year benefit for the program. Although this overestimates the impact for the first year, because the differentials for the last two months were used, it is very conservative overall because the benefits in years two, three, and beyond are omitted from the analysis. Thus, by design, the ROI analysis must stand alone with the first-year benefits. An alternative strategy would have been to use the two-year benefits with the actual values accumulated during the two-year time period.

The same analysis was conducted with turnover. The cost of turnover had not been calculated internally for NCS although it had been estimated by using a variety of studies for construction-related jobs. Several studies indicated that the turnover cost would be in the range of 75 percent to 100 percent of the annual pay, depending on the particular job level. The HR manager suggested using, and the production manager agreed to use, 50 percent of base pay as a conservative and appropriate cost of turnover. Using the average wage rate after implementation and assuming forty-eight weeks of actual work yields a value of $11,606 for the cost of a turnover statistic.

The improvement in absenteeism and job satisfaction were included as intangible measures and not used in the ROI analysis.

PROGRAM COSTS

The costs for developing and implementing the new system is based on the following:

- [ ] The total consulting costs for the project were $40,000.
- [ ] The HR staff devoted 120 hours to the project @ $20 per hour.
- [ ] The plant managers' total time equated to 1,290 hours for the project @ $22 per hour.
- [ ] The total training cost for plant managers was $2,900.
- [ ] Employee time for on-the-job training was estimated at 7,862 hours.
- [ ] Employee time in meetings was estimated at 2,700 hours.

☐ Materials/printing costs were $1,525.
☐ Travel/miscellaneous expenses were $7,540.

Assume a 30 percent average employee benefits factor.

INTANGIBLE BENEFITS

Although measurable and convertible to monetary values in some cases, the intangibles were considered significant but were not used in the ROI analysis. Several intangible benefits were identified, and several quality measures showed improvement although the values of their improvement were not included in the ROI calculation. Other variables influenced quality, and initially it was perceived that this system might have only a minor influence on the variable. Three measures were monitored, and all showed slight improvement:

1. The actual number of customer complaints regarding unacceptable or substandard products was reduced.
2. The actual number of loads of stone rejected by the customer was reduced slightly.
3. The amount of downtime for the plant was reduced slightly. Although this is an efficiency measure, it has impact on the cost and quality of the product.

As anticipated, absenteeism showed slight reduction for the pilot group, compared with the control group. This improvement added value, although it was not included in the ROI analysis. There was no generally accepted value for the cost of an absence. Finally, job satisfaction showed some increase based on both the input from the plant managers and the annual attitude survey conducted by corporate human resources. The differences in the two groups showed improvements in attitude toward the job, company, and career advancement, which are all considered important.

Table 14-5 summarizes the first-year monetary benefits from labor cost savings and turnover reduction. These represent a total value of $2,310,696.

Table 14-6 summarizes the total fully loaded costs—a total value of $255,082.

Table 14-5
Calculation of Monetary Benefits

Monetary Value for Labor Cost Per Ton Savings	
Group difference:	84¢ − 61¢ = 23¢
Adjustment for initial difference:	82¢ − 76¢ = 6¢
Amount attributed to new system:	23¢ − 6¢ = 17¢
Annual benefits:	17¢ × 12.5 million tons = $2,125,000

Monetary Value for Turnover Reduction	
Group difference:	20% − 11% = 9%
Adjustment for initial difference:	21% − 19% = 2%
Amount attributed to new system:	9% − 2% = 7%
Cost of one turnover:	$12.09 × 40 hours × 48 weeks × 50% = $11,606
Turnovers prevented:	203 × 7% = 14 turnovers prevented
Turnover benefits:	16 × $11,606 = $185,696

Table 14-6
Costs of New System

Consulting Costs for Development	$40,000
HR Staff 120 @ 20 × 1.30	3,120
Plant Managers' Total Time 1,290 @ 22 × 1.30	36,894
Employee Time Out 7,862 @ 12.09 × 1.3	123,567
Employee Time in Meetings 2,700 @ 12.09 × 1.3	42,436
Materials/Printing	1,525
Travel/Miscellaneous	7,540
	$255,082

The BCR and ROI are as follows:

$$BCR = \frac{\$2,310,696}{255,082} = 9.05$$

$$ROI = \frac{\$2,310,696 - \$255,082}{255,082} \times 100 = 805\%$$

FORECAST VALUE

For a break-even, the improvement from labor cost per ton should equal the total cost for implementation (0 percent ROI). If we let x equal the improvement in cents per ton, then we have:

$$12,500,000x = 255.082$$

$$x = \frac{255,082}{12,500,000} = .02 = 2¢$$

Thus a net increase of two cents per ton is needed to break even.

QUESTIONS FOR DISCUSSION

1. Critique the data collection plan.
2. Critique the ROI analysis plan.
3. Is the ROI realistic?
4. How should the ROI be communicated to senior management?
5. Should this system be implemented at other locations?
6. Sometimes a pre-program forecast is needed before attempting to implement the new system. If the payoff is forecast of improvements in labor cost per ton only, what improvement would be necessary for a break-even in the first year?

CHAPTER 15

Absenteeism Reduction Program

Metro Transit Authority

By Ron D. Stone

This case illustrates how ineffective human resource policies and selection processes can cause major problems in business operations. The unavailability of bus drivers because of unscheduled absences caused route schedule delays and bottlenecks, which resulted in dissatisfied customers, a loss of revenue, and increased operating costs. New guidelines and disciplinary policies for unscheduled absences, as well as a change in hiring practices, were initiated to correct the situation. The ability to demonstrate the costs associated with the absenteeism problem led to the two solutions being implemented. The evaluation team was able to isolate the effects of each of the two HR initiatives and to calculate the operational savings to demonstrate an impressive return on investment.

BACKGROUND

The Metro Transit Authority (MTA) operates a comprehensive transportation system in a large metropolitan area. More than 1,000 buses function regularly, providing essential transportation to citizens in the metro area. Many passengers depend on the bus system for their commutes to and from work, as well as for other essential travel. MTA employs more than 2,900 drivers to operate the bus system around the clock.

As with many transit systems, Metro was experiencing excessive absenteeism with drivers, and the problem was growing. Just three years before, absenteeism had been 7 percent, compared with the most recent three-month period of 8.7 percent—too excessive to keep the transit system operating in a consistent manner.

To ensure that buses ran on time, a pool of substitute drivers was employed to fill in during unexpected absences. The number of drivers in the pool was a function of the absenteeism rate. At the time of this study, the pool consisted of 231 substitute drivers. When the drivers in the pool were not needed as substitutes, they performed almost no essential work for the Transit Authority although they were required to report to work. When a substitute driver was used, this usually delayed the bus schedule, making the bus late for subsequent stops.

CAUSES OF PROBLEMS AND SOLUTIONS

A needs assessment and analysis was conducted using focus groups, interviews, and an analysis of HR records. Focus groups included bus drivers and their supervisors. Interviews were conducted with supervisors and managers. HR records were examined for trends and patterns in absenteeism. The conclusions from the analysis were as follows:

1. Individuals who were frequently absent had a pattern of absenteeism that dated back to the beginning of their employment and, in most cases, was present in other employment situations.
2. Many of the absences could be avoided. The problem was primarily a motivation and discipline issue.
3. The prevailing attitude among employees was to take advantage of the system whenever possible, up to the threshold of being terminated.

As a result of these findings, Metro initiated two processes:

1. **A no-fault disciplinary system was implemented.** With this policy, an employee who experienced more than six unexpected (unplanned) incidences in a six-month time frame was terminated—no questions asked. A sickness that extended more than one day was considered one incidence. Thus, the policy would not unfairly penalize those who were absent for legitimate sickness or for scheduled surgery and other medical attention. The no-fault system was implemented after extensive negotiations with the union. When union officials realized the impact of excessive absenteeism, they agreed with the new policy.

2. **The selection process for new drivers was modified.** During the initial screening, a list of questions was developed and used to screen out applicants who had a history of absenteeism dating back to their high-school days. The questions, with scoring and interpretation, were added to the current selection process and required approximately thirty minutes of additional time during the initial employment interview.

To bring appropriate attention to the absenteeism issue and to generate results as soon as possible, both initiatives were implemented at the same time.

OBJECTIVES OF THE INITIATIVES

The expected outcomes were established early, in the form of implementation and impact objectives. The objectives of the two initiatives were to:

1. Communicate the no-fault policy, including how the policy would be applied and the rationale for it.
2. Experience little or no adverse reaction from current employees as the no-fault absenteeism policy was implemented.
3. Maintain employees' present level of job satisfaction as the absenteeism initiatives were implemented and applied.
4. Use the new screening process for each selection decision so that a systematic and consistent selection process would be in place.
5. Implement and enforce the no-fault policy consistently throughout all operating units.

6. Reduce driver absenteeism at least 2 percent during the first year of implementation of the two processes.
7. Improve customer service and satisfaction by reducing absenteeism-related schedule delays.

Supervisors were required to conduct meetings with their employees to explain the need for the policy and how it would be applied. Each supervisor completed a meeting report form after the meeting and returned it to the HR department.

The no-fault policy had the potential of influencing employment termination by essentially increasing employee turnover, which could have created problems for some supervisors. Because of this, it was important to demonstrate to the management team that these programs were effective when administered properly. Also, senior executives were interested in knowing the payoff for these types of initiatives; they needed to be convinced that the company was receiving an adequate return on investment.

DATA COLLECTION

Exhibit 15-1 shows the data collection plan for the absenteeism reduction initiatives at Metro Transit Authority. The objectives are defined, and the data collection methods selected are typical for these types of programs. For Level 4 data, absenteeism is monitored on a post-program basis and compared with pre-program data. Table 15-1 shows the absenteeism for the years prior to and after implementing both the no-fault policy and the new selection process. A complete year of data was collected to show the full impact of both initiatives to capture the delayed effect in influencing the absenteeism measure. In addition, schedule delays of more than five minutes caused by unexpected absenteeism were monitored and are reported in Table 15-1.

Also, for Levels 3 and 4 data, a questionnaire was developed and administered to a sample of supervisors to determine the extent to which the programs were implemented and were perceived to be operating effectively. Input was sought regarding problems and issues, as well as success stories and changes in job satisfaction.

For Level 2 data, learning was measured with a simple ten-item true/false test. To ensure that employees understood the

Exhibit 15-1

DATA COLLECTION PLAN—METRO TRANSIT AUTHORITY.

Program: Absenteeism Reduction   Responsibility: Jack Phillips   Date: January 15

Level	Broad Program Objective(s)	Measures	Data Collection Method/Instruments	Data Sources	Timing	Responsibilities
1	REACTION/SATISFACTION and PLANNED ACTIONS • Positive employee reaction to the no-fault policy	• Positive reaction from employees	• Feedback questionnaire	• Employees	• At the end of the employee meetings	• Supervisors
2	LEARNING • Employee understanding of the policy	• Score on post-test: at least 70	• True/false test	• Employees	• At the end of the employee meetings	• Supervisors
3	APPLICATION/ IMPLEMENTATION 1. Effective and consistent implementation and enforcement of the programs 2. Little or no adverse reaction from current employees regarding no-fault policy 3. Use the new screening process	1. Supervisors' response about program's influence 2. Employee complaints and union cooperation	1. and 2. Follow-up questionnaire to supervisors (2 sample groups) 3. Sample review of interview and selection records	1. Supervisors 2. Company records	1. After employee meetings, sample 1 group at 3 months and another group at 6 months 2. Three months and 6 months after implementation	• HR program coordinator
4	BUSINESS IMPACT 1. Reduce driver absenteeism at least 2% during first year 2. Maintain present level of job satisfaction as new policy is implemented 3. Improve customer service and satisfaction through reduction in schedule delays	1. Absenteeism 2. Employee satisfaction 3. Delays impact on customer service	1. Monitor absenteeism 2. Follow-up questionnaire to supervisors 3. Monitor bus schedule delays	1. Company records 2. Supervisors 3. Dispatch records	1. Monitor monthly and analyze 1 year pre- and 1 year post-implementation 2. Three months and 6 months after employee meetings 3. Monthly	• HR program coordinator
5	ROI Target ROI: 25%	Comments:				

policy, the test was developed to be administered by supervisors in their meetings with employees. The scores were attached to the record of the meeting, which noted the time, place, and agenda for the meeting along with a list of the attendees. A sample of the test scores revealed an average value above the minimum acceptable level of 70.

For Level 1 data, reaction was measured with a simple questionnaire using an objective format. The Level 1 questionnaire was distributed at the meetings to obtain reaction to the no-fault policy.

Table 15-1
Absenteeism and Bus Delays Before and After Implementation

	Unscheduled Absenteeism *Percent of Scheduled Days Worked*		Absenteeism-Related Bus Delays *Percent of All Delays*	
	PRE	POST	PRE	POST
July	7.2	6.3	23.3	18.3
August	7.4	5.6	24.7	18.0
September	7.1	5.0	24.9	17.5
October	7.8	5.9	26.1	18.2
November	8.1	5.3	25.4	16.7
December	8.4	5.2	26.3	15.9
January	8.7	5.4	27.1	15.4
February	8.5	4.8	26.9	14.9
March	8.6	4.9	26.8	14.7
April	8.5	4.9	27.8	14.4
May	8.8	4.0	27.0	13.6
June	8.8	4.9	26.4	13.7
Three-Month Average	8.7%	4.6%	27.1%	13.9%

Exhibit 15-2 shows the ROI analysis plan for evaluation of the absenteeism reduction initiatives. Major elements of the plan are discussed below.

ISOLATING THE EFFECTS OF THE INITIATIVES

Several approaches were considered for the purpose of isolating the effects of the two initiatives. At first, a control group arrangement was considered, but it was quickly ruled out for three important reasons:

1. To purposely withhold the policy change for a group of employees could create contractual and morale problems for the individuals in the control group.

Exhibit 15-2

ROI ANALYSIS PLAN—METRO TRANSIT AUTHORITY.

Program: Absenteeism Reduction　　**Responsibility**: Jack Phillips　　**Date**: January 15

Data Items (Usually Level 4)	Methods for Isolating the Effects of the Program/Process	Methods of Converting Data to Monetary Values	Cost Categories	Intangible Benefits	Communication Targets for Final Report	Other Influences/Issues During Application	Comments
1. Absenteeism	1. Trendline analysis and supervisor estimates	1. Wages & benefits and standard values		• Sustain employee satisfaction	• Senior management	• Concern about supervisors' consistent administration	
2. Employee job satisfaction	2. Supervisor estimates	N/A	**Screening Process** • Development • Interviewer preparation • Administration • Materials	• Improve employee morale • Improve customer satisfaction	• Managers and supervisors • Union representatives • HR staff	• Partnering with union reps about how to communicate results of study to employees	
3. Bus schedule delays (influence on customer satisfaction)	3. Management estimates	N/A	**No-Fault Policy** • Development • Implementation • Materials	• Fewer disruptive bottlenecks in transportation grid • Ease of implementation by supervisors			

2. Because the new policy would be known to all employees, contamination would occur in the control group. The policy would have the effect of reducing absenteeism in those areas where it was not implemented.
3. Because of the operational problems and customer service issues associated with absenteeism, it was not desirable to withhold a needed solution just for experimental purposes.

Trendline analysis was initially feasible because only a small amount of variance was noticeable in the pre-program trend data that had developed. Because of the possibility of this option, in the planning stage, trendline analysis was considered as a method to estimate the impact of both absenteeism initiatives. However, because multiple influences on absenteeism later developed, such as a change in economic conditions, the trendline analysis was aborted.

Finally, as a backup strategy, estimations were taken directly from supervisors as they completed the follow-up questionnaire. Supervisors were asked to identify various factors that had influenced the absenteeism rate and to allocate percentages to each of the factors, including the new screening process and no-fault policy.

CONVERTING DATA TO MONETARY VALUES

Because the primary business measure was absenteeism, a monetary value had to be developed for the cost of an unexpected absence. The value could subsequently be used to calculate the total cost of the absenteeism improvement. Although there were several approaches to determine the cost of absenteeism, the analysis at Metro was based on the cost of replacement driver staffing.

Substitute drivers, as well as the regular drivers, were expected to work an average of 240 days per year, leaving 20 days for vacation, holidays, and sick days. The average wage for substitute drivers was $33,500 per year, and the employee benefits factor was 38 percent of payroll. When a regular driver was unexpectedly absent, he or she could charge the absence either to sick leave or to vacation, thus substituting a planned paid day (vacation) for the unexpected absence.

The number of substitute drivers was planned as a function of expected absenteeism. Therefore, the substitute driver staffing level did not always meet the exact level needed for a specific day's unscheduled absences. Because of the service problems that could develop as a result of understaffing, for most days, the company planned for an excessive number of substitute drivers. To minimize potential delays, all substitute drivers were required to report to work each day. Substitute drivers not used in driver seats essentially performed no productive work that could be counted as added value. During the previous year, overstaffing had occurred about 75 percent of the time for weekdays and non-holidays. This overstaffing represented 4,230 days of wasted time. During the weekends and holidays, which represented 114 days, overstaffing had occurred almost half the time, representing a total of 570 wasted days.

On some days, there was actually a shortage of substitute drivers, which caused the buses to run late, and overtime had to be used to make the adjustment. During the previous year, there had been 65 instances in which a driver was not available, and it was estimated that in 45 of those situations, a regular driver was paid double time to fill in the schedule.

A final, and very significant, cost of absenteeism was the cost of recruiting, training, maintaining, and supervising the substitute driver pool, beyond the actual salaries and benefits. These items included recruiting and employment, training and preparation, office space, administration and coordination, and supervision. This item was estimated at 25 percent of the actual annual pay. Here is how the total direct cost of absenteeism was developed from the above information.

Average daily cost of wages and benefits for a substitute driver:

$$\$33,500 \times 1.38 \div 240 = \$192.63$$

Approximate cost of overstaffing, weekdays:

$$\$192.63 \times 4,230 = \$814,800$$

Approximate cost of overstaffing, weekends and holidays:

$$\$192.63 \times 570 = \$109,800$$

Approximate cost of understaffing, overtime (only one salary is used for double-time pay):

$192.63 × 45 = $8,670

Approximate cost of recruiting, training, maintaining, and supervising pool of drivers:

$33,500 × 231 × 0.25 = $1,934,600

COSTS FOR INITIATIVES

The cost for the new screening process contained four components:

1. Development
2. Interviewer preparation
3. Administrative time
4. Materials

The total development cost, including pilot testing, was $20,000. An additional $5,000 was charged for preparing the interviewers to administer the test. The materials and time were variable costs, depending on the number of drivers employed. Approximately 400 drivers were hired each year. For each new driver hired, an average of 3 candidates were interviewed. Thus, 1,200 interviews were conducted each year, with an average time of 30 minutes each. The average wage for the interviewers was $14.50 per hour. The materials cost $2 per test.

The cost for the no-fault policy included development and implementation. The development cost was incurred internally and was estimated to be $11,000, representing the time of internal specialists. The material distributed to employees accounted for another $3,800. The costs of meetings with all supervisors and with employees were estimated at $16,500. The cost for routine administration was not included because the alternative to administering the no-fault policy was to administer a progressive discipline process, and the two were judged to take approximately the same amount of time.

RESULTS: REACTION, LEARNING, AND APPLICATION

Employees expressed some concern about the new policy, but the overall reaction to the change was favorable. They perceived the new policy to be fair and equitable. In addition, employees scored an average of 78 on the true/false test about the no-fault policy. A score of 70 on the end-of-meeting test was considered acceptable.

A follow-up questionnaire, administered anonymously to a sample of supervisors, indicated that the policy had been implemented in each area and had been applied consistently. Although supervisors reported some initial resistance from the habitual absenteeism violators, the majority of employees perceived the policy to be effective and fair. The supervisors also reported that the new policy took less time to administer than the previously used progressive discipline approach.

A review of HR records indicated that 95 percent of the supervisors conducted the meeting with employees and completed a meeting report form. In addition, a review of a sample of interviews and selection records indicated that the new screening process was used in every case.

BUSINESS IMPACT

Absenteeism dramatically declined after the implementation of both processes, yielding an average absenteeism rate of 4.6 percent for the last three months of the evaluation period, compared with the pre-program rate of 8.7 percent for the same period one year earlier. In the Metro situation, a reduction in absenteeism generated a cost savings only if the substitute driver pool was reduced. Because the pool staffing was directly linked to absenteeism, a significant reduction was realized. Table 15-2 shows the cost savings realized, using the calculation-development approach shown earlier in this case.

In addition, on the questionnaires, supervisors estimated and allocated percentages for the contribution of each factor to absenteeism reduction. Table 15-3 presents the results.

The bus schedule delays caused by absenteeism declined from an average of 27.1 percent for the three months prior to the

Table 15-2
Cost of Absenteeism Comparisons

Cost Item	1 Year Prior to Initiatives	1 Year After Initiatives
Cost of overstaffing, weekdays	$814,000	$602,400
Cost of overstaffing, weekends and holidays	$109,800	$51,500
Cost of understaffing	$8,670	$4,340
Cost of recruiting, training, and maintaining driver pool	$1,934,600	$1,287,750
Total cost of absenteeism	$2,867,070	$1,945,990

Table 15-3
Supervisor Estimates to Isolate the Effects of the Initiatives

Factor	Contribution Percentage	Confidence Percentage
No-Fault Policy	67%	84%
Screening	22%	71%
Economic Conditions	11%	65%
Other	1%	90%

initiatives to 13.9 percent for the last three months of the evaluation period.

In addition, several intangible measures were identified, including increased morale, improved customer service, and fewer bottlenecks in the entire system.

MONETARY BENEFITS

Because the total cost of absenteeism for drivers is known on a before-and-after basis (as shown in Table 15-2) the total savings can be developed as follows:

Pre-program	$2,867,070
Post-program	$1,945,990
Savings	$ 921,080

The contribution of the no-fault policy:

$921,080 × 67% × 84% = $518,383 = approximately $518,000

The contribution of the new screening process:

$921,080 × 22% × 71% = $143,873 = approximately $144,000

Total First-Year Benefit = $518,000 + $144,000 = $662,000

Costs

The total costs for both initiatives (shown in Tables 15-4 and 15-5) are as follows:

Table 15-4
Cost of Screening Process

Development Cost	$20,000
Interviewer Preparation	$ 5,000
Administrative Time (1,200 × $\frac{1}{2}$ × $14.50)	$ 8,700
Materials (1,200 @ $2)	$ 2,400
TOTAL	$36,100

Table 15-5
Cost of No-Fault Policy

Development Cost	$11,000
Materials	$ 3,800
Meeting Time	$16,500
TOTAL	$31,300

Total Costs = $36,100 + $31,300 = $67,400

ROI CALCULATION

The BCR and ROI are calculated as follows:

$$BCR = \frac{\$662,000}{\$67,400} = 9.82$$

$$ROI(\%) = \frac{\$662,000 - \$67,400}{\$67,400} = 882\%$$

QUESTIONS FOR DISCUSSION

1. What are feasible ways to isolate the effects of the program?
2. Can the cost of absenteeism be developed for Metro? What additional information is needed?
3. Which cost categories should be developed to determine the overall cost of initiatives?
4. Critique the actual monetary benefits of the reduction in absenteeism.
5. Critique the total cost for the first year of operation of the two initiatives.
6. Could the absenteeism cost be developed in other ways? Explain.
7. Is the ROI value realistic? Explain.
8. How should the results be communicated to various groups?

CHAPTER 16

Stress Management
Midwest Electric Inc.*

By Patricia Pulliam Phillips

This case study begins by describing how the needs for a stress management program were determined and how an organization development solution was evaluated through ROI. The comprehensive approach includes the use of the StressMap® to measure learning, as well as the use of control groups to isolate the effects of the program. A description of how the ROI was measured is included. The specific forms, issues, and processes make this a practical case study for organizations interested in a comprehensive, balanced approach to evaluation.

BACKGROUND

Midwest Electric Inc. (MEI) is a growing electric utility serving several midwestern states. Since deregulation of the industry, MEI has been on a course of diversification and growth. Through a series of acquisitions, MEI has moved outside its traditional operating areas and into several related businesses.

MEI had been experiencing significant workplace changes as it transformed from a bureaucratic, sluggish organization into a lean, competitive force in the marketplace. These changes placed tremendous pressure on employees to develop multiple skills and perform additional work. Employees, working in teams, had to constantly strive to reduce costs, maintain excellent quality, boost productivity, and generate new and efficient ways to supply customers and improve service.

As with many industries in a deregulated environment, MEI detected symptoms of employee stress. The safety and health function in the company suggested that employee stress lowered productivity and reduced employee effectiveness. Stress was also considered a significant employee health risk. Research had shown that high levels of stress were commonplace in many work groups and that organizations were taking steps to help employees and work groups reduce stress in a variety of ways. The vice president of human resources at MEI asked the safety and health department, with the help of the training department, to develop a program for work groups to help them alleviate stressful situations and deal more productively and effectively with job-induced stress.

Needs Assessment

Because of its size and sophisticated human resource systems, MEI had an extensive database on employee-related measures. MEI prided itself as being one of the leaders in the industry in human resources issues. Needs assessments had been routinely conducted at MEI, and the HR vice president was willing to allow sufficient time for an adequate needs assessment before proceeding with the stress management program.

The overall purpose of the needs assessment was to identify the causes of a perceived problem. The needs assessment would:

☐ Confirm that a problem did exist and provide an assessment of the actual impact of this problem.
☐ Uncover potential causes of the problem within the work unit, company, and environment.
☐ Provide insight into potential remedies to correct the problem.

The sources of data for the needs assessment included company records, external research, team members, team leaders, and managers. The assessment began with a review of external research that identified the factors usually related to high stress and the consequences of high stress in work groups. The consequences uncovered specific measures that could be identified at MEI.

This external research led to a review of several key data items in company records, including attitude surveys, medical claims, employee assistance plan (EAP) use, safety and health records, and exit interviews. The attitude survey data represented the results from the previous year and were reviewed for low scores on the specific questions that could yield stress-related symptoms. Medical claims were analyzed by codes to identify the extent of those related to stress-induced illnesses. EAP data were reviewed to determine the extent to which employees were using provisions and services of the plan perceived to be stress-related. Safety records were reviewed to determine if specific accidents were stress-related or if causes of accidents could be traced to high levels of stress. In each of the above areas, the data were compared with data from the previous year to determine whether stress-related measures were changing. Also, where available, data were compared with expected norms from the external research. Finally, exit interviews for the previous six months were analyzed to determine the extent to which the stress-related situations were factors in an employee's decision to voluntarily leave MEI.

During MEI's needs assessment process, a small sample of employees (ten team members) was interviewed to discuss their work-life situations and to uncover symptoms of stress at work. Also, a small group of managers (five) was interviewed with the same purpose. To provide more detail about this input, a 10 percent sample of employees received a questionnaire to explore the same issues. MEI had 22,550 employees with 18,220 non-supervisory team members.

Summary of Findings

The needs assessment process uncovered several significant findings:

☐ There was evidence of high levels of stress in work groups, caused by MEI's deregulation, restructuring, and job changes.

In essence, the change in the nature of work induced high levels of stress in most work groups.

☐ Stress had led to a deterioration in several performance measures, including medical costs, short-term disability, withdrawals (absenteeism, turnover), and job satisfaction.

☐ Employees were often not fully aware of stress factors and the effect stress had on them and their work.

☐ Employees had inadequate skills for coping with stress and adjusting to, managing, and eliminating highly stressful situations.

☐ Managers had more insight into the causes of stress but did not have the skills or mechanisms to deal with most stressful situations.

PROGRAM PLANNING AND DESIGN

Several inherent factors about work groups and data at MEI influenced the program and its subsequent evaluation. MEI was organized around teams, and groups were not usually identical. However, many teams had similar performance measures. The HR database was rich with a variety of measures and with data about employees and work unit factors. Because of the team environment and the important role of the team leader/manager, the program to reduce stress needed to involve the management group in a proactive way. Any efforts to reduce stress needed to shift much of the responsibility to participants and thus reduce the amount of time off the job. Job pressures in the deregulated environment provided fewer off-the-job opportunities for meeting and development activities.

Program Design

Although several approaches could have feasibly satisfied this need, four issues surfaced that influenced program design:

☐ A skills and knowledge deficiency existed, and some type of learning event was necessary.

☐ Several stress management programs were commercially available, which could prevent developing a new program from scratch.

□ Managers needed to be involved in the process to the greatest extent possible.

□ Because of the concerns about time away from the job, the actual classroom/formal meeting activities needed to be limited to one or two days.

With this in mind, the program outlined in Exhibit 16-1 was designed to meet this important need.

Why ROI?

HR programs usually targeted for a Level 5 ROI evaluation are those perceived to be adding significant value to the company, and closely linked to the organizational goals and strategic objectives. The evaluation is then pursued to confirm the added value. Based on the results of the analysis, these programs may be enhanced, redesigned, or eliminated if the results are insufficient. Stress management can be different. If the results are inadequate, the program may not be discontinued but may be

Exhibit 16-1
Stress Management for Intact Work Teams

Departments or work groups of 10 or more people who are committed to improving the satisfaction and effectiveness of their teams will benefit by this more comprehensive approach to stress. The process uses the StressMap® tool as the starting point. Managers and representative employees will participate in focus groups to identify work satisfiers and distressors and then will collaborate on alleviating systemic sources of stress.

What Group Members Will Learn

□ How to identify sources of stress and their personal response to them.

□ That *individuals* have the ability to make a difference in their lives.

□ How to take the first steps to enhance personal health and overall performance.

□ How to access resources, internally and externally, to help teach personal goals.

What the Group/Manager Will Learn

- [ ] Group profile of sources of stress and response patterns.
- [ ] Additional information about sources of both work distress and work satisfaction will be obtained through focus groups. Themes will be identified when possible.
- [ ] New stress reduction skills specific to the needs of the group.
- [ ] Development of recommendations for next steps to improve work satisfaction and productivity.

Highlights

- [ ] Through completion of a comprehensive self-assessment tool called StressMap®, individuals will be able to immediately score themselves on 21 stress scales dealing with work and home life, as well as learn about their preferred coping styles and the thinking and feeling patterns that impact their ability to manage stress. Anonymous copies of each member's StressMap® will be compiled to create a group score.
- [ ] A 3–4 hour StressMap® debriefing session designed to help individuals better interpret their scores will be followed by a 4-hour module suited to the needs of the group (such as situation mastery, changing habits, creating climate for agreement). Total of 1 day.

Precourse Requirements

- [ ] Management commitment to the process. Employees to complete the StressMap® tool and submit a confidential copy.

Length and Format

- [ ] Lead time of 3 to 4 weeks minimum for preparation and communication.
- [ ] Consultant on-site $1\frac{1}{2}$ days
- [ ] Initial follow-up 1 to 2 weeks later on-site or by phone to senior management. Subsequent follow-up on impact of the initiative to occur as negotiated. 3–4 hours of telephone follow-up included.

Cost

- [ ] Approximately $XXXX (plus taxes) US per group of 8 to 25; $XX US per set of materials. Travel and living expenses for consultant are additional.

altered for future sessions, particularly if behavior changes are not identified in the Level 3 evaluation.

At MEI, the stress management program was chosen for an ROI evaluation for two reasons. First, the HR department was interested in the accountability of all programs, including stress management. Second, positive results would clearly show management that these types of programs, which are preventive in nature, could significantly contribute to the bottom line when implemented and supported by management.

Because the program could have been expensive if applied to the entire company, it was decided to try it on a limited basis to determine its success and then to either adjust the program, discontinue the program, or expand the program to other areas in MEI. The evaluation methodology provided the best information to make that decision.

Data Collection Plan

Exhibit 16-2 shows the data collection plan for the stress management program. Broad objectives were established for Levels 1, 2, 3, and 4 data collection. The data collection plan was comprehensive but necessary to meet all of requirements at each of the four levels of data collection. The timing and responsibilities were detailed. For measuring learning, three tools were used. The StressMap® was one measure of learning in the awareness category. Completion of the StressMap® provided insight into stress factors and stress signals. In addition, built into the one-day program was an end-of-course self-assessment to measure learning. Finally, the facilitator had a brief checklist to indicate the extent of learning for the group.

At Level 3 data collection, the completion of the twenty-one-day plan provided some evidence that the participants had changed behavior to reduce stress. A conference call was planned with the facilitator, team manager, and the team twenty-one days after the course. This provided a review of issues and addressed any concerns or barriers to further implementation. A follow-up session was planned with the team, co-facilitated by the manager and facilitator, approximately one to two weeks after the one-day program, to discuss changes in behavior and to address

Exhibit 16-2

Program: Stress Management for Intact Groups   Responsibility: Jack Phillips   Date: _____

Data Collection Plan

Level	Broad Program Objective(s)	Data Collection Method	Timing of Data Collection	Responsibilities for Data Collection
I Reaction, Satisfaction and Planned Actions	• Positive Reaction	• Standard Questionnaire	• End of 1-Day Course	• Facilitator
	• Suggestions for Improvements			
	• Planned Action	• 21-Day Action Plan	• End of Course	• Facilitator
II Learning	• Personal Stress Awareness	• StressMap®	• Prior to Course	• Facilitator
	• Coping Strategies	• Self-Assessment	• End of Course	• Facilitator
	• Stress Reduction Skills	• Facilitator Assessment	• End of Course	• Facilitator
III Job Application	• Change Behavior to Reduce Stress	• Completion of 21-Day Plan	• 21 Days After Course	• No Report
	• Develop Group Action Plan and Communicate to Group	• Conference Call	• 21 Days After Course	• Facilitator
	• Access Internal/External Resources	• Follow-Up Session	• 1-2 Weeks After 1-Day Course	• Facilitator/Manager
	• Application of Skills/Knowledge	• Review Records	• 6 Months After Course	• Program Coordinator
		• Follow-Up Questionnaire	• 6 Months After Course	• External Consultant
IV Business Impact	• Reduce Medical Care Costs	• Group Records	• 6 Months After Course	• Program Coordinator
	• Reduce Absenteeism	• Group Records	• 6 Months After Course	• Program Coordinator
	• Reduce Turnover	• Group Records	• 6 Months After Course	• Program Coordinator
	• Increase Productivity	• Group Records	• 6 Months After Course	• Program Coordinator
	• Increase Job Satisfaction	• Follow-Up Questionnaire	• 6 Months After Course	• External Consultant

barriers. To determine the extent to which the participants were using internal or external resources to address stress-related problems, records of those requests were scheduled to be reviewed for approximately six months. Finally, a detailed follow-up questionnaire was planned for six months after the program to collect both Levels 3 and 4 data. This questionnaire was intended to capture sustained behavior changes, indicate barriers to improvement, and identify impact measures for both groups and individuals.

Group records were expected to reveal changes in medical costs, absenteeism, turnover, and productivity six months after the program. In addition, increased job satisfaction was to be determined from the follow-up questionnaire, which would be administered six months after the program (the same questionnaire described earlier).

ROI Analysis Plan

Exhibit 16-3 shows the ROI analysis plan. For most data items, the method to isolate the effects of the program would be obtained in a control group arrangement in which the performance of the group involved in the program would be compared with a the performance of a carefully matched companion control group. In addition, for most of the data items, trendline analysis was scheduled for use. Historical data were projected in a trend and compared with the actual data to determine the impact of the program.

The methods of converting data involved a variety of approaches, including tabulating direct costs, using standard values, using external data, and securing estimates from a variety of target audiences. The cost categories represented fully loaded costs for the program. Expected intangible benefits from the program were based on the experience of other organizations and other stress reduction programs. The communication target audience consisted of six key groups ranging from corporate and business unit managers to participants and their immediate supervisors.

Management Involvement

Management involvement was a key issue from the beginning and was integrated throughout the design of the program. The

Exhibit 16-3

Program: Stress Management for Intact Groups   **Responsibility:** Jack Phillips   **Date:** _____

ROI Analysis Plan

Data Items (Usually Level 4)	Methods of Isolating the Effects of the Program	Methods of Converting Data	Cost Categories	Intangible Benefits	Other Influences/Issues	Communication Targets
Medical Health Care Costs—Preventable Claims	• Control Group Arrangement • Trendline Analysis	• Direct Costs	• Needs Assessment • Program Development	• Improved Communication • Time Savings • Fewer Conflicts	• Match Groups Appropriately • Limit Communication with Control Group	• Program Participants • Intact Team/Manager
Absenteeism	• Control Group Arrangement • Trendline Analysis	• Supervisor Estimation • Standard Value	• Program Materials • Participant Salaries/Benefits • Participant Travel (if applicable)	• Teamwork • Improvement in Problem Solving	• Check for Team-Building Initiatives During Program • Monitor Restructuring Activities During Program	• Senior Manager/Management in Business Units • Training and Education Staff
Employee Turnover	• Control Group • Trendline Analysis	• External Study—Cost of Turnover in High Tech Industry • Management Review	• Facilitator • Meeting Facilities (Room, Food, Beverages) • Program Coordinator		• 6 Groups Will Be Monitored	• Safety and Health Staff • Senior Corporate Management
Employee Job Satisfaction	• Control Group Arrangement • Management Estimation	• Management Estimation	• Training and Education Overhead • Evaluation Costs			• Prospective Team Leaders
Employee/Group Productivity	• Control Group Arrangement • Trendline Analysis	• Standard Values • Management Estimation				

manager served as the team leader for the program, although a facilitator provided assistance and conducted a one-day workshop. Exhibit 16-4 illustrates the tool used for identifying initial problems as the work group began using the stress management program. With this brief questionnaire, the manager identified specific problem areas and provided appropriate comments and details. This exercise allowed program planning to focus on the problems and provided guidance to the facilitator and the team.

Exhibit 16-4
Manager Input: Potential Area for Improvement
Stress Reduction for Intact Work Teams

Before you begin the stress reduction program for your team, it is important to capture specific concerns that you have about your work group. Some of these concerns may be stress related and consequently may be used to help structure specific goals and objectives for your team. For each of the following potential areas of improvement, please check all that apply to your group. Add others if appropriate. Next to the item, provide specific comments to detail your concerns and indicate if you think this concern may be related to excessive stress.

☐ Employee Turnover. Comments:
_____
_____

☐ Employee Absenteeism. Comments:
_____
_____

☐ Employee Complaints. Comments:
_____
_____

☐ Morale/Job Satisfaction. Comments:
_____
_____

☐ Conflicts with the Team. Comments:
_____
_____

☐ Productivity. Comments:

_____

_____

☐ Quality. Comments:

_____

_____

☐ Customer Satisfaction. Comments:

_____

_____

☐ Customer Service. Comments:

_____

_____

☐ Work Backlog. Comments:

_____

_____

☐ Delays. Comments:

_____

_____

☐ Other Areas. List and Provide Comments:

_____

_____

Exhibit 16-5 illustrates manager responsibility and involvement for the process. This handout, provided directly to the managers, details twelve specific areas of responsibility and involvement for the managers. Collectively, initial planning, program design, and detailing of responsibilities pushed the manager into a higher-profile position in the program.

Control Group Arrangement

The appropriateness of control groups was reviewed in this setting. If a stress reduction program was needed, it would be appropriate and ethical to withhold the program for certain

Exhibit 16-5
Manager Responsibility and Involvement
Stress Management for Intact Work Teams

With the team approach, the team manager should:

1. Have a discussion with the facilitator to share reasons for interest in stress reduction and the desired outcome of the program. Gain a greater understanding of the StressMap® and the OD approach. Discuss recent changes in the work group and identify any known stressors. This meeting could be held with the senior manager or the senior management team.

2. Identify any additional work group members for the consultant to call to gather preliminary information.

3. Appoint a project coordinator, preferably an individual with good organizing and influencing skills who is respected by the work group.

4. Send out a letter with personal endorsement and signature, inviting the group to participate in the program.

5. Allocate 8 hours of work time per employee for completion of StressMap® and attendance at a StressMap® debriefing and customized course.

6. Schedule a focus group after discussing desired group composition with the facilitator. Ideal size is 10 to 22 participants. Manager should not attend.

7. Attend the workshop and ensure that direct reports attend.

8. Participate in the follow-up meeting held after the last workshop, either in person or by conference call. Other participants to include are the HR representative for your area, the Safety and Health representative for your area, and your management team. The facilitator will provide you feedback about the group issues and make recommendations of actions to take to reduce work stress or increase work satisfaction

9. Commit to an action plan to reduce workplace distress and/or increase workplace satisfaction after thoughtfully considering feedback.

10. Communicate the action plan to your work group.

11. Schedule and participate in a 21-day follow-up call with the consultant and your work group.

12. Work with your team (managers, HR, safety and health, facilitator) to evaluate the success of the action plan and determine next steps.

groups while the experiment was being conducted. It was concluded that this approach was appropriate because the impact of the planned program was in question. Although it was clear that stress-induced problems existed at MEI, there was no guarantee that this program would correct them. Six control groups were planned. The control group arrangement was diligently pursued because it represented the best approach to isolating the effects of the program, if the groups could be matched.

Several criteria were available for group selection. Exhibit 16-6 shows the data collection instrument used to identify groups for a control group arrangement. At the first cut, only those groups that had the same measures were considered (that is, at least 75 percent of the measures were common in the group). This action provided an opportunity to compare performance in the six months preceding the program.

Next, only groups in the same function code were used. At MEI, all groups were assigned a code depending on the type of work, such as finance and accounting or engineering. Thus, each experimental group had to be in the same code as the matched control group. It was also required that all six groups span at least three different codes.

Two other variables were used in the matching process: group size and tenure. The number of employees in the groups had to be within a 20 percent spread, and the average tenure had to be within a two-year range. At MEI, as with many other utilities, there was a high average tenure rate.

Although other variables could have been used to make the match, these five were considered the most influential in the outcome. In summary, the following criteria were used to select the two sets of groups:

☐ Same measures of performance
☐ Similar performance in the previous six months
☐ Same function code
☐ Similar size
☐ Similar tenure

The six pairs of groups represented a total level of employment of 138 team members for the experimental groups, and 132 team members and 6 managers for the control groups.

Exhibit 16-6
Manager Input: Group Measures and Characteristics
Stress Management for Intact Work Teams

To measure the progress of your team, a brief profile of performance measures for employees and your work group is needed. This information will be helpful to determine the feasibility of using your group in a pilot study to measure the impact of the stress management program. Changes in performance measures will be monitored for six months after the program.

Listed below are several categories of measures for your work group. Check the appropriate category and please indicate the specific measure under the description. In addition, indicate if it is a group measure or an individual measure. If other measures are available in other categories, please include them under "Other."

Key Performance Measures   Dept. _____

Performance Category	Measure	Description of Measure	Group Measure	Individual Measure
Productivity	1.		❏	❏
	2.		❏	❏
Efficiency	3.		❏	❏
	4.		❏	❏
Quality	5.		❏	❏
	6.		❏	❏
Response Time	7.		❏	❏
	8.		❏	❏
Cost Control/ Budgets	9.		❏	❏
	10.		❏	❏
Customer Satisfaction	11.		❏	❏
	12.		❏	❏
Absenteeism	13.		❏	❏
Turnover	14.		❏	❏

Morale/	15.		❑	❑
Job Satisfaction	16.		❑	❑
Other	17.		❑	❑
(Please specify)	18.		❑	❑
	19.		❑	❑
	20.		❑	❑

Group Characteristics

Average tenure for group _____ years   Group function code _____

Average job grade for group _____   Average age _____

Number in group _____   Average educational level _____

PROGRAM RESULTS

Questionnaire Response

A follow-up questionnaire, Exhibit 16-7, served as the primary data collection instrument for participants. A similar, slightly modified instrument was used with the managers. In all, 73 percent of the participants returned the questionnaire. This excellent response rate was caused, in part, by a variety of actions taken to ensure an appropriate response rate. Some of the most important actions were:

☐ The team manager distributed the questionnaire and encouraged participants to return it to the external consulting firm. The manager also provided a follow-up reminder.
☐ A full explanation of how the evaluation data would be used was provided to participants.
☐ The questionnaire was reviewed during the follow-up session.
☐ Two types of incentives were used.
☐ Participants were promised a copy of the questionnaire results.

(text continued on page 430)

Exhibit 16-7
Stress Management for Intact Work Teams
Impact Questionnaire

Check one: ☐ Team Member   ☐ Team Leader/Manager

1. Listed below are the objectives of the stress management program. After reflecting on this program, please indicate the degree of success in meeting the objectives.

OBJECTIVES	Failed	Limited Success	Generally Successful	Completely Successful
PERSONAL				
☐ Identify sources of stress in work, personal, and family worlds				
☐ Apply coping strategies to manage stressful situations				
☐ Understand to what degree stress is hampering your health and performance				
☐ Take steps to enhance personal health and overall performance				
☐ Access internal and external resources to help reach personal goals				

GROUP

☐ Identify sources of stress for group

☐ Identify sources of distress and satisfaction

☐ Apply skills to manage and reduce stress in work group

☐ Develop action plan to improve work group effectiveness

☐ Improve effectiveness and efficiency measures for work group

2. Did you develop and implement a 21-day action plan?

Yes ☐ No ☐

If yes, please describe the success of the plan. If not, explain why.

3. Please rate, on a scale of 1–5, the relevance of each of the program elements to your job, with (1) indicating no relevance, and (5) indicating very relevant.

___ StressMap® Instrument ___ Action Planning

___ Group Discussion ___ Program Content

4. Please indicate the degree of success in applying the following skills and behaviors as a result of your participation in the stress management program.

Exhibit 16-7
(continued)

	1	2	3	4	5	
	No	Little	Some	Significant	Very Much	No Opportunity to Use Skills
a) Selecting containable behavior for change						
b) Identifying measures of behavior						
c) Taking full responsibility for your actions						
d) Selecting a buddy to help you change behavior						
e) Identifying and removing barriers to changing behavior						
f) Identifying and using enablers to help change behavior						
g) Staying on track with the 21-day action plan						

h) Applying coping strategies to manage stressful situations					
i) Using control effectively					
j) Knowing when to let go					
k) Responding effectively to conflict					
l) Creating a positive climate					
m) Acknowledging a complaint properly					
n) Reframing problems					
o) Using stress talk strategies					

5. List (3) behaviors or skills you have used most as a result of the stress management program.

_____

_____

_____

6. When did you first use one of the skills from the program?

_____ During the program

_____ Day(s) after the program (indicate number)

_____ Week(s) after the program (indicate number)

Exhibit 16-7
(continued)

7. Indicate the types of relationships in which you have used the skills.

☐ Coworkers
☐ Manager or supervisor
☐ MEI employee in another function
☐ Spouse
☐ Child
☐ Friend
☐ Other: (list) _____

PERSONAL CHANGES

8. What has changed about your on-the-job behavior as a result of this program? (positive attitude, fewer conflicts, better organized, fewer outbursts of anger, etc.)

_____

_____

9. Recognizing the changes in your own behavior and perceptions, please identify any specific personal accomplishments/improvements that you can link to this program. (time savings, project completion, fewer mistakes, etc.)

_____

_____

10. What specific value in U.S. dollars can be attributed to the above accomplishments/improvements? Although this is a difficult question, try to think of specific ways in which the above improvements can be converted to monetary units. Use one year of data. Along with the monetary value, please indicate the basis of your calculation.

$ _____

Basis _____

_____

11. What level of confidence do you place in the above estimations? (0% = No Confidence, 100% = Certainty) _____%

12. Other factors often influence improvements in performance. Please indicate the percent of the above improvement that is related directly to this program. _____%

Please explain. _____

_____

GROUP CHANGES

13. What has changed about your work group as a result of your group's participation in this program? (interactions, cooperation, commitment, problem solving, creativity, etc.)

_____

_____

Exhibit 16-7
(continued)

14. Please identify any specific group accomplishments/improvements that you can link to the program. (project completion, response times, innovative approaches)

_____

_____

15. What specific value in U.S. dollars can be attributed to the above accomplishments/improvements? Although this is a difficult question, try to think of specific ways in which the above improvements can be converted to monetary units. Use one year of values. Along with the monetary value, please indicate the basis of your calculation.

$ _____

Basis _____

_____

16. What level of confidence do you place in the above estimations? (0% = No Confidence, 100% = Certainty) _____ %

17. Other factors often influence improvements in performance. Please indicate the percent of the above improvement that is related directly to this program. _____ %

Please explain. _____

_____

18. Do you think this program represented a good investment for MEI?

Yes ☐   No ☐

Please explain. _____

19. What barriers, if any, have you encountered that have prevented you from using skills or knowledge gained in this program? Check all that apply. Please explain, if possible.

☐ Not enough time
☐ The work environment doesn't support it
☐ Management doesn't support it
☐ The information is not useful (comments)
☐ Other _____

20. Which of the following best describes the actions of your manager during the stress management program?

☐ Very little discussion or reference to the program
☐ Casual mention of program with few specifics
☐ Discussed details of program in terms of content, issues, concerns, etc.
☐ Discussed how the program could be applied to work group
☐ Set goals for changes/improvements
☐ Provided ongoing feedback about the action plan
☐ Provided encouragement and support to help change behavior
☐ Other (comments) . . . . _____

Exhibit 16-7
(continued)

21. For each of the areas below, indicate the extent to which you think this program has influenced these measures in your work group.

	No Influence	Some Influence	Moderate Influence	Significant Influence	Very Much Influence
a) Productivity					
b) Efficiency					
c) Quality					
d) Response Time					
e) Cost Control					
f) Customer Service					
g) Customer Satisfaction					
h) Employee Turnover					
i) Absenteeism					
j) Employee Satisfaction					
k) Healthcare Costs					
l) Safety and Health Costs					

Please cite specific examples or provide more details. _____

_____

_____

22. What specific suggestions do you have for improving the stress management program? Please specify.

☐ Content _____

☐ Duration _____

☐ Presentation _____

☐ Other _____

23. Other comments:

_____

_____

_____

(text continued from page 419)

Application Data

The application of the program was considered an outstanding success with 92 percent of the participants completing their twenty-one-day action plan. A conference call at the end of the twenty-one days showed positive feedback and much enthusiasm for the progress made. The follow-up session also demonstrated success because most of the participants had indicated changes in behavior.

The most comprehensive application data came from the six-month questionnaire administered to participants and managers. The following skills and behaviors were reported as achieving significant success:

☐ Taking full responsibility for one's actions
☐ Identifying or removing barriers to change behavior
☐ Applying coping strategies to manage stressful situations
☐ Responding effectively to conflict
☐ Creating a positive climate
☐ Acknowledging a complaint properly

Coworkers were the most frequently cited group in which relationships had improved through use of the skills, with 95 percent indicating application improvement with this group.

Barriers

Information collected throughout the process, including the two follow-up questionnaires, indicated few barriers to implementing the process. The two most frequently listed barriers were:

☐ There is not enough time.
☐ The work environment does not support the process.

Management Support

Manager support seemed quite effective. The most frequently listed behaviors of managers were:

☐ Managers set goals for change and improvement.
☐ Managers discussed how the program could apply to the work group.

Impact Data

The program had significant impact with regard to both perceptions and actual values. On Exhibit 16-7, the follow-up questionnaire, 90 percent of the participants perceived this program as a good investment for MEI. In addition, participants perceived that this program had a significantly influenced:

☐ Employee satisfaction
☐ Absenteeism
☐ Turnover
☐ Healthcare cost
☐ Safety and health cost

This assessment appears to support the actual improvement data, outlined below. For each measure below, only the team data were collected and presented. Because managers were not the target of the program, manager performance data were not included. An average of months five and six, instead of the sixth month, was used consistently for the post-program data analysis to eliminate the spike effect.

Healthcare Costs. Healthcare costs for employees were categorized by diagnostic code; thus, it was a simple process to track the cost of stress-induced illnesses. Although few differences were shown in the first three months after the program began, by months five and six an average difference of $120 per employee per month was identified. This was apparently caused by the lack of stress-related incidents and the subsequent medical costs resulting from the stress. It was believed that this amount would be an appropriate improvement to use. The trendline projection of healthcare costs was inconclusive because of the variability of the medical care costs prior to the program. A consistent trend could not be identified.

Absenteeism. There was significant difference of absenteeism in the two groups. The average absenteeism for the control group for months five and six was 4.65 percent. The absenteeism rate for the groups involved in the program was 3.2 percent. Employees worked an average of 220 days. The trendline analysis appeared to support the absenteeism reduction. Because no other issues were identified that could have influenced absenteeism during this time period, the trendline analysis provided an accurate estimate of the impact.

Turnover. Although turnover at MEI was traditionally low, in the past two years it had increased because of significant changes in the workplace. A turnover reduction was identified using the differences in the control group and experimental group. The control group had an average annual turnover rate of 19.2 percent for months five and six. The experimental group had an average of 14.1 percent for the same two months. As with absenteeism, the trendline analysis supported the turnover reduction.

Productivity. Control group differences showed no significant improvement in productivity. Of all the measures collected, the productivity measure was the most difficult to match between the two groups, which may account for the inconclusive results. Also, the trendline differences showed some slight improvement but not enough to develop an actual value for productivity changes.

Job Satisfaction. Because of the timing difference in collecting attitude survey data, complete job satisfaction data were not available. Participants did provide input about the extent to which they felt the program actually influenced job satisfaction. The results were quite positive, with a significant influence rating for that variable. Because of the subjective nature of job satisfaction and the difficulties with measurement, a value was not assigned to job satisfaction.

Monetary Values

The determination of monetary benefits for the program was developed using the methods outlined in the ROI analysis plan. The medical costs were converted directly. A $120 per month savings yielded a $198,720 annual benefit. A standard value had routinely been used at MEI to reflect the cost of an absence. This value was 1.25 times the average daily wage rate. For the experimental group, the average wage rate was $123 per day. This yielded an annual improvement value of $67,684. For employee turnover, several turnover cost studies were available, which revealed a value of 85 percent of annual base pay. As expected, senior managers felt this cost of turnover was slightly overstated and preferred to use a value of 70 percent, yielding an annual benefit of $157,553. No values were used for productivity or job satisfaction. The total annual benefit of the stress management program was $423,957. Table 16-1 reflects the total economic benefits of the program.

The medical costs were converted directly. A $120 per month savings yielded a $198,720 annual benefit. Other values are as follows:

Unit Value for an Absence

$123 × 1.25 = $153.75

Unit Value for Turnover

$31,980 × 70% = $22,386

Improvement for Absenteeism

138 employees × 220 workdays × 1.45% × $153.75 = $67,684

Table 16-1
Annual Monetary Benefits for 138 Participants

	Monthly Difference	Unit Value	Annual Improvement Value
Medical Costs	$120	—	$198,720
Absenteeism	1.45%	$153.75	$ 67,684
Turnover	5.1% (annualized)	$22,386	$157,553
TOTAL			$423,957

Improvement for Turnover

138 employees × 5.1% × $22,386 = $157,553

No values were used for productivity or job satisfaction.

Intangible Benefits

Several intangible benefits were identified in the study and confirmed by actual input from participants and questionnaires. The following benefits were pinpointed:

- ☐ employee satisfaction
- ☐ teamwork
- ☐ improved relationships with family and friends
- ☐ time savings
- ☐ improved image in the company
- ☐ fewer conflicts

No attempt was made to place monetary values on any of the intangibles.

Program Costs

Calculating the costs of the stress management program also followed the categories outlined in the evaluation plan. For needs assessment, all the costs were fully allocated to the six groups. Although the needs assessment was necessary, the total cost of needs assessment, $16,500, was included. All program development costs were estimated at $95 per participant, or $4,800. The program could have possibly been spread through other parts of the organization, and then the cost would ultimately have been prorated across all the sessions. However, the costs were low because the materials were readily available for most of the effort, and the total development cost was used.

The salaries for the team members averaged $31,980, while the six team managers had average salaries of $49,140. The benefits factor for MEI was 37 percent for both groups. Although the program took a little more than one day of staff time, one day of program time was considered sufficient for the cost. The total salary cost was $24,108. The participants' travel cost ($38 per participant) was very low because the programs were conducted in the area. The facilitator cost, program coordination cost, and training and development overhead costs were estimated to be $10,800. The meeting room facilities, food, and refreshments averaged $22 per participant, for a total of $3,968. Evaluation costs were $22,320. It was decided that all the evaluation costs would be allocated to these six groups. This determination was extremely conservative because the evaluation costs could be prorated if the program was implemented over other areas.

Table 16-2 details the stress management program costs.

These costs were considered fully loaded with no proration except for needs assessment. Additional time could have been used for participants' off-the-job activities. However, it was concluded one day should be sufficient (for the one-day program.)

Table 16-2
Program Costs

Cost Category	Total Cost
Needs Assessment	$ 16,500
Program Development	4,800
Program Materials (144 × $95)	13,680
Participant Salaries/Benefits Based on 1 day 138 × $123 × 1.37 and 6 × 189 × 1.37	24,108
Travel and Lodging 144 × 38	5,472
Facilitation, Coordination, T&D Overhead	10,800
Meeting Room, Food, and Refreshments 144 × 22	3,168
Evaluation Costs	22,320
TOTAL	$100,848

Results: ROI

Based on the given monetary benefits and costs, the return on investment and the benefits/cost ratio are shown below.

$$\text{BCR} = \frac{\$423,957}{\$100,848} = 4.20$$

$$\text{ROI} = \frac{\$423,957 - \$100,848}{\$100,848} = 320\%$$

Although this number is considered quite large, it is still conservative because of the following assumptions and adjustments:

☐ Only first-year values were used. The program should actually have second- and third-year benefits.

☐ Control group differences were used in analysis, which is often the most effective way to isolate the effects of the program. These differences were also confirmed with the trendline analysis.

☐ The participants provided additional monetary benefits, detailed on the questionnaires. Although these benefits could have been added to the total numbers, they were not included because only 23 participants of the 144 supplied values for those questions.

☐ The costs are fully loaded.

When considering these adjustments, the value should represent a realistic value calculation for the actual return on investment.

Communication Strategies

Because of the importance of sharing the analysis results, a communication strategy was developed. Table 16-3 outlines this strategy. Three separate documents were developed to communicate with the different target groups in a variety of ways.

Policy and Practice Implications

Because of the significance of the study and the information, two issues became policy. Whenever programs are considered that

Table 16-3
Communication Strategies

Communication Document	Communication Target	Distribution
Complete report with appendices (75 pages)	☐ Training and Education Staff ☐ Safety and Health Staff ☐ Intact Team Manager	Distributed and discussed in a special meeting
Executive summary (8 pages)	☐ Senior Management in the Business Units ☐ Senior Corporate Management	Distributed and discussed in routine meeting
General interest overview and summary without the actual ROI calculation (10 pages)	☐ Program Participants	Mailed with letter
Brochure highlighting program, objectives, and specific results	☐ Prospective Team Leaders	Included with other program descriptions

involve large groups of employees or a significant investment of funds, a detailed needs assessment should be conducted to ensure the proper program is developed. Also, an ROI study should be conducted for a small group of programs to measure the impact before complete implementation. In essence, this influenced the policy and practice on needs assessment, pilot program evaluation, and the number of impact studies developed.

QUESTIONS FOR DISCUSSION

1. What is the purpose of the needs assessment?
2. What specific sources of data should be used?
3. Critique the data collection plan.
4. What other methods could be used to isolate the effects of the program?
5. Critique the methods to convert data to monetary values.
6. Are the costs fully loaded? Explain.
7. Is the ROI value realistic? Explain.
8. Critique the communication strategy.

CHAPTER 17

Safety Incentive Program

National Steel

By Ron D. Stone

This case addresses measuring the effectiveness of an HR incentive program designed to influence employee behavior and to reduce accidents in a manufacturing environment. Although top executives were concerned about the safety and well-being of employees, they also wanted to reduce the cost of accidents. The cost of accidents was reaching the point that it was an obstacle to the company becoming a low-cost provider of products in a competitive industry. This case demonstrates that an evaluation of an HR intervention can be implemented with minimal resources. It also demonstrates that although some programs may achieve a return on investment, it is sometimes best to communicate the ROI results to a limited audience.

BACKGROUND

National Steel is a large manufacturing operation with divisions in the southeastern, southwestern, and midwestern United States. Each division has multiple plants. The company also has several foreign plants in operation and two others in the construction phase. The plants produce steel products such as bar stock and plate steel. They also fabricate specialized fasteners used in the commercial building industry. The nature of National's manufacturing business requires that safety always receives a top priority with management and the work force. The concern for employee safety is a significant issue. Additionally, domestic and foreign competition is a major factor in National's strategy to become a low-cost producer.

The company had always been always concerned about the human element of a safe work environment, but economic issues were now a significant concern being driven by the cost of accidents. The company had long had a group called the Central Safety Committee in place to continually review safety issues, direct accident investigations, and establish policy and best practices. The committee was made up of a senior line officer (who served as the sponsor), one line manager, two foremen, six members of the work force, the corporate manager of safety, and the VP of HR.

A PERFORMANCE PROBLEM

The committee had recently informed the senior management of National Steel that the midwestern division of the company was experiencing unacceptable accident frequency rates, accident severity rates, and total accident costs. For a two-year period, these costs had been around the $400,000 to $500,000 range annually—much too high for the Central Safety Committee and management to accept.

THE NEEDS ASSESSMENT

The safety manager was directed to meet with managers and employees in the three plants of the midwestern division to seek causes of the problem and to work with the division manager to implement the appropriate solutions. A team of HR specialists completed the assignment. They also analyzed the cost and types of accidents. The team of specialists concluded:

☐ Employees' safety habits were lax, and they were not focusing enough attention on safety.

☐ Employees knew and understood safety guidelines and practices; therefore training was not an issue.

☐ A significant number of accidents and accident-related costs involved injuries of a questionable nature.

☐ Some type of monetary incentive would likely influence employee behavior.

☐ Peer pressure could possibly be used to help employees focus on safety practices and on the need to avoid the costs of seeing a physician when it was unnecessary.

THE HR SOLUTION

As a result of the assessment, the team recommended that the division implement a group-based safety incentive plan at the three plants. A monetary incentive had been successful in another division during previous years. The division manager reviewed the details of the plan and even helped craft some of the components. He accepted the recommendations and agreed to sponsor the implementation. The two objectives of the recommended plan were:

1. To reduce the annual accident frequency rate from a level of 60 to a much lower level of approximately 20 or less.
2. To reduce the annual disabling accident frequency rate from a level of 18 to 0.

THE MEASURE OF SUCCESS

The HR team expressed the need to track certain measures on a continual basis. Once the incentive plan's objectives were established, the team identified the specific data needed to analyze safety performance. The measures identified were:

☐ Number of medical treatment cases
☐ Number of lost-time accidents
☐ Number of lost-time days
☐ Accident costs
☐ Hours worked
☐ Incentive costs

The team decided that data should be collected monthly. Because the data collection system had been in place before the implementation of the safety incentive plan, no additional data collection procedures were needed. The same system was also used by the HR specialists when the Central Safety Committee asked them to review the problem and make recommendations. Management was also interested in a payback for the incentive program. Although accident reduction and severity were major concerns, there was also a need to achieve low-cost provider goals. Management requested to see figures that demonstrated that the benefits from the plan exceeded the costs of implementation. The team members concluded that they could use the same tracking system to determine the return on investment.

THE INCENTIVE PLAN

The incentive plan consisted of a cash award of $75, after taxes, to each employee in the plant for every six months the plant worked without a medical treatment case. A medical treatment case was defined as an accident that could not be treated by plant first-aid and, therefore, needed the attention of a physician. Each plant had a work force of about 120 employees. A team effort at each plant was important because the actions of one employee could impact the safety of another. Peer pressure was necessary to keep employees focused and to remind them to avoid unnecessary physician costs. Therefore, the award was paid at each of the three plants independently. An award was not paid unless the entire plant completed a six-month period without a medical treatment case. When a medical treatment case occurred, a new six-month period began.

IMPLEMENTATION OF THE INCENTIVE PLAN

The plant managers implemented the plan at the beginning of the new year so results could easily be monitored and compared with performance in previous years. Each plant manager announced the plan to employees and distributed the guidelines for payout. The managers communicated the details of the plan and answered questions during the regular monthly safety meeting at each plant. Thorough communication ensured that each employee clearly understood how the plan functioned and what the group had to accomplish to receive an award.

COST MONITORING

Two groups of costs were monitored: the total accident costs and the incentive compensation costs. Total accident costs were monitored prior to the safety incentive plan as part of collecting routine safety performance data. The additional costs related directly to incentive compensation were also tabulated. Because the $75 cash was provided after taxes, the cost to the division was approximately $97.50 per employee for each six-month period completed without a medical treatment case. Additional administration costs were minimal because the data used in analysis were already collected prior to the new plan and because the time required to administer the plan and calculate the award was almost negligible. No additional staff was needed, and no overtime for existing staff could be directly attributed to the plan. However, a conservative estimate of $1,600 per year of plan administration costs was used in the tabulation of incentive costs.

DATA COLLECTION AND ANALYSIS

In addition to the two-year data history, data were collected during a two-year period after the plan implementation to provide an adequate before-and-after comparison. Medical treatment injuries, lost-time injuries, accident frequency rates, and accident costs were all monitored to show the contribution of the safety incentive plan. The data shown in Table 17-1 document the accident costs for the four-year period. The data reveal significant reductions in accident costs for the two-year period after the implementation of the plan.

When comparing the average of years 3 and 4 (after the incentive plan) with the years 1 and 2 average (before the incentive plan), the accident frequency was reduced by 68 percent, while the disabling accident frequency was reduced by 74 percent. The annual cost of accidents (averaging the two years before and the two years after the incentive plan) dropped from $523,244 to $18,701, producing a significant savings of $504,543.

Table 17-1
Accident Costs and Frequency for All 3 Plants

	Year 1 Before Plan	Year 2 Before Plan	Year 3 After Plan	Year 4 After Plan
Accident Frequency	61.2	58.8	19.6	18.4
Disabling Frequency	17.4	18.9	5.7	3.8
Medical Treatment Injuries	121	111	19	17
Lost-Time Injuries	23	21	6.8	5.2
Actual Cost of Accidents	$468,360	$578,128	$18,058	$19,343

The objective of the plan to reduce the annual accident frequency rate to less than 20 was met with a post-plan average of 19. The objective of reducing the annual disabling accident frequency rate from 18 to 0 was not achieved. Although the average after two years dropped significantly from 18.15 annually to 4.75 annually, this was still short of the target. Both calculations are shown below.

BEFORE INCENTIVE PLAN   AFTER INCENTIVE PLAN

Accident Frequency 61.2 + 58.8 = 120   19.6 + 18.4 = 38

Annual Average (÷ 2) = 60 ANNUALLY   = 19 ANNUALLY

Annual Improvmt. 60 – 19 = 41

% Accident Improvmt. 60 → 41 = 68%

BEFORE INCENTIVE PLAN   AFTER INCENTIVE PLAN

Disabling Frequency 17.4 + 18.9 = 36.3   5.7 + 3.8 = 9.5

Annual Average (÷ 2) = 18.15 ANNUALLY   = 4.75 ANNUALLY

Annual Improvmt. 18.15 – 4.75 = 13.4

% Disabling Improvmt. 18.15 → 13.4 = 74%

These impressive results demonstrated a positive business impact. The incentive plan resulted in a safer work environment, fewer accidents, and fewer disabling accidents. Although these results improved the overall safety program considerably, the issue of cost savings remained unanswered. Did the incentive plan bring greater monetary benefits than the cost incurred to implement and administer it? Thus far, all costs have not been identified. Table 17-2 details the additional cost issues. There was also the issue of how much the incentive plan influenced improvement in the measures when compared with other actions that may have influenced improvements.

The needs assessment cost of $2,400 consisted of capturing the time and travel expenses for the HR team to conduct twenty interviews with plant operations and management staff and to develop recommendations. The cost to administer the incentive plan was $1,600 annually. The cost of the incentive plan payout must be captured and included in the total cost of accident

Table 17-2
The Contribution of the Safety Incentive Plan for All 3 Plants

	Year 1 Before Plan	Year 2 Before Plan	Year 3 After Plan	Year 4 After Plan
Needs Assessment Costs (spread)	—	—	$ 1,200	$ 1,200
Plan's Annual Administration and Evaluation Costs	—	—	$ 1,600	$ 1,600
Safety Incentive Plan Payout Costs	—	—	$58,013	$ 80,730
Actual Cost of Accidents	$468,360	$578,128	$18,058	$ 19,343
Total Cost of Accidents and Prevention	$468,360	$578,128	$78,871	$102,873

Plan implemented beginning in year 3

prevention. Payout is determined by calculating the amount of incentive awards paid to employees in years 3 and 4. Table 17-3 provides a breakdown of the payout.

DATA INTERPRETATION AND CONCLUSION

The contribution of the safety incentive plan was determined by adding the accident and administrative costs for years 3 and 4 to the safety incentive plan payout costs and then comparing this total with the accident costs of years 1 and 2. As Table 17-2 shows, the total costs were reduced significantly. Accident costs from years 1 and 2 (see Table 17-2) totaled $1,046,488, for an average of $523,244 annually. Accident and prevention costs for years 3 and 4 totaled $181,744, for an average of $90,872 annually. This was an annual improvement of $432,372.

Table 17-3
The Safety Incentive Plan Payout

Plant 1 Payout, Year 3:	115 employees @ $97.50 115 × 1 PAYOUT	= $11,213
Plant 2 Payout, Year 3:	122 employees @ $97.50 122 × 2 PAYOUTS	= $23,790
Plant 3 Payout, Year 3:	118 employees @ $97.50 118 × 2 PAYOUTS	= $23,010
	Total Payout, Year 3	**$58,013**
Plant 1 Payout, Year 4:	115 employees @ $97.50 115 × 2 PAYOUTS	= $22,425
Plant 2 Payout, Year 4:	122 employees @ $97.50 122 × 2 PAYOUTS	= $23,790
Plant 3 Payout, Year 4:	118 employees @ $97.50 118 × 3 PAYOUTS	= $34,515
	Total Payout, Year 4	**$80,730**
Total Payout, Years 3 and 4		**$138,743**

The Central Safety Committee discussed the issue of isolating the effects of the safety incentive plan. As a group, committee members decided the incentive plan should be credited for most of the improvement. They felt that it was the incentive plan that influenced a new safety awareness and caused peer pressure to work. After much debate, they accepted an estimate from the in-house expert, the manager of safety. The manager of safety brought forth data from an industry trade group that presented convincing evidence that management's attention to safe work habits had been shown to reduce the cost of accidents by 20 percent. Before these data were presented, the improvement was going to be attributed entirely to the incentive plan because no other factors that could have influenced safety performance during this period had been identified. Also, the safety record at the other two divisions showed no improvement during the same time period.

CALCULATING THE RETURN ON INVESTMENT

To determine the return on investment, the costs and monetary benefits of the incentive plan were needed. The annual cost of incentive payouts (two-year average of $69,372) added to annual administration costs ($1,200 plus $1,600) provided a total incentive plan cost of $72,172. The benefits were calculated starting with the annual monetary benefits of $432,372. Because the Central Safety Committee accepted the suggestion of the manager of safety—that management attention played a role in influencing the improvement (20 percent)—then an adjustment had to be made. Thus, 80 percent of $432,372 resulted in an estimated impact of $345,898. The ROI became:

$$\text{ROI} = \frac{\text{Net Benefits}}{\text{Costs}} = \frac{\$345,898 - \$72,172}{\$72,172} = 3.79 \times 100 = 379\%$$

COMMUNICATION OF RESULTS

The results of the safety incentive plan were communicated to a variety of target audiences to show the contribution of the plan. First, the division president summarized the results in a monthly report to the chief executive officer of the corporation. The focal point was on the reduction in accident frequency and severity, the reduction in costs, the improvement in safety awareness, and the return on investment for the incentive plan.

The HR department presented the results in its monthly report to all middle and upper division management with the same focus that was presented to the CEO. Return on investment information was reserved for the eyes of management because it was felt that employees might misunderstand this as being the focus of plant safety.

The results were presented to all plant staff members through the monthly *Safety Newsletter*. This communication focused on the reduction in medical treatment injuries, as well as improvements in lost-time accidents, disabling accidents, and accident frequency. It also commended employees for their accomplishments, as did all the communication.

Finally, the results were communicated to all division employees through the division newsletter. This communication focused on the same issues presented to plant staff members. Communications were positive and increased the awareness of the need for the continuation of the incentive plan.

QUESTIONS FOR DISCUSSION

1. What questions would you have asked during the needs assessment?
2. What are your thoughts about the way the Central Safety Committee decided to isolate the effects of the safety incentive plan?
3. What other alternatives could have been explored to isolate the effects?
4. Would you have sought approval to collect additional data from employees during the follow-up evaluation regarding what caused the improvements? Why would you want additional data? How would you have justified the cost of this additional work?
5. Were there additional costs that should have been included? Should the cost of communication be included?
6. How would you have communicated the results differently?
7. How credible is this study?

CHAPTER 18

Executive Leadership Development

Imperial National Bank

By Patricia Pulliam Phillips

This case shows the monetary impact of a leadership develop-
ment program using an action learning process. The pro-
jected cost of the program was the driving force in this
evaluation and underscores the complexity of measuring the
impact of leadership development. More importantly, this
case shows how changes in program design can significantly
increase the actual return on investment.

BACKGROUND

As with many large global organizations in a competitive
industry, Imperial National Bank (INB)—a large, multi-service
bank operating in fourteen states—recognized that it needed
effective leaders. As a result a comprehensive leadership development program was developed. The program followed a learning-
while-earning model, whereby high-potential leaders worked
together on selected high-priority business issues with access to
just-in-time coaching, advice from senior executives, and a faculty

of subject matter experts. The program structure combined class time and project work.

A process called action reflection learning (ARL) was the principal vehicle used in the leadership development program to assist in learning new approaches to behavioral change and perceptions. The process helped participants associate learning with making things happen in real time. ARL confronted participants with challenges and risks, had them search for information, and had them complete tasks that were outside their regular scope of activities. In essence, ARL took advantage of the fact that when learning is linked to action on real issues, in which there are real consequences and risks, adults are more motivated to learn.

Three critical success factors were identified that needed to be fully operational and executed for the program to achieve the desired success:

☐ A significant amount of time needed to be invested by the management committee, clients, and participants.
☐ Real projects that were enterprise-wide and strategic needed to be developed.
☐ Influential participants needed to be selected based on performance and future potential.

These factors capture the most important issues surrounding this program.

Initiation of the Leadership Development Program

Around the globe, there is a need for more accountability and evaluation in leadership development. In accordance with this need, the director of INB's training function initiated an evaluation of the leadership program. Performance Resources Organization (PRO), a leading international consulting firm that focuses on measuring the return on investment in human resources programs, was called in as an external consultant to direct the evaluation. PRO was not involved in the design, development, or delivery of this program, thus ensuring an independent evaluation.

The leadership program was deemed an ideal candidate for ROI evaluation for several reasons:

The program was INB's first attempt to integrate traditional leadership development with on-the-job, real-life projects, designed to add significant value to the organization.

☐ The program targeted a critical audience at INB—future leaders.
☐ The vision for the program had been developed and refined at the highest levels of the organization.
☐ On a per participant basis, the program was perhaps the most expensive program undertaken at INB. It was also the most visible.
☐ The program was designed to focus on important projects that represented real-life situations and involved key operational and strategic issues.

Several issues apparent at the beginning of the study, however, had the potential to influence the ability to develop a specific return on investment (ROI):

☐ Initially, the program was not designed to deliver a measurable business impact. Consequently, key performance measures were not linked to the program, and specific objectives were not developed to improve measurable performance.
☐ Although the projects were included to add value to INB, the nature of some of the projects made this task difficult. Also, the requirements for developing the projects did not include a process for capturing monetary value.
☐ Data collection systems had not been developed and refined to link with the leadership development program. Performance data were scattered throughout the company and, in some cases, not readily available.
☐ The intangible benefits from this program were expected to be significant and long term, providing non-monetary values that might exceed the monetary benefits.

Even with the presence of the above difficulties, there was a desire to measure ROI, using the most credible processes. Through the implementation of a comprehensive data collection and analysis process spanning a time period of September to June, this evaluation took place, using the ROI process model described throughout this book.

DATA COLLECTION PLAN

An effective evaluation must be carefully planned with appropriate timing established and responsibilities defined. Table 18-1 shows the data collection plan for this evaluation. The data collection plan was initially developed and approved by the support team with additional adjustments made during the program to ensure that appropriate input was obtained from all individuals. Although the amount of data collected might be considered excessive and the multiple methods might provide duplication and overlap, this was considered a necessity because of the importance of the program, the cost of the program in both time and money, and the target audience involved.

Timing of Data Collection

The timing of collection was very critical. End-of-program questionnaires were collected at the end of each session and at the end of the program. Reaction data was also collected from a variety of individuals at the program's completion. Learning data was collected during the session and during on-the-job observations.

The most critical timing issue to address was data collection for application and impact. Although a leadership development program is designed to have a long-term impact, the specific improvements from programs are difficult to capture if assessed years after the program is completed. Although the connection may exist, it is difficult for the participants and participants' managers to make the connection between a training program and specific improvement. In addition, for longer periods of time, additional variables will influence business measures, thus complicating the cause and effect relationship between training and improvement.

The timing of data collection was complicated because senior management wanted the evaluation completed before making a decision about the implementation of future programs. Ideally, the application and impact data should be captured within six months to one year after a program is completed. Following this schedule would push the data collection and completion of the evaluation beyond the requested time frame desired to make decisions about a second program.

The spacing of the sessions further complicated the timing of the study. The first session was held in September and the last in February. The time needed to apply skills learned in the first session would place the evaluation in the spring. For the last session, the follow-up would normally be in the fall. Thus, a period of sixty to ninety days from the last session was selected to allow enough time for application.

End-of-Program Feedback

An essential part of any evaluation is the typical feedback obtained at the end of a training program. A modified version of the standard questionnaire used by the training department captured feedback at the end of each session. This feedback was tabulated and provided to the external consultants, as well as the training support team. Adjustments were routinely made using this feedback data.

Observation

An important part of evaluation was provided by the research component of the program. An expert in action reflection learning research provided observation throughout the program. Although most of the observation occurred during sessions and captured actual learning, some observation took place in work settings as part of an executive shadow program. The results of these observations were provided as feedback to program faculty, the training support team, and program participants. Although results of this research are included in this case as part of the total assessment and evaluation, it is important to note that this research was not designed to serve as program assessment and evaluation.

Questionnaire from Participants

One of the most important data collection methods was the detailed follow-up questionnaire completed by participants in the time frame of sixty to ninety days from the end of the last session. During the third session, participants were briefed about the plans for the questionnaire, and the general topics were discussed. Participants were also reminded about the questionnaire

(text continued on page 456)

Table 18-1
Data Collection Plan

Level	Broad Program Objective(s)	Data Collection Method	Timing of Data Collection	Responsibilities for Data Collection
I Reaction, Satisfaction	☐ Favorable reaction from participants, teams and observers ☐ Suggestions for improvement	☐ Questionnaire from participants (1) ☐ Follow-up questionnaire from participants (2) ☐ Interviews with participants (5) ☐ Observation ☐ Interviews with sponsors (3) ☐ Follow-up questionnaire from manager (4)	☐ End of each session and end of program ☐ 60–90 days after end of program ☐ 60–90 days after end of program ☐ Daily ☐ 60–90 days after end of program ☐ 60–90 days after end of program	☐ PRO ☐ PRO ☐ PRO ☐ Manager ☐ PRO ☐ PRO
II Learning	☐ Enhance knowledge and skills in fourteen areas	☐ Observation ☐ Questionnaire from participants (1) ☐ Values technology instrument ☐ Executive success profile ☐ Follow-up questionnaire from participants (2)	☐ Daily ☐ End of each session and end of program ☐ During program ☐ During program ☐ 60–90 days after end of program	☐ Manager ☐ PRO ☐ Facilitators ☐ Facilitators ☐ PRO

III Application	□ Use of skills and knowledge □ Frequency of skill use □ Interaction with management and policy committee	□ Observation □ Follow-up questionnaire from participants (2) □ Follow-up questionnaire from manager (4) □ Interviews with participants (5) □ Interviews with sponsors	□ During program □ 60–90 days after end of program □ 60–90 days after end of program □ 60–90 days after end of program □ 60–90 days after end of program	□ Managers □ PRO □ PRO □ PRO □ PRO
IV Business Impact	□ Benefits from research, recommendations made by project teams, and resulting savings and/or earnings □ Improvement in business impact measures as each participant applies skills in business unit □ Enhanced quality of executive talent pool	□ Financial performance indicators from project presentations □ Interviews with participants (5) □ Follow-up questionnaire from participants (2) □ Follow-up questionnaire from manager (4) □ HR records	□ 60–90 days after end of program □ 60–90 days after end of program □ 60–90 days after end of program □ 60–90 days after end of program □ 3 years after end of program	□ Program Director □ PRO □ PRO □ PRO □ PRO

(1) Same questionnaire, (2) Same questionnaire, (3) Same questionnaire, (4) Same interview, (5) Same interview

(text continued from page 453)

at the last session, and a final reminder was sent approximately one month after the last session. This reminder came directly from the training director, encouraging them to take appropriate notes of details that could be reported in the questionnaires. As of mid-June, the participant response rate was 73 percent, representing sixteen of the twenty-two participants. In addition, questionnaire responses were very thorough and served as a valuable data source. The questionnaire focused on application and impact data (Levels 3 and 4).

Interviews with Participants

To supplement input from questionnaires, interviews were conducted with each participant. Lasting approximately 1 to 1.5 hours, each interview explored individual application and impact topics. Additional probing was used to uncover business impact applications and to gain further insight into skill applications, barriers, concerns and important issues surrounding the success of the program. These interviews were conducted within sixty to ninety days after the last session.

Questionnaires for Managers

To gain the perspective of participants' managers, a questionnaire was sent directly to them within the timeframe of sixty to ninety days from the end of the program. The managers of participants were involved early in the process when participants were selected. They often had to make adjustments in the business units while participants attended sessions and worked on the project. Manager input was considered important, as their support was necessary for success. As of mid-June, 46 percent of managers had returned the questionnaire.

Interview with Sponsors

Because senior managers' involvement in this program was significant, their interest was high, and consequently, their influence was critical to its success. Interviews with these project sponsors provided a wealth of candid input about the success of the program as well as the concerns from the unique perspective of these key executives.

Questionnaire from the Support Team

To provide additional input from other members critical to the success of the program, a customized questionnaire was distributed to the external consultants and the training support team. Their input focused on reaction to the program, assessment of success, and suggestions for improvement.

Performance Monitoring

Capturing specific data from business impact applications and project evaluation required collecting data from the business records of the organization. This was a factor only in those areas in which impact was identified or on which the projects had a direct influence.

Project Review

To capture the potential value of the projects, the status of the projects was explored with each project owner to determine the extent of implementation and the prospects for future implementations. In some cases, the project review went a step further by placing an actual value on the projects.

Summary

Collectively, these data collection methods yielded a tremendous amount of data, far exceeding expectations. The different perspectives and types of data ensured a thorough assessment of the program and provided a backdrop for insightful recommendations for making improvements.

REACTION AND LEARNING

Table 18-2 shows how the data were integrated for analysis and reporting along the four levels of evaluation as well as the

Table 18-2
Data Integration

	Level 1 Reaction to Program	Level 2 Learning: Skills, Knowledge, Changes in Perceptions	Level 3 Application Implementation and Use on the Job	Level 4 Impact in Business Unit	Costs
End of Session Feedback	X	X			
Research		X	X		
Interviews with Participants	X	X	X	X	X
Questionnaires from Participants	X	X	X	X	
Questionnaires from Managers of Participants	X		X	X	
Interviews with Sponsors	X				
Questionnaires for Faculty/Support Team	X				
Company Records				X	X

Barriers/Concerns →   ROI →

cost of the program. Data on reaction to the program and relevant learning that took place was obtained through end-of-session feedback, interviews with participants, and questionnaires from participants. Questionnaires from managers of participants and faculty/support teams, as well as interviews with sponsors, provided additional reaction data while research provided additional data on relevant learning.

Reaction

The data collected throughout the first leadership development program indicated both high and low points during the program. The participant overall mean score indicated a decline in the value of the sessions. Also, as the participants progressed through the program, a number of issues arose. These issues centered on [1] progress of project team work, [2] lack of time, [3] external presenters/content (2 of 4), and [4] team dynamics.

The components that contributed the most to the participant learning using a five-point scale were: [1] project work (4.6), [2] cross-functional team work (4.6), and [3] being involved in strategic issues at INB (4.5). The components that contributed the least were external resources (2.8) and feedback instruments (3.4).

Therefore, the areas that were sources of frustration during the program were also the areas that contributed the most to the learning—the project work and team dynamics.

Learning

Learning was examined in significant detail as part of the research component for the program. The major findings from the research program are contained in Table 18-3.

APPLICATION

Application of Skills, Knowledge, and Behavior

Although the leadership development program was not designed to develop a number of skills to produce immediate on-the-job results, specific areas were addressed that had immediate applica-

Table 18-3
Major Findings from Research Project

Major Findings from Research Project Measures of Learning

Learning:
- ☐ Learning was "managed" by the participants through the use of several "filters."
- ☐ Learning was impacted by the existing culture of the organization.
- ☐ Executive learning included cognitive re-framing, as well as information transfer and skill development.

Team Skill Development:
- ☐ Development was affected by executive role and position.
- ☐ Skill development was affected by cultural norms and values.
- ☐ Skill development was affected by project focus.
- ☐ Development was affected by interaction with learning coaches.

Projects:
- ☐ Projects were affected by team and individual sponsorship.
- ☐ Projects were affected by program schedule and design.
- ☐ Projects were affected by interaction among teams and by interaction as whole group.

tion potential. The questionnaire response from participants showed significant changes in behavior in several important skill areas. Not surprisingly, "reflection and dialogue" showed the most significant change, followed closely by "thinking strategically" and "communicating effectively." This mirrored, to a certain extent, the results obtained from participant interviews and manager questionnaires. "Using market research and data analysis" showed the least change, principally because it was not developed much in the program, although it was part of the original plan. Surprisingly, "planning personal development" did not show the extent of the transfer to the job as anticipated.

Ironically, the manager questionnaire input provided a more positive assessment of behavior change, particularly with "applying power and influence" and "managing small work groups."

Action Reflection Learning Approach

The action reflection learning approach (ARL) was at the core of the learning process in the sessions. Although the reaction for most of the elements of ARL was positive, there was concern about the overall success of some of the initiatives. The questionnaire responses from participants revealed that the most successful elements of ARL were the abilities to "engage in cross-functional work teams" and "learn from your own experience." The least successful appeared to be "associate learning with making things happen in real time."

BUSINESS IMPACT

Linkage with Key Measures

To achieve results, participants needed to realize a connection or linkage between the application of acquired knowledge and skills and changes in key business measures. According to input from participants and other groups, the strongest linkage occurred with employee satisfaction and customer satisfaction. Building effective leadership skills often improves employee satisfaction while improving the relationship with customers. In addition, the projects contributed significantly to this connection. The weakest linkage with key business measures and this program appeared to be with productivity, revenue generation, profits, cost control, and customer response time. These were some of INB's most important business measures. This assessment was to be expected, unless the program had had mechanisms to provide a connection to these key business variables.

Specific Impact from Individual Projects

Although the team projects were expected to add significant value to INB, it was anticipated that individual participants would undertake specific improvements in their work settings. Participants were asked to identify these improvements, where possible.

Usually when this type of improvement data is desired from a leadership development program, individual business action plans are developed to guide the application of the new skills and report the results. This process of capturing values from individual plans is much more difficult when the action plans have not been developed, as was the case with the leadership development program. Because the team projects were developed for the program, the program designers were not interested in requiring action plans for individual application. Consequently, there was no formal planning for the use of individual skills and no mechanism in place for capturing specific improvements.

In the follow-up questionnaire, participants were asked to explore business results with a series of impact questions, which provided an opportunity to offer details about specific impact. As anticipated, only a small number of participants were able to place values on the questionnaire. Four participants provided values. Two are reported in Table 18-4, which identifies the specific impact derived from the program.

In an effort to capture additional input about business impact, the same series of questions was asked of the participants during the one-on-one interviews whenever there was an opportunity to explore business results. This questioning yielded eleven more instances in which value may be linked to the program. These projects, without monetary values, are listed in Table 18-5.

Collectively, these values do not appear very reliable at this stage. However, this attempt to find specific individual project results related to the program is essential to the evaluation. At the outset, it was concluded that this would be a difficult exercise and that it would be unlikely to generate a tremendous amount of specific and reliable data. Although several individual projects were identified, the values were not used in the ROI calculation.

Turnover Prevention/Reduction

Perhaps an unexpected benefit linked to the leadership development program was staff turnover prevention. The program caused several of the participants to examine their careers and gain a renewed respect for INB. Suddenly they realized that the company valued them as executives, was interested in their careers, and more importantly, was interested in developing critical skills for additional responsibilities. In essence, this program strengthened the bond between the employee and the company, increasing loyalty and commitment. For example, four individuals indicated that this program prevented or probably prevented them from leaving the company within the next couple of years.

Project Results

The team projects were an integral part of the program from the design and delivery perspective and turned out to be the most significant and meaningful part of the process from the participant viewpoint. Without exception, the reaction to the projects was extremely favorable. Participants saw them as extremely frustrating and stressful but very rewarding. Eighty percent of the participants considered the project successful or very successful.

There was, however, some debate and concern about the purpose of the projects. All stakeholders felt that the projects served as excellent learning activities and that even if the recommendations were never implemented, they learned much about themselves, their team, the bank, and the particular topic as a result of the project development and presentation. However, almost all participants indicated that the projects represented real issues that need to be resolved and were concerned that they be implemented.

An important part of the leadership development program design was to use the processes and principles of action reflection learning as participants developed their projects and identified recommendations. Participants gave mixed responses about using ARL as an important and successful part of project success. Some felt ARL was not important to project success.

PROGRAM COSTS

A fully loaded cost profile was used in this study. Table 18-6 shows the listing of cost elements considered in this analysis.

All costs for the program were absorbed by the training department with the exception of some project-related costs incurred by the team members. The fees charged by the consultants and hotels are actual. The rest of the costs are aggregated estimates

(text continued on page 468)

Table 18-4

Impact of Individual Projects from Questionnaires

	Business Impact Examples from Questionnaires			
Description of Project	Monetary Impact	Basis/Time Frame	Contribution Factor	Confidence of Values	Comments
1. This project involves the delivery strategy for the customer-centric enterprise. Combining both business and technology strategies, the project involves a combination of: ☐ Identification, profiling, and delivery of the customer to the most appropriate and cost-effective resource.	$3,625,000 annually	The utilization of call-by-call intelligent network routing will provide load balancing and optimization across the entire organization. The industry estimates 10% to 15% efficiency in the areas of staffing resources and telecommunications expenses. A conservative estimate of 5% for INB would provide the following annual benefit based on current assumptions:	25%	75%	This is an extensive project, which was initiated directly from the program. However, due to other factors and influences that may have brought this project forward in the future, only 25% of the improvement is credited to the

- Enhancement of the customer-employee interaction through effective real time delivery of meaningful customer intelligence to the specialists.

- Collection measurement and reporting on the customer experience and behaviors.

- Agent efficiency based on 2,000 agents @ $30K annual salary with a 5% gain would provide a benefit of $3,000,000 annually.

- Telecommunication costs based on 100,000,000 minutes annually at 7.5 cents per minute with a 5% gain would provide a benefit of $375,000 annually.

- The use of shared equipment at the network level and the repo-sitioning of equipment to provide efficiencies is estimated at a 5% gain on a $5,000,000 annual capital budget resulting in a benefit of $250,000 annually.

program. A more detailed document, including a proposal that was presented to the executive group, is available.

Table 18-4
(continued)

	Business Impact Examples from Questionnaires				
Description of Project	Monetary Impact	Basis/Time Frame	Contribution Factor	Confidence of Values	Comments
2. This project involves designed strategic development and implementation planning to turn INB into a more customer-centric organization.	$20,000,000	When the customer-centric organization is successfully implemented, a 10% impact on customer loyalty, at a minimum, should be realized. A 1-point improvement on any of the loyalty measures is estimated to deliver 30¢ per month, per customer. This produces a $20,000,000 improvement.	The program moved this project ahead by one year. Thus one year of results can be attributed to this program.	N/A	This is only one element of the customer-centric implementation but affects all of the bank. This is being driven by an individual who participated in the program, and the estimates are based only on one element of the project within the scope of that individual.

Table 18-5
Individual Projects from Interviews

Type of Contribution	Brief Description of Improvement
1. Department Initiative	One participant used the communication skills and action-reflection learning skills in an off-site meeting to plan improvements for the department. In this meeting, 14 initiatives were generated from the group using skills taken directly from the leadership development program. This participant estimated that typically in this type of meeting, only 5 initiatives would have surfaced. However, using a different approach with new skills, 14 initiatives surfaced. Thus, 9 initiatives can be credited with the leadership development program.
2. New Product	Two participants are teaming to develop a project for small business. This is a web-based product and the value is generated because the bank will actually provide the service instead of another contractor. Without the leadership development program connection and collaboration, an external resource would have been used instead of the bank.
3. New Customers	One participant has obtained a new customer in the USA as a result of the networking from the leadership development program. The new customer is providing a direct benefit to the bank.
4. Partnership	One participant is building a partnership to share resources, referrals and technology as well as assets with another important and often competing part of the organization.
5. Tool Application	One participant has used the strategic planning process on a particular project for which he/she is responsible. This improved process is adding direct benefits.

Table 18-6
Leadership Development Program Costs

Program Costs	
Design/Development	
External Consultants	$525,330
Training Department	28,785
Management Committee	26,542
Delivery	
Conference Facilities	$142,554
(Hotel)	
Consultants/External	$812,110
Training Department Salaries & Benefits	$15,283
(For Direct Work with the Program)	
Training Department Travel Expenses	$37,500
Management Committee (Time)	$75,470
Project Costs ($25,000 × 4)	$100,000
Participant Salaries & Benefits (Class Sessions)	$84,564
(Average Daily Salary × Benefits Factor × Number	
of Program Days)	
Participant Salaries and Benefits (Project Work)	
Travel & Lodging for Participants	$117,353
Cost of Materials	$100,938
(Handouts, Purchased Materials)	$6,872
Research and Evaluation	
Research	$110,750
Evaluation	$125,875
Total Costs	$2,309,926

(text continued from page 463)

(that is, salary and benefits were calculated by number of participants × average salary × benefit factor × number of hours).

Although there is often some debate as to whether participant salaries and benefits should be included in the cost of the program, in reality the participants were not replaced while they attended this program; therefore, the company did not experience a replacement cost. However, employees are compensated for being on the job every day, and they are expected to make a contribution roughly equal to their compensation. If they are removed from the job for a week, or four weeks in the case of the leadership development program, then the company has lost their contribution for that period of time. To be fully loaded with costs and also be conservative, this value was estimated and included in the overall cost profile.

The issue of prorating costs was an important consideration. In this case, it was reasonably certain that a second session would be conducted. The design and development expenses of $580,657 could therefore be prorated over two sessions. Consequently, in the actual ROI calculation, half of this number was used to arrive at the total value. This left a total program cost of $2,019,598 to include in the analysis. On a participant basis, this was $91,800, or $22,950 for each week of formal sessions. Although this was expensive, it was still close to a rough benchmark of weekly costs of several senior executive leadership programs.

ROI ANALYSIS

When developing the ROI, two important issues had to be addressed: (1) isolating the effects of the program and (2) converting data to monetary values. The role of the participants was extremely critical because the participants provided data on actual improvements, isolated the effects of the program on the improvements, and in some cases converted data to actual monetary values. Although there are many other approaches to isolate the effects of the program and a variety of techniques to convert data to monetary values, several issues prevented the use of a majority of other approaches and techniques:

☐ The timing of the decision to measure the ROI eliminated some of the possibilities. The decision to measure the impact was made after the program had begun and it was too late to influence the design and to use more objective approaches to isolating the effects of the program.

☐ The nature of leadership development eliminated many other techniques. The application and ultimate impact is an individual process and the improvements must come from the participants themselves—who may all influence different performance improvement measures. This situation makes it difficult to link the program to any finite set of performance measures.

☐ The vast number of business units represented and the nature of their issues, challenges, and performance measures made the process difficult to link to any small number of applications.

Challenges in Developing ROI for the Leadership Development Program

Several challenges were encountered as the return on investment was developed for the program:

☐ There was a lack of data tied to specific improvements from each individual. Part of this was caused by lack of design initiatives around the requirement and the focus on achieving results.

☐ There was concern about the nature and scope of the projects and the implementability of their recommendations. A different type of project with specific guidelines for capturing value would have made the ROI values of projects much easier to capture.

☐ The timing issue hampered the ROI analysis. The need to have the evaluation study completed soon after the last session of the program so a decision could be made to proceed or adjust the program led to an earlier-than-desired analysis of the actual impact.

☐ The nature of this program, in terms of its soft skills and the focus on learning without the implications of the impact of what was being learned, made the program more difficult to evaluate at this level.

Collectively, these problems represented critical challenges that had to be overcome to a certain extent to develop values. The result was a less-than-optimum value.

ROI Calculations

The ROI calculations had several components, as illustrated in Figure 18-1. For the first component, project value, two approaches

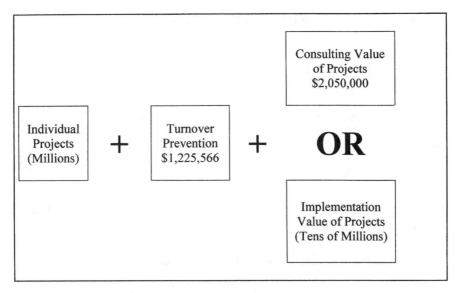

Figure 18-1. Business impact categories.

were considered. The first was to develop the value of a project based on the equivalent value as if a consulting firm had developed the project. This resulted in a value of $2,050,000 and was the most credible way of placing a value on the projects at such an early time frame. The second approach was to place a value on a project at the actual value of an implementation. This value is difficult to develop, but it is estimated to be in the hundreds of millions of dollars. The first approach was used to calculate a project value.

The second component involved the value of the individual projects undertaken by the participants, collected anonymously using questionnaires and confidentially in interviews. It was too early to develop a precise value at the time of evaluation. Thus individual project values, estimated to be in the millions, were not used in the ROI analysis. Finally, the last component was the prevention of turnover. The program conclusively prevented several turnover statistics. Although the exact number will never be known, it was conservative to forecast that four could be attributed to this program, yielding a value of $1,225,566.

The conservative ROI calculation is as follows:

$$ROI = \frac{Net\ Benefits}{Program\ Costs}$$

$$= \frac{(\$2,050,000 + \$1,225,566) - \$2,019,598}{\$2,019,598}$$

$$= 62\%$$

If the value of the other blocks in Figure 18-1 had been included, the value would have been much larger.

Up-Front Emphasis: A Key to ROI Success

The application of the ROI Process model is much more effective when programs are designed to have a specific business impact on the organization. Unfortunately for INB's leadership development program, the decision to calculate an ROI was made after the program was implemented. The original objectives of the programs did not reflect a bottom-line contribution. Consequently, the process of calculating the ROI became a much more difficult issue.

INTANGIBLE BENEFITS

Perhaps the most important results of the leadership development program were the intangible benefits, both short and long term. By definition, these benefits were not converted to monetary value for use in the ROI calculation. They were not measured precisely and are subjective but still important. Most leadership development programs have been evaluated through perceived or actual intangible benefits. The main intangible benefits reported were as follows:

☐ Without exception, each participant considered networking a positive and important outcome. The individuals developed close relationships and, more importantly, they came to understand each other's perspectives, viewpoints, issues, concerns, and problems.

☐ Participants now take a more enterprise view of their jobs, their decisions, and the challenges facing INB. They have a much greater appreciation for the other functions and their relationship to the whole.

☐ Participants are reducing, and sometimes removing, silos that have developed within INB. Participants now see each other as contributors who have the bank's interest at the forefront.

☐ Participants reported that their decision-making capability was greatly enhanced through this program. They are using many of the communication techniques to build the proper rapport with the staff so that they will have free-flowing ideas and input into the decision-making process.

☐ A surprising intangible benefit was increased loyalty to INB as a result of participation in the leadership program. Participation in this program left many participants with the desire and determination to remain with INB and continue to make a contribution.

☐ Through the project teams and other team-related exercises, including those involving the larger group of twenty-two, the participants gained a much greater appreciation for the advantages of teamwork and team building. Many of them are using teams to a greater extent in their own work, and they are encouraging teams to be used in other aspects of the bank.

☐ Some rated this program as a significant personal development experience.

☐ One of the important objectives of this program was the development of an executive talent pool of capable leaders who would be available for future key positions. Some participants think the program did not help build the talent pool, while others feel they are more capable to take on increased responsibility. Two things are certain: Participants understand the enterprise view and are better prepared for a potential promotion, and they know the areas that need improvement to continue to sharpen their skills and enhance their ability for future promotions.

RESULTS

The major objectives of the program were met although not completely successful. Participants rated the most success with the objectives that related to participants taking an enterprise view and acting on synergies within the INB business areas. The least success was achieved with the objective characterized as "participants are prepared to assume senior leadership roles that become vacant or are created based on market needs."

Two major goals were established for the program, and the program was less than successful in meeting these goals. There was more success with the goal to increase the capability of leaders to be high-performing, cross-functional executives. Less success was realized with helping INB become more competitive by tackling and resolving major organizational projects.

There was general agreement about the achievement level for the critical success factors. Less success was attained on the first factor ("a significant amount of time must be invested by the management committee, clients, and participants") because participants did not perceive that, on the whole, the executive and management committee invested significant time in the program. The most success was realized with the second factor, "real projects must be developed that are enterprise-wide and strategic." The success achieved in the third factor, "influential participants must be selected based on performance and future potential," however, was mixed. The selection of the participants was an issue of much concern and debate. It was generally assumed that the participants were high potential executives with the ability to move into key senior management positions. In reality, most participants think this did not occur. The selection criteria was not followed consistently across both major operational units or within those units.

There was general agreement about the success of major outcomes both from the organizational perspective and the individual perspective. There were mixed results in terms of the outcomes of enhancing the quality of executive talent and on the outcome of research and recommendations for solutions to key strategic issues. There was general agreement that success was realized with management committee interaction with high potential leaders. Generally, the individuals felt that the outcomes related directly to them faired much better. There was consistent agreement that they were exposed to a broader range of INB businesses and to establishing networks across business lines. There was less agreement relative to building skills in systems and strategic thinking, communication, and building high-performance teams. There were varied results identified for reaching accelerated personal and leadership development.

Frequently, a program is only as successful as the support provided to ensure that it functions efficiently, effectively, and achieves its desired goals. The overall support was rated quite good, with some specific issues raising concerns. Learning coaches were rated effective, as was executive support. In the interviews, most indicated that executive support improved during the program and was at its peak toward the end during the presentations. There was a perception of a "wait and see" attitude. The mentor role was misunderstood and not appreciated and most felt it was not very effective. The clients generally received good remarks, although the results were mixed for certain individuals. The clients were often referred to as sponsors and met with the individual teams to help develop the projects. The faculty received good ratings; the subject-matter experts, however, did not receive favorable ratings. Although some were outstanding, others were considered extremely ineffective. The support provided by the program director was rated as somewhat effective.

There was expectation that the program would be one of the most significant personal development experiences encountered by the participants. However, most participants disagreed, and only 27 percent rated the experience as very effective. In the interviews, almost every participant indicated that he or she had experienced a more effective leadership and personal development program.

Overall, the success versus the plans was mixed, with several areas requiring adjustments in the future.

Questions for Discussion

1. Discuss why intangible benefits were perhaps the most important results of the leadership program.
2. How might the background of this organization have affected the program?

3. If you had been in charge of this program, would you have done anything differently?
4. What is the rule of the supplier in this type of evaluation?
5. Critique the data collection plan.
6. Critique the method to isolate the program.
7. Critique the approach to costing the program.
8. How many years should the benefits be monitored? Explain.
9. Is the ROI realistic? Explain.
10. What rule could ROI forecasting play in this evaluation?
11. Choose another case presented in this book—similar in some way to this one—and compare and contrast it with this case. Specifically, decide why the different situations called for different approaches.

CHAPTER 19

Technology-Based Learning

United Petroleum International

By Ron D. Stone and J. Patrick Whalen

This case addresses measuring the effectiveness and return on investment of a technology-assisted learning solution in an international sales environment. This can be especially challenging when management wants the program to pay for itself in the first year. This case demonstrates that, with a proper needs assessment and support from the organization, a well-designed training program can influence business measures significantly. The program contribution to sales and other business measures are determined by using one or more methods to isolate the effects of the program. Isolating the effects of each influencing factor can provide convincing evidence of the value of a program. The $500,000 projected price tag of the training was a key factor in management's decision to support an impact study to determine the return on investment.

BACKGROUND

United Petroleum International (UPI) is an international organization headquartered in the southwestern United States. UPI operates several refineries and engages in the sales and service of petroleum products worldwide. UPI has approximately 17,500 employees. International sales of petroleum products have plummeted during the last three quarters, and the outlook shows this trend will continue.

Increased competition abroad and a diminishing quality of sales relationships with customers/prospects were determined to be the major reasons for the lack of performance. The results from quarterly customer satisfaction surveys revealed specific areas of low performance. The executive vice president (EVP) of international sales asked for an assessment of the performance improvement needs of the UPI International Sales Organization (ISO). International Sales has 117 sales engineers and 8 sales managers. They are supported by 50 administrative employees who maintain the customer/prospect database, develop sales quotes for the sales engineers, maintain pricing and inventory lists, and provide HR services.

A senior representative from corporate HR and two of UPI's internal consultants teamed with an external consultant from Performance Resources Organization (PRO), to implement PRO's Performance Assessment and Analysis Process™ to identify problems, opportunities, and solutions in ISO. The report provided to the EVP identified overall findings, performance gaps, and recommended solutions. At the end of the presentation, the EVP agreed to fund an intense improvement effort, including sales training and restructuring of the ISO incentive pay plan, which was no longer competitive in the changing markets. Funding was also made available for using PRO and its ROI Process™ to design and implement a comprehensive evaluation system to determine business impact and return on investment. The EVP was particularly interested in the contribution of the training. A business objective was established to improve three business measures. Measures to be tracked were identified as sales, monthly closing ratios, and customer satisfaction. Because measurement is an inherent component of PRO's process, the methods and timing were designed and put in place. Baseline data were collected from UPI's performance records.

DESIGNING AND IMPLEMENTING THE SOLUTIONS

The HR department worked with the design team to design and implement a more appropriate and competitive incentive plan. This new incentive plan was designed after a review of several models and an analysis of application to UPI's markets. The plan was approved and scheduled for implementation in June.

The second solution, addressing the skill and knowledge needs within the sales force, was more difficult to design and implement. Client workload, time constraints, and the scattered locations of the sales engineers were impediments to implementing traditional instructor-led training. Electronic learning methods were considered a viable alternative. A plus for this delivery method at ISO was that all sales engineers had electronic online and CD capabilities at their laptop computers. Another plus was that the flexibility of the electronic delivery method allowed it to be available at any time of the day. This flexibility is attractive to participants who are compensated principally through incentive pay and who desire to spend their available time making customer contacts. The decision was made that the 117 sales engineers and 8 sales managers would receive an electronically delivered interactive sales training process to improve their skills and effectively achieve the business objectives. During the performance analysis, it was discovered that the corporate HR group had identified sales competencies from a previous project and had already begun developing a curriculum. Much of this in-work product served as an important input for the new initiative and greatly assisted the on-time completion of the project.

The design called for a more focused training effort, paying specific attention to the sales relationships engaged in by sales engineers and allowing for significant practice of the required skills. The training had to present numerous job scenarios and challenges currently being encountered in the marketplace. The EVP of International Sales assigned the training project to the manager of sales training, who subsequently established a project team to provide the coordination, design, and development of this project.

Several modules were developed with the support of corporate professionals, including technical writers, learning technology specialists, graphic designers, information technology specialists, and consultants. The team consisted of five full-time employees and four external training consultants. Given a very short time frame for completion (management allowed a few months to design and implement the program), work began immediately to develop focused training based on the desired business impact (the business objectives), job performance competencies, and field sales encounters. Several members of the design team were concerned that traditional face-to-face learning methods could not be replaced by an interactive electronic program. The learning technology specialists addressed these concerns, and field testing established the electronic technology design as a success in achieving learning goals. The electronic training process that was developed for the sales engineers became known affectionately as the TLC Program, the Technology Learning Competency Program. After design completion, it was implemented in June and July, shortly after the new incentive plan was implemented.

THE TECHNOLOGY LEARNING COMPETENCY PROGRAM (TLC)

The TLC Program was an interactive, self-paced learning process designed to assess current skill level and needs of the sales engineer. Each module was designed to build on a specific set of UPI sales skills (that is, client partnerships, product pricing and contracting, selling more profitable products, uncovering objections, handling objections, defining product features as unique benefits for the customer, expanding existing contracts, handling dissatisfied customers, building community awareness of UPI, and UPI product awareness/knowledge).

The TLC Program was designed to allow the participant to respond to various sales-relationship scenarios and to determine the appropriate decision to move closer to a sale. Each decision made by the engineer activated another scenario, which allowed additional choices or decisions to be made. The program continued on a predetermined path initiated by the engineer until a string of choices confirmed the responses as appropriate or until the decision was redirected. Video of a subject matter expert provided analysis of decision choices and helpful suggestions. This took maximum advantage of learning opportunities presented when a participant worked through the program. The engineer experienced real-world issues and situations, had the help of an expert, and was able to learn from mistakes in a nonthreatening manner.

A pre-test at the beginning of each module was used to determine the skill areas that needed improvement and to load the appropriate learning modules. All the 117 sales engineers were pre-tested to establish a baseline. The program then linked participants to recommended modules that addressed their skill gaps. Each engineer was allowed a two-month window to complete the required electronic training, either during or after hours as his or her schedule allowed. So that they could be more effective coaches, the 8 managers completed all modules plus a coaching module.

The TLC Program contained a programmed mechanism that captured the results from the various decision paths chosen by the participant. After each learning module, an individual report was generated, which highlighted the learning achievement and the decisions made by the engineer. This report was provided to each participant and his or her manager for discussion in the follow-up coaching session. This provided additional learning opportunities and a means for recognition and feedback. Sales engineers were asked to schedule the follow-up planning and coaching meeting with their managers to occur within two weeks of their TLC Program implementation.

MEASUREMENT METHODS AND DATA ANALYSIS

Measures to evaluate the effectiveness of a program can be designed and tracked through five distinct levels, as shown in Table 19-1.

In addition to the five levels of data illustrated in this table, intangible benefits are reported for important outcomes that cannot be converted to monetary values.

The executive vice president of international sales requested that the return on investment (Level 5) be calculated for this

Table 19-1
Five Levels of Data

Level and Type of Measure	Measurement Focus
Level 1. Reaction/Planned Action	Measures participant satisfaction and captures planned actions
Level 2. Learning	Measures changes in knowledge, skills, and attitudes
Level 3. Job Application	Measures changes in on-the-job behavior
Level 4. Business Results	Measures changes in business impact variables
Level 5. Return on Investment	Compares program benefits with the costs

program because of the high cost and potential business impact of the TLC Program. Therefore, it became necessary to gather and analyze data at the five levels plus any intangible benefits.

ROI MODEL AND PROCESS

Executive management expressed concern that the process used to evaluate TLC be a credible process. Figure 19-1 illustrates the process PRO used to address this concern. This process has been applied in virtually every industry and in numerous international settings to evaluate training programs, HR programs, technology initiatives, and performance improvement programs. The process flows sequentially from step to step until the ROI is developed. The impact study captures both Level 3 (application) and Level 4 (business impact) data. The ROI (Level 5) is developed from Level 4 data. Improvements that cannot be converted to monetary values are reported as intangible benefits. A conservative approach is used by PRO to ensure that only benefits that can be legitimately attributed to the program are captured.

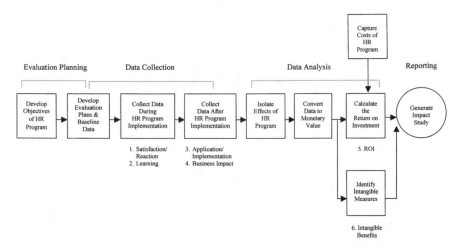

Figure 19-1. ROI model.

THE DATA COLLECTION PLAN
AND ROI ANALYSIS PLAN

After the business measures were determined and the framework for the TLC Training Program was known, the data collection plan focusing on Level 3 (job application) and Level 4 (business results) measures was developed. The Level 3 measures were behavior changes and frequency of application linked to the TLC Program objectives. After exploring performance data availability in the ISO unit, the quality of the specific data, and the perceived linkage to the TLC Program, the Level 4 measures were targeted and included in the data collection plan: The data collection plan is presented in Exhibit 19-1.

The Level 4 data items were then transferred to the ROI analysis plan so that the planning process could be completed. The methods for isolation, data conversion, cost categories, and other items were determined and documented on the ROI analysis plan. The ROI analysis plan is presented in Exhibit 19-2.

(text continued on page 486)

Exhibit 19-1

DATA COLLECTION PLAN □ UNITED PETROLEUM INTERNATIONAL

Program: Technology Learning Competency Program (TLC)   **Responsibility:** Ron Stone   **Date:** 1999

Level	Objective(s)	Measures/Data	Data Collection Method	Data Sources	Timing	Responsibilities
Level I *Reaction and Satisfaction*	Employee positive reaction to: • appropriateness of the technology delivery program • usefulness of the TLC • TLC application to the job	• Participants' perception and attitude	• online questionnaire	• participant	• end of each segment (3-5 modules) • end of program	• program coordinator
Level II *Learning*	• Module learning assignments based on knowledge/skill gaps: • client partnerships • product pricing & contracting • identification & handling objections	A. skill gaps identified B. learning occurs as gaps closed through each module implemented	A. online pre-test questionnaire on all modules B. online post-test by module	• participant	A. prior to training to establish baseline A. prior to each module as required B. at end of each module	• program coordinator
Level III *Application & Implementation*	1. review post-course report and participate in follow-up planning meeting with manager 2. application of skills to achieve business goals	1. goals set and achieved 2. skills applied in sales planning and sales situations	1. and 2. follow-up questionnaire	1. and 2. Participants 1. and 2. Managers	1. Coaching and planning session within two weeks of TLC 1. and 2. Follow-up questionnaire four months after TLC	• program coordinator initiates follow-up • manager and participant initiate planning and coaching
Level IV *Business Impact*	1. improved closing ratio 2. increased revenue 3. customer satisfaction	1. increase in monthly closes 2. increase in profit margin 3. customer satisfaction index	1. performance monitoring 2. performance monitoring 3. customer survey (existing)	1. sales record – marketing 2. sales record – marketing 3. customer quarterly survey	1. monthly 2. monthly 3. quarterly	• program coordinator
Level V *ROI*	Because of the strict requirement for development costs (see comments) an ROI at 20% will be acceptable.		**Comments:** Because training will be completed for all current engineers within first year of roll-out, management desires to achieve a return on investment during the first year. Therefore, development costs will not be prorated over the life of the program as is customary.			

Exhibit 19-2

ROI ANALYSIS PLAN ☐ UNITED PETROLEUM INTERNATIONAL

Program: *Technology Learning Competency Program (TLC)* **Responsibility:** *Ron Stone* **Date:** *1999*

Data Items (Usually Level 4)	Methods for Isolating the Effects of the TLC Program	Methods of Converting Data to Monetary Values	Cost Categories	Intangible Benefits	Communication Targets for Final Report	Other Influences/ Issues During Application	Comments
Closes per month	• participant estimates • manager estimates	*n/a; captured in monthly revenue below*	• development costs • materials and software • equipment • time of subject matter experts • salaries and benefits during training (while on company time) • analysis and evaluation costs	• recruiting tool • increase in employee satisfaction • improved partnership and communication between manager and sales engineer	• sales engineers • leadership of sales organization • UPI executive management	• customers may not be able to identify if or how "engineer skills" impact their satisfaction • influence of other factors on the three measures • quality of coaching/ expectations session • short time frame inhibited ability to field test the TLC modules	• *must capture % of time that training occurs on company time*
Monthly revenue	• participant estimates • manager estimates	*profit margin of revenue*					
Customer satisfaction index	• customer estimates	*executive management estimate*					

(text continued from page 483)

LEVELS 1 AND 2 DATA

Level 1 data were captured through an online feedback question-naire that assessed course content, usefulness of the TLC Program, and job applicability. Participants rated questions on a Likert-type scale from 1 to 7. Participant average for the overall course content was 6.6, and overall usefulness of the system was 6.5. Applicability of the course to the job was rated 6.8. Level 1 data are consolidated in the first three columns of Table 19-2.

Level 2 data were assessed using pre- and post-testing. The pre- and post-testing for TLC was designed based on job performance expectations. Subject matter experts (SMEs) determined the testing components, which were then validated by sales managers. The SMEs, working with the program designers, validated program content based on competency requirements and skill gaps of the sales organization. They also provided input to design pre- and post-tests. Pre-tests were administered electronically online at the beginning of each learning module to determine individual knowledge and skill gaps. The results showed that participants averaged a 50 percent knowledge level on the pre-test and averaged a 91 percent knowledge level on the post-test. These Level 2 data are consolidated in the last two columns of Table 19-2.

LEVELS 3 AND 4 DATA

Level 3 (application of skills) included three components to evaluate results (1) follow-up planning and coaching sessions between sales engineers and sales managers, (2) self-assessment of skill application using a follow-up questionnaire, and (3) managers' assessment of skill application using a follow-up questionnaire.

Engineers completed follow-up planning and discussion meetings with their respective managers within two weeks of completing the TLC Program. A plan including goals and expectations was created as a result of each discussion. To allow appropriate time for evaluation and application of skills, it was imperative for managers to have these planning and coaching sessions as close to the end of the training as possible. The sessions occurred

Table 19-2
Reaction and Learning Results—1 to 7 Scale

Reaction: Overall Course	Reaction: Overall Usefulness of TLC	Reaction: Job Applicability	Learning: Pre-test Overall Score	Learning: Post-test Overall Score
6.6	6.5	6.8	50%	91%

during July and August and averaged two hours in length. Because of the dispersed locations of the engineers and managers, some of these meetings were conducted face-to-face and some by telephone or video conferencing.

The follow-up questionnaire was developed during the program design phase and field-tested with a random sample of sales engineers and sales managers. By advice of the sales managers, the questionnaire was administered four months after the completion of the TLC Program. Four months was deemed an appropriate time frame to determine the successful application of skills. A series of questions on the follow-up questionnaire also focused on engineers' progress with the improvement goals established in the follow-up discussions between managers and sales engineers. In addition, sales managers each received a follow-up questionnaire focusing on the performance of sales engineers and isolating the effects of the TLC Program. These performance data were consolidated and documented in the final evaluation report. Figure 19-2 presents a summary of the follow-up questions from the sales engineers' questionnaire.

Business impact data (Level 4) were monitored by reviewing the quarterly customer satisfaction index scores, the monthly sales closing averages, and the profit margin of monthly sales revenue. These data were readily available within the organization, and all but customer satisfaction were used in the determination of business impact and return on investment of the TLC Program. Customer satisfaction data were reviewed for progress, but a standard monetary value did not exist for improvements; thus there was no conversion to a monetary value.

1. Did you have a follow-up coaching session with your sales manager?
2. Did you complete a follow-up plan and set related goals?
3. How do you rate the quality of the planning and discussion session with your manager?
4. Based on the discussion and planning session you had with your manager, what specific improvement goals have you completed? What improvement goals still need to be completed?
5. How have you and your job changed as a result of participating in TLC?
6. How are you specifically applying what you learned as a result of participating in TLC?
7. What is the impact of these changes for the customer and the ISO organization?
8. Rank (estimate the percentage) the effect each of the following had on any improvement in your sales performance. Allocate from 0 to 100% to the appropriate factors (the total percentage of all items selected must equal 100%):

   TLC Training Program ___%   Executive Management ___%
                                      Influence

   Market Influences   ___%   New Monetary Sessions ___%

   Manager Coaching   ___%   Other _____%
   Incentives   (specify)

9. What barriers (if any) were a deterrent as you applied what you learned?
10. List any skills you did not have an opportunity to apply during the evaluation time frame?
11. Estimate the total hours you were involved in accessing/completing TLC training during regular company work hours: _____ hours

Figure 19-2. Summary of follow-up questions.

ISOLATING THE EFFECTS

To assess the Levels 4 and 5 data accurately, it was imperative that the various influences on any improvement in sales performance be isolated. To isolate the effects of how each factor influenced sales (that is, TLC training, the new incentive plan, market changes, management influence, etc.), each had to be assessed by a credible source. The influence of each factor was determined by using participant and manager estimates regarding each factor. The data were gathered from the participants in the Levels 3/4 follow-up questionnaire and from the managers in a separate follow-up questionnaire. Table 19-3 reports the consolidated data.

DESIGN AND IMPLEMENTATION COSTS

The development costs of $354,500 for this project included the salaries for development time of one project manager, five full-time employees, and four contract consultants. The costs associated with time spent in meetings and interviews with executive management, senior sales staff, and subject matter experts were also included. This included the time of the interviewer as well as the people being interviewed. The cost of travel, meals, and lodging during development was also included.

Table 19-3
Consolidated Estimates—Isolating the Effects

Influencing Factor	*Sales Engineers* Average from 104 Respondents	*Sales Managers* Average from 8 Respondents	Combined Average
New Incentive Plan	35%	37%	36%
TLC Training Program	38%	36%	37%
Executive Management Influence	8%	6%	7%
Coaching by Sales Manager	16%	18%	17%
Other (market changes, new products, product improvements, etc.)	3%	3%	3%

The material costs of $68,500 included a comprehensive work-book for participants, distribution of tutorial CDs, and some additional dial-up networking software.

The equipment cost of $91,000 included upgrades (systems, processors, and video/graphics capability) to the specified hardware setup. This cost category also included the purchase of several new laptops for the sales engineers, digital editing equipment for editing the video and graphics in each module, and two platform servers capable of handling the multioperational usage.

Eight subject matter experts were assigned to the project. These eight lead sales engineers were paid their sales average ($150 per day) for the eighteen days each spent on the module designs, video shoots, and other project duties.

The analysis and evaluation costs of $71,000 included all costs associated with the initial performance analysis and evaluation process (for example, employee time during interviews and question-naires). This cost category also included the use of an outside consulting firm (Performance Resources Organization) to plan and implement the performance analysis and evaluation methodology for this project.

All the 117 sales engineers reported completing all modules during their personal time. Because they were compensated mostly by commissions, they usually spent their work hours conducting sales planning and call activities. Table 19-4 summarizes the fully loaded costs for the TLC Program.

Table 19-4
Fully Loaded Costs

Development Costs	$354,500
Materials/Software	$68,500
Equipment	$91,000
SME Time (commission paid to expert sales engineers for lost opportunity) 8 people @ $150/day × 18 days	$21,600
Analysis and Evaluation Costs	$71,000
TOTAL	**$606,600**

Because no sales were occurring for SMEs during the eighteen project days, the commission payments may represent a cost to the sales bottom line. The management team felt the lead sales engineers would be able to maintain their average sales throughout the year even with their involvement in this project. Therefore, they did not feel that lost sales should be included as an opportunity cost. Salaries and benefits and opportunity costs for the "actual training time" are not included in the calculations because none of the 104 sales engineers reported implementing the TLC training during normal company work hours.

LEVELS 3 AND 4 RESULTS

The results of the initiative were encouraging. Prior year sales records revealed that sales engineers' overall performance showed an average of 14 closes per month at $980 profit margin per close. Six months after the implementation of TLC, the engineers averaged 16.65 closes per month at $1,350 profit margin per close. From the previous year, this was an average increase of 2.65 closes per month and an additional $370 profit margin on revenue.

The design team decided to use PRO's conservative process when calculating the ROI based on revenue generated from new or increased closes. This decision helped to enhance the credibility of the data because participant and manager estimates were the only methods used to isolate the impact of training. Only the profit margin portion of the revenue increase attributable to the training (TLC) was used as a basis for the ROI calculation.

The Level 5 data were calculated by comparing the cost with the net benefits attributable to the TLC implementation. The benefit attributed to the use of TLC for improvement was considered to be 37 percent based on the combined participant and manager estimates from Table 19-3.

The benefits, except for improved customer satisfaction, were then converted to a monetary value, and a return on investment was calculated. Customer satisfaction improvements and other data that could not be converted to monetary values were captured as intangible benefits. Level 3 and Level 4 performance data and intangible benefits were documented in the final evaluation report. The ROI was calculated as follows:

$$\text{ROI}(\%) = \frac{\text{Benefits} - \text{Costs}}{\text{Costs}} \times 100 = \underline{\qquad} \%$$

ROI RESULTS

Monitoring the performance records revealed the total increase in sales attributable to all influencing factors was $5,022,810. There was an average of 2.65 additional closes per month (16.65 – 14.0). However, based on the participant and manager estimates, only 37 percent of this increase in sales was influenced by the TLC Program.

The conservative adjustment of benefits resulting from the TLC training was a factor of 0.98 additional closes per month (2.65 × 0.37). This resulted in an average of $1,323 profit margin per close ($1,350 × 0.98). Multiplied by 12 months and 117 engineers to annualize, this produced $1,857,492 in monetary benefits attributable to TLC.

- ☐ 2.65 closes × 0.37 = 0.98 factor for additional closes attributable to TLC Program
- ☐ 0.98 × $1,350 per close = $1,323
- ☐ $1,323 × 12 months = $15,876 × 117 sales engineers = $1,857,492

The total cost of the TLC Training Program was $606,600. After rounding the benefits from the program, the ROI for the TLC Program was calculated as follows:

$$\text{ROI}(\%) = \frac{\$1,867,000 - \$606,000}{\$606,600} \times 100 = 206\%$$

In addition to the impact of the TLC training, participants and managers reported the new incentive plan implemented in June had influenced an increase in sales by 36 percent, or $1,808,000.

INTANGIBLE BENEFITS

The results from quarterly customer satisfaction surveys were used to compare the previous year with the current year. Positive improvements and trends were identified. These data were not converted to a monetary value because management had no standard monetary value for an increase in customer satisfaction. It was also difficult to determine how much the skills/behavior from the training actually influenced the improvement in customer satisfaction. Data to isolate and substantiate this would need to come directly from customers because many factors could influence their satisfaction level. When using estimates, only customers are likely to know the extent of such influences. However, executive management felt the customer satisfaction scores were a good indicator of how the organization was responding to the market.

The customer satisfaction scores showed an average improvement of 23 percent since the previous year. Sales engineers and sales managers reported additional intangible benefits, such as increased job satisfaction, better understanding of expectations, reduced turnover, and increased recruiting effectiveness of future sales engineers.

LEARNING ISSUES FROM THE STUDY

This program demonstrated very favorable results. The results can be attributed to several things: a comprehensive front-end analysis process that accurately identified the appropriate gaps and solutions, the support of corporate HR, the support of executive management, and the sales organization providing the resources and clarification of expected outcomes prior to designing this initiative.

A major learning issue involved meeting management's requirement for a short lead time to design and implement the program. Executive management expected the program to be implemented within a few months because the competitive environment and need for improved skills were having a negative impact on sales. This created little time to conduct a pilot program. Also, there was not enough time to create all the modules needed for the full range of competency and skill needs of the sales organization. The most salient competencies were targeted and given development priority.

The need to more accurately isolate the effects of this initiative was another learning issue. Several factors influenced the results. Although participant estimates can be effective (participants know what influences their performance), additional methods, like a control group arrangement or trendline analysis, can often isolate the impact more convincingly.

REPORTING TO STAKEHOLDER GROUPS

The target population for this initiative included four groups: the sales engineers, the leaders of the sales organization, the subject matter experts, and the executive management team of UPI. All played a critical role in the success of the TLC Program. All were provided a final report showing the results from the impact study.

The primary group was the 117 sales engineers who actually participated in the TLC Program. They were the most instrumental of the groups in creating the success enjoyed by TLC. They dedicated the time to the system and took full advantage of the opportunity to improve performance based on what they learned from the technology-supported training. They also provided tremendous constructive feedback to enhance the system for future engineers.

The second group consisted of the leaders of the sales organization, who were responsible and accountable for the success of sales at UPI. Ten people—including one executive vice president, one director, and eight sales managers—were key factors in the success. They supported the up-front analysis and the validation of the job skills and gaps that were to be measured. By conducting planning and coaching sessions with sales engineers and by discussing expectations, the leaders of the sales organization were essential factors in the transfer and application of skills on the job.

The third group was the SMEs, who provided timely and accurate feedback about each module being developed, and the corporate professionals and consultants, who demonstrated diligence and expertise. On frequent occasions, they worked beyond normal work hours to keep the project on track.

The fourth group was the members of the executive management team of UPI, who funded the project and showed interest in the entire training process. The executive management team supported the project by allocating the necessary resources and setting the expectations for outcomes.

QUESTIONS FOR DISCUSSION

1. Identify the influencing factors that contributed to the success of the TLC Program.
2. How would you convince management that a control group arrangement would be beneficial to the study?
3. What recommendations would you make to management to convert customer satisfaction improvements to a monetary value?
4. How credible are the estimates in this evaluation?
5. How credible is this study?

Self-Test: How Results-Oriented Are Your Human Resources Programs?

Select the response that best describes the situation in your organization and circle the letter preceding the response.

1. Performance measurements have been developed and are used to determine the effectiveness of:
   A. All human resources (HR) functions
   B. Approximately half of the HR functions
   C. At least one HR function

2. Major organizational decisions:
   A. Are usually made with input from the HR function
   B. Are usually made without input from the HR function
   C. Are always made with input from the HR function

3. The return on investment in HR is measured primarily by:
   A. Intuition and perception by senior executives
   B. Observations by management and reactions from participants and users
   C. Improvements in productivity, cost savings, quality, etc.

4. The concern for the method of evaluation in the design and implementation of HR programs occurs:

A. Before a program is developed

B. After a program is implemented

C. After a program is developed but before it's implemented

5. New HR programming, without some formal method of measurement and evaluation, is:

    A. Never implemented

    B. Regularly implemented

    C. Occasionally implemented

6. The costs of specific HR programs are:

    A. Estimated when the programs are implemented

    B. Never calculated

    C. Continuously implemented

7. The costs of absenteeism, turnover, and sick leave of the organization:

    A. Are routinely calculated and monitored

    B. Have been occasionally calculated to identify problem areas

    C. Have not been determined

8. Benefit/cost comparisons of HR programs are:

    A. Never developed

    B. Occasionally developed

    C. Frequently developed

9. In an economic downturn, the HR function will:

    A. Be retained at the same staffing level, unless the downturn is lengthy

    B. Be the first to have its staff reduced

    C. Go untouched in staff reductions and possibly be beefed up

10. The cost of current or proposed employee benefits are:

    A. Regularly calculated and compared with national, industry, and local data

    B. Occasionally estimated when there is concern about operating expenses

    C. Not calculated, except for required quarterly and annual reports

11. The chief executive officer (CEO) interfaces with the senior HR officer:

A. Infrequently; it is a delegated responsibility

B. Occasionally, when there is a pressing need

C. Frequently, to know what's going on and to provide support

12. On the organizational chart, the top HR manager:
    A. Reports directly to the CEO
    B. Is more than two levels removed form the CEO
    C. Is two levels below the CEO

13. Line management involvement in implementing HR programs is:
    A. Limited to a few programs in its area of expertise
    B. Nil; only HR specialists are involved in implementing programs
    C. Significant; most of the programs are implemented through line management

14. The HR staff involvement in measurement and evaluation consists of:
    A. No specific responsibilities in measurement and evaluation with no formal training in evaluation methods
    B. Partial responsibilities for measurement and evaluation, with some formal training in evaluation methods
    C. Complete responsibilities for measurement and evaluation; even when some are devoted full time to the efforts, all staff members have been trained in evaluation methods

15. Human resources development (HRD) efforts consist of:
    A. Full array of courses designed to meet individual's needs
    B. Usually one-shot, seminar-type approaches
    C. A variety of education and training programs implemented to improve or change the organization

16. When an employee participates in an HR program, his or her supervisor usually:
    A. Asks questions about the program and encourages the use of program materials
    B. Requires use of the program material and uses positive rewards when the employee meets program objectives
    C. Makes no reference to the program

17. Pay for performance programs (bonuses, incentive plans, etc.):
    A. Exists for a few key employees
    B. Is developed for all line employees
    C. Is developed for most employees, line and staff

18. Productivity improvement, cost reduction, or quality of work life programs:
    A. Have not been seriously considered in the organization
    B. Are under consideration at the present time
    C. Have been implemented with good results

19. The results of HR programs are communicated:
    A. Occasionally, to members of management only
    B. Routinely, to a variety of selected target audiences
    C. As requested, to those who have a need to know

20. With the present HR organization and attitude toward results, the HR function's impact on profit:
    A. Can be estimated but probably at a significant cost
    B. Can be estimated (or is being estimated) with little additional cost
    C. Can never be assessed

Scoring and Interpretation

Scoring: Assign a numeric value to each of your responses to the questions based on the following schedule: 5 points for the most correct response, 3 points for the next most correct response and 1 point for the least correct response. Total your score and compare it with the analysis that follows.

The following schedule shows the points for each response:

POINTS	POINTS	POINTS	POINTS
1. A - 5	6. A - 3	11. A - 1	16. A - 3
B - 3	B - 1	B - 3	B - 5
C - 1	C - 5	C - 5	C - 1
2. A - 3	7. A - 5	12. A - 5	17. A - 1
B - 1	B - 3	B - 1	B - 3
C - 5	C - 1	C - 3	C - 5
3. A - 1	8. A - 1	13. A - 3	18. A - 1
B - 3	B - 3	B - 1	B - 3
C - 5	C - 5	C - 5	C - 5

4. A - 5	9. A - 3	14. A - 1	19. A - 3
B - 1	B - 1	B - 3	B - 5
C - 3	C - 5	C - 5	C - 1
5. A - 5	10. A - 5	15. A - 3	20. A - 3
B - 1	B - 3	B - 1	B - 5
C - 3	C - 1	C - 5	C - 1

Rationale: Explanations for responses are given below.

1. Performance measurements should be developed for all HR function. When that is not feasible, at least a few key measures should be in place in each function; otherwise, a function may be perceived to be unimportant or not a contributor.

2. *Major* organizational decisions should always involve input from the HR function. HR policy makers should have input into key decisions in which human resources are an issue.

3. Whenever possible, the investment in human resources should be measured by improvements in productivity, cost savings, and quality. Although other types of evaluation are important and acceptable, these measures are the ultimate proof of results.

4. The concern for the method of evaluation should occur before the program is developed. In the early stage, some consideration should be given to how the data will be collected and how the program will be evaluated. This ensures that the proper emphasis is placed on evaluation.

5. HR programs should never be implemented without a provision for at least some type of formal method of measurement and evaluation. Otherwise, the contribution of the program may never be known.

6. The costs of all individual HR programs should be continuously monitored. This provides management with an assessment of the financial impact of these programs at all times—not just when the program is implemented.

7. Because these important variables represent a tremendous cost for the organization, the cost of absenteeism, turnover, and sick leave should be routinely calculated and monitored.

8. Benefit/cost comparisons of HR programs should be conducted frequently, particularly when a significant investment is involved. Even rough estimates of payoffs versus estimated costs can be helpful in the evaluation of a program.

9. In an economic downturn, the HR function should go untouched in staff reductions or possibly beefed up. Ideally, the function should enhance the bottom line by improving productivity or by reducing costs that can keep the organization competitive in the downturn.

10. Because employee benefits represent a significant portion of operating expenses, they should be routinely monitored and compared with national data, industry norms, and localized data. Projected future costs of benefits should also be periodically reviewed.

11. The CEO should frequently interface with the executive responsible for human resources. It is important for the CEO to know the status of the HR function and receive input on employee morale. This provides an opportunity for the CEO to communicate concerns, desires, and expectations to the HR executive. Frequent meetings are important.

12. The top HR executive should report directly to the CEO. A direct link to the top will help ensure that the HR function receives proper attention and commands the influence necessary to achieve results.

13. Line management involvement in the implementation of HR programs should be significant. Line management's participation in the design, development, and implementation of HR programs will help ensure its success. Line management should be considered in a partnership with the HR staff.

14. The entire HR staff should have some responsibility for measurement and evaluation. Even when some individuals are devoted full time to the effort, all staff members should have a partial responsibility for measurement and evaluation. Staff members should also have training in measurement and evaluation methods. This comprehensive focus on evaluation is necessary for successful implementation.

15. Human resources development (HRD) efforts should consist of a variety of education and training programs

implemented to increase the effectiveness of the organization. HRD involves more than just courses or short seminars. It should include a variety of instructional methods aimed at improving organizational effectiveness.

16. When an employee completes an HR program, his or her supervisor should require use of the program material and reward the employee for meeting or exceeding program objectives. This positive reinforcement will help ensure that the appropriate results are achieved.

17. Pay-for-performance programs should be considered for most employees, both line and staff. Although usually limited to a few key line employees, these programs can work for all employees. Through gain sharing plans, bonuses, and incentives, employees can see the results of their efforts and are rewarded for their achievement. This is fundamental to a results-oriented philosophy for the HR function.

18. Productivity improvement, cost reduction, or quality work like programs should be implemented in many locations and should achieve positive results. These programs are at the very heart of bottom-line HR contributions and have been proven successful in all types of settings. The HR function should take the lead to ensure that these programs are administered efficiently and are successful.

19. The results of HR programs should be routinely communicated to a variety of selected target audiences. Different audiences have different interests and needs, but several important audiences should receive information on the success of HR programs. While some may need only limited general information, other audiences need detailed, bottom-line results.

20. The impact of the HR function on the bottom-line contribution can be estimated with little additional costs. If measurement and evaluation is an integral part of the organization's philosophy, data collection can be built into the human resources information system. It adds a little cost but should generate data necessary to calculate program results.

Analysis of Scores

Total score should range from 20 to 100. The higher the score, the greater your organization's emphasis on achieving results with the HR function.

Score Range	Analysis of Range
81–100	This organization is truly committed to achieving results with the HR function. Additional concentrated efforts to improve measurement and evaluation for the HR function is not needed. There is little room for improvement. All HR sub-functions and programs appear to be contributing to organizational effectiveness. Management support appears to be excellent. Top management commitment is strong. This HR department is taking the lead in measurement and evaluation by showing the contribution it can make to the organization's success. Chances are, it is a vital part of an effective and successful organization.
61–80	This HR department is strong and is contributing to organizational success. The organization is usually better than average in regard to measurement and evaluation. Although the attitude toward achieving results is good, and some of the approaches to evaluation appear to be working, there is still room for improvement. Additional emphasis is needed to make this department continue to be effective.
41–60	Improvement is needed in this organization. It ranks below average with other HR departments in measurement and evaluation. The attitude toward results and the approach used in implementing HR programs are less than desirable. Evaluation methods appear to be ineffective and action is needed to improve management support and alter the philosophy of the organization. Over the long term, this department falls far short of making a significant contribution to the organization.
20–40	This organization shows little or no concern for achieving results from the HR function. The HR department appears to be ineffective and improvement is needed if the department is to survive in its current form and with its current management. Urgent attention is needed to make this department more effective in contributing to the success of the organization.

This instrument has been administered to HR managers and specialists attending local, regional, or national HR conferences. The typical respondent has been the individual responsible for the HR function. The instrument was administered anonymously and the respondents were provided ample time at the beginning of the meeting to complete it. Questions and answers were allowed during the administration of the instrument. To date, there have been more than 700 usable responses representing an average score of 61.4 with a standard deviation of 7.7.

The score can reveal much about the status of human resources in an organization and the attitude toward measurement and evaluation. A perfect score of 100 is probably unachievable and represents utopia; however, it is the ultimate goal of many HR executives and a few other key executives. On the other extreme, a score of 20 reveals an ineffective organization, at least in terms of the contribution of the HR function. The organization will probably not exist for long in its current form or with the current staff.

Although the analysis of these scores is simplistic, the message from the exercise should be obvious. Achieving results from the HR function is more than just evaluating a single program or service. It represents a comprehensive philosophy that must be integrated into the routine activities of the HR staff and supported and encouraged by top executives.

Index

505

About the Authors

Jack J. Phillips, Ph.D., is a world-renowned expert on measurement and evaluation, who provides consulting services for Fortune 500 companies, as well as workshops for major conference providers around the globe. The author or editor of more than twenty books—eight about measurement and evaluation—and more than one hundred articles, Dr. Phillips' expertise in measurement and evaluation spans more than twenty-seven years of corporate experience in five industries (aerospace, textiles, metals, construction materials, and banking). He has served as training and development manager at two *Fortune* 500 firms, senior HR officer at two firms, president of a regional federal savings bank, and management professor at a major state university.

Dr. Phillips' background in training and HR led him to develop the ROI Process™—a revolutionary process that provides bottom-line figures and accountability for all types of training, performance improvement, human resources, and technology programs. In 1992, he founded Performance Resources Organization (PRO), an international consulting firm that provides comprehensive assessment, measurement, and evaluation services for organizations. In 1999, PRO was acquired by the Franklin Covey Company and is now known as the **Jack Phillips Center for Research.** Today the center is an independent, leading provider of measurement and evaluation services to the global business community. Dr. Phillips consults with clients in manufacturing, service, and government organizations in the United States, Canada, Sweden, England, Belgium, Germany, Italy, Holland, South Africa, Mexico, Venezuela, Malaysia, Indonesia, Hong Kong, Australia, New Zealand, and Singapore. He leads the center's research and publishing efforts, which support the knowledge and development of assessment, measurement, and evaluation.

Dr. Phillips' books include *The Human Resources Scorecard*, Gulf Publishing, Houston, TX, 2000; *The Consultant's Scorecard*, McGraw-Hill, New York, NY, 2000; *HRD Trends Worldwide: Shared Solutions to Compete in a Global Economy*, Gulf Publishing Company, Houston, TX, 1999; *Return on Investment in Training and Performance Improvement Programs*, Gulf Publishing Company, Houston, TX, 1997; *Handbook of Training Evaluation and Measurement Methods*, 3rd edition, Gulf Publishing Company, Houston, TX, 1997; and *Accountability in Human Resource Management*, Gulf Publishing Company, Houston, TX, 1996. He is series editor for ASTD's In Action Series and serves as series editor for Gulf Publishing's Improving Human Performance Series.

Dr. Phillips has undergraduate degrees in electrical engineering, physics, and mathematics from Southern Polytechnic State University and Oglethorpe University, a master's degree in decision sciences from Georgia State University, and a Ph.D. in human resource management from the University of Alabama. In 1987 he won the Yoder-Heneman Personnel Creative Application Award from the Society for Human Resource Management.

Ron D. Stone is director of workshops and consultants for the Jack Phillips Center for Research, a division of Franklin Covey. Prior to joining the center, Ron was vice-president and chief consulting officer for Performance Resources Organization, where he specialized in measurement processes and directed the international consulting practice for four years. He currently conducts return on investment (ROI) studies and consults with clients in manufacturing, service, and government organizations in the United States and abroad. He provides consulting services in measurement and evaluation, training function management, the establishment of results-based policies and procedures, performance management systems, and strategic planning. Ron also certifies practitioners in the ROI Process™, conducts a full range of public and in-house workshops, and is a certified change consultant.

Mr. Stone has more than thirty years of experience in human resource management, engineering, and training in the aerospace, electric utility, and industrial development industries. He has considerable experience in employment processes, compensation and benefits, performance management, healthcare delivery system management, budgeting and account classification processes, training curriculum design, safety, organizational development, executive development, and needs assessment and evaluation. In addition, he served eighteen years in a managerial capacity while working for two subsidiaries of the Southern Company, served as manager of corporate training for twelve years, was supervisor of skills development, manager of management and executive development, manager of research and evaluation, and manager of human resources. He also served on the design team to develop and implement the Southern Company's performance management process and incentive pay plan. He also consulted with the pilot project team to design and implement team structures within the Southern Company.

As chair of the Edison Electric Institute's Executive Leadership Program for senior officers in the electric utility industry, Mr. Stone led the design, delivery, and evaluation of the industry's premier executive development program. He served on the Alabama's Adult Education Advisory Council and the University of Alabama Management Development Program Advisory Council, and has designed industry management programs that were delivered through continuing education functions at the University of Alabama, Auburn University, and the University of Georgia.

Mr. Stone currently serves on the steering committee and faculty for the University of Alabama Human Resource Development Program. He received the Pioneer Award in 1993 from the Alabama Healthcare Council for his leadership of a three-year major change initiative and his visionary work in influencing improvement in the quality and efficiency of Alabama's healthcare delivery system. He is a member of the Society for Human Resource Management and the American Society for Training and Development.

In addition to his made numerous contributions to perfecting the ROI Process™, Mr. Stone has contributed several case studies to ASTD's In Action Series, which appear in the casebooks titled *Measuring Return on Investment* (1997) and *Measuring Learning and Performance* (1999). He is a contributing author to the ASTD Info-Line Series and the ASTD Tool Kit Series (1999). He is co-author of *The Human Resources Scorecard*, Gulf Publishing Company, and the upcoming book *How to Measure Training Success—A Practical Guide to Teaching the Six Key Indicators*, McGraw-Hill (2000). Ron received his BBA from Georgia State University.

Patricia Pulliam Phillips is chairwoman and CEO of the Chelsea Group, a consulting and publishing company focused on accountability issues in training, HR, and performance improvement. Building on the work of Jack J. Phillips, developer of the ROI Process™, Ms. Phillips offers a practical and cost-savings approach to implementing ROI within organizations. She works closely with the ROI Certification™ process and helps promote accountability practices through research and publications. Through the Chelsea Group, Ms. Phillips works with publishers, editors, and authors to develop publications on accountability, including the American Society for Training and Development's In Action Series and Gulf Publishing's Improving Human Performance Series. She also serves on the board of directors for the ROI Network™, a professional organization of practitioners of measurement and evaluation.

Formerly, Ms. Phillips served as vice-president of business development at Performance Resources Organization. In this role, she was responsible for the development of international and domestic strategic alliances, client relations, and sales and marketing initiatives. Prior to her work with Performance Resources Organization, she worked in the electric utility industry for the Southern Company. Her thirteen-year career there included the role of manager of market planning and research, in which she was responsible for the development of marketing programs for residential and commercial customers. She also played an integral part in the development of Marketing University, a learning environment that supported the needs of new sales and marketing representatives.

As manager in the Corporate Services organization, Ms. Phillips initiated and implemented the operation evaluation process. This evaluation process included the development and analysis of surveys, interviews with line management and employees, and participation in line operation activities. The results of this evaluation process served as a planning tool for establishing purchasing procedures for line equipment and tools, an internal process-planning tool to support line operations, and a model for future operation evaluation initiatives.

Ms. Phillips has an MA in public and private management from Birmingham-Southern College, is certified in ROI evaluation, and serves as co-author on the subject in such publications as *Corporate University Review* (1998), *The Journal of Lending and Credit Risk Management* (1997), and *Evaluating Training Programs*, 2nd edition, by Donald L. Kirkpatrick, Berrett-Koehler Publishers Inc. (1998). She is also contributing author to *HRD Trends Worldwide*, by Jack J. Phillips, Gulf Publishing (1999), and co-author of the American Society for Training and Development's Info-Line Series, *Level 5 Evaluation: ROI* (1998); *ROI on a Shoestring* (2000); and *The Human Resources Scorecard*, Gulf Publishing (2000).